Late Stage

Late Stage

Theatrical Perspectives on Age and Aging

Edited by Benjamin Gillespie and Cindy Rosenthal
with Elinor Fuchs

University of Michigan Press ANN ARBOR

Published in the United States of America by the
University of Michigan Press
First published March 2026

A CIP catalog record for this book is available from the
British Library.

Library of Congress Cataloging-in-Publication data has been applied for.

ISBN 978-0-472-07796-0 (hardcover : alk. paper)
ISBN 978-0-472-05796-2 (paper : alk. paper)
ISBN 978-0-472-90573-7 (e-book)

DOI: http://doi.org/10.3998/mpub.14408934

Cover image: Chantel C. Lucier, Judith Malina as Maudie in the Living Theatre's production of *Maudie and Jane*. New York, 2007.

The authorized representative in the EU for product safety and compliance is Easy Access System Europe, Mustamäe tee 50, 10621 Tallinn, Estonia, gpsr.requests@easproject.com

This book is dedicated to Elinor Fuchs (1933–2024), whose profound insights and enduring brilliance in her own late stage illuminated this work.

Before making judgments, we must ask questions. This is the deepest meaning of the idea, often-repeated but little understood, that the study of art shows us how to live.

—ELINOR FUCHS, "VISIT TO A SMALL PLANET"

Contents

Digital materials related to this title can be found on the Fulcrum platform via the following citable URL: https://doi.org/10.3998/mpub.14408934

Illustrations

Acknowledgments

This book was born in the brilliant mind of Elinor Fuchs. We are privileged to have been her comrades and co-travelers early on as the argument and organization of this book took shape—at theater and performance studies conferences, at age studies conferences, on panels, and in working groups, grabbing coffee in the in-between moments. Ultimately, however, we were tasked with fulfilling Elinor's vision for this book without her. We believe that her spirit and intellect live on in these pages.

We are extremely grateful to each of the passionate, generous scholars who joined us as contributors in this volume. We are also immensely appreciative of Margaret Morganroth Gullette for her insightful foreword.

LeAnn Fields, our original editorial director and dear friend at the University of Michigan Press, was a huge champion of this project from the start. She has begun her well-deserved retirement, but we remain forever in her debt for her astute guidance, kindness, deep wisdom, and wicked-sharp wit. We were delighted to work closely with Sara Cohen, who stepped in for LeAnn upon her retirement and brought boundless energy to the project. We would also like to thank other members of the production team—Kianna Delly, Danielle Coty-Fattal, Marcia LaBrenz, Cheryl Bowman, and Jessica Hinds-Bond—for their work on the book.

We are grateful to our respective academic institutions—Santa Clara University and Baruch College, and Hofstra University—for their support of this book project. This project was directly supported by funding from a PSC-CUNY Grant Award and the Hofstra Faculty Research and Development Grant. We are also indebted to the friends, mentors, and artists who have generously shared their time, knowledge, and creativity in support of this work: Kate Bredeson, Brad Burgess, Dorothy Chansky, Sean Edgecomb, Bertie Ferdman, James Harding, Kimberly Jannarone, Bess Rowen, Pat Russell, Annette Saddik, Peggy Shaw, Lois Weaver, and James F. Wilson. Tom Walker contributed to this process in important ways but sadly passed away a few months before we submitted the final manuscript. His loss is deeply felt in New York City's downtown theater community and by his many friends across the globe.

We are incredibly fortunate to have patient, loving partners. We thank Cindy's husband, Emanuel Levy, and Benjamin's husband, Michael J. S. Moran, for keeping us sane on the roller coaster of our scholarly lives.

Finally, we wish to acknowledge and thank some of our dearest elders, whose support sustains us: Cindy's mother, Lola (age ninety-seven at this writing), and Benjamin's grandparents Edith and Harold, whose extraordinary late stages continue to inspire us.

Foreword
Age Critics Help Transform Theater and Performance

Margaret Morganroth Gullette

1

Theater and performance, here celebrated for their confluence with age studies, can have amazing virtue as agents of change. Elinor Fuchs, as an actor of her own material, is one instance. At the inaugural European Network in Aging Studies (ENAS) conference in Maastricht, which I attended in 2011, Elinor performed conversations she had exchanged with her mother, Lil, as Lil's utterances became apparently nonsensical. Doing both parts, Elinor played her mother's sentences with exuberance, enabling us to hear Lil striving for meaning. Instead of answering with embarrassed silence or unfriendly laughter, Elinor played her own as easy rejoinders.

ELINOR: How are you, Mother?
LIL: Oh, in a fast muff, getting out of the wet ditches.
ELINOR: Wet ditches, well, that's interesting.
LIL: Oh, I'm in a dedeford, they're, they're having a bedurz. I mean, they're having a cressit. And would be considered hajardi. Would be picking dependent stuff. I mean they're showing up prepays and other things.
ELINOR: That's good!

Basing her text on audiotapes, Elinor incorporated Lil's strange nouns in American speech rhythms. Lil responded without agitation to her daughter's enthusiastic tones.[1]

As theater, this performance was innovative. As persuasive teaching in bioethics, it was effective. There *was* after all a way to be with—to talk

Fig. 0.1. Elinor Fuchs and Margaret Morganroth Gullette at the North American Network for Aging Studies (NANAS) conference, Miami University of Ohio. 2015. Photo courtesy of NANAS.

with—a person whose cognitive impairment had progressed to a point that might have floored others.

By her own brilliant meaning-making performance, Elinor was undermining the audiences's potential "dementism." In our competitive society, expected to be hyperverbal, we may learn to feel alienated from people living with apparent obstacles to sociability. As long as Alzheimer's is more feared than cancer, how can plays not sensationalize and terrorize? When I hear that a veteran actor is getting cast in the "deeply forgetful person" role, I shrink away.[2]

Elinor's performance changed me. Later, I used the memory to listen to people with such impairments and respond by looking them in the eye, so they felt they were heard. Bold theorists had told us this—the field-changing Tom Kitwood, the ethicist and TED talker Stephen Post. But Elinor's sweet hour of instruction taught me the *practice*—the skills and patience. The practice need not be verbal. At Maastricht, clowns mimed amiable expressive silence, sidling up, waiting for silent acceptance, stroking, waiting, offering gentle touch to those who miss it.

Live theater in some hands can overcome factors that might even obviate performance. In a *Sonic Elder* concert in Vancouver, one musician with memory losses was enabled, by cues and empathy, to deliver his song successfully, as Julia Henderson explains (chapter 12). Peggy Shaw used her show *Ruff* "to present [the] physical and cognitive impacts [of her stroke] unapologetically to audiences" so they could "imagine a world beyond the privileging of linear timelines" (Benjamin Gillespie, chapter 13).

Echoing Walt Whitman, Tony Kushner said about creative people: "You willfully loosen some of the inner straps that hold your core together. You become more porous and multivalent and multivocal, so that the multitudes you have inside yourself can start to get up and walk around and emerge."[3]

2

Theater and film sometimes glory in representing formerly overlooked injustices. Contemporary impresarios seize on gripping themes, "fostering dialogue between contentious racial and cultural groups of people," as Robbie McCauley notes (chapter 11). Actors relish high-impact conflicts. I think of *Fun Home* (the London production). *Killers of the Flower Moon. BlacKkKlansman. Grenfell* (the Brooklyn production). *Prima Facie. The Jungle. Conclave.* Drawing attention to the varied violences of homophobia, racism, classism, sexism, xenophobia, and transphobia can change consciousness and feelings.

"Writing age" and "performing age" can be similarly transformational. In Sophocles's *Oedipus at Colonus*, Frankie Faison (in the version I saw from Theater of War)[4] magnificently played the righteously angry, homeless immigrant so anyone could understand the age justice he demanded. Pedro Almodóvar's *The Room Next Door* (2024) enacts a rare relationship, between a midlife character seeking end-of-life companionship and a same-age friend afraid of death. Audiences get practice dealing with their own reactions imaginatively.

Like any other creative mimicry of the human, however, representation of older adults can be convincing, or not: perfunctory, flatteringly phony, factually wrong, or simply implausible, as well as mean, grotesque, satirical, disgusting, condescending.

The violences of *ageism* (merging with ableism, sexism, racism, dementism, or classism) are less well understood. Elinor reminds us that our ways of thinking age are still strange to some scholars in theater and performance studies. The concepts are also strange to many theater- and moviemakers, and to audiences, including untrained reviewers.

As an avid New York theater audience member from the age of twelve and a writer of anti-ageist nonfiction, I find that my pleasure in an intense immersive artistic experience is spoiled if I am wrangling in my mind against insensitivity. (I wish the media hired age critics to write reviews; potential audience members who "look like me" sometimes deserve trigger warnings, or spoiler alerts.) Audiences, reviewers, other scholars, actors—many accept insulting, obsolete choices as "everyday life." How could they not?

Well, the right kinds of attention and resistance disrupt that status quo. Brecht could have been calling for the help of age critics in the arts when he wrote: "Before familiarity can turn into awareness, the familiar must be stripped of its inconspicuousness; we must give up assuming that the object in question needs no explanation. However frequently recurrent, modest, vulgar it may be, it will now be labelled as something unusual."[5]

Almost forty years ago, a vanguard of age critics started stripping recurrent, vulgar ageist stuff of its "inconspicuousness." By now, no need to wait for a movement, picketing theaters to yell "AGE MATTERS" or standing outside the Dolby Theatre to shout "#OscarsSoYoung." The current cultural atmosphere, for critics capable of focusing on age and theater arts *together*, as in this anthology, is thus heady with urgency and curiosity. Such critics have taken on responsibilities as guardians of later life.

3

Specifying age-related elements that others still overlook is delicate, creative work. "The most important thing for a critic," Bonnie Marranca says, "is to cultivate an individual voice" (chapter 14). It needs to be enlightening and subtle (not preachy), observant and learned, fresh and friendly.

Writers in this volume took me *behind the scenes*, to reveal how playwrights, screenwriters, directors, actors, and producers, as well as for-profit businesses, not knowing any better, reflect the ways we are negatively aged by culture. When youth is prized for energy, sexuality, looks, and cultural "fit," we often find "a punishingly youth-focused theater and film industry" (Dorothy Chansky, chapter 7). As scriptwriters grow older, acquiring a huge cultural reserve, how many can find producers to support interesting stories centering on older characters? Some scripts exhibit "the viciousness toward older women that characterizes youth-centric societies" (Núria Casado-Gual and Inesa Shevchenko-Hotsuliak, chapter 4). Casting directors "may dismiss everyone over age fifty or so as too unreliable to hire, . . . [because] the social imaginary deems that body on the precipice of illness and death" (Valerie Barnes Lipscomb, chapter 6).

Creative criticism enjoys showing where professionals do well (in writing, casting, directing, performing live, or talking autobiographically, onstage or off, about phases of life). Critics stay open to noticing aspects that war with one another. "A gendered narrative of decline" may also "allow for mature actresses to exhibit their craft and talent through characters that are extremely demanding, both physically and emotionally" (Casado-Gual and Shevchenko-Hotsuliak, chapter 4).

Many writers in this volume *seat us in the audience* by describing productions that feature age, which many readers have no chance to see. Heunjung Lee describes Belgian dance theater company laGeste's 2021 restaging of *Gardenia—10 Years Later* with "six older drag performers who have lived as LGBTQ individuals, born between the 1940s and 1960s" (Lee, chapter 9). We vicariously expand our experiences with "the performed identity, presence, and materiality of aging" (Lee, chapter 9) and "depth performances of age" (Henderson, chapter 12).

Observant praise teaches. "The visibly adult default bodies of the performers [in *Dance Nation*] enable easier identification with these [adolescent] experiences" (Bess Rowen, chapter 8). Oral histories and reminiscences of admired artists like Judith Malina and Robbie McCauley spread fresh theatrical ideas and acting and directing practices. Creative critics build on important literary/cultural/gerontological/dramaturgical/technological concepts. They debate dramatic theories. They imply the "unknowable potential," transfer a "proleptic impulse" (to borrow from R. Darren Gobert, chapter 5), and offer utopian "glimpses of how it could *feel* to resist ageism" (Henderson, chapter 12).

Sage commentaries will influence scripts, rehearsals, published reviews, talkbacks, classroom discussions, and future scholarship. Some appraisals constitute interventions beyond these spaces—into arenas such as "applied theater," nursing home care, AI, and social media. Scott Magelssen reports that wearing "suits" that allegedly simulate old age confirmed "fears of aging as scary, disorienting, and uncomfortable" (chapter 15). Readers (including adult children) can relish the use of Zoom and lament the limitations of robo-pets or robo-husbands in "the care economy," through Jennifer Parker-Starbuck's chapter.

Theater, performance, and age studies—when these approaches merge, the results are what I am calling *virtue*. It's a privilege to watch a dynamic process, intent on dazzling artistry and consciousness-raising, ever unfurling.

NOTES

1. In 2005, Elinor published those dialogues in an admired memoir. Reading *Making an Exit*, however, didn't let us *hear* those two different voices. Elinor Fuchs, *Making an Exit: A Mother-Daughter Drama with Alzheimer's, Machine Tools, and Laughter* (Metropolitan Books, 2005).

2. It is Stephen Post who invented the name, "deeply forgetful persons." See Post, "Hope in Caring for the Deeply Forgetful: Enduring Selfhood and Being Open to Surprises," *Bulletin of the Menninger Clinic* 77, no. 4 (Fall 2013): 349–68. He also invented the label "dementism." Stephen Post, *The Moral Challenge of Alzheimer Disease: Ethical Issues from Diagnosis to Dying* (Johns Hopkins University Press, 2002), 29–32.

3. Tony Kushner, interviewed by Catherine Steindler, "The Art of Theater no. 16," *Paris Review*, no. 201 (Summer 2012), https://www.theparisreview.org/interviews/6153/the-art-of-theatre-no-16-tony-kushner

4. Theater of War Productions, "The Oedipus at Colonus Project," https://theaterofwar.com/projects/the-oedipus-at-colonus-project

5. Brecht was trying to train *actors*. Bertolt Brecht, "Short Description of a New Technique of Acting, Appendix, #17," in *Brecht on Theatre: The Development of an Aesthetic*, ed. and trans. John Willett (Radha Krishna Prakashan, 1978), 143–44.

Introduction
time she stopped

Benjamin Gillespie and Cindy Rosenthal

How does time behave on this planet? Does "time stand still"? Is time frantic and staccato on this planet? Is it leisurely, easy-going time? How is time marked on this planet? By clock? By the sun? By the sound of footsteps? What kind of time are we in? Cyclical time? Eternal time? Linear time? What kind of line? One day? One lifetime?
—ELINOR FUCHS[1]

This volume was fifteen years in the making. In 2011, pathbreaking critic, scholar, professor, and playwright Elinor Fuchs—a monumental figure in the field of theater and performance studies—conceived of an anthology dedicated to illuminating and interrogating an emerging, hybrid scholarly territory: the intersection of age studies with theater and performance studies. Fuchs was a vital mover and shaker of this new hybrid field, publishing foundational essays in her own "late-stage" career; indeed, Fuchs was in her late seventies when she invited Rosenthal (two decades her junior) to join her as co-editor of *Late Stage*. Gillespie (three decades younger still) came on board the project first as a key contributor. When Fuchs was no longer able to work on the volume due to the progression of her Alzheimer's disease symptoms, Gillespie took over as co-editor. The book was envisioned by Fuchs as multivocal, multigenerational, and interdisciplinary, including the work of a diverse community of scholars and artists to discuss the unexplored facets of aging in theater and drama. The title for the book, *Late Stage*, was also Fuchs's inspiration. The day we submitted this book to the press, to our shock and devastating sadness, Fuchs passed away.

As we work, then and now, we are inspired and influenced daily by Fuchs's pioneering legacy in both fields. As with many contributors in this volume, Fuchs was also a significant mentor to both of us. She advised Gillespie early on in the writing of his dissertation about the later work of the lesbian-feminist theater company Split Britches, and she was a keen conversant on the work of downtown New York experimental theater ensembles with Rosenthal (Fuchs and Rosenthal were frequent theatergoing companions as well).

The idea of this anthology was first seeded in Fuchs's mind in 2011, after she attended the inaugural European Network in Aging Studies (ENAS) conference in Maastricht, the Netherlands. At that conference, the idea for a North American Network in Aging Studies (NANAS) was formed, with Fuchs later becoming a key contributor.[2] At the conference, Fuchs was struck by how underrepresented her own field of theater and performance studies was at a conference on age and aging, especially as an embodied art form. In response, Fuchs organized a special working session at the 2012 annual American Society for Theatre Research (ASTR) conference, titled "Performing Age"—the first session (to our knowledge) on theater and aging offered at any US theater conference. The following year, Fuchs and Rosenthal discussed the possibility of working together on *Late Stage* at the 2013 Performance Studies International (PSi) conference in Palo Alto, California. With great fervor and excitement, and with a few necessary stops and starts along the way, Fuchs led the charge and sought collaborators to leap in with her to bring her idea for the volume to life. It wasn't until 2017, during the ASTR-curated panel "Aging and Its Extra/Ordinary Differences" in Atlanta (including Fuchs, Rosenthal, Gillespie, and Valerie Barnes Lipscomb), that the volume began to really take shape. Heartbreakingly, by 2022, Elinor could no longer work on *Late Stage*; in 2023, Rosenthal and Gillespie confirmed the final roster of contributors included in this volume, ensuring that Fuchs's vision for the book remained intact.

In Anne Davis Basting's brief memory play included as the volume's final chapter, the line "time she stopped" from Samuel Beckett's *Rockaby* calls the reader/spectator to attention. Basting's *At This Time (or My Friend Elinor)* situates the reader/spectator in a recent, intimate moment in time, an encounter between Basting and Fuchs, longtime comrades and colleagues. Fuchs, who, in her late seventies, helped forge a new intersectional field of research and writing about age and performance. Fuchs, who, since 2022, had advanced symptoms of Alzheimer's disease. We, *Late Stage* co-editors and contributors, still find it impossible to comprehend that Elinor Fuchs—theater studies and age studies groundbreaker, mentor, friend, teacher, and most esteemed colleague—had been stopped in her tracks by dementia.

There is painful irony along with deep appreciation for the brilliance of the author when rereading Fuchs's heartrending and often hilarious *Making an Exit: A Mother-Daughter Drama with Alzheimer's, Machine Tools, and Laughter* (2005). The book is an account of her mother's journey with Alzheimer's and Fuchs's own experience as her mother's primary caregiver. We know full well that the layers of Alzheimer's care moved on to another generation—Fuchs's daughters. We are incredibly blessed to have had the chance to work closely with Fuchs on this crucial, timely passion project for almost a decade before it became too difficult for her to continue. As Fuchs once wrote in her influential essay "Visit to a Small Planet," "You can construct meaning in this world in many different ways. Construct it in the most inclusive way you can. There will still be more to see."[3] It is because of Elinor Fuchs's powerful vision that this volume exists in the world.

THEORIZING AGE IN/AS PERFORMANCE

> How do figures appear on this planet? Are they inward or two-dimensional? Subtle? Exaggerated? Are they like puppets? Like clowns? Like you? (Are you sure?)
> —ELINOR FUCHS[4]

Undoing the notion that we maintain a singular, continuous self as we age—an assumption that negatively positions old age in opposition to youth—this volume challenges biological imperatives imposed by essentialist views of aging.[5] Echoing Judith Butler's well-known theory of the social construction of gender developed in the early 1990s, *Late Stage* presents age as a performative facet of identity tied to the changes produced over time on, and in, the material body.[6] Together, contributors to *Late Stage* demonstrate how aging and the construction of self are embedded within sociocultural and corporeal systems that continuously evolve over time and are therefore never fixed, despite ageist cultural representations. Across these chapters, individual age differences counter dominant representations of the later life course that attempt to naturalize aging as a homogeneous and undesirable experience.

In contrast, *Late Stage* celebrates performances of age and representations of aging onstage that reposition later life in more complex narratives. We emphasize the importance of liveness and living artists as opposed to filmed or digitized performance works in the research and scholarship in the volume in order to underscore how theater is an ideal space for considering aging because it includes embodied performers and audiences who are also always aging. It is our hope that this volume encourages scholars to incorporate age as an intersectional facet of all identity in theater and performance.

The chapters that follow explore age as a performative identity tied to the changes produced over time on the material body. As with gender, the performative qualities of aging imbue subjects with the potential to destabilize normative age roles. A performative view of aging seeks to eliminate strict divisions between life stages deeply embedded in our cultural imaginations, thereby considering how age and aging are constructed through a series of social acts performed throughout one's life rather than being a biological imperative. As age scholars Aagje Swinnen and Cynthia Port outline, a performative age approach highlights the possibilities for subversion of the negative societal scripting of age:

> Theories of performativity claim that age identities are formed and perpetuated through the repetition of behavioral scripts connected to chronological ages and life stages. Since a repetition can never be identical to its original script, there is always the possibility of subversion and change. The concept of performativity has particular significance in performance studies, as actors both enact age upon the stage and negotiate behavioral norms associated with their own chronological ages. But it also offers an illuminating conceptual approach to understanding the actions and behaviors of individuals and groups across the life span.[7]

To this end, we consider the performativity of age both on and offstage, both in theater and in life. If we take as a given that identities become *more* richly complex with age as time is layered and sedimented on the body, what are the possibilities for older artists and citizens to transform and evolve with lived experience? Just as Judith Butler described the repetitive acts that produce and congeal gender identity for the subject over time, so too is age identity formed through a temporal ordering of the life course, which constructs our concept of both age and aging.

Being old is unquestionably a stigmatized identity in US society and culture.[8] As age scholar Kathleen Woodward observes, given the growing populations of older people in the US and around the globe, "age may assume more importance than any of the other differences which distinguish our bodies from others, including gender."[9] So-called successful aging narratives are exceedingly visible: from the proliferation of *anti-aging* products on the market, to the ubiquity of plastic surgery that attempts to minimize the effects of age.[10] Problematically, "success" is measured not by productivity or well-being, but by the erasure of the signs of age through the *imitation* of youth. Leading age scholar and *Late Stage* contributor Margaret Morganroth Gullette has demonstrated that the negative association with middle to old age in the United States is the result of an omnipresent "master narrative of decline" that pushes culture to devalue the old in favor of youth.[11] The negative impact of *ageism*, a term first coined by gerontologist Robert N. Butler in 1975, is prevalent across our culture, from the sidelining of elderly populations in governmental policymaking to age-based stereotypes represented in more mainstream venues and media.[12] Robert N. Butler emphasizes the exponential growth of older populations on a global scale as an outcome of the "longevity revolution" of the last century, resulting in people living longer lives on average than ever before in Western history.[13] According to the 2020 US Census, one in six people are sixty-five and over (making up 16.8 percent of the population). This portion of the population also grew nearly five times faster than the total population over the one hundred years from 1920 to 2020.[14] These remarkable figures should undoubtedly push scholars to further consider the impact and presence of older populations in all forms of cultural production, but especially for theater and performance as an embodied art form where the body can be represented outside the dominant ideologies of aging as decline. Today, sixty-five seems relatively young in comparison to the mid-twentieth century, and yet those over that age marker in the United States still face an onslaught of ubiquitous ageism in our society.

As a field, age studies began in the 1990s to address the ramifications of negative attitudes toward aging, particularly old age. While age studies considers *all* ages and stages across the spectrum of the life course, the field has primarily focused on middle to old age. Strongly influenced by feminist and gender studies, age studies focuses on how culture affects individual embodiment and subjectivities, especially for older people. The field also encompasses the area of "cultural gerontology," more distinctly defined by sociological studies, health studies, and anthropological research.

Perhaps the most important critique to evolve in the field of age studies surrounds the cultural binarization of youth and age that results in decline ideology. While aging leads to very real physical and cognitive shifts, criticism around age in the humanities should not be oriented toward a framework in which aging equals debility or death.[15] Since the 1990s, scholars have worked to expose how assumptions about aging and old age are part of a larger societal system dependent on the privileging of *chronological age* as an institutionalized measurement of the human life course, ultimately producing a master narrative of decline and a cult of youth.[16] As with other hegemonic narratives, these internalized ideologies were found to both normalize and collapse disparate populations of people into entrenched categories that discipline identity and existence and "restrict the potential richness and fulfillment of later life."[17] Age studies incorporates feminism, psychoanalysis, performance theory, queer theory, and other approaches, many of which, according to age studies scholar and sociologist Stephen Katz, came out of "poststructuralism, discourse analysis, governmentality, phenomenology, the sociology of the body, social studies of science and technology, and feminist, LGBT, and disability studies" nearing the end of the twentieth century.[18] Issues surrounding identity formation, embodiment, and representation have helped reposition the aging experience as wide ranging, intersectional, and pluralistic.[19]

This collection establishes a necessary dialogue between the fields of age studies and theater and performance studies by exploring aging subjectivity already extant in performance while engaging in more "age-conscious" criticism, to borrow Fuchs's useful terminology.[20] The previous lack of engagement with age and aging in theater and performance studies is perhaps indicative of the cultural erasure of old(er) ages, especially in comparison to other aspects of identity, like race, gender, and sexuality. In reality, of course, age intersects with each of these identities and affects the ways in which we see and experience the world. In her earlier work, Anne Davis Basting usefully describes the manifestation of time on the aging body through a "depth model of aging," highlighting the phenomenon of seeing age onstage: "Our past roles remain with us, written in our memories and on our bodies . . . offsetting theories of rigidity and an inability to change with possibilities for continued growth. Because any social act of aging is always done in concert with the past, present, and future, no single representation of age can be a stable identity."[21] In Basting's pathbreaking *The Stages of Age: Performing Age in Contemporary American Culture*, she convincingly demonstrates the temporal depth harnessed by the aging actor onstage and insists on the older subject having "layers of selves created throughout one's life, making it impossible to isolate a *single* sign of one's age" in performance.[22] Her work is echoed frequently throughout *Late Stage*.

As theatre and age studies scholar Valerie Barnes Lipscomb has previously asserted, "while other branches of the arts and humanities have finally begun a critical exploration of what it means to age in our culture, theatre has lagged behind, focusing more on theatre projects with older people than on theorizing age on stage."[23] Following Lipscomb's example, this book develops a critical model for understanding older age embodiments as social and aesthetic performances. While much of mainstream theater continues to produce narratives that leave elderly characters decrepit by the end of the play, there are many counterexamples that work against such damaging normative age scripts in their move away from realism and peak-and-decline ideologies. Many of those examples are analyzed in detail in the pages that follow.

This book offers a revised conception of aging in theater and performance studies that works against the grain of age expectations, and calls attention to the unique ability of the veteran artist to embody past and present simultaneously onstage. Judith Malina, Robbie McCauley, and Peggy Shaw are but a few examples explored here, and there are many more out there to consider. We hope readers will continue to expand on the examples collected here. Taking a performative approach, the authors in this volume consider traditional forms of acting and performance onstage, but also engage age as a performative facet of identity in everyday life.

In *Out of Time: The Pleasures and the Perils of Ageing*, feminist philosopher Lynne Segal reflects:

> As we age, changing from year to year, we also retain, in one manifestation or another, traces of all selves we have been, creating a type of temporal vertigo and rendering us psychically, in one sense, all ages and no age . . . the older we are, the more we encounter the world through complex layerings of identity, attempting to negotiate and shift the present while also grappling with discovering images of the old thrust so intrusively upon us.[24]

This does not mean that we avoid understanding the body's real physical changes by defining age as a purely social construction. As Kathleen Woodward contends in *Figuring Age: Women, Bodies, Generations*, "unlike other markers of difference, old age cannot be theorized or understood as a social construction only, one that erases the real changes of the body that can come with aging and old age. There is a point at which the social and cultural construction of aging must confront the physical dimensions, if not the very real limits of the body."[25] While a focus on the body's physical limits is an important factor in the analysis provided in these chapters, the scripting of age is also widely acknowledged to be produced by culture as much as biology—the central claim of Gullette's field-changing book *Aged by Culture* (2004), which includes the chapter "Acting Age on Stage: Age-Appropriate Casting, the Default Body, and Valuing the Property of Having an Age," referenced by several scholars in this volume. We are deeply grateful to have Gullette's singular voice as the foreword to this volume.

Over the past decade, the work of earlier pioneers in the field has been picked up by new generations of scholars within age studies, including Marlene Goldman, Cynthia Port, Sally Chivers, Aagje Swinnen, Kate de Medeiros, Thomas Cole, Andrea Charise, Leni Marshall, Amelia DeFalco, and others, each introducing more recent theoretical movements to the field.[26] Chivers asserts that while age studies and disability studies remain in critical conversation with each other, there has been a separation of these two fields with little crossover until recently, due to the problematic association of the two identities—often a stigma the elderly face in society that age is itself a disability.[27] While this volume does not equate disability with aging, it does engage with age-related complications that shift the artist's perceptions or embodied physical abilities.

Theater and performance studies could learn much from the developing theoretical discourses surrounding age and aging, especially as they intersect with questions of temporality and embodiment already embedded in theatrical scholarship. In many ways, aging reflects a "haunted" body that brings the past into the present, not unlike Marvin Carlson's theories in *The Haunted Stage: The Theatre as Memory Machine*, referenced in a number of the essays here.[28] In the introduction to the 2016 special issue of *Modern Drama* on "Aging and the Life Course," guest editor Lawrence Switzky argued that theater and performance "can both model and challenge narratives, affects, and cultural understandings (and misunderstandings) about aging."[29] This special issue of *Modern Drama* came out of the "Playing Age" conference at the University of Toronto in 2015.

Playing Age was the first conference of its kind in North America dedicated to exploring aging in theater and performance, with scholars from across the arts, humanities, and social sciences. A special issue of *Theatre Research in Canada* (co-edited by Benjamin Gillespie, Julia Henderson, and Núria Casado-Gual) published in November 2021, expanded age studies perspectives in theater and performance.[30] A special issue of the UK-based journal *Performance Research*, "On Ageing (& Beyond)," was published in 2019, edited by Richard Gough and Nanako Nakajima (including essays by Fuchs, Rosenthal, and Gillespie).[31] There were also two other special issues of note: first, the interdisciplinary online journal *Occasion* published an issue on "Aging, Old Age, Memory, Aesthetics" in 2012, including essays on opera, film, and theater, and considering "the relationship between memory and aging, the notion of embodied experience and its relationship to gender, and, finally, contemporary modes of conceiving of and caring for the elderly."[32] Second, also in 2012, *Women & Performance: a journal of feminist theory* curated a special issue on "Aging" from a feminist performance perspective.[33] The open-access journal *Age, Culture, Humanities* (*ACH*), on its ninth volume as of 2025, has proven to be a major venue for new scholarship on aging, including articles by a range of scholars working internationally on theater and performance.[34] *ACH* is the journal affiliated with both ENAS and NANAS—the two major organizations dedicated to age studies internationally, referenced above—which have featured panels on theater and performance at their major biannual conferences, and most recently at their co-sponsored conference Take Back Aging, hosted at Trent University (Ontario, Canada) in 2019.[35] The 2024 volume *The Palgrave Handbook of Literature and Aging*, edited by Lipscomb and Swinnen, included two chapters on theater and performance.[36] *Late Stage* will contribute substantially to the discourse of age in theater and performance studies, providing much for future scholars, practitioners, and students to draw from and be inspired by as they focus on age and aging in their work.

Late Stage extends and deepens the discourse already begun in pioneering books on theater and aging, including Basting's *The Stages of Age: Performing Age in Contemporary American Culture* (1998) and *Forget Memory: Creating Better Lives for People with Dementia* (2009); Fuchs's *Making an Exit: A Mother-Daughter Drama with Alzheimer's, Machine Tools, and Laughter* (2005); Lipscomb and Leni Marshall's *Staging Age: The Performance of Age in Theatre, Dance, and Film* (2010); Lipscomb's *Performing Age in Modern Drama* (2016); and Michael Mangan's *Staging Ageing: Theatre, Performance and the Narrative of Decline* (2013).

Following the work of Basting, this volume moves beyond dramatic analysis to explore age and its intersections with performative identity on and offstage. While age and aging are finally establishing a presence at major theater and performance studies conferences and journals in the United States, this volume solidifies the greater need for explicit engagement with age and aging in the field, to an extent equal with other categories of identity such as race, gender, and disability. *How* and *why* we should analyze and deconstruct age onstage are fundamental questions of this book. Age represents a social and political identity deeply embedded in theater and performance practices, one that is in need of more thorough analysis. The essays, interviews, and dialogic pieces gathered here are an answer to that call.

AIMS AND STRUCTURE

In most dramatic worlds there are hidden, or at least unseen, spaces. Ask questions about them as well. What are their characteristics of space, time, tone, and mood? How do they relate to the represented world, the world you can see?
—ELINOR FUCHS[37]

The diverse contributors to this book represent a wide range of theater and drama expertise, spanning historical and contemporary performance, while also drawing on the fields of gender studies, critical race studies, phenomenology, AI, animal studies, memory studies, and feminist and queer theories. Expanding beyond a dramaturgical focus, *Late Stage* considers embodied performance of age onstage and the performance of aging offstage across the life course to mark, and ultimately challenge, ageism in theater and society. Themes explored in the book are broad ranging, but connected by their interrogation of the narratives of ageism and decline ideology; ageist and sexist casting practices; the representation of age-based stereotypes; disability, race, gender, sexuality, and class; age and robotic technologies; community-building and intergenerational dialogues; theatrical legacies; age and autobiography; time, memory, and memory loss; and empathy and care.

Late Stage is divided into four discrete but related parts. Part I, "Dramaturgies of Aging and Late Style," draws on the intersections of dramaturgy, dramatic theory and criticism, late style, and aging. We begin with two foundational essays from Elinor Fuchs: "Estr*age*ment: Toward an 'Age Theory' Theater Criticism" from *Performance Research* (2014) and "Rehearsing Age" from *Modern Drama* (2016). "Estr*age*ment" (without the *n*) focuses on integrating age studies with the dramatic theories of Bertolt Brecht while incorporating an analysis of Henrik Ibsen's later plays, featuring aged characters in exile encountering strange new landscapes. Alongside Brecht, Fuchs considers the experience of aging through her work on "landscape theory," noting how age metaphors are often geographic and spatial in theater and life. "If one is attuned to theatrical discourse, one cannot miss the architectonics," she writes. Fuchs explores how age can influence the portrayal of theatrical characters and their relationships, and how theater and drama can reflect and challenge societal attitudes toward aging. "Estr*age*ment," she explains, "is not so much a perceptual/political moment, as in Brecht, but a late-life developmental moment in which the familiar also becomes strange. In an age-conscious *Verfremdung* scene the aging figures may see as if for the first time, or the scene may depict a late-life experience in which the old are estranged from their former selves and look back with astonishment on their past limitations."

Fuchs calls for a more nuanced and inclusive approach to theater criticism that recognizes the importance of age as a vital component in the analysis of dramatic literature and performance. These ideas are built on in "Rehearsing Age," where Fuchs reinforces the theoretical link between theater studies and age studies. Presenting case studies of older individuals confronting aging, and analyzing these through Brecht's theory of estrangement, Fuchs contrasts the dramatic theater with the epic theater, noting how these dramaturgical approaches align well with the prevailing theories of aging. In both essays, Fuchs exposes how dramatic structure has the potential to disrupt age-old narratives centered on decline. She writes, "This dimension has perhaps been awaiting our own age of longevity for a fuller understanding, both in art and in life."

In "Aging and the Time of Estr*age*ment in Chekhov's Drama," Yana Meerzon draws directly on Fuchs's concept of estr*age*ment to argue that aging is a central feature of Anton Chekhov's major characters as they reevaluate and reassess the meaning of their own lives, looking to the past in order to (re) define the present (known as the "life review" in age studies terms). As they become older, Meerzon writes, Chekhovian characters "try to learn how to appreciate their present time and to acknowledge their aging within it," which "becomes important for them to see themselves from the distance of another time," thereby creating a space of estr*age*ment or exile for these characters. Analyzing this phenomenon primarily in *Three Sisters* and *The Cherry Orchard*, Meerzon shows how Chekhov's tragicomic mode allows characters to acknowledge their aging in ways that constitute a gesture of recognition, forcing us (the audience) to reflect on our own aging in return. In "Pathologizing Aging Femininity," Núria Casado-Gual and Inesa Shevchenko-Hotsuliak continue responding to the pioneering work of Fuchs in their comparative study of Tracy Letts's *August: Osage County* and Florian Zeller's *The Mother*. Focusing on characterization of the female protagonists in these plays, and the madness they intend to evoke, the authors demonstrate how the stereotype of the "mad" mother persists in drama, constructing both age and gender in a negative light and rescripting decline narratives. Their essay demonstrates that the so-called illness role of the mother reflects a sexist stereotype of aging femininity as well as deeply ingrained anxieties surrounding female aging more broadly. Offering close readings of these plays, the authors showcase how important it is to return to canonical plays in order to explore age stereotypes in ways that have been previously ignored.

In "Caryl Churchill's Late Style," R. Darren Gobert introduces readers to the aesthetic concept of late style by applying it to the latter part of the seven-decade career of Caryl Churchill. In close readings of her recent plays, including *Escaped Alone*, *Here We Go*, and *What If If Only*, among others, Gobert looks at the refracted, ruptured, and anachronistic qualities associated with artistic lateness. He explores the minimalistic or "distilled" qualities of Churchill's later work, showing how her plays have been abbreviated and condensed in recent years. Gobert also notes the catastrophic elements present in Churchill's late plays (not dissimilar to those of Beckett), another hallmark of late style according to Theodor Adorno and Edward Said. While appropriately critical of this framework as an aesthetic category in relation to aging, Gobert recognizes the unique ability of the aging Churchill to capture the crises of the present.

In part II, "(Re)Casting Age," the focus shifts to an array of very different contemporary plays in production and the work of a panoply of multigenerational actors on these scripts. In Valerie Barnes Lipscomb's essay, casting against "age-type" raises questions for some community theater performers because of their concerns about audiences'—and other performers'—reactions. What are the stakes and the outcomes of "age-passing"? This autoethnographic account challenges assumptions about what happens when an actor (Lipscomb) plays an ingenue at age fifty-six. Dorothy Chansky's essay points to who is doing the storytelling (younger playwrights) and who is cast (mid- and later-life actors) in New York's Public Theater's production of *Out of Time*, which sheds light on the lives of five Asian American elders. Chansky sets this production and its artistic team's choices against the backdrop of other recent works written and/or performed by Asian American artists in the New York theater scene; she also documents and analyzes ongoing issues in representation (including the absence) of Asian Americans on the American stage. Next, with close readings of stage directions, Bess Rowen draws connections and sharp contrasts between the works of three contemporary playwrights that directly challenge the age/youth binary in casting choices. Whereas the age gap in casting described by Lipscomb in her essay was pragmatic, based on actor availability (or lack thereof), in Rowen's analysis of *Dance Nation*, *Log Cabin*, and *Kimberly Akimbo*, the age gap between actor and character is specific and intentional. Rowen makes clear that stage directions and casting notes matter greatly in performing resistance to age, gender, and sexual identity stereotypes. In Heunjung Lee's examination of trans and queer performers' work over time, she tracks how the dance-theater production *Gardenia*, and its restaging with most of the original cast in *Gardenia—10 Years Later*, offers a rich site for excavating the intersections of gender, sexual identities, and age as they illuminate the nonlinearity of trans and queer aging. Lee draws on Basting's depth model of aging in her reading of the resistance and power in older trans performers' bodies, "retrospective gaze," and survivor stories onstage, in juxtaposition with the choreography of pain performed by two young cisgender dancers in *Gardenia—10 Years Later*.

Part III, "Autobiography and the Aging Body/Self," turns the spotlight on significant performers of later life. Each essay in this section is the result of live encounters "in the room" between the author and their late-stage artist-subject(s). These pieces time-travel and foreground the voices, bodies, experiences, and perspectives of the artists themselves, along with the interpretations, responses, and analyses of their interlocutors/witnesses. This section reflects the feminist tradition of "auto/biography" as theorized by Liz Stanley and, more recently, Deirdre Heddon, among others.[38] Cindy Rosenthal illuminates how Living Theatre cofounder Judith Malina's pacifist/anarchist/utopia-inspired theater work evolved to challenge the decline narrative of aging in her later performances. Malina's feisty performance in *Maudie and Jane*, her play "The Triumph of Time" (based on the life course narratives of Lillian Booth Actors Home residents), and her role in leading the final liberatory Living Theatre seder are markers of how she "set an example" during the late stage of her activist art. For Malina, this meant putting her body on the line, raising her voice, and engaging others in the struggle whenever and wherever she saw injustice and oppression. Next, Daniel Alexander Jones riffs in a dream-form memory-dialogue with Black feminist performance pioneer Robbie McCauley. This moving, intergenerational exchange between two pathbreaking performance artists/playwrights/educators/collaborators highlights the enduring strength of McCauley's mentorship and her inspiring legacy. Here we see Fuchs's theory of estr*age*ment highlighted in the vibrant shift in form and feel of this chapter, which challenges more traditional academic discourse with its freshly empowered (re)view of youth, age, and aging in performance. Jill Dolan's concept of the "utopian performative" ("an affective rehearsal of what utopia could *feel* like," as Julia Henderson explains) is a through line in Rosenthal's analysis of Malina's performances, and also sits at the heart of Henderson's moment-to-moment examination of later-life performers' and multigenerational spectators' intersubjectivity at a performance of the "live autobiographical 'onstage documentary'" *Sonic Elder*. Henderson explores the hope and the resistance to ageism embedded in the empathic, intimate actor-audience connections that emerged from the life storytelling, the collective music-making, and the hallowed, memory-laden resonance of the performance venue itself. In the last chapter of this section, Benjamin Gillespie turns our attention to butch lesbian icon Peggy Shaw and her first production after surviving a stroke in 2011, *Ruff*, as well as to the challenges and transformations in creating and producing work with an age-related illness. Integrating myriad forms of technical support and multiple collaborations, rehearsal and performance practices were remade to be newly sustainable for Shaw. Gillespie argues that *Ruff* is a queered memory play with Shaw at its center, and that the fragmentation and nonlinearity of this work highlight and celebrate the resistance of queer aging.

Part IV represents a range of contributions and writing styles centering on themes of "Time, Empathy, and Care." We begin with a long view of history and the impact of time on the life of the critic in an interview with Bonnie Marranca. Hillary Miller's conversation with Marranca in "The Melody of Aging" focuses on Marranca's lifelong dedication to writing, editing, and publishing in the field of theater and performance. Marranca has cultivated a distinctive perspective and writing style centered on experimental theater and performance practices over multiple decades. The interview highlights the evolving life of a critic in a dynamic field, reflecting on decades of engagement with the avant-garde. Marranca, who has addressed aging in her own work, especially in her writing on the life and legacy of María Irene Fornés, here contemplates her own aging as she prepares, in 2024, to conclude the long-running *PAJ: A Journal of Performance and Art*, which she has curated for almost fifty years with nearly 140 issues. Reflecting on her extensive background and experience, Marranca challenges limiting clichés about aging in the arts and considers how her own processes and perspectives have transformed over time.

We turn then to issues of technology and care. The following two chapters shift the focus from theater studies to an analysis of age performativity. In "Age Simulation: The Ultimate Dress Rehearsal," Scott Magelssen interrogates the fast-growing aging simulation industry with techniques geared toward those who work closely with older people, investigating how the recreation of precise memory spaces from the past helps support and comfort individuals suffering memory loss. His essay begins with the example of Town Square, an immersive environment that simulates San Diego in the 1950s and early 1960s for individuals who are experiencing the impact of Alzheimer's disease. By immersing participants into their youthful past, this simulation uses memory to "prompt them to open up and tell stories, connect with each other and their family members and Town Hall staff." This is just one example of many in the chapter exploring how immersive age simulations promise to benefit those facing the physical, emotional, and mental challenges that come with aging, but also how they can also perpetuate and reinforce negative stereotypes about aging adults, such as with the controversial use of "aging suits." Questions surrounding technology and aging continue with Jennifer Parker-Starbuck's "Bringing Down the Curtain: Robotic Animals and Technologies of Aging." Parker-Starbuck begins by detailing the brutal loss of her own mother during the COVID-19 pandemic while both she and her mother were living in forced isolation. As she writes, "Zoom became a time-travel machine of sorts. Although we didn't know it, our weekly meeting with my mother became for her an extended goodbye to those she loved." Expanding on her own experiences with the loss of an aging parent, Parker-Starbuck details the pandemic of loneliness and isolation experienced more widely by seniors in care homes, and the technology used to help "solve" this problem, including telecommunications like Zoom, FaceTime, and Skype, but also animatronic robots for adults. While noting that robotic technologies do not replace human contact, Parker-Starbuck argues that they can play a valuable role in combating the loneliness pandemic. Parker-Starbuck connects this phenomenon to Jordan Harrison's futuristic play *Marjorie Prime*, in which "Prime" robots replace deceased loved ones for families to benefit from. "Let us continue to look at the agents for aging that balance and facilitate, that assist and comprise, and let us acknowledge the humans and nonhumans that surround us at the end, for they too, are us."

In the final chapter, Anne Davis Basting offers an openhearted reflection on her friendship and final meeting with Elinor Fuchs in the form of a short memory play. It is apt that we end the book with this testament to Fuchs's brilliant life, memorialized by a scholar who has also shaped the field of age studies immensely through the lens of performance and techniques for assisting those with dementia-related memory loss. As Basting visits Fuchs, now experiencing dementia herself, she contemplates their parallel professional and personal journeys through theater scholarship, playwriting, age studies, parenting, daughtering, dementia, and friendship.

The eighteen authors gathered here—a multigenerational group including senior, mid-career, and emerging scholars—represent a broad spectrum of research, identities, and backgrounds, as well as diverse approaches to theorizing age and aging in theater, drama, and performance. *Late Stage* offers a unique array of materials and approaches, including performance analyses and critiques, biographical and autobiographical presentations of aging, the aesthetic concept of "late style," and essays on theory and dramatic literature. Chapters include traditional academic essays, interviews with artists and critics, and performative writing. Our goal has been to capture as many voices as possible to showcase the nuanced and variegated ways age and aging are experienced and lived differently. Focusing mostly on Europe and North America, this volume expands existing concepts of age and aging and firmly embeds them within existing discourses in the field. We hope that, moving forward, theater and performance studies will become, at last, a home for work on age studies.

NOTES

1. Elinor Fuchs, "EF's Visit to a Small Planet: Some Questions to Ask a Play," *Theater* 34, no. 2 (Summer 2004): 6.

2. For more on the ENAS, see https://temp.agingstudies.eu/. For more on the NANAS, see https://agingstudies.org/NANAS/

3. Fuchs, "EF's Visit to a Small Planet," 9.

4. Fuchs, 7.

5. The notion that our identities and constructions of age do not change over time is challenged by numerous scholars. Fuchs argues that this misunderstanding of the life course positions aging in an Aristotelian "rise and fall" structure, with aging told as a narrative of decline. See her chapter "Estr*age*ment: Toward an 'Age Theory' Theater Criticism," reprinted here. Also see Kathleen Woodward's foundational book, *Aging and Its Discontents: Freud and Other Fictions* (Indiana University Press, 1991).

6. Judith Butler, *Gender Trouble: Feminism and the Subversion of Identity* (Routledge, 1990), 146–47.

7. Aagje Swinnen and Cynthia Port, "Aging, Narrative, and Performance: Essays from the Humanities," *International Journal of Ageing and Later Life* 7, no. 2 (2012): 12.

8. See Robert N. Butler, *Why Survive? Being Old in America* (Johns Hopkins University Press, 2002); Lawrence R. Samuel, *Aging in America: A Cultural History* (University of Pennsylvania Press, 2017); and Margaret Cruikshank, *Learning to Be Old: Gender, Culture, and Aging*, 3rd ed. (Rowman and Littlefield, 2013).

9. Woodward, *Aging and Its Discontents*, 16.

10. For more on successful aging narratives, see Stephen Katz and Toni M. Calasanti, "Critical Perspectives on Successful Aging: Does It 'Appeal More Than It Illuminates'?," *Gerontologist* 55, no. 1 (2015): 26–33.

11. Margaret Morganroth Gullette, *Aged by Culture* (University of Chicago Press, 2004), 130.

12. See Butler, *Why Survive?* For an overview of the concept of "cultural aging," see Gullette, *Aged by Culture*.

13. See Robert N. Butler, *The Longevity Revolution: The Benefits and Challenges of Living a Long Life* (PublicAffairs, 2009).

14. See Zoe Caplan, "U.S. Older Population Grew from 2010 to 2020 at Fastest Rate Since 1880 to 1890," US Census Bureau, May 25, 2023, https://www.census.gov/library/stories/2023/05/2020-census-united-states-older-population-grew.html

15. Julia Henderson, "Challenging Age Binaries by Viewing *King Lear* in Temporal Depth," *Theatre Research in Canada* 37, no. 1 (2016): 43.

16. See Gullette, *Aged by Culture*; Stephen Katz, *Disciplining Old Age: The Forma-*

tion of Gerontological Knowledge (University Press of Virginia, 1996); and Woodward, *Aging and Its Discontents.*

17. Jan Baars, *Aging and the Art of Living* (Johns Hopkins University Press, 2012), 4.

18. Stephen Katz, "What Is Age Studies?," *Age, Culture, Humanities* 1, no. 1 (2014): 19, https://ageculturehumanities.org/WP/what-is-age-studies/

19. See Stephen Katz, *Cultural Aging: Life Course, Lifestyle, and Senior Worlds* (University of Toronto Press, 2009).

20. See Fuchs, "Estragement."

21. Anne Davis Basting, "Performance Studies and Age," *Handbook of the Humanities and Aging*, 2nd ed., ed. Thomas R. Cole, Robert Kastenbaum, and Ruth E. Ray (Springer, 2000), 268.

22. Anne Davis Basting, *The Stages of Age: Performing Age in Contemporary American Culture* (University of Michigan Press, 1998), 141.

23. Valerie Barnes Lipscomb, "Age in *M. Butterfly*: Unquestioned Performance," *Modern Drama* 59, no. 2 (2016): 193 (emphasis added).

24. Lynne Segal, *Out of Time: The Pleasures and the Perils of Ageing* (Verso Books, 2014), 4.

25. Kathleen Woodward, *Figuring Age: Women, Bodies, Generations* (Indiana University Press, 1999), xxii.

26. Perspectives from each of these authors, along with many others, can be found in Marlene Goldman, Kate de Medeiros, and Thomas Cole's edited collection *Critical Humanities and Ageing* (Routledge, 2022). See also Julia Twigg and Wendy Martin, eds., *Routledge Handbook in Cultural Gerontology* (Routledge, 2015).

27. Chivers is one of the few scholars bridging these two fields, through her study of old age representation in cinema. She claims that "while illness and disability arguably differ, age, disability, and illness are tightly linked in most popular interpretations of late life . . . rather than conflate disability and aging, these signs designate two separate groups and yet imagine that they belong together in a shared space . . . critical gerontology has similar goals, methods, and politics to those of disability studies in that it seeks to revise a set of interpretations of late life against the grain and for the political benefit of older people, but scholars in the field have not yet fully engaged with one another's work." See Sally Chivers, *The Silvering Screen: Old Age and Disability in Cinema* (University of Toronto Press, 2011), 8–9. See also Erin Gentry Lamb, "Age and/as Disability: A Call for Conversation," *Age, Culture, Humanities* 2 (2015): 313–22; and Christine Overall, "Old Age and Ageism, Impairment and Ableism: Exploring the Conceptual and Material Connections," *NWSA Journal* 18, no. 1 (2006): 126–37.

28. Marvin Carlson, *The Haunted Stage: The Theatre as Memory Machine* (University of Michigan Press, 2003).

29. Lawrence Switzky, "Introduction: Modern Drama, Aging, and the Life Course," *Modern Drama* 59, no. 2 (2016): 137, 141.

30. Benjamin Gillespie, Julia Henderson, and Núria Casado-Gual, eds., "Age and Performance," special issue, *Theatre Research in Canada* 42, no. 2 (November 2021).

31. Richard Gough and Nanako Nakajima, eds., "On Ageing (& Beyond)," special issue, *Performance Research* 24, no. 3 (2019).

32. Marlene Goldman, "Aging, Old Age, Memory, Aesthetics: Introduction to the

Special Issue," *Occasion* 4 (June 2012), https://shc.stanford.edu/arcade/publications/occasion/aging-old-age-memory-aesthetics/

33. Pam Cobrin and Debra Levine, eds., "Aging," special issue, *Women & Performance: a journal of feminist theory* 22, no. 1 (2012).

34. *Age, Culture, Humanities* is available online at https://tidsskrift.dk/ageculturehumanities/

35. See https://agingstudies.org/NANAS/?page_id=903.

36. Valerie Barnes Lipscomb and Aagje Swinnen, eds., *The Palgrave Handbook of Literature and Aging* (Springer, 2024).

37. Fuchs, "EF's Visit to a Small Planet," 7.

38. For more on feminist auto/biography, see Liz Stanley, *The Auto/Biographical I: The Theory and Practice of Feminist Auto/Biography* (Manchester University Press, 1992); and Deirdre Heddon, *Autobiography and Performance: Performing Selves* (Palgrave Macmillan, 2008).

Part I
Dramaturgies of Aging and Late Style

1

Estragement
Toward an "Age Theory" Theater Criticism[1]

Elinor Fuchs

This paper is an attempt at a theater criticism informed in part by age theory and in part by dramatic and theatrical theory put to a new use.[2] It is a response to a question only recently being asked in the fields of theater and performance: how is it possible, after more than thirty years of identity theory, in which, in our researches in the humanities and not least in theater and performance studies, we have "undone" an entire rosary of binary oppositions—male and female, white and black, straight and queer, abled and disabled, human and animal—how is it possible that we have largely ignored the vast undeconstructed binary of youth and age? My hope is to suggest new ways of understanding the depiction of age, in this case meaning the condition of being old, in drama and theater, and, by extension, in cultural representations of age and aging as well.

THE CULTURAL CONSTRUCTION OF AGE

Age studies (or in the UK, "ageing studies") has emerged, since the 1990s, out of a resistance and an inspiration—resistance to accepting decline as the primary fact of advancing age, from early middle age on, and inspiration from the "materialist" identity theories, especially the body-based theories of race and gender that have pierced the screen of biological determinism to expose cultural constructions of the self. Feeling her way toward a new paradigm of age in *Declining to Decline: Cultural Combat and the Politics of the Midlife* (1997), the pioneering American age critic Margaret Morganroth Gullette has written that many who study aging "keep in circulation the sleepy illusion that age and aging are ahistorical, prediscursive—natural." The illusion can only be maintained, she observed, because age "is still at the stage where gender and race used to be: hidden by its supposed foundation in 'the body.'"[3] Seven years later, in *Aged by Culture*, Gullette found that age remained "an impoverished concept, not only because of its undertheorized relationship to the body, but also because of its poorly defined relationship to market forces, neoliberal politics, and ideology."[4]

In *Cultural Aging: Life Course, Lifestyle, and Senior Worlds* (2009), the Canadian sociologist Stephen Katz foregrounds the concept of culturally constructed age bias. Katz criticizes the medicalized and social-scientized fundamentalisms of traditional gerontology, and supports the emergence of a critical gerontology that reaches out "nomadically" to theory in other body-based fields that have led the way in resisting biological fatalism.[5]

We may well recall the feminist protest of thirty and forty years ago—"We are not our bodies!"—yet despite analogous efforts in the critical age community, the body persists at the center of virtually all media attention, social discourse, "natural wisdom," and public policy on aging. Nora Ephron picked up the theme in the title of her book *I Feel Bad About My Neck: And Other Thoughts on Being a Woman* (2006).[6] Why has a broad-based movement against ageism, or at least against the body obsession that underlies it, not "taken off," as did other body-based movements, even as a movement seems to gather force in academic conferences, journals, and many book-length studies? Among the reasons: old age and death do not offer the liberatory horizon promised by the theorization of race, gender, and sexual identity; it is harder to organize older constituencies against the master narratives of age, as they are the "truths" of the old as well as the young; and youth and age present a unique form of binary opposition. As Gullette writes, "Age may be the hardest of the body-linked constructs to dispute because two of its properties, change and continuity, seem unavoidable, yet when considered together, contradictory."[7]

No one is born old; no one, short of early death, escapes it; yet even the old deny age. (This writer's father, something of a public figure, convincingly put out the story that he was exactly one year younger than his actual age: the year he chose, as he thought, served to identify him with a more youthful decade.) "Youth culture" ages us and individuals correspondingly "de-age" themselves; the dividing line between youth and age is constantly elusive. Thus youth and age may be the most unstable of deconstructable binaries. Finally, one cannot neglect the power and persistence of what I see as the Sublime of Age, a visceral horror of physical decrepitude.

Today this horror is exploited in Western society to support the anti-aging industry. Chilling examples of the latter may be found in a study by Toni Calasanti, Amy Sorensen, and Neal King entitled "Anti-Ageing Advertisements and Perceptions of Ageing," published in Virpi Ylänne's anthology *Representing Ageing: Images and Identities* (2012). Analyzing the content of ninety-six anti-aging websites, they found, along with cheery age-denial sales pitches, language that appeared to be borrowed from fairy-tale descriptions of evil witches: "At the grossest level, that of the human body, the aging process . . . is directly tied to the bulging, wrinkling, saggy, flabby, draggy creatures that we all sooner or later start to see in the mirror."[8] Thus, the active age movement, particularly in the United States, is not against ageism but against growing old itself.

The anti-aging enterprise, with its utopian goal of stopping the ageing process or at least of prolonging "youth" and masking the marks of age on the body, is the only true "age movement" in popular culture. One can note, for instance, the noxious, discriminatory, and ageist slogan and varied program of "successful aging," which is popularly accepted as an individual mandate and societal goal. To the failure of growing old, now add the failure of not growing old "successfully." Embedded within the success ideology is a further charge against women as chief failures, as displayed, for instance, in the age-centered performances of commercials accompanying late evening news programs. The helpless female (played by a not-yet-old actress wearing flattering makeup and hairstyle) lies collapsed on the floor. She cries, "I've fallen and I can't get up!" A strong male voice responds that a rescue team has been dispatched, as a help-on-the-way siren wails its reassurance. In an adjacent commercial, a vigorous white-haired male promotes a medication for older men. He is seventy-two and feels "great." Far from not getting up, he takes testosterone and—can't get down, so to speak. Here are the apocalypse and millennium of contemporary aging.

AGE THEORY

My own interest in age was sparked by my ten-year experience as caregiver to a mother with dementia and by the results of publishing a memoir about the experience. The book led to invitations to speak at caregiver conferences, in turn leading to participation in academic age and disability studies conferences. I have been spurred along this path not only by my personal progress in aging, but also by the realization that my own field of theater theory and criticism has been almost entirely unrepresented within the multidisciplinary range of these conferences. At the American theater conferences that

I frequent and in our theater journals, age is scarcely a category of research or even notice. Anne Basting's two books *The Stages of Age* (1998) and *Forget Memory* (2009), the anthology by Valerie Barnes Lipscomb and Leni Marshall, *Staging Age* (2010), and Mick Mangan's recent *Staging Ageing* (2013) have not yet penetrated the silence on the subject of age and aging in American theater and performance studies.[9]

What thinking can we turn to in cultural age theory that will begin the question-raising and consciousness-lifting that launched the earlier critical movements and their theatrical and performance analogues? The major shift in age theory over the past few decades has been the accumulating rejection of the "peak-and-decline" narrative of age. Margaret Morganroth Gullette is the main architect of this argument. "The master narrative starts," she writes, "as a story of progress and becomes a peak-and-[increasingly early]-decline story." Using theatrical language, she writes that aging is a "script" that we tailor to ourselves. "According to the prevailing script, even if we also make progress, we are supposed to internalize decline as our dominant private age identity."[10]

Cultural gerontologists now speak widely of the rejection of decline ideology and its replacement by the "life course" narrative, or sometimes the "creativity across the life course" narrative.[11] This perspective argues for each individual the peculiar nature, shape, virtue, problems, and interest of the stages of the life course, with social/historical factors taken into consideration. For each individual, the possibility of self-reinvention beckons along that spectrum. Life course thinking rejects the fatalism of the declinist story. Among other accomplishments, this perspective has spawned a growing literature on the "late style" of composers and artists, familiarly known in the literature as OAS, or Old-Age Style.

Yet as adopted and adapted in popular culture, even the nuanced "life course" does not avoid the body trap that the age critics deplore, but rather may serve as another route back to the narrative of ineluctable decline, leading this time to its avoidance. The optimism of life course thinking has become a rich foundation for selling as new and happily treatable diseases what were formerly considered "natural" manifestations of the inevitability of decline; for instance, "overactive bladder" has replaced incontinence, and "Low T" or the vague "blood flow" has replaced "erectile dysfunction," itself a replacement for the inevitable "impotence" of later age.[12] These new diseases and their accompanying treatments have resulted in novel forms of health and a restoration of "natural" youth and vigor to those who, by neglect or chance and no longer by necessity, find themselves afflicted. Thus, peak-and-decline itself is inscribed back into life course narrative as an image of personal failure. The terrifying sublime of the aging body reappears less as a fate than an avoidable choice, an option.

Life course theory, or sometimes the life course perspective, began to come together in the 1960s from many different disciplines, leading, at the level of the individual, to widening interest in and respect for the resiliency and variability of older people. In 1975, Dr. Robert Butler, widely recognized as the father of modern American age consciousness and policy, published his Pulitzer Prize–winning book, *Why Survive? Being Old in America*, in sympathy with this perspective.[13] Butler was the first to identify discrimination against the elderly as "ageism." Among his ideas that will have some bearing later in this essay, is Dr. Butler's valorization of life review as an active and essential practice of the old, however popularly derided as mere reminiscence and a symptom of decline. (Inevitably, life review therapy has emerged as a flourishing economic offshoot of Butler's book.)

Notwithstanding market exploitations, these are the sturdy roots to age consciousness derived from the "criticality" of age thinking: an awareness of social agendas masquerading as the "natural" narrative of decline, the acceptance of life course thinking and the positive value of life review. They have helped me to begin to think about the possibility of an age-related theater criticism. Stephen Katz's encouragement to "nomadic" theorization in the field of age—the "fracturing, transfiguring, borrowing, and recombining" of theoretical ideas from other fields (he mentions Bourdieu, Deleuze and Guattari, and Foucault, among others)—further pushes me to consider whether theatrical and dramatic theory can make its own contribution to a theatrical age theory.[14]

FROM AGE THEORY TO DRAMATIC THEORY

To begin, then: We, we theater people! invented peak-and-decline. We (with Aristotle) mapped it in classical plot structure—in reversals, recognition, and suffering. We (with Sophocles) memorialized it in the riddle of the Sphinx and her "three legs at night." We codified it in Freytag's Pyramid.[15] And then, after two or so millennia, we scrapped it for the life course structures of Epic Theater. Fifty years after that, we accused peak-and-decline of spreading the contagion of phallocentrism and left it for dead. Thus, gerontology, unbeknown to itself, has moved from Aristotle to Brecht and perhaps beyond. Oh my goodness, the reader may ask, are we going to have to comb through all of dramatic literature now to expose ageist decline narratives, just as Elin Diamond once exposed realism as the carrier, or let us say, the narrative enforcer, of gynophobia?[16]

But perhaps there's a shortcut. We could look for counterexamples. Do critical gerontology or cultural age studies provide any examples of non-declinist narratives of aging? And do these have theatrical analogues? Here I must introduce a new figure, whose notebook on her experience of advancing age, *The Measure of My Days*, was first published in 1968 when she was eighty-five. Although Florida Scott-Maxwell is not widely known outside professional fields studying age, the book has been in print for most of its forty-six years. Scott-Maxwell, an American writer and playwright, who moved to Scotland and later became a Jungian analyst, is gerontology's inoculation against the ideology of decline; she is also its bulwark against the *reductio ad corpum* of traditional age discourse. "We who are old," she writes, "know that age is more than a disability. It is an intense and varied experience, almost beyond our capacity at times."[17] Her eighties become a time of revelation. "My dear fellow octogenarians," she exclaims, "how are we to carry so much life, and what are we to do with it?" Fierce with new insight she writes, "I cannot conceive how age and tranquility came to be synonymous." "Though drab outside inside we flame with a wild life that is almost incommunicable."[18] She strains to find language to describe this new experience: "We have reached the place beyond resignation, a place I had no idea existed until I had arrived here," and later: "All is uncharted and uncertain, we seem to lead the way into the unknown. Here we come to a new place of which I knew nothing. Further on, go further on, one finds that one has arrived at a larger place still."[19]

Age scholars cite Scott-Maxwell's curiosity and sense of wonder about age. Her book becomes a personal testament to the possibilities of human development and growth even at advanced age. As a theater person, I see something else: her discovery of age as a series of "places." If one is attuned to theatrical discourse, one cannot miss the architectonics. Her late years have become a journey inscribed in scenes of increasing magnitude, a station drama of unfolding age. This vocabulary of landscape as related to age is a vast subject—it appears in autobiography, fiction, poetry, and drama. However, the metaphor beckons me to take up Stephen Katz's invitation to "nomadically" bring dramatic theory to age theory.

"Landscape theory" has made an incursion into theatrical discourse. Gertrude Stein's essay "Plays" (1935) marks a modernist beginning, and my own chapter in *The Death of Character* (1996) and the project that I and my colleague Una Chaudhuri of New York University pursued in our anthology *Land/Scape/Theater* (2002) have contributed to it.[20] Una Chaudhuri and I argue the limits of a conventional characterological approach to dramatic structure, claiming that landscape, whether seen onstage as a design element, imagined as offstage or more distantly embedded in the "landscape imaginary" of a dramatic world, can play a crucial role in the deep dramaturgy that underlies every dramatic text.[21]

Since I began thinking age and theater together, I have become curious about the role that landscape plays in the great works of the dramatic canon that concern themselves with aging figures (I think of *Oedipus at Colonus*, *King Lear*, the conclusion of *Faust 2*, Ibsen's late plays, perhaps *Endgame*). With his seeming interest in what we would today call life course perspective and life review, and especially in his pictorial rendering of the peak-and-decline narrative, Henrik Ibsen will provide for the rest of this paper my thought experiment: what new insights can age theory wring from his much-discussed late plays?

THE IBSEN TRIPTYCH

Neither designated nor commonly seen as such, three of Ibsen's final four plays compose a triptych on age—"over the hill" age. (Even our clichés of age come wrapped in landscape.) Omitting another kind of age play, *Little Eyolf* of 1894, the three others—*The Master Builder* of 1892, *John Gabriel Borkman* of 1896, and the 1899 *When We Dead Awaken*—can be read together as an evolving debate between Ibsen and himself on the respective values represented by or assignable to youth and age, their mutual conflict, and the way to live in the face of approaching death. Of the three, *When We Dead Awaken* puzzled and even embarrassed many of Ibsen's early modern champions for its departure from realism and seeming regression to the earlier romanticism of *Brand*'s symbolic landscape. On the other side of what became a debate in the Ibsen literature, the play's admirers pointed to Ibsen's emerging symbolist style, the chamber music elegance of its quartet of principals, and its intimate assessment of the value of a human life dedicated to the creation of art. I myself have read it as a revisiting of apocalyptic and millennialist themes at the turn of the century. Not to my knowledge ever regarded as directly concerned with the values of youth and age (or youth versus age), the play seems to me now to lay out the entire age-critical territory I have sketched above, especially when read in relation to the earlier two plays.

This three-play meditation on age, on what it means to cycle off the planet and be succeeded by new life, begins with a corny but memorable moment in the first act of *The Master Builder*. The great architect Solness confesses to the family doctor his terror that one day he will be displaced by the next generation.

SOLNESS. It racks me, this fear—it racks me, morning and night. Because someday things have to change, you'll see.
HERDAL. Oh, rot! Where's this change coming from?
SOLNESS. (*with firm conviction*). From the young.
HERDAL. Hah! The young! I'd hardly say you're obsolete. . . .
SOLNESS. The change is coming. I can sense it. . . . Someone or other will set up the cry: Step back for me! And all the others will storm in after, shaking their fists and shouting: Make room—make room—make room! Yes Doctor you better look out. Someday youth will come here, knocking at the door—[22]

At that moment comes Ibsen's famous knock-knock joke: enter youth.

The Master Builder is a difficult play with a startlingly unsympathetic protagonist. Rarely has a playwright treated a central character with the contempt that Ibsen showers on Solness: ironically inflated as a kind of sun king ("sol" means "sun" in Norwegian), whose satellites are blinded by his radiance, Solness withholds professional advancement from a younger colleague, has an open sexual dalliance with his secretary (the young man's fiancée), lies to his mentally unstable wife, was indirectly responsible for the deaths of his infant twin sons, and on at least one occasion may have sexually molested a twelve-year-old girl. Now twenty-two, it is that girl, Hilde Wangel, who knocks at the door and in the course of the drama ushers Solness to his suicidal death, playing out Solness's premonition on the role of youth in the grinding generational cycle. Yet don't blame youth: Ibsen seems to say that Solness's own frightened assessment reveals him as already "in decline" and headed for death. Ibsen has constructed an almost parodic peak-and-decline narrative, the trajectory of a human lifetime understood as rise and fall.[23]

This vertical shape changes in Ibsen's final act from an outline of a well-worn dramatic theme to a visual image. Offstage—the account is excitedly narrated—Solness mounts the high tower on the new home he has built for himself and his wife, his latest architectural triumph, to hang a dedicatory wreath. Hilde had urged him on to this act of bravado, remembering his similar dedicatory performance in her hometown, where as a child ten years earlier she was smitten with Solness. Now he topples instantly to his death, crushed in an adjacent rock quarry, as if into an already prepared grave. The play ends abruptly. This harsh theatrical conclusion, with no additional scene of pious mourning or suffering survivors, signals a similarly harsh conclusion to an "age" reading of *The Master Builder*: the old will die with their insatiable lives incomplete, never finally "home," and the young will surge forward over their necessary bodies, taking possession of all they left behind. The play ends with Hilde Wangel in a transgenerational delirium. Like an excited child, she celebrates Solness's daring and seems not to note his death. Yet in the same words that she shouts "with wild intensity," one also hears the cry of the emerging generation claiming ownership, "My—my master builder!"[24]

In *John Gabriel Borkman*, Ibsen looks again at this generational rite of passage. He brings little more sympathy to the old than he did in *The Master Builder*, but here the old have become older, and clearly represent an entire generation. Three principal elders (and a fourth from the play's comic subplot) will be left to die; three young people all but run them over in their urgent need to escape to freedom, pleasure, and warmth.

John Gabriel Borkman's splendid "peak" of wealth, power, and influence lies far behind him. Having embezzled the funds of the bank he directed in the service of a vast industrial dream of controlling all the mineral resources of the region, he has served his prison sentence, and now endures life trapped in his own home. He has lived a meteoric rise, and a terrible fall, sixteen years in duration. The vertical image of peak-and-decline is not scenically mapped onto this story until the play's last act, yet is consonant with the play's three scenic "worlds." For three acts onstage Ibsen's familiar domestic space is on display, here weirdly divided into noncommunicating lower and upper levels. Below, Mrs. Borkman sits in her cold parlor, defiantly expecting restitution; above, John Gabriel paces the floor like a "sick wolf," awaiting vindication.[25] Trapped between shame and arrogance, they are two frozen visions of decline. They are joined by a rare visitor, Mrs. Borkman's estranged twin sister, Ella. A more normative version of age-in-decline, Ella will soon die of a terminal disease and intends to spend her last days on the Borkman estate, cared for by the Borkman son, whom she had raised after the financial calamity struck. The vertical house with its harsh division between upper and lower levels is framed by a greater scenography of the map of Europe—ice- and duty-bound in the north; warm and sensual as one moves south. Ibsen's characters, the trio of dying elders, and the trio of pleasure-seeking young people among whom is young Erhart Borkman, divide the map between them in the course of the action.

And then there is the literal plein air mountain scene of the play's astounding final act, to which I return shortly.

It is not always noticed by stage directors, actors, and indeed critics that Ibsen paints the three principal elders as vampires. All have their hopes fastened on young Erhart, who will in their view variously redeem honor, revive business, or serve the dying. The younger generation, led by the ripe, sexually experienced "widow" or divorcée—it is unclear—Fanny Wilton, lives in a far more playful universe. Within hours, they will flee the frozen north for Italy. The third of this party, the young Foldal girl, who plays piano nicely, will give the expedition the color of respectability. At least she won't have to play the *Danse macabre* for Borkman on her regular visits to his quarters as hired pianist.

Spectators who have been waiting to see which of the three parents will enlist young Erhart as an ally are often confused at the end of the third act as the young dash south, and the play appears to change genre. The audience discovers that it has not after all been watching a realist contest over an issue of value and is not about to witness a scene that brings the generations into a common understanding. It turns out that there never was a question, there were no "stakes," and that the agendas of age were defeated before the play even began. Ibsen has been shaking with laughter at his three deluded old people. But now he switches from the real-world coordinates of north/south, ice/sun, Christian/pagan, and their emotional analogues, which had so often appeared in his earlier plays, and turns to the more symbolic vertical landscape first seen in his 1865 *Brand*. In the final act of the play, the three elders converge on the mountain ascent directly outside the Borkman home.

With Borkman, as it will soon appear, moments from death, the sick sister Ella not far behind in dying, and Mrs. Borkman like Mrs. Solness in some sense already dead, the three aging figures now throw themselves out on the whitened mountain scene in the dark of night. Ibsen takes them to the ironic "peak" of his tale of decline, their losses composed of old age, disgrace, poor health, bad temperament, and now their coveted adult child.

Suddenly we have arrived at one of Scott-Maxwell's new "places," a place of discovery knowable only to the aged. On the mountain John Gabriel shouts out his love and deranged vision for the great hidden treasure of the earth; in this speech he rises beyond the level of sordid capitalist to a kind of tragic figure, "a spiritual hero," as Brian Johnston writes, even as he collapses and dies; here, too, over Borkman's dead body, the sisters reach out to each other in the tepid warmth of a late-life reconciliation.[26] The scene, one of new life surging forth in a wild, unsheltered environment, is a harbinger of the discoveries Ibsen may have made as he turned for a third time to weigh the values (and value) of the older and younger generations.

WHEN WE DEAD AWAKEN

In his final play, *When We Dead Awaken*, Ibsen reconsiders the age problem, and rather astonishingly, sees it differently. He musters up his career-long dialectic of conflicting values—north/south, ice/sun, Christian/pagan, duty/

pleasure, spirit/flesh, art/life—but the decline narrative that Ibsen hung over the Borkman family like a shroud, and with which he taunted Solness to his death, is now in question. The peak of the career of the aging sculptor Rubek may be behind him, but it is also before him, spiritually and scenically. The triumph of the young in the contest over values is no longer assumed. Ibsen's rethinking of the "age problem" is much advanced in this last dramatic work by jettisoning domestic realism and shifting to a total plein air scenography.

The renowned, aging sculptor Rubek and his young wife, Maya, have arrived at a sea-level health spa, located at the foot of a mountain, in preparation for a summer voyage on the fjords. In this green, parklike environment, seen only in act 1, two unexpected figures appear and the four will share entwined destinies. One is Ulfhejm, the bear hunter, a coarse if genial figure, "of indeterminate age," whose vitality at once fascinates Maya; the other is Irene, Rubek's long-ago model, who had posed for his world-famous sculpture, Resurrection Day. Irene, a more expressionistically drawn version of the living dead previously encountered in *John Gabriel Borkman*, is a wraithlike figure in white, persistently trailed by her nurse, a black-clad nun. Two independent compacts are made that lead all four up the mountain to a high plateau at tree line where they will share entwined destinies.

In that liminal space there ensues one of the strangest scenes Ibsen ever wrote, one that suggests his ongoing reevaluation of the disaster of age. Just after Rubek and Maya have a frank talk about the limits of their marriage, and without fear or recrimination agree to pursue their lives independently—a scene remarkable enough in itself—Rubek and the ghostly ruin of his former model Irene sit on an outcropping of rock with a stream trickling through it, and discuss the failures of their former relationship as artist and model. The scene is also a reenactment, for they have taken the exact positions their two figures assume relative to rock and stream in the revision Rubek made to the celebrated sculpture on which they famously collaborated. This complex doubling of past and present in a metatheatrical inset, the echoing of stone sculpture by live, or perhaps, walking dead, bodies, complicates the question of whether art or life is more alive. The long, reflective scene is itself almost as immobile as statuary; some of it seems lost in reminiscence. The audience grows impatient with the scene; critics skip over it. But in the homely language of critical gerontology, theirs is not the mere reminiscence of two aged figures; this is "life review" of a most serious and passionate urgency. After it, now "flaming with a wild life that is almost incommunicable," as Scott-Maxwell describes her discoveries of advancing age, the couple will ascend higher still, to the highest peak, the "peak of promise."[27]

The third and final act is Ibsen's *Lear* scene, a wild craggy waste high up the mountain with no human mark save a broken-down hovel. A life-threatening storm is about to break. It is dawn, the sun not yet risen. Ulfhejm the bear hunter and young Maya—her name suggests not only the youth of May but the veil of illusion—clamber down from above. In short order Irene and Rubek ascend from below. Here two life-and-death decisions will be made. The younger couple flees the dire landscape, singing of freedom and looking forward to rape by permission. They are heading back down to a verdant garden that is in truth a spa filled with sick people surrounded by fetid water. They happily agree that in their future life together they will banish art and hunt animals. No peak for them in Ibsen's staging, only a retreat, and, quite literally and schematically, a "decline." The older couple, aflame with the conviction that they may, even at the end of life, recapture its promised fullness, climb upward and disappear into the cloud that portends the avalanche that will sweep them away. So here, laid out as if on a graph, decline is for the young, and peak for the old. Except that on this graph of the stations of the life course, all levels have been explored by all ages, and now choices, whether discriminating or illusory, have been made. For the younger couple, the choice of robust action and sexual happiness will mean death in life; for the elders, the belated aspiration to spiritual and sexual union leads directly to death. The terror reign of peak-and-decline, as narrated by Solness, is dead. Human life may be played out on a vast scenography of peak-and-decline, but the metaphor is no longer master; it is the ground on which we shape our individual destinies. There is life or death at all levels, at all ages.

ESTRA*GE*MENT

This paper has been intended not as a study as such of Ibsen's late plays, but as an attempt to sketch out for further thought a newly emerging territory opened by considering theater and age together. The Ibsen/age readings here are not intended to displace many other rich readings of these plays by Rolf Fjelde, Brian Johnston, James McFarlane, Joan Templeton, Toril Moi, and even myself, nor are they complete in themselves. But here I will just make space for the pun and neologism of my title. In the great plays that depict age and impending death not as comic spectacle, but from the inside, as living experience, there often comes a moment that could impel the nomadic gerontologist back to Brecht to borrow his term *Verfremdung*, usually translated as "alienation" or "estrangement." "Estr*age*ment," as I conceive it, without the *n*, producing a hybrid of "age" and "strange," is not so much a perceptual/political moment, as in Brecht, but a late-life developmental moment in which the familiar also becomes strange. In an age-conscious *Verfremdung* scene the aging figures may see as if for the first time, or the scene may depict a late-life experience in which the old are estranged from their former selves and look back with astonishment on their past limitations. "O, I have ta'en / Too little care of this," cries Lear.[28]

The aging are almost out of life—the blind Oedipus, the near-deranged Lear, the embittered Rubek, Maeterlinck's stranded Blind, the blind Hamm. Viewed from the perspective of age, these plays seem to require a landscape, staged or told, that itself becomes a place of estrangement or exile—a forest, a heath, a mountain height, an apocalyptic waste. Here the limitations of age may terrify, yet a new horizon of old age may open. These dramatic moments are sometimes quite literally performed, often with a flourish of metatheatricality. These places suggest to me, as her own did to Scott-Maxwell, an immensity of the conscious experience of age barely glimpsed in the discourse of normative life, where the failing body-as-decline numbly presides. These places and their developmental import, unimagined by the characters' earlier selves, have frequently been missed by actors, directors, spectators and critics alike. It is this condition that I am thinking of as "estr*age*ment," an internalized *Verfremdungseffekt* specific to the old. This dimension has perhaps been awaiting our own age of longevity for a fuller understanding, both in art and in life.

NOTES

1. Republished with permission from *Performance Research* 19, no. 3 (2014): 69–77.

2. I would like to thank Margaret Morganroth Gullette, Annabelle Winograd, Paul Walsh, and Valerie Barnes Lipscomb for their generous readings of this essay in draft.

3. Margaret Morganroth Gullette, *Declining to Decline: Cultural Combat and the Politics of the Midlife* (University Press of Virginia, 1997), 202.

4. Margaret Morganroth Gullette, *Aged by Culture* (University of Chicago Press, 2004), 105.

5. Stephen Katz, *Cultural Aging: Life Course, Lifestyle, and Senior Worlds* (University of Toronto Press, 2009), 85–100.

6. Nora Ephron, *I Feel Bad About My Neck: And Other Thoughts on Being a Woman* (Random House, 2006).

7. Gullette, *Aged by Culture*, 107.

8. Toni Calasanti, Amy Sorensen, and Neal King, "Anti-Ageing Advertisements and Perceptions of Ageing," in *Representing Ageing: Images and Identities*, ed. Virpi Ylänne (Palgrave Macmillan, 2012), 24.

9. Anne Davis Basting, *The Stages of Age: Performing Age in Contemporary American Culture* (University of Michigan Press, 1998); Anne Davis Basting, *Forget*

Memory: Creating Better Lives for People with Dementia (Johns Hopkins University Press, 2009); Valerie Barnes Lipscomb and Leni Marshall, eds., *Staging Age: The Performance of Age in Theatre, Dance, and Film* (Palgrave Macmillan, 2010); Michael Mangan, *Staging Ageing: Theatre, Performance and the Narrative of Decline* (Intellect, 2013).

10. Gullette, *Aged by Culture*, 130.

11. Katz, *Cultural Aging*, 101–18.

12. I here pick up on the PSi #19 conference theme of "Now Then." Impotence, so *then*; Low T, very *now*.

13. Robert N. Butler, *Why Survive? Being Old in America* (Johns Hopkins University Press, 1975).

14. Katz, *Cultural Aging*, 15.

15. Gustav Freytag, *Die Technik des Dramas* (1894); see Wikipedia, "Story Structure," last modified April 25, 2014, http://en.wikipedia.org/wiki/Story_structure

16. See Elin Diamond, "Mimesis, Mimicry, and the 'True-Real,'" *Modern Drama* 32, no. 1 (1989): 58–72.

17. Florida Scott-Maxwell, *The Measure of My Days* (Penguin Books, 1979), 5.

18. Scott-Maxwell, 139, 131, 132.

19. Scott-Maxwell, 132, 139–40.

20. Gertrude Stein, "Plays," in *Lectures in America* (Random House, 1935), 91–131; Elinor Fuchs, *The Death of Character: Perspectives on Theater After Modernism* (Indiana University Press, 1996), 92–107; Elinor Fuchs and Una Chaudhuri, eds., *Land/Scape/Theater* (University of Michigan Press, 2002); see also Elinor Fuchs, *Making an Exit: A Mother-Daughter Drama with Alzheimer's, Machine Tools, and Laughter* (Metropolitan Books, 2005).

21. Elinor Fuchs, "Reading for Landscape: The Case of American Drama," in Fuchs and Chaudhuri, *Land/Scape/Theater*, 30.

22. *Henrik Ibsen: The Complete Major Prose Plays*, trans. Rolf Fjelde (Farrar, Straus and Giroux, 1978), 799–800.

23. Although Solness is represented in Ibsen's text and in all productions I have seen as being in vigorous good health, the recent Wallace Shawn/André Gregory film adaptation of *The Master Builder*, titled *A Master Builder* (2013), forcefully recognizes the "decline" plot by beginning the action with Solness confined to a hospital bed in his own studio, wired to beeping hospital apparatuses and surrounded by nurses. Shawn's original title for the adaptation, *Fear of Falling*, suggested his sensitivity to the decline narrative.

24. *Henrik Ibsen*, 860.

25. *Henrik Ibsen*, 951.

26. Brian Johnston, "The Demons of *John Gabriel Borkman*," *Comparative Drama* 13, no. 1 (1979): 31.

27. Scott-Maxwell, *The Measure of My Days*, 32; *Henrik Ibsen*, 1091.

28. William Shakespeare, *King Lear*, ed. Kenneth Muir (Methuen, 1972), III.iv.108.

2

Rehearsing Age[1]

Elinor Fuchs

Some years ago, as my mother slid into dementia, I adopted another mother and took care of them both. This was my friend Gertrude, who lived in a fifth-floor artist's loft on 29th Street in Manhattan. A former concert pianist and metal art worker with the WPA during the Depression, Gertrude was now a jeweler. For clients hardy enough to climb the four flights of steps to her apartment, she created astonishing new pieces made from dealers' discards—broken Georgian necklaces, Victorian bracelets, and Edwardian cuff links.

Claiming that she didn't understand business, Gertrude operated entirely in cash. Now in her eighties, she had, as a result, none of the social benefits we Americans rely on in later age: no health insurance, no social security, no Medicare or Medicaid, not even a bank account. To pay her rent each month, she worked her way down the stairs with her cane and walked to the central post office at 34th Street to buy a money order. Somehow, I convinced her to open a joint bank account in our two names so that I could mail the landlord a monthly $96 check for her rent-controlled apartment.

One day, I arrived at the loft to find Gertrude recovering from a panic. The day before, she had braved the stairs to accept an invitation from her friend Sarah to see a display of ancient jewelry at a store in Midtown. "I went to 57th and Madison," Gertrude told me, in a wavery voice. "I was completely lost. I couldn't find the place where we were supposed to meet. Everything had changed. I didn't recognize a thing." Unable to find her friend or the exhibit, she fled home.

I was stunned by this story. I considered: Was this what it meant to grow old? Do we become "old" when the familiar world around us has changed beyond recognition, when people and places are gone and social organization is transformed—and then we die? Was this Brecht's *Verfremdungseffekt* of life? Was the *V-effekt* not just a theatrical method to awaken spectators to their true political situation but some kind of sociobiological law of nature?

I tried to drape Brecht's pattern across the human lifespan. So, from birth to midlife, there is the making familiar, the socializing, the fitting in? And then, at least for many of us, in the middle years, there is the perfect fit of our own growth to the shape of our world? (This was a progress mordantly charted by the Austrian playwright Peter Handke in his play inspired by that archetypal misfit, Kaspar Hauser.)[2] And finally, in later years, comes the fitting out, so to speak, the defamiliarizing? So that we find our way to old age through a progressive not fitting in? A progressive *estrangement*? Gertrude never again walked those stairs alone, or perhaps not at all—I can't recall. Soon I was handling all her medical needs, and she restlessly complied. That day had been a kind of hinge between denial of, and collapse into, old age.

Simone de Beauvoir catches André Gide at a similarly liminal, albeit somewhat younger, moment of aging. She quotes a passage from his diary of 1941, in which he laments his physical age, seventy, when in spirit he feels much younger: "My heart has remained so young that I have the continual feeling of playing a part, the part of the seventy-year-old that I certainly am; and the infirmities and weaknesses that remind me of my age act like a prompter, reminding me of my lines when I tend to stray. Then, like the good actor I should like to be, I go back into my role, and I pride myself on playing it well." Writing in the month of March, Gide notes that he would simply prefer to abandon himself to the arrival of spring the next month, but regrets that "I no longer have the costume that it calls for."[3]

Poor Gide, this performer of age, disciplining himself, in the spirit of French decorum, into the "role" of the seventy-year-old. No doubt he would find—would have found—performing the forty-year-old while looking seventy even more grotesque a spectacle of old age than Proust's Marcel sees written on the guests assembled at the Guermantes's salon (so brilliantly described by Kathleen Woodward in "The Mirror Stage of Old Age").[4] Gide offers a double estrangement, for as he clings to youth but adopts the mask of seventy or tries to maintain the mask of youth while accommodating himself to the reality of seventy, he struggles to decide which is the "real" age and which the theatrical performance—which age, in other words, is the familiar that is being made strange.

A third example of estrangement is drawn from my own life. In the past year or so, after I passed a significant birthday marker, I found myself performing a ritual in the privacy of my bedroom. When I was dressing or packing my overnight bag to travel to teach in New Haven, I would sometimes break into an "elder walk," shuffling, feet flattened, back curved, head jutting forward, arms pumping back and forth like little pistons. I was an age puppet, of which I myself was the puppeteer. I seemed to be trying on age, rehearsing age, by splitting myself into two, one a caregiver, the other growing frail and needing care. The first would reassure the second, "You'll be all right dearie, I'll take care of you." The presumption of need was on the side of the puppet. Then the presumption shifted: the puppet was a mere performance; her "needs" were just an act. Elinor would scold, "Elinor! What are you doing? Why are you walking like an old lady?" The puppet would melt away as Elinor straightened up and walked briskly.

Gertrude, Gide, and Elinor—all living these different "estrangements." In the summer of 2014, I published a paper that used a new word I had stumbled on, which attempted to describe a certain split consciousness belonging to aging—"estr*age*ment" I called it—estrangement without the *n*.[5] The present article continues that earlier essay's project—to explore the value, if any, of theater theory for age studies. I will return to these three homely examples.

BRECHT'S ESTRANGEMENT

Brecht's idea of a political theater using techniques of estrangement evolved between the late 1920s and the mid-1930s. It was indebted to his study of Marx, to the influence of the political theater director Erwin Piscator, and to his resistance to the "culinary" entertainment theater of his day. Brecht's ideas about estrangement, or alienation, were implicit in his definition of "epic theater," which appeared in his 1930 notes to the Brecht-Weill opera *Rise and Fall of the City of Mahagonny*.[6] He articulated estrangement as a theory of performance, however, only after he went into exile in early 1933 and took his famous trip to Moscow in 1935. There, it is thought, the Russian playwright Sergei Tretyakov may have introduced him to the term *ostranenie*, coined by the Russian formalist Viktor Shklovsky. The term names what Shklovsky saw as a fundamental literary device, which he described as "distantiation," or making the familiar strange. It was shortly after this trip that Brecht wrote his famous essay on "Alienation Effects in Chinese Acting," where, for the first time, John Willett tells us, he uses the term *Verfremdungseffekt* and, for short, *V-effekt*.[7]

A less well-known essay of about the same time—probably a little earlier—with the Horatian title "Theatre for Pleasure or Theatre for Instruction" touches on the theme, using Marx's Hegel-derived term for the alienation of labor, *Entfremdung*.[8] Brecht's essay contains the following description of the estranged style as seen in epic theater: "The spectator was no longer in any way allowed to submit to an experience uncritically . . . by means of simple empathy with the characters in a play. The production took the subject matter and the incidents . . . through a process of alienation: the alienation that is necessary to all understanding. When something seems 'the most obvious thing in the world' it means that any attempt to understand the world has been given up."[9] Unpublished in Brecht's lifetime, according to Willett, this essay is remarkable in promoting estrangement or alienation as a faculty *necessary to all understanding*. Alienation becomes the law of all intellectual life, the foundation of human development itself. The concept bears comparison with Lacan's mirror stage, to which I'll also return.

The final phase of Brecht's thinking about estrangement appears in the appendices to his most sustained theoretical essay, *A Short Organum for the Theatre* (1948).[10] Here Brecht extends his discussion of the *V-effekt*, now stressing the importance of dialectical thinking in the theater: "The bourgeois theatre's performances always aim at smoothing over contradictions, at creating false harmony, at idealization," he writes. "Conditions are reported as if they could not be otherwise; characters are drawn as . . . incapable by definition of being divided, [as] cast in one block. . . . None of this is like reality, so a realistic theatre must give it up."[11] In other words, the postbourgeois theater, the theater of today, must give up the idealism of the "solid block" for the realism of division and contradiction.

Far from being rigidly or falsely unified, the theater of estrangement thrives on a separation of dramaturgical elements. In theater practicing estrangement (or, in its many variants, distancing, defamiliarization, making the familiar strange, alienation), the spectator's experience in every dimension of the dramatic spectacle is divided and even conflicted: the actor stands aside from her character, whom she "demonstrates"; the action is framed by commentary, or in Brecht's term, "literarized"; the action reflects the material conditions of the stage figures, or is "historicized"; and the stage picture itself is broken up to reveal how theater is made—no more seducing the viewer into a fictive elsewhere. Above all, Brecht wanted to avoid the sentimental fusion of spectator and spectacle through the manipulation of "empathy." To this end, he wanted the spectator to stand back from the performance and think about it critically, adopting the laid-back "gest" of the cigar smoker at a sports event. Brecht recognized, in the appendices to the *Short Organum*, that all these examples of estrangement added up to a demonstration of dialectical materialism in the theater.[12] He even considered renaming his entire approach to theater-making "dialectical," but he had long employed the term "epic theater" and was stuck with it.

The opposition between dramatic and epic theater was intended by Brecht, and is so understood by his critics and commentators, as a sign of Brecht's competition with Aristotle. In chapters 23, 24, and 26 of the *Poetics*, Aristotle admires the epic form but ultimately ranks it lower than tragedy, in large part because it is less unified: "Indeed, any epic provides the subject matter for several tragedies."[13] Brecht liked to see himself not only as "non-Aristotelian" but also as Aristotle's successor. His turn away from dramatic to "epic," in effect adopting Aristotle to fight Aristotle, accomplished both these aims. Recently revisiting Brecht's famous chart comparing dramatic and epic forms at a time when I was thinking about age theory, I made a startling discovery. The two sides of the chart can be seen as corresponding to the two major developmental narratives of aging that have emerged from age studies and critical gerontology.[14]

The chart describes two genres of theatrical text, two styles of performance, and two types of spectator. We see at once that, in Brecht's telling, dramatic theater is linear, unified, and centered on emotion and individual experience, while epic theater describes a loose bundle of freestanding theatrical effects and affects.

But now, let's take the two sides of this chart to be a comparison not only of types of theater but also of two schemas of life trajectory, perhaps of our own lives. One can map onto the chart the two kinds of life narrative that emerge from the literature on aging. The first is the decline narrative, or the decline *script*, as Margaret Morganroth Gullette has called it.[15] Criticized by Gullette as in large part an ideological construction, the decline story enrolls all elderly people in a process of inevitable decay, both physical and mental, a state that erases individual distinctions and differences. The dramatic (read "Aristotelian") theater's linearity and determinism, the dramatic character's helplessness in the face of "the finish"—these can be read as dramatic corollaries to the trajectory of deterioration that is still today the society-wide "normal" youth assigns to age and older people themselves have absorbed from our youth-centered culture.

The second narrative emerges out of gerontology over the past half-century. In the 1960s, gerontologists began to bring historical, sociological, economic, and broadly cultural perspectives to bear on their study of human development. The emerging critical gerontology no longer posited a rigidly ordered life trajectory. This new thinking about aging came to be called the "life course" perspective or approach. The epic theater side of Brecht's chart corresponds to this more flexible account of the life trajectory, where a human life (as in one of Brecht's plays) would be seen as a "process" and the human subject as both "alterable" and "able to alter." A life on this side of the ledger moves in surprising ways, in "curves and jumps," not simply in foretold steps leading to the grave. Brecht's epic theater description, taken as human-life trajectory, could almost be seen as making room, en route to the grave, for today's emerging world of "encore careers" and "life-long learning" institutes.

FROM IDENTITY THEORY TO ESTRANGEMENT THEORY

Materialist feminist theory blasts apart nature and culture, revealing the myriad ways in which anatomical differences were (and still are) enlisted in support of systematic gender discrimination. Humanities-based age criticism and critical gerontology borrow from feminist theory to similarly expose the social component in the narrative of natural decline. Yet there are two key obstacles to the optimistic project of deconstructing the assumed binary of youth and age through the medium of identity theory. First, as these same critics recognize, age is a continuum and not a binary construction. It does not submit easily to deconstructive analysis. But perhaps of more importance, feminist and other identity theories are liberatory in intention and effect; they restore wholeness to the lopped-off self. The battle against ageism differs from the battle against sexism and racism, for it is marked by the realization that nothing can liberate us from disease and death.

A theatrical view of the self may be of special interest to age theory as it contemplates this impasse. Here, a psychoanalytic theory of self-formation that has attracted leading figures in the recent age discourse, Lacan's theory of the mirror stage of development, might be included in this discussion. Like Brecht, Lacan presents a riven view of the human self and one that, with its "stage" and its great "prop," the mirror, is intrinsically theatrical. With some hesitation, I venture beyond my competence to speculate on the comparative value for age studies of Brecht's epic theater and Lacan's mirror.

If estrangement is fundamental to the very project of human thinking as Brecht asserts, then for Brecht, to be human is to be divided at the root. It hardly makes sense to observe sentimentally that we are estranged *from ourselves*, for Brecht would seem to imply that, without estrangement, there is, in effect, no self. This fundamental insight underlies each specific characteristic of his theater, as it does his radical concept of realism. It was also Lacan's insight, traceable to Freud as Brecht's is traceable to Marx, that there is no intrinsic, inborn sense of self. Rather, the sense of being or having a self is based on a kind of necessary error; it can only be recognized as a double, an image or reflection. The developmental moment of recognizing oneself outside oneself must precede the child's entry into language or into the "Symbolic," as Lacan puts it. The mirror can be real (Mother to Child: See? This is *you*!), but it is also metaphorical, for the self is constituted in the eyes of other (albeit similarly alienated) selves in whose systems of meaning we are granted continuity and constituted as selves.

In "The Mirror Stage of Old Age," Kathleen Woodward posits a second mirror stage that works a reversal on the first. Here, the ager no longer recognizes herself in her own mirror image or relates to her aged appearance in others' eyes. Woodward cites Lacan as suggesting, as Leni Marshall elaborates in a later article, that this *méconnaissance*, or misrecognition, may be a positive, protective development of later age.[16] Nevertheless, the late mirror stage, like the first, is a kind of error, for now the gaze of age sees continuity and relative youth where the law of estrangement should be evident. The aging figure might properly observe, "I am not who I was," but instead supplies an image that reassures: "I am as I always was."

It is hardly necessary to point out to a theatrical readership how "performatized" Lacan's concept of the self is and how it might be compared to the emergence of a character that is sustained in a compact between actor and audience. If feminist theory revealed how traditional gender behavior with its binary "roles" is "performative" and has given us a frame in which to discover our greater selves in a more capacious reality, Brecht and Lacan help us to see something like the reverse—that the self-consciousness of performance is not opposed to an underlying reality but is constitutive of it.

If Brecht and Lacan teach similar lessons from their positions in different disciplines, what does the theater theorist add to the estrangement described by the psychoanalyst? Easy to answer: she adds practice. It is the practicality of the theater that leaps out from Brecht's chart. Unlike Lacan's mirror, Brecht's theater of estrangement—estr*age*ment, as I call it elsewhere—gives us a way to think and even something to do about aging.[17] The mirror may reify and magnify the self-absorption and fear that aging can bring. But the dialectical habit, shall we call it, can keep the epic performer of age alert and objective, playing roles to the audience-of-herself as character, spectator, and critic. She is not lost in empathic identification with her own aging; she is not trapped in the dramatic theater's (that is, Aristotle's) pity and fear. Such multiple awareness may be what is meant by the wisdom of age.

REHEARSING AGE

Brecht would have questioned my street scene of the elderly Gertrude lost and frightened in a transformed Manhattan. He might say that falling into a whirlpool of panic was only one of the possible actions she might have performed that day. She might have protested the commodification of 57th Street; she might have contemplated the inevitability of change in her world or even in herself; and—by the way—did she ask for directions? She could have saved herself from falling through the looking glass, so to speak, by a constructive estrangement. She could have assumed control by being not only the figure in the story who was acted on but Brecht's spectator, who "historicizes" the scene from many perspectives, like a cubist portrait. (Why have so few critics understood Brecht as a dramaturgical cubist?) She might then have seen—and without negative interpretation—that the lost woman was attached to an image of the city and herself in it that no longer matched an outer reality. In short, there was more than one way to tell Gertrude's story of that fateful day, and had she told the story differently, or had her friends listened differently, it might have had a different outcome. Had Gertrude been able to treat her defamiliarized moment as more of a rehearsal, as an episode offering a choice of responses rather than as an absolute reality demanding submission, she might have gone into her older age with greater freedom. Gertrude is the least performance-conscious ager here. Her story lies on the dramatic side of Brecht's ledger.

The story of the cannily self-aware Gide offers its own complications, as elegant as he may be in his manipulation of the theatrical metaphor. For as Gide clings to a younger age and assumes the age of seventy, he finds it hard to say which is the reality and which the theatrical performance. Unable to choose a "real" age with assurance, he becomes proof of the central idea of de Beauvoir's chapter, the "unrealizable" nature of old age.[18] Yet, in Brecht's terms, we see that Gide is still caught up in the dramatic theater, unable to give up the credo of unalterability or the pathos of its loss. The mirror reflects his dilemma—*I can't be seventy!*—but offers him no way to move beyond its conflicted message.

As for my own masquerade, Elinor is not so much caught between two ages, like Gide, or two periods and settings, like Gertrude, but between two bodies. One of us is "trying on" physical frailty. The other is performing the role of comforter—there would always be "Elinor" to take care of "Elinor." Of the three versions of estrangement here, this one might be estranged by performance itself. Elinor's "roles" could be modeled less on observed life than on other performances. Where, after all, did that shuffle come from? Is her decline narrative a mere citation of a decline narrative, an act copied from actors? Yet, while arguably closest to the saving self-awareness of the actor and the critical spectator of Brecht's epic theater, her/my puppet show is still infected with the fear of decline and the empathy of the dramatic.

RECOGNITION

If Gertrude were a play, her story would demand a recognition scene. And I note here that a failure of recognition is central to all three of my stories, whether of the urban landscape or of the central character. Appearing in Aristotle's *Poetics* in what could be taken to be a dry analysis of dramatic form, *anagnorisis*, or recognition, appears as the second of three essential "parts" of plot, which itself is one of—and the most essential of—Aristotle's six elements of tragedy. For Aristotle, recognition comes after and develops out of a series of reversals and leads to the third part of tragedy: *pathos*, or suffering (Aristotle does not claim that the parts appear in the order in which he names them, but the priority of order pervades his thinking). Yet "recognition" is not only a narrative device; it is, at the same time, one of the most resonant terms in all accounts of narrative structure, for it brings into perfect alignment a place in a story and a place in the human heart in its longing to be individually seen and known—that is, recognized. I am talking not about a yearning for fame and celebrity but about the need to know that one's life has mattered.[19] The decline narrative is most terrible not in its fatalism but in its erasures, terrible not that the elder dies, but that she is reduced to pure body. Her selfhood is wiped out by those very "mirrors," other people's eyes, that once affirmed her individuality. She is unrecognized by herself as well as others, as Woodward writes, for she now rejects the mirror image of her own face. One wincingly recalls poet Donald Hall's account in the *New Yorker*, reprinted in his *Essays After Eighty*, of a visit to the National Gallery in a wheelchair, accompanied by his attendant Linda. After a cafeteria lunch, a museum guard bends over Hall's chair to ask, "Did we have a nice din-din?"[20]

The Aristotelian plot scheme would seem to be an abstracted form of the decline narrative. Plots begin in reversal and end in suffering. Just before that terminal suffering, they pass through a moral reckoning, where all figures of the play accept the same truth, where, as Aristotle says, changes in bonds of love or hate occur and are acknowledged. From that point, the last steps of remorse and mourning will follow. This is the shape of the decline narrative, which ancient Greek theater may be thought to have incised into narratology. Yet if Sophocles and his explicator, Aristotle, launched the decline narrative, we might, on reflection, note that what most troubles critics of decline is not decline itself; it is the absence of recognition! Decline's worst sin is not in fact the overdetermined trail of suffering leading to death; it is absence of recognition; it is the humiliation of being reduced to mere body and the denial of personhood.

Here, theater theory and age theory must part ways, one might suppose, for it would seem that Brecht's "estrangement," a condition, he says, that enables us to think critically, and Aristotle's "recognition," a condition in which we are reconciled with ourselves and others, cannot coexist in the same dramatic and human profile. But we are not quite finished with Brecht. Look once again at Brecht's chart.

It might have escaped our notice the first time that "recognition" makes a sneak appearance. Opposite dramatic theater's observation that "instinctive feelings are preserved," the epic side notes that the spectators (or perhaps the characters—Brecht doesn't say) are "brought to the point of recognition." It is not hard to guess that, by "instinctive feelings," Brecht means pity and fear. Gertrude's story was overwhelmed by her fear and our pity; Gide struggled to keep his own toggling between these feelings in check. But for Brecht is "recognition" merely an illusory validation of "instinctive feelings"?

As the moment in a classical drama of truth and its acceptance—in its best form, a moment of change in a bond of love or hate—recognition is the dramatic moment best designed to stir the empathy of the spectator. Brecht would thus be suspicious of recognition scenes but appears to approve of them as an absence, as potentiality. Brecht can organize an entire play around a dawning recognition, as in *The Mother*, where it accompanies an advance in age. It is even more central in its absence in *Mother Courage*, whose title character loses three children to the war. She is "brought to the point of recognition" that war is bad, but she does not cross the threshold into the action needed to reject it. One could say that estrangement brings spectators and characters to the point of change, but change will be realized only in the future. Recognition may be a millenarian idea, always deferred.

What I learn from Brecht at this moment is hard to accept: that I must give up narrative idealism in my own personal life, the hope that loose ends will be tied up, that misunderstandings will be cleared away, that I can "die in peace." I must accept that there will never be a conclusion, a moment of recognition, a finish, in which "I" close the gap of estrangement in a scene of recognition between—well, between my puppet and myself. On the chart, Brecht opposes "eyes on the finish" to "eyes on the course." And now I see that Brecht goes beyond life course analysis in his scheme of epic theater, for this chart—not as drama but as a gerontological prescription—is telling us, telling *me*, that there is no finish. The epic theater of estrangement shrugs off the empathic scene of recognition to tell me that Brecht's characters are specks in an unending process and that every point of recognition becomes only a new illusion in an ever-evolving dialectic. The only way to break the grip of decline ideology, he might say, is to stop seeking that state so valued in pop psychology discourse—closure. This is tough love! Embrace the estranged way, Brecht tells the aging actor, tells *me*; give up the certainty of drama for the open path of epic. Take on the risk of improvisation and the discipline of rehearsal.

NOTES

1. Republished with permission from *Modern Drama* 59, no. 2 (2016): 143–54.
2. Peter Handke, *Kaspar and Other Plays* (Hill and Wang, 1970).
3. Quoted in Simone de Beauvoir, *The Coming of Age*, trans. Patrick O'Brian (G. P. Putnam's Sons, 1972), 296.
4. De Beauvoir, *The Coming of Age*, 189–90; see also the chapter "The Mirror Stage of Old Age" in Kathleen Woodward, *Aging and Its Discontents: Freud and Other Fictions* (Indiana University Press, 1991), 53–72.
5. For this 2014 paper, "Estr*age*ment: Toward an 'Age Theory' Theatre Criticism," see the preceeding essay in this volume.
6. *Brecht on Theatre: The Development of an Aesthetic*, ed. and trans. John Willett (Hill and Wang, 1964), 33–42.
7. *Brecht on Theatre*, 99n.
8. *Brecht on Theatre*, 76n.
9. *Brecht on Theatre*, 71.
10. *Brecht on Theatre*, 179–205, and 276–81.
11. *Brecht on Theatre*, 277.
12. *Brecht on Theatre*, 276–77.
13. *Aristotle: On Poetry and Style*, trans. G. M. A. Grube (Hackett, 1989), 62.
14. For this chart, see *Brecht on Theatre*, 37.
15. Margaret Morganroth Gullette, *Aged by Culture* (University of Chicago Press, 2004), 132, and see 129–37.
16. See Woodward, *Aging and Its Discontents*, 53–72; and Leni Marshall, "Through (with) the Looking Glass: Revisiting Lacan and Woodward in 'Méconnaissance,' the Mirror Stage of Old Age," *Feminist Formations* 24, no. 2 (Summer 2012): 52–76.
17. For "estr*age*ment," see the preceding essay in this volume.
18. De Beauvoir, *The Coming of Age*, 296.
19. See Elinor Fuchs, "Waiting for Recognition: An Aristotle for 'Non-Aristotelian' Drama," *Modern Drama* 50, no. 4 (Winter 2007): 532–44.
20. Donald Hall, *Essays After Eighty* (Houghton Mifflin Harcourt, 2014), 8–9.

3
Aging and the Time of Estr*age*ment in Chekhov's Drama

Yana Meerzon

"Among many themes that make up Chekhov's dramaturgy," the Russian Soviet theater scholar Boris Zingerman wrote, "the most important one is time."[1] Time in Anton Chekhov's plays is naturally connected to aging, which can be understood as a progression of one's life and history, and as a structural marker of dramatic narrative. A key source of characters' neurosis, time is made tangible and visible in Chekhov's dramaturgy *through age*: whenever his characters come onstage, they talk about their aging, and they meticulously count the years that have passed and those yet to come; they measure their success and failure in temporal dimensions; and they reminisce about old days and philosophize about the distant future. Beyond characters' neurosis, Chekhov's time is evoked too as a calendar of history, manifested in such events as a town's fire, state holidays, and religious celebrations, and in the cyclical time of nature, with many of Chekhov's plays opening in the early spring with nature's first blossoming, and closing in the autumn, when the colors of life begin to fade. In *The Cherry Orchard*, for example, the orchard is "in blossom as the play opens, leafless and due for destruction as it closes." In *Three Sisters*, the change of time is signaled through "the passage of migratory birds, swans or geese."[2] Furthermore, time and aging are inseparable from the settings of Chekhov's plays. The house of the Prozorovs in *Three Sisters*, the lake in *The Seagull*, and the nursery in *The Cherry Orchard* serve as containers of each play's temporality and of memories that make up their dramatic environments. These environments can be trivial—in Stanislavsky's rendering of *Three Sisters*, the house of the

Prozorovs was to be "ordinary" and "cheaply furnished"—but they are also mythical.[3] In Chekhov's plays, "man's inner struggle against the power of triviality" is revealed as "the conflict between character and environment"; and so, in his plays, "the limitations of age may terrify, yet a new horizon of old age may open."[4]

In this chapter, I draw forth both age and aging as defining elements of Chekhov's dramatic storytelling. Drawing on the work of Elinor Fuchs, I demonstrate that Chekhov uses time as a technique of estr*age*ment (age estrangement), which is revealed through the structure of the plots of his plays as a new script of aging, "in which the old are estranged from their former selves and look back with astonishment on their past limitations getting older" within the inner workings of his characters, and in the symbolism of his spatial/temporal settings.[5] I examine aging as a feature of Chekhov's characters through estr*age*ment, or making character strange, which describes one's act of renewal and reevaluating of their life strategies when reaching an older age.[6] This arrival at old age and the recognition of this arrival affect the physical and symbolic landscapes in which Chekhovian characters dwell. Chekhov reflects the calendar time of history and the cyclical time of nature in his settings. As Chekhov's characters try to learn how to appreciate their present time and to acknowledge their aging within it, it becomes important for them to see themselves from the distance of another time, in which the immediate action, space, and time turn into the spaces of transition and "becom[e] a place of estrangement or exile."[7]

Like Beckett's plays decades later, Chekhov's dramaturgy "makes age itself thematic in a new way."[8] In Chekhov's plays, age is, first, a source of laughter and irony. Following conventions of comedy and realism, which "[tend] to represent age negatively," Chekhov often typecasts his aging characters as comic relief and makes them "funny through their ill-fittedness for the practicalities of life."[9] At the same time, Chekhov presents his characters' preoccupation with time and aging as existential questions of life and death, or as questions of modern tragedy. Time and again, Chekhov's plays begin with a gesture of discovery, enacted as characters' encounter of someone new, as in Vershinin's arrival at the house of the Prozorovs in *Three Sisters*. There can also be a discovery as an encounter between the characters and their environments—as in Professor Serebryakov's and his wife Elena's arrival at the family estate in *Uncle Vanya*, or in Lubov Ranevskaya's homecoming in *The Cherry Orchard*. This encounter puts Chekhov's characters into a state of internal estrangement; and it keeps them standing still for the duration of the action, waiting for reversal and resolution to take place. Borrowing from the bravura of the comedic plot, which rapidly unfolds toward a happy ending with the wedding celebration or a similar festivity in its finale, Chekhov's plays turn the audiences' expectations upside down. Chekhov deliberately slows down the action of his plays; specifically, he "decelerates it by the finale."[10] In Chekhov's slow endings, one can recognize the slow burning action of *an extended recognition*; it invites Chekhov's readers and audiences "to focus not on what is taking place in front of them on stage, but on what will happen after the curtain closes."[11] To address how aging works in Chekhov's dramaturgy, I will first discuss it as a device of plot construction, then as a "sobering up" moment of a character's development, and finally, as the dramaturgical work of space and time.

CHEKHOV'S PARADOX: ON THE TRAGICOMEDY OF RECOGNITION

Dramatic recognition, famously defined by Aristotle as "a change from ignorance to knowledge," is one of the central dramaturgical forces that distinguish plot and action structures in Chekhov's plays.[12] Traditionally, recognition is an action that takes place at the closure of a play. It leads to a reversal of the characters' fortune and a resolution of the play's conflicts, so the characters can "acknowledge the truth of a shared history," while the protagonist "understands his/her own implication in the preceding reversals."[13] In Chekhov's plays, recognition functions both as a feature of plot-making and as a device of character development. As a structural device, it can take place more than once and lead neither to reversal nor to resolution, thus turning into what I would call an *extended recognition*. As a device of characterization, recognition is tightly connected to the age of Chekhov's characters: age is used here as the characters' personal trait but also as a unit of time measurement. Chekhov's plays trade in the unrealized potentials of his characters, who are summoned onstage to face their tragic fault and fate.[14]

The opening sequence of *Three Sisters*—the arrival of Lieutenant Colonel Vershinin, the new battery commander, to the Prozorovs' house—serves as a good example of using extended recognition and character's unrealized potential as a device of encounter and estrangement. Vershinin's arrival affects every character present onstage and all the others, kept temporarily off of it. An overture of a kind, the scene unfolds from *potentials* to *(non) realizations*,[15] and thus it foreshadows the future developments in the story:

TUZENBAKH. Lieutenant-Colonel Vershinin.

VERSHININ [*to Masha and Irina*]. May I introduce myself? I'm Vershinin. Delighted, absolutely delighted to be here at last. Well, you *have* grown up and no mistake.

IRINA. Please sit down. This is a great pleasure.

VERSHININ [*gaily*]. I'm more pleased than I can say, I really am. But there should be three of you sisters. I remember three little girls. Can't remember your faces, but that your father, Colonel Prozorov, had three little girls I remember quite clearly, saw you with my own eyes. How times flies, dear me, how time does fly.

TUZENBAKH. The colonel comes from Moscow.

IRINA. From Moscow? You come from Moscow?

VERSHININ. Yes, I do. Your father was battery commander there and I served in the same brigade. [*To Masha.*] Now I think I do just remember your face.

MASHA. I don't remember you, I'm afraid.[16]

The dialogue points at the act of recognition: Vershinin's arrival brings a promise of change, and it forces each character's internal estrangement, their involuntary acknowledgment of the fact that time has passed and each of them has significantly aged. Vershinin's arrival incites a new configuration as well: since the last time the characters saw one another, the lovesick major has become a lieutenant colonel, while the little girls have come of age. One of them got married, another became an aging spinster, and the youngest is about to leave her nest, although she feels a bit bored, being overeducated and emotionally understimulated, with nothing to do. This recognition is startling for all characters, and it makes the encounter uncomfortable, if not slightly embarrassing. It costs Vershinin an uncalled-for emotional oversharing.[17] The scene unfolds from one innuendo to the next, with Masha keeping away from the initial exchange and Vershinin trying to please each of the sisters. For Irina he comes in the aura of familiarity: he is now a battery commander like her late father used to be. For Olga, he represents a promise of stability if not happiness in one's older age (we learn earlier that Vershinin is not that old, "forty or forty-five at the most").[18] And for Masha, his arrival forces her to accept that her marriage was rushed and is unhappy, an arrangement that she will never be able to shake or change. This arrival scene, in other words, contains the essence and the outline of the future dramatic action. It foreshadows the four years of the plot span, in which the characters will not move beyond this initial state of stillness. The sisters seem to come to life only when and because Vershinin is onstage, and when he leaves for good there will be no other hopes or encounters for them.

MASHA. . . . [*Eagerly.*] Now I remember. Olga, you remember how we used to talk about "the lovesick major." You were a lieutenant then and you were in love, and everyone teased you and called you a major for some reason.

VERSHININ [*laughs*]. Oh yes, the lovesick major. You're quite right.
MASHA. You only had a moustache in those days. Oh, you look so much older. [*Through tears.*] So much older.
VERSHININ. Yes, when I was known as the lovesick major, I was young and in love. Things have changed since then.[19]

This dialogue outlines the contours of their love affair, with Masha already seemingly knowing how it will end. She is in tears because she recognizes that their time, when they could be happy and together, has inevitably passed. He looks much older, and she herself is trapped in a loveless marriage. What would serve as a scene of promise within the traditional structure of a romantic melodrama functions in *Three Sisters* as a vision of unresolvable sadness, a failure, to which this love story is already fated, before it had a chance to begin.

However, as Fuchs reminds us, recognition—a smaller pattern of storytelling in a larger scheme of an overall plot—must also be defined by its own patterns of action:

> Like the trajectory of reversal, [recognition] has an interior pattern as well, a beginning–middle–end not unlike that which Aristotle identifies as the shape of the overall action itself. A recognition has duration: it begins in reversal . . . passes through the moment of clear seeing, and typically, opens out onto a terrain of moral and physical suffering (the "pathos"), though Aristotle also concedes that suffering may be averted and that endings may be positive.[20]

In Chekhov's plays, recognition is presented in relation to the structures of time, aging, and plot-making. It is also played in relation to characters' personal potentials and "the inevitability of its non-realization," in which their aging and their affairs are staged.[21] Hence, characters' aging and their immediate realization that they have aged constitutes a special time marker in Chekhov's dramaturgy.

STAGING CHARACTERS' RECOGNITION OR "SOBERING UP"

"Modern characters"—Chekhov wrote—"should be not younger than thirty to thirty-five years of age,"[22] and so they must appear in the moment of their "tragic sobering, when they suddenly realise with frightening clarity that life is short and has not been lived as it should be, but for them it is too late to change anything."[23] For the tragic characters of the past, someone like Oedipus Rex, for example, this act of "tragic sobering" was tangible and immediate, and it was followed by the reversal of fortune, including self-punishment. In Chekhov's world, however, characters avoid taking on this act of sobering or recognition: they seem to live inside it, refusing to confront their past or acknowledge their future. Often, we meet Chekhov's characters at a midlife crisis—a time of transition, when one's youth with its promise of limitless opportunities and choices has already gone, and when the sobriety of adulthood announces the speedy arrival of old age. To this extent, Chekhov's characters seem to be living in a permanent state of estr*age*ment, a different logic to the decline script of getting old.[24]

A term inspired by Brecht's *Verfremdung*, estr*age*ment is "a hybrid of 'age' and 'strange'"; but it is not "a perceptual/political moment, as in Brecht, but a late-life developmental moment in which the familiar also becomes strange. In an age-conscious *Verfremdung* scene the aging figures may see as if for the first time, or the scene may depict a late-life experience, in which the old are estranged from their former selves and look back with astonishment on their past limitations."[25] Estr*age*ment, in other words, presumes a reevaluation of one's life strategies when reaching an older age and is based on the acknowledgment of one's arrival at that old age, seen now as a new physical and symbolic landscape of possibilities and techniques of life-making. Stories of old age—from Ibsen to Maeterlinck and Beckett—"seem to require a landscape, staged or told, that itself becomes a place of estrangement or exile—a forest, a heath, a mountain height, an apocalyptic waste. Here the limitations of age may terrify, yet a new horizon of old age may open."[26]

Chekhov's universe, at first glance, does not provide much of an alternative to the decline script. A doctor himself, who was writing his plays while constantly registering the signs of his own deteriorating health, Chekhov does not give space to the new horizons of old age or to his characters' *renouvelement*. They all age accordingly, most of the time nondramatically and anticlimactically. Privileging a monotone routine of the everyday as the background to his modern tragedy, Chekhov registers time as something that passes by, not as something that optimistically moves forward. To Chekhov's characters time drags and staggers, and somehow, almost in Beckettian terms, it moves on. A playwright of the twentieth century, Chekhov does not pay attention to the so-called "culmination of human existence" because those events, those culminations, are too short lived and insignificant in the larger scheme of things.[27] For Chekhov, these culminations are incongruences of life, a game of chance, which could or could not take place. Thus, in Chekhov's plays, the plot does not develop from intrigue to resolution, but instead unfolds without any visible ups and downs, with neither firmly defined beginnings nor definitive resolutions at the end.[28] What happens in Chekhov's plays, however, is the estr*age*ment of the characters' consciousness. From one dramatic event to the next, Chekhov's characters find themselves in new-to-them psychological and temporal landscapes. With every new displacement, they feel even more confused and disoriented, as any traveler arriving at a new destination can be. As a consequence of this dramatic structure, each character must regroup; they must reevaluate and re-understand something profound about themselves and about their age.

However, this act of estr*age*ment is rarely put into words or actions. Often, Chekhov's characters refuse to take any real action that could lead to making a concrete decision or changing their situation. Often they eat and drink and talk and quarrel as their lives pass. Putting this state of nonaction onstage is Chekhov's special dramaturgical principle, which he formulated at the dawn of his career,[29] and put into practice in many of his plays from *Three Sisters* to *The Cherry Orchard*. This is how Chekhov articulated his views on the state of nonaction in theater:

> They say that in theater there should be a hero, a heroine, stage effects. But in real life, people do not shoot, hang themselves, or declare love in every minute of their existence. And they do not say clever things all the time, either. They spend much more time eating, drinking, flirting, and saying foolish things—this is what should happen on the stage. One should write a play in which people come and go, have lunch, talk about the weather, and play cards, . . . but not because the author wants them to, but because this is exactly what happens in real life. . . . One should not look for any kind of dramatic framework. Life should appear onstage as it is, and people should be as they are.[30]

In *The Cherry Orchard*, one can argue, Chekhov fully mobilizes his theory of dramatic nonaction, in which time and life pass by, whereas the characters talk and drink, and eat and flirt. For many of them, specifically for Lubov Ranevskaya and her brother Gayev, the owners of the estate, who appear onstage in the glory of their respective midlife crises, "the elusive life no longer frightens their imagination." Ranevskaya and Gayev seem to be "carefree," and they "tend to think of their age with the same lightness as they think of the approaching date of the sale of the estate."[31] At the end, Gayev did spend his fortune on "boiled sweets."[32] In their refusal to act or to do something practical—that is, in their desire to keep up the appearance of being carefree—Ranevskaya and Gayev display their lack of responsibility, but also their acceptance of their own inevitable finale. Aging from day to day, but not wishing or being able to change, Ranevskaya and Gayev step onto Chekhov's stage somewhat frozen in time or suspended within it in the gesture of permanent estrangement—and they seem to prefer to see their present time from the distance of their uncertain future.[33]

Zingerman compares this dramatic device of time distancing to a *glaze painting*. In Chekhov's plays, he writes, each character exists in several temporalities, with one temporal dimension imposed onto another:

> This method of blending the present into the past and the future into infinity reminds one of a glaze painting, looking at which one can simultaneously see two or several layers of colors, put one over the other. Each underlying color is made visible using a transparent glaze, where one layer of glaze is put on top of the other. Similarly, in Chekhov's plays, as the plot approaches its conclusions, the events that take place in the present, in front of our eyes, become more transparent, whereas the time of eternity becomes more visible, it touches everything that happens onstage in the present moment.[34]

The gaze of Chekhov's characters is often directed at their past, which is already gone, and at the future, yet to come, and so their dramatic time of the present turns into that of eternity. Such treatment of dramatic time suggests a turn to epic or predramatic structures, and so, Chekhov's "chamber plays mark the beginning of modern epic theater. They expand the drama of an individual and directly connect theatrical time to human time, the past and the future, and to the succession of generations."[35] Much like Brechtian *gestus*—the device of character and text estrangement—Chekhov's plays invite us to recognize the act of aging onstage within this moment of standing still.

Perhaps the most notorious example of this dramatic technique is in Chekhov's portrayal of Ranevskaya's servant Firs, who seems to have fully embraced the challenge of estr*age*ment. Chekhov describes Firs as "an old man of 87 years of age," to whom, one can argue, the time of estr*age*ment, a chance to regroup and reevaluate his own life and self, has passed. Firs, however, appears to be fully content, if not happy, with his old age, and specifically now, when his mistress (Ranevskaya) has finally returned home: "The mistress is home," he exclaims gaily; "Home at last! Now I can die happy. [*Weeps with joy.*]"[36]

Like many other characters in *The Cherry Orchard*, Firs defines his present existence and time in relation to his past, not future:

FIRS. In the old days, forty or fifty years ago, the cherries used to be dried, preserved, and bottled. They used to make jam out of them, and time was— . . . Time was when dried cherries used to be sent to Moscow and Kharkov by the wagon-load. They fetched a lot of money. Soft and juicy those dried cherries were, sweet and tasty. People had the knack of it in those days.

MRS. RANEVSKY. But where's the recipe now?

FIRS. Forgotten. No one remembers it.[37]

This acceptance of the inevitable, as displayed by Firs—his time has passed, and the secrets of the past disappeared together with it—can also be read as a state of nonaction. Firs's contentment, his acceptance of the state of inaction, reminds the audience of the eternal stasis that awaits every one of us. Firs, Chekhov's spokesperson of age and aging, remains content even when he realizes that his masters have abandoned him in the old house; they have left him to die alone, in his old age:

FIRS [*goes to the door and touches the handle*]. Locked. They've gone. [*Sits on the sofa.*] They forgot me. Never mind, I'll sit here a bit. And Mr. Leonid hasn't put his fur coat on, I'll be bound, he'll have gone off in his light one. [*Gives a worried sigh.*] I should have seen to it, these young folks have no sense. [*Mutters something which cannot be understood.*] Life's slipped by just as if I'd never lived at all. [*Lies down.*] I'll lie down a bit. You've got no strength left, got nothing left, nothing at all. You're just a—nincompoop. [*Lies motionless.*]

A distant sound is heard. It seems to come from the sky and is the sound of a breaking string. It dies away sadly. Silence follows, broken only by the thud of an axe striking a tree far away in the orchard.[38]

The moment of stage silence, when we hear only the sounds of the axe striking the trees, invites deep self-reflection on the part of the audience. Presenting us with many different examples of aging and scenarios of character estr*age*ment, Chekhov encourages us to think of our own processes of getting old. Chekhov's plays force us to stop and look at ourselves as from outside our own time and aging. This moment where Chekhov's reader or spectator pauses to self-reflect connects with Elinor Fuchs's notion of estr*age*ment. Watching Ranevskaya lose her lightness of being as she ages in front of us or watching Firs die onstage brings forward a rush of recognition for viewers, when suddenly we look at ourselves across the distance of time, and we experience our own sobering up, our own acknowledgment that we have aged.

ON MNEMONIC RESERVES AND KEEPSAKES IN CHEKHOV'S POETICS

The settings of Chekhov's plays can be considered types of living organisms, whose history is marked by the characters' past actions; they are also the *mnemonic reserves* of everything that took place before the curtain opened or of what will transpire after it falls. Accordingly, one can read Chekhov's treatment of a dramatic space after Joseph Roach as a metaphor of a human body and as a type of landscape that functions through a series of performance genealogies that "draw on the idea of expressive movements of mnemonic reserves."[39] As a mnemonic reserve, the Prozorovs' house of *Three Sisters* contains the memories of the space and serves as a repository of characters' actions, emotions, and experiences, as they get constructed or lived through in front of us. Because of these tight interconnections between the dwelling and its inhabitants, Chekhov's dramatic space becomes a special time marker of the characters' aging. His characters tend to either lead a very settled life (like Uncle Vanya and his niece, Sonya, in the play *Uncle Vanya*, or like the sisters Prozorov in *Three Sisters*) or return to their family's estates (like Arkadina in *The Seagull* or Lubov Ranevskaya in *The Cherry Orchard*).

At the same time, in Chekhov's plays, the home settings and the physical environments of the characters seem to lead separate lives from the characters themselves. The characters tend to come and go, leave and return to their homes, whereas the objects, the furniture, and the spaces remain the same, untouched by time and by aging, by the absence or presence of their owners. In this way, the physical environments of Chekhov's plays—the rooms, the houses, the lake, and the orchard—serve as mnemonic reserves of these characters' pasts, keepsakes of the characters' aspirations and desires, and reminders of their half-forgotten events and emotions. When Chekhov's characters return to their homes, their memories are activated and their old hopes and needs present themselves again, now marked by the characters' nostalgia for a past that they have lost forever but that continues to live in the objects these characters left behind.

The nursery in *The Cherry Orchard*, where the play begins and ends, exemplifies such a mnemonic reserve. An environment that traditionally represents the intimate connection between the child and their mother and that is the locus of one's formative and vulnerable years is now a space of transition: the nursery in *The Cherry Orchard* is a hallway exposed to strangers, which is then "emptied of its furniture during the play itself," and thus becomes even more public.[40] First we see the servant Dunyasha in this space. She comes in carrying a candle. Then a merchant, Lopakhin, a close acquaintance of the family, joins Dunyasha in this room. They hold a brief conversation about the hosts' arrival, the point of which is to inform the reader that for Lopakhin the nursery functions as an emotional anchor. It is here that his first encounter—if not intimacy—with Lubov Ranevskaya took place. Once, when he was fifteen, Lopakhin's father punched him in the face, and Ranevskaya, "quite a slip of a girl," brought the little peasant into this room, the place where she grew up and where her late son would have lived. "She brought me over to the wash-stand here in this very room, the nursery as it was. 'Don't cry, little peasant,' she said. 'You'll soon be right as rain.'"[41] Now, the estate and the nursery are about to be sold, and if this happens, the new owners will change its history and erase its memories. Lopakhin, it seems, is the only one who takes this problem seriously, who cares about the house and its aging memories.

When Ranevskaya joins these characters onstage, we learn that her recollections of this old nursery are radically different from those of Lopakhin. They are unique to her personal experiences here, and they are as much about her past, her age when they were formed, as they are about her present state of mind:

> MRS. RANEVSKY [*happily, through tears*]. . . . The nursery! My lovely, heavenly room! I slept in here when I was a little girl. [*Weeps.*] And now I feel like a little girl again. [*Kisses her brother and Varya, and then her brother again.*] Varya hasn't changed a bit, she still looks like a nun. And I recognized Dunyasha. [*Kisses Dunyasha.*][42]

To Freddie Rokem, Chekhov's dramaturgy mobilizes the device of "multiple points of view"; in his plays, "each character views his surroundings and fellow characters according to his or her own measure and understanding. In this method of theatrical presentation, nothing is fixed, and everything is constantly given new meanings."[43] Spaces keep their own memories of the past, but as the example above demonstrates, different characters activate different memories, and hence the past, much like the present, emerges in its multiplicity reflecting each character's personal experiences and feelings, their unique ways of reacting to the passing time. After years away, Ranevskaya is finally back home. Her reactions, one could argue, reveal Ranevskaya more like that little girl, who has never left her nursery, someone who—as a grown-up—has not learned how to take responsibility for her actions. She ran away from the estate; she barely recognizes those who stayed behind and took care of it; and she has spent, sold, or lost all means for survival that she has ever had: "she'd already sold her villa near Menton and had nothing left, nothing at all," her daughter Anya says. "I hadn't any money either, there was hardly enough for the journey. And Mother simply won't understand. If we have a meal in a station restaurant, she asks for all the most expensive things and tips the waiters a ruble each."[44] This failure or reluctance to recognize her own troubles, this refusal to face the famous "sobering up" moment of recognition, is the major character trait of Ranevskaya—an aging woman who decided not to grow up. Encountering the old nursery on her day of homecoming gives Ranevskaya the pleasure of finding herself in her own element—it is not a place of memory or recognition for her, but the place of Ranevskaya's personal past, which one could argue has never ended for this character.

The other characters of *The Cherry Orchard*, specifically those who stayed behind on the estate, volunteer facts and information about what has passed there while Ranevskaya lived in Paris. Gayev mentions the nanny, who died while Ranevskaya was away, and speaks of other servants who used to be close to them but who have either left or passed away. Firs famously ruminates about the good old days, the balls they used to host, and the cherries they used to sell.[45] To most of this information, Ranevskaya responds absent-mindedly, as if she does not want to acknowledge or focus on any of those changes, because, one could argue, if she stops and takes the information in, she will also need to accept that time has passed and that she has changed and aged, and so must recognize her responsibilities and act on them. Instead, she continues to brush off all the unpleasant news, as if trying to do everything possible not to arrive at the actuality of the moment, to keep her inner little girl intact; this is how she reacts to most of the information she receives:

MRS. RANEVSKY [*laughing*]. Varya, you haven't changed a bit. [*Draws Varya toward her and kisses her.*] I'll just drink this coffee, then we'll all go. . . .

. . .

MRS. RANEVSKY. Is it really me sitting here? [*Laughs.*] I feel like dancing and waving my arms about. [*Covers her face with her hands.*] But perhaps I'm only dreaming. God knows, I love my country, I love it dearly. I couldn't see anything from the train, I was crying so much. [*Through tears.*] But I must drink my coffee. Thank you Firs. Thank you, dear old friend. I'm so glad you're still alive.

. . .

MRS. RANEVSKY. I can't sit still, I really can't. [*Jumps up and walks about in great excitement.*] I'll die of happiness. Laugh at me if you want, I'm silly. My own dear little book-case [*kisses the book-case.*] My own little table—

GAYEV. Nanny died while you were abroad.

MRS. RANEVSKY [*sitting down and drinking her coffee*]. Yes, God rest her soul. Someone wrote me about it.[46]

In this scene, a little bookcase and a little table serve as the *time markers* of the action and as Ranevskaya's personal mnemonic anchors or keepsakes. Seeing and touching these objects helps Chekhov's characters keep the time still, stay in the past, without acknowledging the present, and so remain in the state of estrangement or inner stillness. In *Three Sisters*, the clock that the doctor Chebutykin breaks is the token of the sisters' memory of their late mother; in *Uncle Vanya*, the books that Professor Serebryakov reads are the mementos of his past academic glory; and in *The Cherry Orchard*, the old bookcase that Ranevskaya kisses and to which Gayev addresses his famous speech is silent witness to the characters' past embarrassments and new mistakes. "This book-case was made exactly a hundred years ago," Gayev says. "We might celebrate its centenary. It's an inanimate object, but all the same it is a book-case, you can't get away from that."[47] In Chekhov's plays, however, not only the objects but also the characters themselves can function as markers of time. "Nanny died while you were abroad," Gayev says, then quickly adds: "Anastasy has died too. Petrushka—remember the chap with the squint?—left me for another job, he's with the chief of police in town now."[48] These events—Nanny's death and the laborer's departure for another job—indicate a passage of time and the fact that everybody on the estate and off it has aged. Anya also worries as Peter Trofimov (the onetime tutor for Grisha, Ranevskaya's child who drowned on the estate) steps into the room: "he might bring back memories."[49] Curiously, it is Anya, Ranevskaya's daughter and the youngest character onstage (she is seventeen years old), and Varya, her adopted daughter of twenty-four years, who seem to worry about the past and what it might do to them or to Ranevskaya the most. Anya keeps track of the months and years: "its six years since Father died," she says. "And a month after that our brother Grisha was drowned in the river. He was a lovely little boy, only seven years old. It was too much for Mother, she went away, just dropped everything and went."[50] But Ranevskaya lets all these facts and memories slip, very much in the same way as she chooses not to pay any attention to Lopakhin's pragmatic advice on how to save her property. In a moment, in the same manner of brushing things off, she will tear a telegram from Paris without reading it, declaring that she is finished with it, and then she will ask Charlotte to do a trick.[51]

As with *Three Sisters*, with *The Cherry Orchard* Chekhov challenges the dramatic function of recognition. In *Three Sisters*, recognition defines both the action of the play's opening sequence and its overall dramatic structure, whereas in *The Cherry Orchard*, recognition plays out differently. Chekhov opens *The Cherry Orchard* by zooming in on the leading character, who refuses to "sober up" with age. In her floundering, Ranevskaya suddenly freezes her gaze and movement. When she notices the cherry orchard, we swiftly recognize where the real focal point of the play lies. A mnemonic reserve as well, the cherry orchard, the only "interesting, in fact quite remarkable, thing in the whole county," occupies the center of this play and signifies deep emotional value for its characters.[52] It is tied directly to Ranevskaya's youth and the most intimate memories and experiences she had; and so, it appears to be the reason for her homecoming. The monologue below attests both to the character's desire to return to her happy place and to the great failure of her grand return. It also serves as another example of the character's estr*age*ment or internal recognition:

> MRS. RANEVSKY [*looking through the window at the orchard*]. Oh, my childhood, my innocent childhood! this is the nursery where I slept and I used to look out at the orchard from here. When I woke up every morning happiness awoke with me, and the orchard was just the same in those days. Nothing's changed. [*Laughs happily.*] White! All white! Oh, my orchard! After the damp, dismal autumn and the cold winter there you are, young again and full of happiness. The angels in heaven have not forsaken you. If I could only shake off the heavy burden that weighs me down, if only I could forget my past.[53]

The feeling of happiness that Ranevskaya describes in the first part of this speech can be experienced only by innocent children, and so this monologue connects the place and the character. In the second part, she emerges as a disappointed older woman, who is desperately trying to hold on to an image of herself as a foolish child. When Ranevskaya finally admits that the burden of the past has aged her, she directs her gaze and her words toward the orchard, which she believes will always be there. It will keep its yearly returns and rejuvenations, following the rules of the cyclical time of nature. The orchard Ranevskaya describes arises at the end of this speech as something everlasting, mythological, and eternal, marked in its present time by the power of natural returns and reincarnations.

Ranevskaya's monologue is also reflective of the character's estr*age*ment: on the one hand, Chekhov evokes a clear sense of separation between the character and her orchard; on the other, he gives Ranevskaya a chance to connect with a sense of eternity. She is certain the orchard will be there even after she passes on. However, when Lopakhin starts cutting down the trees, he brings forward the time of the present, and thus he allows the calendar time of history to invade the mythological time of the orchard. This loss of her favored moment in time, this loss of eternity, with which Ranevskaya identifies her orchard, is a much more terrifying loss than just the demise of the estate. In Lopakhin's action of cutting through and irrevocably marring Ranevskaya's precious hold on eternity, Chekhov predicted the horrible atrocities to come; within the calendar time of twentieth- and twenty-first-century history, we find the wars, the genocides, and the mass killings that are rife in modern and contemporary experience.

CONCLUSION

Time is a central component of Chekhov's dramaturgy, and one that profoundly affects the structure of Chekhov's plots, which consist of an extended recognition. For Chekhov's characters, acknowledging their age and aging also constitutes a gesture of recognition. The result for some of his characters is immersion into a state of inaction or stillness. Facing this outcome, readers and spectators of Chekhov's theater may feel the need to turn their gazes inward, onto their own aging selves.

In Chekhov's universe, the action focuses not on the order of a sequence of events, but on what takes place between these events, events that are brushed off as insignificant, or as pure chance. In Chekhov's world, "time is estranged from the human; it is imposed, impersonal, and external to the individual. Time manifests itself through the inevitable violent event, which is thrust on the characters along with a predetermined date in their calendars."[54] In the two plays of Chekhov that I chose to examine in this chapter, *Three Sisters* and *The Cherry Orchard*, time serves as a marker of the characters' aging and as a special device of dramatic storytelling. The calendar time of history is used to denote the physical age of the characters and to present this through the prism of the historical events in which Chekhov's plays are embedded. Building on Fuchs's theoretical framework on aging as a form of dramatic and psychological distancing, we see that aging and time are tightly interconnected in Chekhov's universe, knotted together within the layout and structure of his plays, the dramaturgies of his characters' development, and the plays' spatiotemporal settings. Among the innovations of Chekhovian drama is his ability to do what Fuchs calls making character strange—when a dramatic turn of events makes a character reevaluate their life strategies, or not, when reaching an older age.[55] Chekhov's theater, hence, paves the way to a new epic drama, in which theatrical time is juxtaposed with human lifetime, our aging with the time of history, and humanity with the metaphysical world of eternity, based on "the infinite succession of generations."[56]

NOTES

1. Boris Zingerman, "Vremia v p'esakh Chekhova," in *Ocherki istorii dramy 20 veka* (Nauka, 1979), 84. When not indicated, all translations from Russian to English are mine.

2. John D. Goodliffe, "Time in Chekhov's Plays," *New Zealand Slavonic Journal* 7, no. 7 (1971): 35.

3. Freddie Rokem, *Theatrical Space in Ibsen, Chekhov and Strindberg: Public Forms of Privacy* (UMI Research Press, 1986), 33.

4. Stanislavsky, quoted in M. N. Stroyeva, "*Three Sisters* at the MAT," in *Re:Direction: A Theoretical and Practical Guide*, ed. Rebecca Schneider and Gabrielle Cody (Routledge, 2002), 40; Elinor Fuchs, "Estr*age*ment: Towards an 'Age Theory' Theatre Criticism," *Performance Research* 19, no. 3 (2014): 77.

5. Fuchs, "Estr*age*ment," 77.

6. Elinor Fuchs, "Rehearsing Age," *Modern Drama* 59, no. 2 (2016): 143–54.

7. Fuchs, "Estr*age*ment," 77.

8. Christopher Murray, "Beckett and the Representation of Age on Stage," *Princeton University Library Chronicle* 68, nos. 1–2 (2007): 434.

9. Murray, 435, 436.

10. Zingerman, "Vremia v p'esakh Chekhova," 101.

11. Chekhov, quoted in Zingerman, 102. In his comments to the actors of the Moscow Art Theatre, Chekhov suggested they not play any of the closing scenes exuberantly, wildly, or too fast. On the contrary, the significant events that take place close to the final curtain—the goodbye scene between Masha and Vershinin in *Three Sisters*, or the kiss that Astrov and Elena share in *Uncle Vanya*, or the failed marriage proposal between Varya and Lopakhin in *The Cherry Orchard*—must be played in a slow tempo, with actors searching for pianissimo and not forte in their actions, "opposite to all regulations of a proper dramatic art." Chekhov, quoted in Zingerman, 101.

12. Aristotle, *Poetics*, trans. S. H. Butcher (Macmillan, 1895), 39.

13. Elinor Fuchs, "Waiting for Recognition: An Aristotle for 'Non-Aristotelian' Drama," *Modern Drama* 50, no. 4 (2007): 534.

14. Harai Golomb, "Music as Theme and as Structural Model in Chekhov's *Three Sisters*," *Israel Studies in Musicology Online* 17 (2020): 108.

15. Golomb, 107.

16. Anton Chekhov, *Three Sisters*, in *Five Plays*, by Anton Chekhov, trans. Ronald Hingley (Oxford University Press, 2008), 177.

17. Chekhov, 178.

18. Chekhov, 173.

19. Chekhov, 178.

20. Fuchs, "Waiting for Recognition", 534.

21. Golomb, "Music as Theme," 108.

22. Chekhov, quoted in Zingerman, "Vremia v p'esakh Chekhova," 87.

23. Zingerman, 88.

24. Margaret Morganroth Gullette, *Aged by Culture* (University of Chicago Press, 2004), 132.

25. Fuchs, "Estr*age*ment," 76–77.

26. Fuchs, 77.

27. Zingerman, "Vremia v p'esakh Chekhova," 145–47.
28. Zingerman, 91.
29. Geoffrey Borny, *Interpreting Chekhov* (Australian National University E Press, 2010), 65.
30. Quoted in Dmitrii Gorodetskii, "Mezhdu 'Medvedem' i 'Leshim': Iz vospominanii o Chekhove," *Birzhevye vedomosti*, no. 364 (July 18, 1904), reproduced in N. S. Grodskaia et al., "Primechaniia," in *Anton Chekhov: Polnoe sobranie sochinenii*, vol. 12, *P'esy, 1889–1891*, ed. N. F. Bel'chikov et al. (Nauka, 1978), 45.
31. Zingerman, "Vremia v p'esakh Chekhova," 87.
32. Anton Chekhov, *The Cherry Orchard*, in Chekhov, *Five Plays*, 262.
33. Zingerman, "Vremia v p'esakh Chekhova," 87.
34. Zingerman, 104.
35. Zingerman, 147.
36. Chekhov, *The Cherry Orchard*, 247.
37. Chekhov, 250.
38. Chekhov, 294.
39. Joseph Roach, *Cities of the Dead: Circum-Atlantic Performance* (Columbia University Press, 1996), 26.
40. Rokem, *Theatrical Space*, 35.
41. Chekhov, *The Cherry Orchard*, 241.
42. Chekhov, 243.
43. Rokem, *Theatrical Space*, 32.
44. Chekhov, *The Cherry Orchard*, 245.
45. Chekhov, 249–51.
46. Chekhov, 248–49.
47. Chekhov, 250–51.
48. Chekhov, 249.
49. Chekhov, 247.
50. Chekhov, 247.
51. Chekhov, 250.
52. Chekhov, 249.
53. Chekhov, 253.
54. Zingerman, "Vremia v p'esakh Chekhova," 146.
55. Fuchs, "Rehearsing Age," 143–54.
56. Zingerman, "Vremia v p'esakh Chekhova," 147.

4
Pathologizing Aging Femininity
The Mad Older Woman in Tracy Letts's August: Osage County *and Florian Zeller's* The Mother

Núria Casado-Gual and Inesa Shevchenko-Hotsuliak

Research in different fields of aging studies has amply proved that the narrative of decline persists in current representations of old age. Despite the recent increase in explorations of later life on the contemporary stage, the theater continues to retell the experience of aging through a story of crisis, failure, and loss. This declinist tendency, which Michael Mangan identified as establishing continuities with the tradition of classical drama,[1] and which pioneering age scholars like Elinor Fuchs associated with the ongoing influence of Aristotelian structures,[2] is sometimes conveyed through plays that do not evolve around old age per se, and yet present mature or older protagonists in a state of mental breakdown or, even more, as the source of the chaos in their dramatic universe. Whereas in the Western theatrical tradition the intersection between age and bodily failure has its classical roots in patriarchal figures such as Oedipus or King Lear, on the contemporary stage it is more frequently signified through mature or aging female characters. Indeed, a quick look at recent examples of modern age-centered American and European dramaturgies confirms the redirection of the focus from older male to female characters as the new conventional models of old age,[3] a trend that is particularly notable from the 1980s onward in other cultural media, too.[4]

While this tendency could be celebrated as a sign of diversity within the new narratives of later life, the broader visibility of older women on the stage is often obscured by their ambiguous portrayals, in the theater and elsewhere, as either "successfully" aged individuals (that is, as physically attractive, young looking, and healthy, without any of the "prejudicial" signs of aging)[5] or, conversely, as stereotyped objects of fun and ridicule,[6] disgust and horror,[7] and decay and dependency,[8] all of which limit cultural representations of aging and old age, in Sherryl Wilson's terms, "to a series of somewhat retrogressive images."[9] In the best of cases, narratives of later life endow older people (and older women in particular), as Anna Harpin puts it, with "a troublingly untroubled presence."[10] Significantly larger in number, negative representations of mature and older women stand out over their "successful" versions, on the contemporary stage and through other media, which proves that, despite myriad life experiences, female aging is mostly aligned with decline. This cultural attitude is a clear reflection not only of our social denial of old age, but also of the "double standard of aging" of which Susan Sontag warned more than five decades ago,[11] and to which older women remain submitted in the sexist, youth-centered societies of the so-called advanced world.

Amid the prevalence of declinist scripts of female old age, the generalized association of old age with disease, physical and mental decay, senility, and infirmity, commonly accepted within the field of traditional gerontology,[12] has been particularly reflected in literary narratives with female protagonists either in their middle age[13] or later years,[14] thereby generating a gendered pathologization of old age in popular culture. In the theater, dramatic renderings of female old age often focus on dementia,[15] to the extent of making older women characters their iconic embodiment.[16] Through the conflation of aging with disease, older women have also been typically associated with mental health issues, often symbolically related to the trope of "madness."[17] While Harpin considers "madness" a more appropriate term to discuss complex forms of subjectivity that do not always comply with restrictive and consensual definitions of mental illness,[18] Brant Wenegrat contends that seeing a malady as part of a dramatic enactment implicitly indicates that it fulfills a "social role" or, as the scholar alternatively terms it, an "illness role."[19] The interpretation of female aging as a form of "madness" or "illness" is particularly significant since, as Harpin affirms, in the theater age is often "constructed as an illness role" whereby female characters are codified as "old."[20]

This chapter offers a comparative study of two well-known contemporary plays, Tracy Letts's *August: Osage County* (henceforth *August*, 2007)[21] and Florian Zeller's *The Mother* (2010),[22] by analyzing the characterization of their female protagonists, the different forms of madness they evoke (through both their illnesses and various addictions), and the constructions of age and gender they connote. Despite the international success of the two plays, little (*August*) or no attention at all (*The Mother*) has been given to the role that age plays in the protagonists' "mad" characterizations. The analysis is framed within the textual tradition of theater and age studies that Elinor Fuchs pioneered,[23] and that scholars like Michael Mangan[24] and Valerie Barnes Lipscomb[25] have helped establish on both sides of the Atlantic. It draws on insights derived from the intersecting critical study of age and gender while at the same time adopting Harpin's broad use of "madness" as a term that can accommodate the polychromatic subjectivities of Letts's and Zeller's characters. On the whole, this study demonstrates that the "illness role" ascribed to the protagonists of these two plays is directly associated with sexist notions of aging femininity as well as with deeply ingrained anxieties around female aging. By making older women the embodied receptacles of these cultural prejudices and fears, and by placing them within dramatic structures that isolate them or even punish them, these plays reproduce persistent patriarchal and declinist ideologies through which female old age becomes a double sign of failure.

THE MADNESS OF THE AGING MATRIARCH—*AUGUST: OSAGE COUNTY*

Nominee for and winner of various prestigious awards, Tracy Letts is considered a leading contemporary American playwright, and, among his numerous plays, *August* remains his best-known piece. Following its premiere in Chicago in 2007 with a production by Steppenwolf Theatre Company, it transferred to Broadway the same year, and it has been performed internationally since then.[26] Winning the 2008 Pulitzer Prize for Drama, the Tony Award for Best Play, and the New York Drama Critics' Circle Award (among other prizes), *August* has become one of the few plays to gain "the triple crown of American playwriting."[27] In 2013, a screen adaptation, scripted by Letts, directed by John Wells, and starring Meryl Streep as Violet Weston and Julia Roberts as Barbara Fordham (Violet's oldest daughter), premiered at the Toronto International Film Festival (TIFF) before its worldwide release in 2014; it is now available through streaming platforms, contributing to the play's ongoing international appeal.

Part of the play's success relies on its resort to one of the main themes of American theater, namely, the dysfunctional family, which Letts revisits through gallows humor and a plot full of unexpected twists. Following the tradition established by Eugene O'Neill, Arthur Miller, Edward Albee, and Sam Shepard, who plays Beverly Weston (Violet's husband) in the film version, Letts sets his own story of a deeply troubled family in "a rambling country home outside Pawhuska, Oklahoma" (9), where the Westons gather after the disappearance (and, as revealed later on, suicide) of the patriarch, Beverly. Divided into three acts, the dramatic action unfolds around the widowed matriarch, Violet, while the rest of the family (Violet's three daughters, Barbara, Ivy, and Karen; together with the partners of two of them; Barbara's teenage daughter; and Violet's sister, her brother-in-law, and "Little Charles," her nephew) receive different moments of attention whereby their convoluted lives and personal frustrations are disclosed. The play's poignant epigraph from Robert Penn Warren's *All the King's Men*, which compares the parents' affection for their children to "a kind of blood greed," and family gatherings to "diving into the octopus tank at the aquarium" (7), signals the dysfunctionality of the Weston clan. Indeed, the members of the family are characterized as "dysfunctional" in different ways: through addiction (to alcohol or drugs), mental instability (including suicide), deviant sexual behavior (ranging from adultery to attraction to adolescents and, albeit unconsciously, incestuous relationships), and their resort to violence (verbal and physical) as a result of all these disorders. Significantly, the family's multiple troubles are closely connected to Violet's characterization as a "mad," monstrous matriarch, who is both perpetrator and victim of the various mayhems she generates.

The complexity of Violet's personality is based on the combination of archetypal and sociocultural features in her character creation. On the one hand, her ambiguous portrayal, either as a source of conflict or as a "tragic" character who ends up deranged and alone, echoes other famous "madwomen" of the stage, such as Eugene O'Neill's Mary Tyrone, Tennessee Williams's Amanda Wingfield or Blanche DuBois, Lillian Hellman's Regina Giddens, Federico Garcia Lorca's Bernarda Alba, Edward Albee's Martha, or Martin McDonagh's Mag, to name just a few. Nevertheless, as noted by some theater critics, "Violet puts all the rest in the shade"[28] through her pill addiction, toxic maternal love, manipulative tactics, and, especially, vicious tongue. On the other hand, the sociocultural components of her characterization—that is, her "national" and social symbolism, as a white, upper-middle-class American (86), representative of settler culture (25, 37)—as well as her familial roles, as wife, mother, grandmother, and sister, coalesce with her personal identity: while evoking the stereotype of the "abandoned" woman and "deceived" wife, she is also constructed as extremely egotistical, cruel, interfering, and disempowering toward her loved ones, and, aggravating it all, as having to cope with cancer and a damaged brain. Violet's age (sixty-five), in combination with her gender, intensifies and further complicates her multi-

Fig. 4.1. Deanna Dunagan as Violet (foreground) and Amy Morton as Barbara (background) in *August: Osage County* by Tracy Letts for the U.S. premiere at Steppenwolf Theatre Company, Chicago, 2007. Photo: Michael Brosilow.

faceted characterization while simultaneously revealing the cultural politics of female aging re-created in Letts's play.

Violet's portrayal as an older woman highlights social[29] and cultural[30] interpretations of female aging by rendering her a victimized and, at the same time, horrifying individual. The matriarch's double "fragility" is accentuated through different kinds of illness that—albeit unrelated to her age—can be seen as natural and/or symbolic consequences of her life(style). In this way, Violet's cancer, defined by the *Oxford English Dictionary* as "anything that frets, corrodes, corrupts, or consumes slowly and secretly,"[31] is encumbered by a clearly metaphorical meaning. Although in her book *Ill-*

ness as Metaphor Sontag warned that "perhaps nobody will want any longer to compare anything awful to cancer," since this is a disease "overlaid with mystification" and "charged with the fantasy of inescapable fatality."[32] Violet's "mouth cancer," which keeps her tongue "on fire" (27), is ironically referred to as "a punch line" by Beverly (16), as it is closely connected to the caustic effect that the matriarch's verbal attacks have on the entire family. The effect of Violet's corrosive tongue, already reflected in the prologue, in which she is shown insulting her husband (11), is intensified by her addiction to pills, which she gets as a result of manipulation of and threats to various physicians (100). In fact, this is the first thing the readers/audience learn about her through Beverly's words: "Violet. My wife. She takes pills, sometimes a great many. And they affect . . . among other things, her equilibrium" (11), which, in great part, impairs the family's own balance. The aggressivity with which she threatens whomever dares to take her "little blue babies" (96–97) renders her characterization a self-destructive, violent version of the "illness role," which, as Wenegrat contends, can have divergent and, for the most part, contradictory, "rational, goal-directed" behavioral patterns aimed at obtaining benefits such as "attention, care, concern, and relief," or at expressing one's dissatisfaction.[33] In fact, "healthy" and "unhealthy," like "insane" or "insanity," are recurrent words in the play, hence showing the symbolic importance of health and (ir)rationality in the moral universe of Letts's piece.

Yet, Violet's fragility as a brain-damaged drug addict affected by cancer is also enhanced by her aging body and mind. Their gradual deterioration—manifested through her inability to manage some administrative formalities of the house, which was her husband's ordinary task (25), or even to fulfill some basic domestic routines, as signified by her "wrinkled clothes" (13); her need for treatment and care (15), underscored by her constantly having pills in her hand (25, 27, 57, 58); and her states of mental confusion (33, 138), in which fear is a predominant emotion (27, 32)—not only accentuates her "illness role" but also evokes the so-called "feminization of aging,"[34] whereby the vulnerabilities of old age and stereotypical views of femininity as "weak"[35] are perfectly conflated. While Violet's victimization clearly serves dramatic purposes (it effectively justifies some of her actions and, in this way, enables a certain degree of identification with her plight), it also perpetuates ageist and sexist assumptions about female aging.[36] Violet herself has absorbed the culturally enforced beliefs around her own age and gender: she is worried about her beauty (14) and accepts its disappearance by mocking the "symbols" of her youthful femininity (the pretty clothes and high-heeled shoes she would never wear again) and by sarcastically referring to her aging body as "downgrading" and "downsizing" (93). In the same vein, she feels repulsed by her "swollen ankles," "varicose veins," and "toenails [that] could dig through cement" (65), and firmly believes that women "are beautiful when they're young, and not after," while men, she continues, "still preserve their sex appeal well into old age" (65). Mattie Fae, Violet's younger sister, age fifty-seven, tries to confront her blatant manifestation of the "double standard" of aging;[37] however, Violet's vehemence and powerful rhetoric clearly win in the debate. As women age, Violet asserts, they "get ugly" (93), "old and fat and wrinkly" (66)—this is "the truth" she must tell (66, 93), a discourse of internalized sexism and self-inflicted ageism that not only victimizes her further, but also distresses her middle-aged daughters at a particularly unstable moment of their sentimental lives, either as divorcée-to-be (Barbara), as an officially single woman with a secret affair with her cousin Little Charles (Ivy), or as the future bride of a man who, like Barbara's husband, feels attracted to young girls (Karen).

Beyond her (self-)victimizing qualities, Violet's unruly and extremely cruel personality renders her monstrous, almost nonhuman—another feature commonly attached to contemporary cultural representations of older women.[38] Ranging from the depiction of her "sealed" house (9–10), in which Violet lives like a beast and preys on the "weaker" members of her family ready to "eat [them] alive" (96), to the expressions of the woman's grotesque femininity in her almost-animalistic behavior of smuggling drugs in her vagina—revealed in the dialogue between Violet's three daughters, which resorts to the ultimate taboo about one's mother (and older woman's) genitalia to create a comic effect (101)—to the signals of the woman's incapacity to love and care for her family, the play constantly portrays the character of Violet as a dehumanized individual, almost reptilian in her demeanor and habits. Her lifelong partner, Beverly, describes his wife as "cold-blooded and not just in the metaphorical sense" (12). Her monstrous, mad personality makes her capable of keeping a terrible secret about the relationship between her husband and her sister (which resulted in the birth of Little Charles), and of letting her husband die so that she could have the money from the deposit that both of them kept to secure their later life (135–37).

The combination of fragility and monstrosity in Violet's characterization results in a declinist portrayal of female old age that amplifies sexist and ageist stereotypes. Although the "age effects" of her characterization—to draw from Bridie Moore's adaptation of Judith Butler's theory[39]—elicit more terror than pity (in Aristotelian terms), Violet's "excessive" vulnerability also awakens some compassion within the rich emotional scope of Letts's modern tragedy. In this respect, the realistic character basis of Violet as a representative of a decadent white middle class from Oklahoma, and as a woman who has faced and overcome several forms of abuse or oppression throughout her life, facilitates a more nuanced interpretation of her personal madness. Thus, throughout the play, Violet is also portrayed as a woman who once loved and was loved (36, 46); as a "suffering" (17) and cheated-on wife, even though she knew about her husband's secrets (93, 133); as a mother who needs her children (41) and was "heartbroken" when they left (104), and yet does not want to be patronized and invalidated by them (94, 109); as a victim of the meanness and cruelty of her own mother (91, 106, 107), as well as of the attacks of one of her mother's "many gentlemen friends" (94); as a survivor of poverty (94–95) who loses control of her own house; as a shy girl or, in Mattie Fae's words, as "Shrinking Violet" (18), who, seeing her daughters together, remembers what it was like to be young (106); or as an ill person, who feels scared (27) and is in a lot of pain (40), and yet dances to the music of Eric Clapton whenever she feels lost (21, 28, 55), claiming, "I'm not old, you know" (28). The intersectional aspects interwoven within Violet's fictionalized life and characterization explain and demonstrate the complexity of her identity as an older woman by placing it within the broader spectrum of her dramatized life course.

Especially in connection with her social class– and gender-determined roles, which highly account for cultural aspects of old age, Violet's aging femininity is loaded with what Ricca Edmondson calls "generational meaning," that is, "the place of individuals . . . within the flow of generations."[40] Within the dysfunctional Weston family, such generational meaning is tainted with negative value, thereby enhancing the play's declinist portrayal of female old age. Violet insistently, yet unsuccessfully, tries to identify herself with "her generation," in which "families stayed together" (27); but the accounts of her childhood are quite ambiguous and deprived of any sense of "honor," and her daughters (especially Barbara) refuse to recognize the sense of moral superiority that Violet defends through her generational identification (100–101). Clearly influenced by Violet's own abusive mother, the matriarch's intergenerational relationships have mutated from victimhood to perpetration of abuse and malice, therefore sustaining and eternalizing the generational divide, which, as Chris Gilleard and Paul Higgs contend, evolves over time yet constantly perpetuates the schism between the young and the aged.[41] In the dramatic universe of *August*, the generational breach generates, in fact, a form of collective madness. From this perspective, and despite the rich characterization that Violet receives at the heart of her own tragedy, this character can also be read as a symbol of a depraved, corrupt, almost apocalyptic world, whereby the play's sense of "lateness" is given a specific human shape: that of an older woman.

AGING FEMININITY AS (SELF-)ALIENATION: *THE MOTHER*

The Mother (2010) is part of the family trilogy that, in recent years, has turned Florian Zeller into "the French prodigy" of contemporary theater.[42] Even though the other two pieces of the trilogy, *The Father* (winner of the Molière Award for Best Play in 2014) and *The Son* (which premiered at the Comédie des Champs Élysées in 2018), have received broader attention through their film adaptations, cowritten and directed by Zeller himself, *The Mother* has also gained significant international acclaim, especially through the productions it received in the UK (2015–16) and New York (2019), with actresses Gina McKee and Isabelle Huppert in the lead role, respectively. Neither their stellar casting nor the author's own reputation saved these productions (especially the American one) from somewhat ambivalent critical reviews, which considered *The Mother* a weaker play in comparison with *The Father*. Yet, Zeller's capacity to create haunting central roles and to elicit reflection on the complexities of the human psyche, particularly in connection with cognitive processes or mental health, was equally enhanced.[43] As a matter of fact, it is the play's exploration of a late-middle-aged woman's failing mind that makes *The Mother* a "timely" piece given the contemporary concern toward mental health, as considered in a recent review,[44] as well as the object of new productions within a relatively short period of time.

Zeller's drama is characterized by its disorienting plots and subjective representation of dramatic time, through which the readers/audience must interpret (often without a clear resolution) whether what happens in front of their eyes is reality, the memory of a past moment, the projection of a wish, or just the product of the imagination of the characters' fragile minds. In *The Mother*, Zeller uses this postmodern take on multiperspectivism and overlapping temporalities to generate the disconcerting portrayal of Anne, a forty-seven-year-old woman whose perception of her own life drifts away from reality to hallucination. Through a series of scenes that often refer back to themselves in altered versions, Anne's conviction that she is being betrayed by her husband, Pierre, that she will be "abandoned" by her two adult children, especially Nicolas, and that she will somehow end up replaced by her son's girlfriend (Élodie), is constantly repeated, connecting the character's midlife crisis to a clearly deteriorating mental condition. In this way, Zeller's play troublingly explores the cumulative effect of a series of turning points associated with the late middle years (such as facing the dissolution of a long-lived marriage or seeing one's children become adults) on the human (in this case, female) psyche.

Fig. 4.2. Isabelle Huppert as the Mother in *The Mother* by Florian Zeller for the U.S. premier at the Atlantic Theater Company, New York City, 2019. Photo: Ahron R. Foster.

Just like with Violet in *August*, Anne's acute feeling of alienation within her family (and, ultimately, social) domain renders her midlife crisis a form of madness or, more specifically, of hysteria. As Eleanor Bowen and Laura González assert, hysteria "is a process, a state of mind, rather than a condition"; closely related to femininity and the body, it "captures something inherently human, ambivalent and conflicted."[45] In this sense, Anne's hysteria is closely related to the negative effect that aging has both on her "feminine" social roles as a wife and mother (which she now thinks she cannot fulfill anymore) and on her own body, which she is also obsessed with. In a society that does not accommodate aging, especially in women, Anne must adopt an "illness role"[46] through hysterical behavior. As Bowen and González contend, this includes "a struggle with gender, a manifestation of symptoms of the body, and the asking of a question . . . 'What do you want from me?'"[47]—precisely the question that Anne repeatedly poses to those around her (47, 48, 53, 56). The multiple demands of attention Anne imposes on her husband and son lead her to (if the ending of the play is to be interpreted in realistic terms) a profound clinical depression.

Defined by the author as a "black farce" on the title page, the play suggests a strong archetypal basis for the characterization of the eponymous Mother.

In fact, she is named after the role she plays (or thinks she has lost), just like the other characters of the play, whose names are revealed only later. The scope and symbolic load of her archetypal "matriarchal role" are negatively reduced through the strong alignment between her characterization and the negative stereotype(s) of the deceived and obsessive wife, particularly notable in act 1 (with the Mother and Father as the only characters), and the suffocating mother (especially to her son), which is fully developed in the remaining acts. From a more victim-oriented perspective, her characterization also echoes the image of the depressed "empty nester," which makes the character prone to self-destructive behavior: this is manifested through Anne's addiction to alcohol (6, 10, 11) and pills, which she both takes "to stay alive" (41, 54, 59–60) and, conversely, implicitly leans on in her suicide threats (23–24, 46). Feminist authors like Betty Friedan have long reacted against the social strictures that tie middle-aged and older women to the mother role, elaborating on the positive changes that may follow the stage of the empty nest.[48] However, the play presents Anne's empty-nest syndrome as both a traumatic and an alienating experience, which, besides leading her to a mental breakdown, estranges her from her daughter (she hardly remembers Sara's age and recalls having felt "strangely repelled" at her face when she was born [7]) and renders her a potentially dangerous progenitor to her son (as shown when she offers pills to him [41]). Anne's loss of her mothering role also makes her a revengeful and defiant wife, who speaks openly about her constant unhappiness, makes her husband feel responsible for it—"You know perfectly well my day was shitty" (1)—and undertakes petty tricks such as switching off the alarm clock so that her husband misses his train to a supposed seminar (21, 25).

Through her "unmotherly" and "unloving" reactions to her sense of abandonment, Anne is depicted as a grotesque expression of aging femininity. This expression, on the one hand, endows the aging woman with "monstrous" qualities precisely, as Lynne Segal contends, due to "the combination of age and gender,"[49] and, on the other hand, depicts gendered old age, now borrowing from Kathleen Woodward, as "the figure of horror and catastrophe."[50] This is especially poignant within Zeller's dramatic universe because Anne is deprived of an identity of her own outside her roles as mother and wife. In this respect, Zeller's play is constructed on a suppressive patriarchal structure, which, in its intricate entanglement of family dynamics, desire, misperception, and suppression around the creation of Anne's "feminine" identity, reflects the subjugation or, even more, the invalidity of women outside the social/family roles ascribed to them and, therefore, favors the pernicious "age effect"[51] of associating women's maturity with the demise of their personal life. Despite all the features that render Anne both a victim and a source of conflict in the play, she is also shown to continue fulfilling the "domestic roles" to which mature and older women remain bound.[52] Coherent with the allegedly farcical tone of the play, Anne constantly makes sure that her husband and son are not hungry (8, 45), or ensures that they have everything they need (33), or simply wonders about their day, despite her permanent anxiety and even in the oddest of conversations (7, 10, 11).

Nonetheless, on a more specific level, the trauma of Anne's empty-nest syndrome is completely connected to her own understanding of the experience of aging, which is only manifested in terms of the narrative of decline that has become deeply ingrained in the woman's psyche. Her everyday reality is hence defined in deeply negative terms and characterized by Anne's rather static portrayal as someone stuck in a kind of limbo, trapped in a loop of inertia (2), uselessness (5, 12), and constant struggle with her own mental fragility (16, 25, 58), from which she cannot escape. The world the Mother dwells in offers her no space for self-fulfillment or growth, reflecting in this way the combination of aging and gender as a perilous form of marginalization.[53] Anne's personal and social forms of passivity, underscored through her constant act of waiting for Nicolas to call her—"I stayed in, did nothing. Waited." (2)—transform the Mother into a character reminiscent of the theater of the absurd. Her continuous sense of isolation, together with her repetitive (almost demented) statements, re-creates a highly symbolic representation of the absurdist drama of female aging in an ageist and sexist world. In this sense, Anne's invisibility as a mother, poignantly expressed through her claim that "he never comes by to see me. Never. He behaves as if I didn't exist" (2) when referring to her son, is an allegorical sign of her own invisibility as an older woman, which she continuously (yet, unsuccessfully) tries to defy.

In a similar vein, Anne's references to her beauty should be understood as laments for her gradual loss of youth—a double loss that is typically entangled for women in the aging process,[54] especially because, as Margaret Morganroth Gullette contends, in our patriarchal cultures the feared and loathed signs of aging are always made more visible on women than on men.[55] In an attempt to disguise her biological and social age, and complying with the idea that age can also be a performative category,[56] Anne puts on a red dress she has bought for herself and shows it to her son while asking him: "What age do you think I look in this dress?" (38–39). Anne's recurrent, unsuccessful attempts to look younger (and with them, to cease to look like a mother to her adult son) situate her age at the center of her "Oedipal performance." Significantly, she enacts it in front of a mirror (38–39, 51), a highly symbolic prop in psychoanalytic terms, which, in the play, also enhances the essential role that declinist understandings of "age" play in the character's mental crisis. In this case, the Mother's attempt to escape her own age through her disguised self-reflection in the mirror signifies her "mirror stage of old age," that is, the stage in which, according to Woodward's adaptation of Lacanian theory,[57] the (female) aging subject (and viewer) becomes dissociated from herself through the distorting self-image that the mirror refracts, which also contains her social age.

The Mother's seemingly absurdist or farcical "drama of aging" is also expressed through her painful "life review" of sorts, in Robert Butler's terms,[58] as reflected in her regret of life-changing decisions such as starting a relationship with her husband, Pierre, when she was young and unexperienced (6), unaware of "the extent of the disaster" that marriage would bring with it (4, 6), and having children with him (9). Even though these reflections could be understood in feminist, even anti-ageist terms, they do not generate the constructive reexamination of one's life that, according to Butler, helps older individuals reintegrate unresolved conflicts of the past into their present perspective, often in the light of their approaching death or "dissolution."[59] Rather, the Mother's declinist views about her own life complicate the "Oedipal" overtones of the play, especially when she is visibly racked by jealousy every time her son's girlfriend is mentioned or is present (9, 22, 28–29). Élodie is a clear image of what Anne is not anymore—that is, a young, beautiful, and sexually appealing woman who is loved by a (young) man. Anne's "excessive" love for her son, as reflected in Élodie's interpretation of her "maternal" relationship (29), transforms her into a pathetic Phaedra-and-Jocasta-like figure. Anne's doubly tragic image as a desiring-yet-undesired aging mother is exacerbated through her fantasy about having a night out with Nicolas and going "as far away as possible" with him (42, 49). In the duel between the Girl and the Mother, and conforming to the sociocultural discomfort with an older (or mature) woman's sexuality,[60] the Mother is inevitably portrayed as desexualized, not only because she is represented as a lonely older woman whose sole pleasure will be found in eating biscuits at her home while the young couple are having sex (45), but also because Nicolas's girlfriend will also call her "Mum" as a final act of "cruelty" (46) that invalidates her as a sexual agent and, putting an end to her "Oedipal" performance, resituates her within the (appropriate) confinements of her mothering role.

Élodie's heartless responses to Anne's suffering mirror the viciousness toward older women that characterizes youth-centric societies and that is deeply ingrained in our cultural history.[61] More generally, though, Zeller's dramatic world not only substantiates the cultural idea that female aging equals decline but also, similarly to Letts's play, assigns metaphorical meanings to the protagonist's fragile mental state, connecting her age and gender to a form of pathology. At the beginning of the play, the Mother's depressed and neurotic state is associated with her physical and social passivity, to which the Father reacts by insisting on Anne's finding herself something to do (4), hence echoing culturally ingrained beliefs in the effects of staying active as a sign of health and social worth.[62] Especially as of Nicolas's appearance in the play, the Mother's "unsuccessful" mental state is defined as "fragile" (25) and "exhausted" (36), and becomes cause for the Father's concern (25). Yet, Nicolas's telling his father he will look after her during his father's trip (26) already presents the Mother as disabled, even incapable of taking care of herself. Throughout the play, Anne's depression gradually evolves into a dangerous form of neurosis or "madness" that can only be "cured" or "controlled" by the healthy characters (for whom she is rendered "the other" through their difference in gender or age, or both). This is reflected through Pierre's (mental, physical, social, and moral) superiority over his wife in his offering Anne some sleeping pills to calm her down (11); or, more harshly, in Élodie's threats to force Anne to get into bed (57–58); or, even more symbolically, in Anne's feeling the burden of social mockery as two stagehands suddenly enter during the last scene of act 3 and, after laughing at her fragile mind, eventually force her to the hospital bed they bring on the stage (58).

On the whole, the Mother's characterization complies with the image of the "madwoman" (20, 34, 40), which is long established in the patriarchal history of literature, as identified by Sandra Gilbert and Susan Gubar,[63] and which, in this case, refers to the double "otherness" that defines the character through her gender and age. Nevertheless, toward the end of the play, and contrary to Violet's corrosive "madness" in *August*, the Mother gets scared about the effects the pills are having on her (54, 57), and acknowledges her mistakes to her son in a desperate attempt to keep him with her (56). The final destabilization of the Mother's mad and maddening characterization, through which a groove for empathy is slightly opened, represents her as an ambivalent figure whose state of mind is in a continuous struggle with her subconscious, which dominates the scene. Both her contradictory behavior and her unreliable statements make her an extremely "uncanny" character, in the Freudian sense, composed of both familiar elements (reinforced by archetypal and stereotypical aspects of her characterization) and unfamiliar ones (evocative of her "hysteria"), which merge in her "ordinary" life. At the same time, the intimate connection between her mental dissolution and her traumatic experience of female aging endows her uncanniness with deep cultural meaning. As elucidated by Amelia DeFalco, who, like many other scholars, argues that gender is the category that "most dramatically" interacts with age, aging "opens our eyes to the ubiquity of uncanniness, and most unsettlingly, to the contradiction that is constitutive of selfhood."[64] Zeller expresses the ubiquity of the strangeness of aging on the female subject by tinging the entire play with a "strange atmosphere" (1) that is constantly reinforced through sound effects and intriguing pauses, besides the recurrence of repetitions. These theatrical strategies, which are meant to underline the psychological tension of the piece, mainly reveal the subjective world of Anne's mind amid the traumatic experience of becoming "othered" as an aging mother: facing the contradictions of her new sense of self within a world founded on ageist, patriarchal values, Anne is deprived of her own vital purpose and, evoking Julia Kristeva's thought,[65] becomes "a stranger to herself."

CONCLUDING THOUGHTS

In *Illness as Metaphor*, Sontag claimed that "the modern metaphors suggest a profound disequilibrium between individual and society, with society conceived as the individual's adversary. Disease metaphors are used to judge society not as out of balance but as repressive."[66] As demonstrated in this chapter, the pathologized older women in *August: Osage County* and *The Mother* reinforce declinist views of aging that especially repress women within societies in which aesthetic pressure and domestic roles continue to define the female experience of growing older. Far from generating counternarratives of aging femininity, whereby the value of the older woman and her continuous process of growth are vindicated,[67] Letts's and Zeller's pieces instead construct their protagonists through the mold of the "madwoman." Instead of suggesting the feminist image of rebellion that other "madwomen in the attic" have inspired,[68] they generate a sinister view of female aging in either pathetic (Violet) or intriguingly uncanny (Anne) versions, which clearly equates female old age with decadence and failure. More particularly, and albeit in completely different dramaturgical styles, both plays assign their main characters an "illness role" that blends the process of aging with the women's altered mental states, addictions, and toxic behavior, hence generating a specific form of "madness" that conflates negative interpretations of age and femininity with unacceptable, grotesque, or even monstrous manifestations of the irrational. Through such deeply ingrained interpretations of age and gender, Violet's and Anne's unpredictable, "nonnormative," and, ultimately, abhorrent behavior mainly renders them not only the main sources of dramatic conflict, but also the "objects of horror" of their patriarchal societies, which "monster" them in their maturity or incipient old age in the same way that, when they were young women, these societies had regarded them as objects of desire.

In the same vein, and although in more subtle ways, *August* and *The Mother* also victimize their protagonists, thereby underlining the powerful effect of ageism and sexism on their characterizations as well as their personal and social spheres. In this respect, the similar symbolic treatment that both plays make of the house as their presentational space is worth noticing. If, as some scholars assert, the house (or home) can be understood as a reflection of the occupant's self or identity,[69] then the deteriorated and "deranged" facade of the Westons' house, "literally falling apart" (25) and blind to the world, claustrophobically darkened by "cheap plastic shades" and "black duct tape" that cause the effect of "a complete absence of outside light" (10), is a striking metaphor for Violet's frail corporeality and dark inner world, as well as for the toxic effect that her "madness" has on everyone living under the same roof. The Westons' home is hence defined as "a goddam madhouse," where Violet's "shrill insanity" affects the entire family (76), especially her daughters—and Barbara in particular, who is accused of becoming a "monster" like her (134–35). Also evoking the intimate connection between the house and its dwellers, the "disappearing" house of *The Mother*, radically replaced by a mental hospital through the unexpected entrance of the stagehands dressed like paramedics (57), similarly symbolizes the gradual self-alienation and final dissolution of Anne's psyche, processes that run in parallel to her social disappearance as a mature woman. While in the naturalistic world of Letts's piece the house reflects the matriarch's ghoulishness by taking on "a ghostly cast" (128), its sheer disappearance in Zeller's allegorical piece signifies Anne's total disintegration. As clear projections of the two women's failing minds and bodies, the house is inextricably connected with Violet and Anne not only through its psychoanalytic power (that is, as the presentational space in which the protagonists' troubling fears and desires are revealed), but also, and mainly, through the declinist qualities that underscore their symbolic "illness" and ultimate "demise" as aging matriarchs in male-dominated, youth-centered domains.

Despite the more or less overt use of humor in the two plays (which makes *August* an extremely successful tragicomedy, and *The Mother* a symbolic farce with a peculiar sense of irony), the endings of the two pieces are equally tragic. Complying with the declinist tendency of the peak-and-decline structure that Fuchs perceptively observed in Aristotelian plots—which Letts's realistic piece fulfills completely and which Zeller's play, despite its anti-Aristotelian appearance, also evokes through the centrality of the main character—both texts present their protagonists as eventually becoming completely helpless and alone, and needing care themselves.[70] The fact that the care Violet and Anne receive at the end of their respective plays is not provided by members of the family underscores their personal feeling of alienation: in *August*, it is, Johnna, the Native American domestic worker whom Violet belittles due to her racist and class-derived prejudices, who will end up taking care of her; whereas in *The Mother*, Anne is eventually looked after by the nurses at the hospital. Even more significantly, the two plays transform the protagonists' fear of being abandoned by their own into a self-fulfilling prophecy, which is regarded as following "the nature of things," as Pierre puts it, from the privilege of his male, ableist position, at the end of Zeller's piece (63). Yet, there is nothing "natural" in the denouements of the two texts. Violet is last shown "on all fours," crawling up the stairs of her house "to the attic" and putting her head on Johnna's lap, while the maid sings, "This is the way the world ends . . ." to her—an apocalyptic image that, besides confirming her as another "madwoman in the attic," practically transforms her into an abandoned animal. Anne, meanwhile, wonders, "What was all that for? Mm? When it comes down to it . . . What was all that for?" (64) while lying in her hospital bed, unable to make sense of an entire life exclusively constricted by her domestic roles, and incapable of imagining anything else beyond it but the repetition of the same obsessive cycle she is bound to (as reflected by her son's last, silent and ominous, appearance) within her own destitution.

All in all, the dramatic strategies employed in *August* and *The Mother* not only reassert the narrative of decline by presenting it as an inevitable destiny, but also highlight the pathologization and, ultimately, *dehumanization* of female aging within cultural frameworks in which femininity and old age are either diminished or feared, or both, not only by the male or younger "others," but by the female aging subjects themselves. At the same time, however, the "age effects" of these two plays, to use Moore's term once again,[71] should not be read exclusively in declinist terms. In fact, in the same way that Violet's and Anne's rich characterizations allow for a compassionate interpretation of their grotesque reactions and deviant behavior, the potential performances inscribed in the two playscripts signal the extremely rich and rewarding parts that these roles turn out to be for the actresses that play them. Beyond the predominant projection of a gendered narrative of decline through the stories they tell, *August* and *The Mother* allow for mature actresses to exhibit their craft and talent through characters that are extremely demanding, both physically and emotionally (Violet being particularly the case, as an almost-

Lear-esque role in which fury and fragility, power and disempowerment, are constantly combined), and which also require an extremely high level of concentration and theatrical savoir faire, either due to the scope of the play (especially *August*) or (particularly in *The Mother*) because of its intricate pseudo-repetitive structure. As demonstrated by the extremely positive reviews that actors who have actually performed these roles have received, such as Deanna Dunagan (winner of a Tony Award for her performance as Violet in her late sixties), or Gina McKee (the protagonist of the original British production of *The Mother* while in her fifties), the two plays not only place the older woman in the spotlight (a dramatic choice that, although more frequent, remains exceptional) but also generate a sense of empowerment among mature and older actresses at a stage in their careers that may be strongly affected by sexism and ageism. Ironically enough, by allowing for an alternative (and extremely powerful) performance of female old age to emerge through the art of the mature woman actor, *August* and *The Mother* undermine the narrative of decline that their dramatic worlds firmly delineate.

NOTES

1. Michael Mangan, *Staging Ageing: Theatre, Performance and the Narrative of Decline* (Intellect, 2013).
2. Elinor Fuchs, "Rehearsing Age," *Modern Drama* 59, no. 2 (2016): 147.
3. Anna Harpin, "The Lives of Our Mad Mothers: Aging and Contemporary Performance," *Women & Performance: a journal of feminist theory* 22, no. 1 (2012): 71.
4. Sherryl Wilson, "She's Been Away: Ageing, Madness and Memory," in *Alive and Kicking at All Ages: Cultural Constructions of Health and Life Course Identity*, ed. Ulla Kriebernegg, Roberta Maierhofer, and Barbara Ratzenböck (Transcript Verlag, 2014), 187.
5. Wilson, 187.
6. Harpin, "The Lives of Our Mad Mothers," 71.
7. Anne Billson, "'Hagsploitation': Horror's Obsession with Older Women Returns," *Guardian*, January 18, 2018, https://www.theguardian.com/film/2018/jan/18/hagsploitation-horrors-obsession-with-older-women-returns; Liz Byrski, "Conscientious Objections: Feminism, Fiction and the Phoney War on Ageing," in *Ageing, Popular Culture and Contemporary Feminism: Harleys and Hormones*, ed. Imelda Whelehan and Joel Gwynne (Palgrave Macmillan, 2014), 16–17; Kathleen Woodward, *Aging and Its Discontents: Freud and Other Fictions* (Indiana University Press, 1991).
8. J. Brooks Bouson, *Shame and the Aging Woman: Confronting and Resisting Ageism in Contemporary Women's Writings* (Palgrave Macmillan, 2016); Imelda Whelehan, "Not to Be Looked at: Older Women in Recent British Cinema," in *British Women's Cinema*, ed. Melanie Bell and Melanie Williams (Routledge, 2010), 170–83.
9. Wilson, "She's Been Away," 187.

10. Harpin, "The Lives of Our Mad Mothers," 68.

11. Susan Sontag, "The Double Standard of Aging," *Saturday Review* 23 (1972): 29–38.

12. Mikhail V. Blagosklonny, "Disease or Not, Aging Is Easily Treatable," *Aging* 10, no. 11 (2018): 3067–78; Gunnar De Winter, "Aging as Disease," *Medicine, Health Care and Philosophy* 18, no. 2 (2015): 237–43.

13. Emma Domínguez-Rué, *Of Lovely Tyrants and Invisible Women: Invalidism as Metaphor in the Fiction of Ellen Glasgow* (Logos Verlag, 2011).

14. Sara Zadrozny, "Women's Ageing as Disease," *Humanities* 8, no. 2 (2019): 75.

15. Morgan Batch, "Demarcating Dementia on the Contemporary Stage," in *The Routledge Handbook of Disability Arts, Culture, and Media*, ed. Bree Hadley and Donna McDonald (Routledge, 2019), 148–60; Anne Davis Basting, *Forget Memory: Creating Better Lives for People with Dementia* (Johns Hopkins University Press, 2009); Janet Gibson, *Dementia, Narrative and Performance: Staging Reality, Reimagining Identities* (Palgrave Macmillan, 2020).

16. Cases in point are *A Wedding Story* by Bryony Lavery (2007), *Salt, Root and Roe* by Tim Price (2011), *Autobiographer* by Melanie Wilson (2012), *The Humans* by Stephen Karam (2016), and *Elegy* by Nick Payne (2016), among many others.

17. Harpin, "The Lives of Our Mad Mothers"; Wilson, "She's Been Away," 194.

18. Anna Harpin, *Madness, Art, and Society: Beyond Illness* (Routledge, 2018), 2.

19. Brant Wenegrat, *Theater of Disorder: Patients, Doctors, and the Construction of Illness* (Oxford University Press, 2001), 4.

20. Harpin, "The Lives of Our Mad Mothers," 79.

21. Tracy Letts, *August: Osage County* (Theatre Communications Group, 2008). Subsequent citations are given parenthetically in the text.

22. Florian Zeller, *The Mother*, trans. Christopher Hampton (Faber and Faber, 2010). Subsequent citations are given parenthetically in the text.

23. Elinor Fuchs, "Estr*age*ment: Towards an 'Age Theory' Theatre Criticism," *Performance Research* 19, no. 3 (2014): 69–77.

24. Mangan, *Staging Ageing*.

25. Valerie Barnes Lipscomb, *Performing Age in Modern Drama* (Palgrave Macmillan, 2016).

26. In Catalonia, from which this chapter is written, *August* was produced by the Teatre Nacional de Catalunya for the 2011–12 season. Its reception was so successful that the production was programmed again in 2012–13: this was the first time Barcelona's National Theater gave a production a second season.

27. E. Teresa Choate, "August: Osage County," *Theatre Journal* 61, no. 1 (2009): 105.

28. Charles Isherwood, "A Matriarch After Your Attention, If Not Heart," *New York Times*, August 13, 2007, https://www.nytimes.com/2007/08/13/theater/reviews/13augu.html

29. Robert Butler, *The Longevity Revolution: The Benefits and Challenges of Living a Long Life* (Public Affairs, 2008), 24; Margaret Cruikshank, *Learning to Be Old: Gender, Culture, and Aging*, 3rd ed. (Rowman and Littlefield, 2013).

30. Byrski, "Conscientious Objections"; Woodward, *Aging and Its Discontents*.

31. Susan Sontag, *Illness as Metaphor, and AIDS and Its Metaphors* (Anchor Books, 1990), 10.

32. Sontag, 87.

33. Wenegrat, *Theater of Disorder*, 5.

34. Patricia M. Davidson, Michelle DiGiacomo, and Sarah J. McGrath, "The Feminization of Aging: How Will This Impact on Health Outcomes and Services?," *Health Care for Women International* 32, no. 12 (2011): 1031–45.

35. Maren Wehrle, "Becoming Old: The Gendered Body and the Experience of Aging," in *Aging and Human Nature: Perspectives from Philosophical, Theological, and Historical Anthropology*, ed. Mark Schweda, Michael Coors, and Claudia Bozzaro (Springer, 2020), 75–96.

36. Betty Friedan, *The Fountain of Age* (Simon and Schuster, 1993); Germaine Greer, *The Change: Women, Aging and the Menopause* (Penguin Books, 1992); Martha B. Holstein, "On Being an Old Woman in Contemporary Society," *Generations: Journal of the American Society on Aging* 41, no. 4 (2017): 6–11; Sontag, "The Double Standard of Aging"; Kathleen Woodward, ed., *Figuring Age: Women, Bodies, Generations* (Indiana University Press, 1999).

37. Sontag, "The Double Standard of Aging."

38. Woodward, *Aging and Its Discontents*, 8.

39. Bridie Moore, "Depth, Significance, and Absence: Age-Effects in New British Theatre," *Age, Culture, Humanities: An Interdisciplinary Journal*, no. 1 (January 2014): 163–95.

40. Ricca Edmondson, *Ageing, Insight and Wisdom: Meaning and Practice Across the Lifecourse* (Policy Press, 2015).

41. Chris Gilleard and Paul Higgs, *Ageing, Corporeality and Embodiment* (Anthem Press, 2013), 26, 31.

42. Laura Cappelle, "'I Know What Anxiety Is. And Guilt': Florian Zeller on His Nightmarish New Play," *Guardian*, January 31, 2022, https://www.theguardian.com/stage/2022/jan/31/florian-zeller-father-oscar-forest-nightmarish-new-play

43. Lyn Gardner, "Gina McKee Is Ghost-Like in Haunting Empty Nest Drama," review of *The Mother*, *Guardian*, May 29, 2015, https://www.theguardian.com/stage/2015/may/29/the-mother-review-gina-mckee-empty-nest-syndrome-ustinov-bath-florian-zeller; Alexis Soloski, "Isabelle Huppert Shines in Otherwise Stale Play," review of *The Mother*, *Guardian*, March 11, 2019, https://www.theguardian.com/stage/2019/mar/11/the-mother-review-isabelle-huppert-shines-in-otherwise-stale-play; Matt Trueman, review of *The Mother*, *Variety*, January 27, 2016, https://variety.com/2016/legit/reviews/the-mother-review-play-florian-zeller-1201690099/

44. Dewi Nurjuwita, review of *The Mother*, *TimeOut*, August 6, 2021, https://www.timeout.com/singapore/theatre/the-mother

45. Eleanor Bowen and Laura González, "The Hysteric as Mad: Unfolding and Exquisite Corpse," in *Beyond These Walls: Confronting Madness in Society, Literature and Art*, ed. Helen Goodman, Bernadette V. Russo, and Joana Zózimo (Inter-Disciplinary Press, 2013), 169.

46. Wenegrat, *Theater of Disorder*.

47. Bowen and González, "The Hysteric as Mad," 169.

48. Friedan, *The Fountain of Age*, 144–46.

49. Lynne Segal, *Out of Time: The Pleasures and the Perils of Ageing* (Verso, 2014), 13.

50. Woodward, *Aging and Its Discontents*, 8.

51. Moore, "Depth, Significance, and Absence."

52. Miriam Bernard et al., eds. *Women Ageing: Changing Identities, Challenging Myths* (Routledge, 2005).

53. Cruikshank, *Learning to Be Old*; Holstein, "On Being an Old Woman in Contemporary Society"; Sontag, "The Double Standard of Aging."

54. Sontag, "The Double Standard of Aging."

55. Margaret Morganroth Gullette, *Declining to Decline: Cultural Combat and the Politics of the Midlife* (University Press of Virginia, 1997), 105.

56. Valerie Barnes Lipscomb and Leni Marshall, eds., *Staging Age: The Performance of Age in Theatre, Dance, and Film* (Palgrave Macmillan, 2010); Valerie Barnes Lipscomb, "'The Play's the Thing': Theatre as a Scholarly Meeting Ground in Age Studies," *International Journal of Ageing and Later Life* 7, no. 2 (2012): 117–41; Mangan, *Staging Ageing.*

57. Woodward, *Aging and Its Discontents.*

58. Robert Butler, "The Life Review: An Interpretation of Reminiscence in the Aged," *Psychiatry* 26, no. 1 (1963): 65–76.

59. Butler, 66.

60. Laura Hurd Clarke, *Facing Age: Women Growing Older in Anti-Aging Culture* (Rowman and Littlefield, 2011), 4.

61. Segal, *Out of Time*, 42.

62. Stephen Katz and Toni Calasanti, "Critical Perspectives on Successful Aging: Does It 'Appeal More Than It Illuminates'?," *Gerontologist* 55, no. 1 (2015): 26–33.

63. Sandra Gilbert and Susan Gubar, *The Madwoman in the Attic: The Woman Writer and the Nineteenth-Century Literary Imagination* (Yale University Press, 1979).

64. Amelia DeFalco, *Uncanny Subjects: Aging in Contemporary Narrative* (Ohio State University Press, 2010), x–xi, 17.

65. Julia Kristeva, *Strangers to Ourselves*, trans. Leon S. Roudiez (Columbia University Press, 1994).

66. Sontag, *Illness as Metaphor*, 73.

67. Anna Freixas, *Yo vieja: apuntes de sobrevivencia para seres libres* (Capitán Swing, 2021); Friedan, *The Fountain of Age*; Greer, *The Change*; Gullette, *Declining to Decline*; Segal, *Out of Time*; Barbara Frey Waxman, *From the Hearth to the Open Road: A Feminist Study of Aging in Contemporary Literature* (Greenwood Press, 1990).

68. Gilbert and Gubar, *The Madwoman in the Attic.*

69. Gaston Bachelard, *The Poetics of Space*, trans. Maria Jolas (Beacon Press, 1994); Clare Cooper Marcus, *House as a Mirror of Self: Exploring the Deeper Meaning of Home* (Nicolas-Hays, 2006); Shelley Mallett, "Understanding Home: A Critical Review of the Literature," *Sociological Review* 52, no. 1 (2004): 62–89.

70. Fuchs, "Estragement."

71. Moore, "Depth, Significance, and Absence."

5
Caryl Churchill's Late Style

R. Darren Gobert

Mortality has hardly been absent from Caryl Churchill's career, now (if we count her undergraduate debut at Oxford University's Oriel College in the autumn of 1958) in its sixty-seventh year: it is right there in the title of 1962's *Easy Death*, also produced at Oxford, and it suppurates through her work starting with her first professionally produced play, *The Ants*, with its annihilated insects and nuclear terrors. Deaths propel the plots of *Serious Money*, *Icecream*, and *Far Away*, for instance, and suicides in particular abound—both offstage, as in *Identical Twins*, and onstage, as in the final scenes of the phenomenal *Fen*. Neither is grief a new theme: to name only one example, *A Number*'s patriarch, Salter, mourns a son who kills a brother before killing himself. So audiences may have been unsurprised at the opening of Churchill's most recent play, *What If If Only*, when a man sitting alone onstage quickly invokes death ("If I was the one who was dead would you still be talking to me?") and clearly grapples with the loss of a partner ("I miss you I miss you I miss you I miss you. I miss you").[1]

But despite the thematic revenants,[2] the production and reception of *What If If Only*—directed by James Macdonald at London's Royal Court in September 2021[3]—were distinctive, and not only because the show represented its maker's return to the theater after the fatal disruptions of COVID-19. The production was unavoidably colored by the death, earlier that year, of Churchill's husband of over six decades; the reception seemed shadowed by Churchill's own advanced age. Publications that had failed to specify that Churchill was forty-three when she premiered *Top Girls*, for example, or seventy-three when she premiered *Love and Information*, felt compelled to specify this time around. Her age, eighty-three at the time, was signaled by multiple reviewers, their praise perfumed with admiration or ageist astonishment.[4]

The mourner's supplications for a sign from the afterlife in *What If If Only*—"Just a wisp . . . any small thing"—do in fact conjure an otherworldly visitor. Churchill's stage directions announce "*there's someone there*" as a scene partner materializes: "Here I am."[5] Having been summoned by a wish for things to be otherwise ("I tasted your what if if only"), this partner introduces itself plainly as the Future, as do the script's speech prefixes:

> FUTURE: I'm the ghost of a future that never happened. And if you can make me happen then . . . what happened will never have happened[.][6]

Even in live performance—the realm, we have been told, of the here and now—this Future by its characterological nature directs us elsewhere and later, to where and when it might happen. In this way, *What If If Only* seems to repudiate the present circumstances of its plot (which is to say mortality) and also its offstage context (mortality again). "I'm a Future you'd really like," we are promised, "Equality and cake and no bad bits at all."[7] Critics praised Churchill for *What If If Only*'s sui generis quality: "Into her 80s but as innovative as ever," the *Arts Desk* reviewer opined.[8] But while the originality and experimentality of the playwright's vision are beyond dispute, the play's aesthetic peculiarities—especially its representation of time as materially situated in space—in fact follow closely the logic of what Edward Said called "late style," which "does not admit the definitive cadences of death; instead, death appears in a refracted mode."[9]

Said derived his theory from Theodor Adorno, who contemplated the late style of Beethoven in a much-analyzed essay fragment from 1937, "Spätstil Beethovens." It begins: "The maturity of the late works of significant artists does not resemble the kind one finds in fruit. They are, for the most part, not round, but furrowed, even ravaged. Devoid of sweetness, bitter and spiny, they do not surrender themselves to mere delectation."[10] In four dense pages, Adorno grapples with what he sees as the difficulties of Beethoven's late works. That they seem marked by impending mortality is indisputable, he claims, and yet the biographical fact is misemphasized in Beethoven criticism, which fails to apprehend the coded, even allegorical ways in which death is presented. Late works, he suggests, bear the intensified presence of the creator who, having achieved aesthetic maturity, feels freer to experiment. Yet even thus tinged by their author's subjectivity, late works transcend the creator's mortality: it is an objective fact, after all, that the Ninth Symphony lives on. "Touched by death," Adorno writes, "the hand of the master sets free the masses of material that he used to form: its tears and fissures, witnesses to the finite powerlessness of the I of Being, are its final work."[11] The discontinuity that characterizes late Beethoven—that is, the refusal of synthesis and harmony—thus serves to express both the greatness of the work of art and the greatness of its creator. The resulting contradiction between objective and subjective elements is unresolved and "catastrophic," a term that seems to encompass both the conclusion of the artist's life as well as the artist's disruption of traditional art forms. For key to late work's disjunct temporality is its ability to presage or foment later aesthetic developments, and in this way the late work subverts the art form's history and redirects its future.

From Adorno's remarks and a reading of artists including Glenn Gould, Richard Strauss, and Luchino Visconti, Said developed his own theory of work that "expresses lateness through the peculiarities of its style."[12] First among these peculiarities is the unresolved and catastrophic quality emphasized by Adorno: the work's "apparent disregard for its own continuity" and its consequently perplexing effects.[13] The second aesthetic quality emerges from Adorno's remarks about time: "Late style is *in*, but oddly *apart* from the present," Said writes.[14] Its anachronistic force is future oriented, with an eye to both the pioneering and everlasting qualities of great art. The third and related quality is late style's habit of converting "time into space"[15]—a strategy to quarrel more effectively with time and its consequential companion, death. Of course any such description of "late style" risks seeming totalizing and deterministic, not least Said's, with its transcultural and transhistorical scope. And it may be telling that his description contradicts those of others who followed in Adorno's wake by asserting the singularity of late works, or at least the late works of presumptively great artists.[16] A "certain wariness about 'late style' as a category" is therefore advisable, to quote Gordon McMullan and Sam Smiles, whose collection *Late Style and Its Discontents* interrogates the assumptions undergirding the term.[17] At the same time, for a reader or spectator looking to navigate the puzzling terrain of *What If If Only*, Said's remarks provide adroit guidance. Meanwhile, if the play's forward-looking qualities do in fact presage further developments in theatrical form—if it makes the theater's future possible, to paraphrase the play—it can also help us understand in retrospect some of Churchill's earlier experiments and to determine, at least provisionally, if and when a late style emerged in a body of work that spans seven decades.

The aesthetics whose "sudden discontinuities" Adorno admired recur in Churchill's plays of the last few years.[18] For example, *Here We Go* features a triptych of scenes each in a different form. The first scene offers eight pages of dialogue, unattributed to characters (Churchill dictates "not fewer than three . . . and not more than eight").[19] This omission of speech prefixes the playwright essayed with *Seven Jewish Children* in 2009 and has reprised repeatedly, most notably in 2012's *Love and Information*. As in that play, she also provides ancillary text to be "*inserted randomly into the previous dialogue in any order*," in this case soliloquies to be chosen, one speech for each of the three to eight actors, from a list of ten options.[20] Thus the first scene of *Here We Go* toggles between its randomly inserted soliloquies and fragmentary dialogue thematically related to its setting, "*a party after a funeral*."[21] The scene ends abruptly—

> he could tell a joke
> yes I can never remember[22]

—and is followed by a second scene, a five-page monologue from beyond the grave. (Although the dialogue is broken up in the same way and there are still no speech prefixes, the stage directions dictate: "*One person. Very fast*.")[23] This speech ends equally abruptly—

> and there you all are for a short time
> that's how it's put together for a short time
> and oddly you are actually are one of those
> and it goes on and on and you're used to it and then suddenly[24]

—before ceding to a wordless third scene of a "*very old or ill person and a carer*."[25] The latter helps the former to dress and undress, dress and undress ("*slowly and with difficulty because of pain and restricted movement*"), alternating between clothes and nightclothes, over and over, over and over, "*for as long as the scene lasts*."[26]

The premiere of *Here We Go*, directed by Dominic Cooke at the National Theatre, Lyttelton, in November 2015, smoothed over some of the play's difficulties. The production was perplexing, to be sure, but by casting the same actor (Patrick Godfrey) in both the second and third scenes, Cooke created continuity among dissonant sections: the audience could apprehend a backward trajectory from funeral to death to late-life suffering. In fact, the script is disarmingly casual about such continuity. The absent speech prefixes leave matters open ended, and Churchill writes only that the mourned (scene 1)

Fig. 5.1. Patrick Godfrey in *Here We Go* by Caryl Churchill. National Theatre, 2015. Photo: Alastair Muir.

and dead (scene 2) characters "can be but needn't be" the same: a comically irrelevant distinction since the audience doesn't meet the mourned man in any case.[27] Tellingly she says nothing at all about those characters' relationship to the ailing person in scene 3. A few years earlier, *Love and Information* had used its absent speech prefixes and variable scene order to match its subject: preoccupying itself with information, the play appears as infinitely reconfigurable dramatic data. *Here We Go* is less reconcilable. The earlier play, filled with sharp turns of phrase, vividly implied its settings, characters, and plot intrigues. But *Here We Go* offers little plot or characterization—only banal dialogue for the mourners (e.g., "We miss him / of course"),[28] free-associative clichés for the second-scene monologue (a light-filled tunnel and pearly gates, Saint Peter and Cerberus, purgatory and reincarnation), and a stripped-down dumb show for as long as the last scene lasts. The vocabulary of theater contracts in ways that recall Adorno's formulation. For earlier Beethoven, as in most of Churchill's career, conventions of the form existed to be synthesized, transcended, and (to paraphrase Adorno) transformed according to the artist's intention.[29] Think of *The Skriker*, with its intricately integrated physical theater; *Traps*, with its Möbius-strip setting; or even *Love and Information*, which, despite its pared-down style, expertly matches form to content by bending theatrical conventions to its will. In *Here We Go* the theatrical form is left skeletal. Conventions appear "bald, undisguised, untransformed" (Adorno again): they "find expression as the naked representation of themselves."[30]

Of course, Adorno insists that late style does not represent death directly, as Churchill clearly does in a play whose cover describes it as "about dying and being dead." Here we all go, Churchill says, as we alternately mourn and wait for death, as long as each of us lasts. But the disjunct chronology in which she offers those alternatives hints at transformations to come. *Here We Go*'s soliloquies, randomly scattered through the small talk of a post-funeral party, pull us out of the present and proleptically forward to other deaths. Each begins the same way: "I die the next day" or "I die eleven years later" or "I die sixty-two years later."[31] More radical temporal ruptures mark *Escaped Alone*, Churchill's next play. In it she represents four women—"*all at least seventy*," she specifies—sitting in a backyard garden and chatting about topics expected (their children and grandchildren) and unexpected (what superpower they'd like to have).[32] But more jarringly than in *Here We Go*'s first scene, their naturalistic dialogue is disrupted by decidedly unnaturalistic monologues. In the fifth scene of *Escaped Alone*, Sally's ailurophobia erupts ("a cat could be in the teapot with the keys a cat could be on the ceiling . . . a cat could be under my hand when I put out my hand"),[33] and in the seventh scene, Lena's agoraphobia. In the eighth scene, Vi—who years ago killed her husband and served a prison term—abruptly vents her repressed trauma, not long before Mrs. Jarrett takes her own turn: "Terrible rage terrible rage."[34]

The stylistic incongruity between dialogue and monologues within *Escaped Alone*'s scenes hints at larger temporal disruptions between the scenes, for just as mental suffering erupts into individual life courses, apocalypse rives the geological timescale. Churchill describes the play as taking place on a "*Summer afternoon. / A number of afternoons but the action is continuous*,"[35] but this time is rent when Mrs. Jarrett steps away from the domestic scene for seven speeches in a different key. Each provides an account of environmental cataclysm. Mrs. Jarrett describes "senior executives" burying a populace that "feed[s] off the dead" and constructs folklore about "those above ground."[36] It is not the beginning of a new evolution but a drawn-out end: "Torrential rain leaked through cracks and flooded the tunnels enabling screams at last before drownings. Survivors were now solitary and went insane at different rates."[37] Mrs. Jarrett describes a citizenry flooded after "water was deliberately wasted in a campaign to punish the thirsty."[38] She describes a world where "chemicals leaked through cracks in the money" and one where "food was diverted to tv programmes . . . so the dying could watch cooking" and one where "wind developed by property developers . . . soon turned heads inside out."[39] The scenarios differ in their horrific (if blackly comic) details, but each culminates with a more final end on the horizon. "The last survivors had immunity and the virus mutated, exterminating plankton," Mrs. Jarrett tells us in another speech, describing a planet whose marine food chain would collapse and oxygen supply would fail.[40]

Note the difference between these proleptic interruptions and those in *Here We Go*. In that play, each soliloquy uses the present tense to mark a specific event in the future of the character (for example, "I die six months later. I hang myself. I should have thought about who'd find me")[41] and thus temporally locates the death neatly vis-à-vis the present of the performance, which is to say the day of the first-scene funeral. Mrs. Jarrett, by contrast, in *Escaped Alone*, uses the past tense to describe the dying days not of an individual but of the Anthropocene. This eschatological time, when one recognizable human describes events that no human could live to see, invokes as it inverts the allegorical time of the Bible, in which a week suffices to create light and dark, land and water, life on earth. In other words, with her seven monologues—a number that in the Judeo-Christian tradition contains beginning and end—Mrs. Jarrett recalls the days in Genesis, as she narrates the undoing of what was there created. Her messages both unnerve and confuse, riddled as they are with contradictions: sometimes the extinction event is flood, sometimes fire, sometimes cancers that "began in the lungs and sometimes on the fingertips or laptops."[42]

Churchill draws her title from the Book of Job, in which four messengers describe the tragedies that have befallen Job's family and declare, "I only am escaped alone to tell thee."[43] But each uses that same phrase, and thus the Bible undermines their claims to singularity in a manner that Churchill amplifies when she also cites Herman Melville's *Moby-Dick*, which includes the line before Ishmael's epilogue narration.[44] Thus her title encapsulates the irreconcilability at the heart of the play and, for Said like Adorno before him, late style more generally. For Mrs. Jarrett cannot be understood as singular in the manner of most people, even the "not fewer than three . . . and not more than eight" that populate *Here We Go*'s flexible first scene. She sits at once in the represented present of the summer afternoon and in the real time of the audience at this or that performance. Indeed, she sits outside

Fig. 5.2. Linda Bassett as Mrs. Jarrett in *Escaped Alone* by Caryl Churchill. Royal Court Theatre, 2016. Photo: Johan Persson/ArenaPAL; www.arenapal.com.

time altogether. It is no accident that the script sets each of her monologues on its own page, unnumbered and separate from the play's numbered scenes. To quote Revelation—the biblical book that *Escaped Alone* most resembles—Mrs. Jarrett "was, and is, and is to come."[45] The advanced age of the play's quartet, sitting and chatting and singing in a backyard garden, turns out to be a red herring in just the manner that Said described when he noted that late style "abjures mere bourgeois aging" and "insists on the increasing sense of apartness and exile and anachronism, which late style expresses and, more important, uses to formally sustain itself."[46] Mrs. Jarrett enacts such a temporal exile every time she steps out of the play's action—literally, in the case of the premiere production, directed by James Macdonald at the Royal Court in January 2016. For each of the seven monologues, actor Linda Bassett moved in front of a blazing proscenium of light and into the darkness downstage. If Mrs. Jarrett's message was catastrophic (global disaster awaits), Churchill's message is catastrophic in Adorno's sense. It anticipates changes to theatrical form.

Fig. 5.3. Linda Bassett in *What If If Only* by Caryl Churchill. The Royal Court Theatre, 2021. Photo: Johan Persson / ArenaPAL; www.arenapal.com.

This conversion of time into space represented by Mrs. Jarrett is, Said argues, an aesthetic strategy by which the late-style artist represents death. The idea blossoms in *What If If Only* with its onstage Future, who is joined soon enough by still other personifications of time. "*And there's lots of them*," Churchill's stage directions instruct, as a character called Futures enters: "Yes yes yes me me and me."[47] This wraith, who like Mrs. Jarrett is both singular and many, disappears only when it is cursed as in a fairy tale ("you never happened") and thus someone else appears, "the only Future that didn't die":

PRESENT: I'm the Present, I'm here now I'm here I'm now now now now every second gone to the past but always here now now now now. Do you like me?[48]

Scholars of theater and performance studies will recognize, in this talk of the present receding into the past, our field's preoccupation with the now, now, now of theater—most famously articulated in Peggy Phelan's formulation that "performance's only life is in the present."[49] This ontology of performance, as Phelan describes it, might offer a unique challenge to "late style" if we follow Said in imagining an exile from the present as one of the defining characteristics. After all, Future may beg *to be* ("Please please help me make me happen make me happen"),[50] but by virtue of live performance Future already *is*—especially as vividly played in the Royal Court production, again by Linda Bassett. Onstage, the character is every bit as materially apparent, as real, as Churchill's mourner, who, despite the anchoring specificity of John Heffernan's performance, remained generic and unnamed and whose identity the script denominates only as "Someone." Theater's natural allegiance with the present might appear as its own bulwark against death, as Present ventriloquizes when reminding Someone that he "*thought* what if if only" whereas "I'm now now now now."[51] However, the play's present is hobbled by grief, and Present's argument fails. Future disappears in the play; Futures disappears too. By contrast, even in the presence of Present a newly emergent character called Child Future simply won't leave. "Careful . . . you don't know what it is," cautions Present, but the child is insistent.[52] Churchill is expert at using the material of her actors' bodies: think of *Cloud Nine*, with its cross-gender casting, or *Top Girls*, with its resonant doubling across acts. Here she slyly deploys a child actor as she gives futurity the defiant last word. "I'm going to happen," the child repeats multiple times, including as the play's final line.[53]

These themes were supported by Macdonald's staging, which threw the future into relief by leveraging Churchill's long history on the stage. By casting Bassett as three of the four temporal personifications—Future, Futures, and Present—the director allied not only the present and future(s) but also both of them to the past. After all, Bassett and Churchill's history of collaboration stretches more than four decades. The two met in 1982, when Bassett worked on the workshop-based *Fen*, directed by Les Waters, and subsequently she has inaugurated many iconic Churchill characters: in *Serious Money* for director Max Stafford-Clark, in *Far Away* for Stephen Daldry, and in multiple Churchill plays for Macdonald, including, of course, Mrs. Jarrett in *Escaped Alone*. Especially for a longtime London theatergoer, this past shadows *What If If Only*. In performance theory, Rebecca Schneider rebuked the idea that live performance "takes place in a 'now' understood as singular, immediate, and vanishing" by reminding us how often performance yearns to reenact the past.[54] Onstage, Churchill's rebuke is somewhat different. She (and Bassett) invoke their shared history only to abdicate the present in favor of the Child Future and all the unknowable potential that its child body represents. (In fact, children's bodies: the multiplicity of potential was underscored by casting two children to perform in alternation, one girl [Jasmine Nyenya], one boy [Samir Simon-Keegan], and both uncoincidentally non-white.) Again Churchill brings time into space in the manner Said described. "*A small child future is there*," her stage direction emphasizes.[55]

Thus the play quells Someone's grief. It repudiates the past, marked by a partner's death both in the plot and offstage, just as it repudiates the present in the manner said to be typical of late style. Subverting the theater's very ontology—at least if we follow Phelan—the artist also takes a "self-imposed exile from what is generally acceptable," "surviving beyond it" by changing its future contours, as Said wrote.[56] Stathis Gourgouris's précis of Said's book might summarize Churchill's play equally well. "Late style," he writes, "is precisely the form that defies the infirmities of the present, as well as the palliatives of the past, in order to seek out this future, to posit it and perform it, even if in words and images, gestures and representations, which now seem puzzling, untimely, or impossible."[57] Recall that in *Here We Go* Churchill had offered ten soliloquies, one per actor, to the first-scene cast, who number at least three but cannot exceed eight. Like the soliloquies left unrealized—at least two, perhaps a resonant seven—*What If If Only* imagines an objective future for itself that stands outside the present of its performance, held (it may be relevant to note again) in a COVID-constrained time.

Even more than Churchill's other recent works, *What If If Only* invites a consideration of late style by beginning as it does:

SOMEONE: I was reading about this man who spent ten years trying to paint an apple so it looked just like an apple. That was eighteen to twenty eight.

Then he spent seven years trying to paint an apple so it looked nothing like an apple.

Then he died.[58]

From its first moments, in other words, the play juxtaposes an arresting death with Churchill's longtime preoccupation with representation. Thus the play recalls the unresolved tension, which characterized late style for Adorno, between the aesthetic objectivity of the artwork and the mortal subjectivity of its maker. The author's subjectivity cannot help but intrude, which we register whenever reviewers mention Churchill's advanced age.[59] In spite of it, *What If If Only* defies death with its proleptic impulse, its appeal to an unrealized future. "I was thinking," Someone muses, "if he'd lived another ten years what would he have done next."[60]

I don't claim the play offers "a Future you'd really like," as its first wraith promises Someone. Instead Churchill's late works recall those of Ibsen, which for Said "tamper irrevocably with the possibility of closure, and leave the audience more perplexed and unsettled than before."[61] In *Here We Go* the random affordances of the "I die" soliloquies—and especially the unusual fact that some are always deferred—may speak to the ever-renewing quality of Churchill's plays, which in the telling terms of her medium are perennially *revived*. But what goes unrealized is just more death. In *Escaped Alone* Churchill uses her geriatric cast as a feint: "always nice to be here," the quartet agree at the play's end, and whatever their ages the characters live eternally.[62] But a more consequential end is nigh. In Churchill's critique of capitalism and the culture industry—recall that the play's doomsday is accelerated by "senior executives" and "tv programmes"—we may see still more affinity with Adorno, whose remarks on late style rest on a broader critique. As Robert Spencer has argued, for Adorno late works are remarkable not (or not only) because of the artist's closer proximity to death but rather because they articulate the "lateness or moribundity of capitalism itself."[63]

Skeptical of a generalizable "late style" that uniquely afflicts older masters, I am sympathetic to the critique of Laura Tunbridge, who sees the designation as a tool critics use to confer otherwise unfashionable claims of genius.[64] And even if I have no reservations about asserting Churchill's greatness, the typical periodization of early work/mature work/late work seems worrisome: her corpus, as I have written elsewhere, generally defies chronology.[65] All the same, she is closer to the end of her career than to its beginning, and in retrospect we can trace distinct phases: an early period, too frequently ignored due to the unavailability of unpublished scripts, or the period starting in 1976, when collaborations with Monstrous Regiment (on *Vinegar Tom*) and Joint Stock (on *Light Shining in Buckinghamshire*) catalyzed Churchill's politics and shifted her writing practices. Elaine Aston has convincingly argued that another chapter began in 1997, when a crisis of

UK politics (New Labour) occasioned a crisis of creativity—Churchill's triumph over which would soon produce plays such as *Far Away* and *A Number* and cement her position as the most formally innovative playwright in the English language.[66] I hesitate to apply the term "mature" to such plays, so different from the earlier but equally matured *Fen* or *Mad Forest*, and yet they do marry content to form so expertly as to distill a lifetime's exploration of theater and its possibilities into scripts of startling economy, to achieve the elegance that Samuel Beckett achieved by reducing his dramatic material. For me, *Love and Information*, one of her most formally daring experiments, marks an apotheosis.[67]

In his book *Beyond Minimalism*, Enoch Brater—with no debt to Adorno and in advance of Said—defined Beckett's late style as one in which "genre is under stress . . . and the play is on the verge of becoming sometime else," a threshold Beckett had crossed by the time of *Not I*.[68] In Churchill, I locate a threshold at *Here We Go*. At the time of its premiere I thought it lacked the refined minimalism of plays such as *A Number*, already then more than two decades old. In retrospect, I see it as a step into thornier territory—the sort of ravaged terrain that Said found in Ibsen, Brater in Beckett. Shorter and shorter, Churchill's late works are also more fragmentary: sometimes obscure (for example, *Glass* or *Kill* [both 2019]), sometimes polemical (*Tickets Are Now on Sale* [2015] or the Trump-preoccupied *Beautiful Eyes* [2017]). Following Adorno, Said had contrasted Beethoven's "organically whole" mature works with his "wayward and eccentric" late style. "Near the end of their lives," he writes, the work of "great artists . . . acquires a new idiom."[69] Whatever my hesitations about a universal late style, I concede that we see a more wayward and eccentric idiom lately. Churchill describes *Air*—premiered in 2020—thus: "In early 2019 . . . I started each day writing whatever came into my head, not trying to make sense or make it into a play. It did settle into something like dialogue, and after about a dozen I stopped because it began to feel more deliberate and so less interesting."[70]

No longer trying to make plays—the art form she has indisputably mastered—Churchill plainly recalls Beethoven's late period in Adorno's account, with its abbreviated style and refracted representation of death. Paraphrasing this account, Said changed one word: Adorno had written that death appeared "in a refracted mode, as allegory"; Said, that "death appears in a refracted mode as irony."[71] "The irony," he explained, "is how often lateness as theme and style keeps reminding us of death."[72] This irony proliferates. *On Late Style* was finished by others; Said died while writing it. Adorno predicted that late-style works escape such ends, since death cannot be imposed on immortal forms of art.[73] Churchill—now eighty-seven—is less sanguine, her art form less separable from people, who make it happen. All the same she offers a glimpse of the future for as long as the theater lasts, as when Mrs. Jarrett leaves her old friends in the garden and steps into what Aston, in her review of *Escaped Alone*, called the "death space."[74] Well downstage from the rest of the action, it is in fact on our side of the proscenium.

NOTES

1. Caryl Churchill, *What If If Only* (Nick Hern Books, 2021), 4, 5.

2. Suicide's specter returns, too: "You know what it takes to kill yourself." Churchill, 3.

3. Macdonald's stage production was not quite the play's premiere. Churchill authorized a six-performance, live-streamed pandemic production three months earlier, produced by the New York–based National Asian American Theatre Company and codirected by Les Waters and Jared Mezzocchi.

4. See, for example, Nick Curtis, "An Audacious Theatrical Miniature from Caryl Churchill," *Standard*, October 4, 2021, https://www.standard.co.uk/culture/theatre/what-if-if-only-review-royal-court-theatre-caryl-churchill-b958615.html; or Mark Lawson, "Short and Sharp, with Shades of Scrooge," *Guardian*, October 1, 2021, https://www.theguardian.com/stage/2021/oct/01/what-if-if-only-review-short-and-sharp-with-shades-of-scrooge

5. Churchill, *What If If Only*, 5.

6. Churchill, 6–7.

7. Churchill, 8.

8. See Gary Naylor, "Short If Not Sweet," *Arts Desk*, October 5, 2021, https://theartsdesk.com/theatre/what-if-if-only-royal-court-review-short-if-not-sweet

9. Edward W. Said, *On Late Style: Music and Literature Against the Grain* (Vintage Books, 2007), 24.

10. Theodor Adorno, "Late Style in Beethoven," trans. Susan H. Gillespie, in *Essays on Music*, ed. Richard Leppert (University of California Press, 2002), 564.

11. Adorno, 566.

12. Michael Wood, introduction to Said, *On Late Style*, xii, quoting Said's syllabus for the course "Late Works/Late Style."

13. Said, *On Late Style*, 10.

14. Said, 24 (emphasis in original).

15. Wood, introduction to Said, *On Late Style*, xii, again quoting Said's syllabus.

16. Joseph N. Straus catalogs dozens of different descriptions in "Disability and 'Late Style' in Music," *Journal of Musicology* 25, no. 1 (2008): 8–11. It is notable that "late style" is sometimes characterized as "irascible, discordant, and recalcitrant" (as for Said) and sometimes, contradictorily, as "serene, synthetic, and consummatory." See Gordon McMullan and Sam Smiles, introduction to *Late Style and Its Discontents: Essays in Art, Literature, and Music*, ed. Gordon McMullan and Sam Smiles (Oxford University Press, 2016), 2. This introduction also surveys the wider critical landscape.

17. McMullan and Smiles, introduction to *Late Style and Its Discontents*, 2.

18. Adorno, "Late Style in Beethoven," 567.

19. Caryl Churchill, *Here We Go*, in *Plays: 5*, by Caryl Churchill (Nick Hern Books, 2019), 120.

20. Churchill, 129. Compare Caryl Churchill, *Love and Information*, in Churchill, *Plays: 5*, 88, where Churchill offers an appendix called "Random," whose speeches "*can happen in any section*."

21. Churchill, *Here We Go*, 121.

22. Churchill, 128.

23. Churchill, 130.

24. Churchill, 134.

25. Churchill, 135.

26. Churchill, 135.

27. Churchill, 120.

28. Churchill, 121.

29. Adorno writes that middle Beethoven took conventions and "transformed them according to his intention." Adorno, "Late Style in Beethoven," 565.

30. Adorno, 565, 566.

31. Churchill, *Here We Go*, 129.

32. Caryl Churchill, *Escaped Alone*, in Churchill, *Plays: 5*, 142.

33. Churchill, 164.

34. Churchill, 179.

35. Churchill, 142.

36. Churchill, 146.

37. Churchill, 146.

38. Churchill, 150.

39. Churchill, 155, 160, 166.

40. Churchill, 167.

41. Churchill, *Here We Go*, 129.

42. Churchill, *Escaped Alone*, 155. In this way too Mrs. Jarrett's allegorical narrative might remind us of Genesis, which famously gives differing accounts of creation.

43. Job 1:15–19, King James Version (KJV).

44. See Churchill, *Escaped Alone*, 141, and compare Herman Melville, *Moby-Dick* (Oxford University Press, 1988), 509.

45. Rev. 4:8, KJV.

46. Said, *On Late Style*, 17. We might contrast Churchill's use of an older cast in *Escaped Alone* to her earlier play *Blue Heart*, where the age of several characters is, in fact, thematically significant.

47. Churchill, *What If If Only*, 9.

48. Churchill, 10, 11, 11.

49. Peggy Phelan, *Unmarked: The Politics of Performance* (Routledge, 1996), 146.

50. Churchill, *What If If Only*, 7.

51. Churchill, 11, 12 (emphasis added).

52. Churchill, 13.

53. Churchill, 13, 13, 13, 13, 14.

54. Rebecca Schneider, *Performing Remains: Art and War in Times of Theatrical Reenactment* (Routledge, 2011), 87.

55. Churchill, *What If If Only*, 13.

56. Said, *On Late Style*, 16.

57. Stathis Gourgouris, "The Late Style of Edward Said," *Alif: Journal of Comparative Poetics* 25 (2005): 45.

58. Churchill, *What If If Only*, 3.

59. One such review also likened late Churchill to the "late sketches" of Picasso. See Sarah Crompton, "Caryl Churchill's 20-Minute Play Premieres at the Royal Court," *WhatsOnStage*, October 2, 2021, https://www.whatsonstage.com/news/what-if-if-only-review-caryl-churchills-20-minute-play-premieres-at-the-royal-court_55043/

60. Churchill, *What If If Only*, 3.

61. Said, *On Late Style*, 7.

62. Churchill, *Escaped Alone*, 179. A different essay could be written on the relationship of age studies to theories of, on the one hand, "late style" or *Spätstil* (work written when the artist is close to death, irrespective of age) and, on the other, "old-age style" or *Altenstil* (work written when the artist is elderly).

63. Robert Spencer, "Lateness and Modernity in Theodor Adorno," in McMullan and Smiles, *Late Style and Its Discontents*, 221.

64. She notes that late style can "raise the aesthetic status" of an artist and "perhaps even sav[e] him (typically) from oblivion." Laura Tunbridge, "Saving Schubert: The Evasions of Late Style," in McMullan and Smiles, *Late Style and Its Discontents*, 121.

65. R. Darren Gobert, *The Theatre of Caryl Churchill* (Bloomsbury, 2014), xi–xii.

66. See Elaine Aston, "But Not That: Caryl Churchill's Political Shape Shifting at the Turn of the Millennium," *Modern Drama* 56, no. 2 (2013): 145–64.

67. The lines between these phases are of course arguable and blurry. For example, 2006's jagged *Drunk Enough to Say I Love You?* could be seen to anticipate later plays, just as the precise constrained-writing experiment from 2012, *Ding Dong the Wicked*—whose second act reshuffles every word of its first act into a new and semantically dissonant order—recalls earlier conceptual work such as *Blue Heart*.

68. Enoch Brater, *Beyond Minimalism: Beckett's Late Style in the Theater* (Oxford University Press, 1987), 3. It is worth noting that one of Beckett's last plays, premiered in 1982, is entitled *Catastrophe*.

69. Said, *On Late Style*, 10, 6.

70. Caryl Churchill, *Air*, in Churchill, *What If If Only*, 17.

71. Compare Adorno, "Late Style in Beethoven," 566; and Said, *On Late Style*, 24.

72. Said, *On Late Style*, 24.

73. See Adorno, "Late Style in Beethoven," 566: "Death is imposed only on created beings, not on works of art."

74. Elaine Aston, "*Escaped Alone*—Caryl Churchill," *Drama Queens Review*, February 8, 2016, https://dramaqueensreview.com/2016/02/08/escaped-alone-caryl-churchill/

Part II

(Re)Casting Age

6
Age-Conscious Casting
Comedy and the Middle-Aged Ingenue

Valerie Barnes Lipscomb

My goal in this chapter is to advance the questions currently being examined in age studies at its intersection with theater studies. I offer an unusual choice of case study to raise those questions: an autoethnography of acting in a community theater production.[1] While most drama-focused age studies scholars have addressed the performance and performative nature of age,[2] we are becoming increasingly vocal about identifying and fighting ageism in all aspects of theater. I have argued, for example, against the traditional practice of casting younger actors to play older characters.[3] Our Western theater training system helped establish that convention, as college programs tend to draw their actors from a narrow, eighteen- to twenty-two-year-old age pool, then cast them as all the characters across the life course. I have advocated for more age-appropriate casting, particularly in memory plays, in which the character is older and remembering younger selves. While Anna Harpin explains, "One could reason that such efforts towards physical veracity in theatre are superfluous given that an audience is already in a willful contract with an imaginative transformation of bodies and space,"[4] we agree that many productions that strictly adhere to verisimilitude in other aspects do not consider the age of the actors cast as important to that aesthetic. I also have advocated that senior theater troupes, which likewise draw from a limited range of ages, have formulated an intriguing, promising model of older actors playing younger people. As pioneering age critic Margaret Morganroth Gullette has pointed out, older actors should have inherent credibility playing younger, because they actually have "been younger, psychologically and physiologically," as opposed to the younger actors playing ages they have not yet experienced.[5] I have asserted that a move toward age-conscious casting could contribute to exposing and eradicating our culture's endemic ageism. This chapter's position might be summarized as "Be careful what you argue for."

The production I analyze here of a play-within-a-play farce, *Play On!* by Rick Abbot, incorporated age-defying casting, raising a number of topics for scholars at the juncture of age and theater studies. From the effects of age "passing" onstage to the construction of humor at the intersection of age and gender, opportunities proliferate to raise awareness of ageism through script and casting choices. While in this production, gender norms intertwine with and sometimes supersede age norms, the project crystallizes the concept that age-conscious casting can be a weapon against ageism.

When the director called to offer me a part, I was confused: "Violet? Which character was Violet?" Then I remembered I had summarily dismissed her when reading because she is the one designated in the character list as the stock ingenue. The plot of *Play On!* traces a community theater group's attempts to rehearse and stage a period murder mystery. Everything goes wrong; hilarity ensues. (It has been called the poor man's *Noises Off*, as it is easier to mount.) The character list describes the six who take part in the play within a play not only by both their "actor" names and their "character" names, but also by the stock type: "Villain," "Juvenile," "Character Actor," and, for Violet, "Ingenue." I had attended to the five female parts that could be played by any adult, not to the two relegated to youth. However, no younger women had auditioned, and the director chose to make the casting work with the actors available. Moreover, he explained that he was also casting a woman whose apparent age was in her sixties as the teenager; he said that she had been a longtime actor at that theater, so all the subscribers knew her and it would be "hilarious." At age fifty-six, I wondered whether my casting against age was also to be hilarious. I thought: here is a chance to put my money where my mouth is.

I concluded that performing in this show would provide an opportunity to journal through the entire production process, to record what I felt as well as what others who were involved said and did regarding the issues of age in casting. (In this chapter, when it is necessary to refer to specific castmates, I will use the play's stock character designation, such as "Villain.") The resulting analyses I offer here follow the guidelines for autoethnography summarized and demonstrated by Carolyn Ellis and Arthur P. Bochner, who acknowledge the challenges as well as the benefits of personal-narrative methodologies. As they explain, Patricia A. Adler and Peter Adler coined the term "complete-member researchers," who "explore groups of which they already are members or in which, during the research process, they have become full members with complete identification and acceptance."[6] That description aligns with my experience, as I joined not only this specific production's cast but also the larger pool of actors who identify with and contribute to the efforts of this community theater. The decision to journal through the process was predicated on the anticipation of experiencing some discomfort with my being cast in a part written for the twenty-two-year-old love interest, while there were five women in my age group cast in the age-appropriate roles that I had noted when first reading the script. My awareness of the endemic ageism in American culture, persisting more than fifty years after Robert N. Butler coined the term "ageism,"[7] does not mean, after all, that I am exempted from it. Weighing my options, I ultimately believed it would be most productive to observe and analyze the situation rather than to consciously crusade against ageism during the production process.

My first concern about being cast as Violet was that she has a love scene; actually, she kisses two of the play's three male characters (Juvenile and Villain). I had an immediate age-based reaction, that I had assumed I was past the age for that kind of part—which was absolutely fine with me. Parts for older women tend to be minor and seldom involve sexual physicality, particularly for characters who are clearly past childbearing age. Those who do continue to express themselves as sexual beings are subject to ridicule, typically comic in nature. In "Fallen, Falling, Clinging, and Crawling: The Everyday Age Effects of Drama and Performance," critic Bridie Moore notes, "From ancient times, post-menopausal female sexual desire has been condemned in literature and drama"; her argument traces examples from Horace to contemporary times.[8] Would I become an object of ridicule as a post-menopausal woman thrust into a sexualized role? At the first read-through, I saw that the man playing Juvenile appeared to be quite a bit younger than I, closer to the age of twenty-five that the script specifies. That choice certainly complicated my reaction to the casting. He said, "You're my love interest?" and I heard incredulity. Uncomfortable, I quipped: "I'll wear a lot of stage makeup." Although I had been forewarned at auditions that this community theater tended to cast older people in younger roles, which I welcome, casting a couple against age compatibility is quite a different matter.

My discomfort reminded me not only of our societal ageism, but also of the specific ageism regarding companionate relationships that is leveled at couples who are not age compatible, especially when the woman is significantly older. Early in the rehearsal process, I voiced my concern that my love interest was much younger and wondered how the audience would react to the difference. One male cast member in my age group told me not to worry, that there would be plenty of "cougars" in the audience who would love it if they did notice. I rolled my eyes at his reference to this relatively recent addition to the ageist lexicon. I told Juvenile that there is an advantage to our age difference: our spouses should be reassured that we would not fall into the cliché of backstage romance because I was about twice his age. He replied that this was not true—and sounded sincere. He did not seem to realize how close I was to being twice his age, as I learned that Juvenile was in his early thirties.

The male dismissal of the age difference was among events that occurred early in rehearsal that raised the issue of age-passing offstage as well as on—I started to feel that people working on the production thought I actually was classifying myself as younger than the other women in the cast, whom I considered to be peers. Age-passing may be censured in everyday life in a similar pattern to noncompanionate pairing, but at smaller intervals—attempting to pass for a decade younger, for example. This potential condemnation remains a dilemma for actors: when they reach middle age, they value appearing as youthful as possible because theater still tends not to cast older people in major roles. That difficulty materializes earlier for women than for men and is complicated by the current technological simplicity of looking up someone's chronological age. I dealt with particular discomfort over passing for younger offstage because it was my first show at that theater; I felt the importance of establishing rapport with the cast and crew. The director and assistant director appeared to be in my age group; the costumer and hair stylist were perhaps a decade older. Judging by apparent age and their conversations, three of the female cast appeared to be in their sixties, three others with me in our fifties. When we took rehearsal photos, one woman expressed discomfort about her size by asking not to be in a photograph that showed her in contrast to—or covering up—her friend, who was very petite. So, I joked to everyone that it would be great if the photos did not make it obvious that I was old enough to be Juvenile's mother. The director looked genuinely surprised, peered at the two of us more closely, and said that it would not be obvious, employing that useful literary device of litotes: "It's not implausible." The onstage issue was not a major concern: Juvenile's apparent age was ambiguous. I had learned that he was thirty-three, but he could play older, and of course, knowing one's performing age range is simply a facet of being an actor. Since his chronological and apparent ages were not out of line with the character he portrayed, the discomfort revolved around my playing significantly younger. As I clarified that I considered myself in the same age group as the older women who were appropriately age cast, I felt the tension about age-passing offstage dissipate. While I believe my reaction was typical within a Western context, I do not know whether the tension was entirely in my head. Regardless, I deemed it prudent to avow that I was not trying to pass for younger.

As the weeks went on, Juvenile indicated that he thought I was exaggerating about our age difference, about its being uncomfortable to have a love scene with someone young enough to be my son. He implied that I was just demonstrating a normal insecurity about my physical appeal to the actor who had to profess passion for me; he reassured me that he was a "red-blooded male" and knew an attractive woman when he saw one, regardless of my age. I decided to put that subject to rest and informed him that I was not exaggerating, that the last time I had been cast in a full-length play, he was in elementary school. Then I gave him the year, 1988, to prove my point. He looked surprised and said I wear it well. Later, I actually did the calculation—and he was not quite in elementary school yet. When we had the occasion to celebrate Juvenile's birthday during the rehearsal period, I joked that he would now be only twenty-two years younger than I, and one of the cast expressed denial and surprise; she had thought I must be in my forties. When I told her that I was fifty-six, she responded, "No wonder you were fussing about the age difference." I was finally classified in the appropriate age category, and she had affirmed my ageist anxiety as justified. As I have concluded in analyses of canonical plays, a ten-year age difference is not typically a problem, but twenty years between potential lovers matters.[9] A generation's difference has undertones of incest, Freudian attraction to a parent figure. The topic does arise when the man is older, but it is much more pronounced as being "unnatural" when the female is older. Although there were other references to my being younger than characters played by actors in my age range, it was the incestuous-undertoned generational difference with my love interest and the assumption of my trying to pass for the same age that bothered me most. I believe that the issue of passing was more pronounced for me because I have been adamantly vocal about comments regarding my looking younger than my age; that is one area where I have not hesitated to educate strangers that I have no qualms about being exactly the age I am. When I have been asked about what it means that I study ageism and performance, part of my standard response has been, "I am __ years old, and our culture says I should do everything in my power to ensure you do not find that out."

The issue of passing would not have been so foregrounded for me if the other actor cast against age had been in the same position. A woman apparently in her sixties was cast as a teenager, whose part in the play within a play was the maid, a "Supporting Character," according to the cast list. The teenager in rehearsal complains about having to study for a high school biology exam and facing her mother if she gets home late. At the table reading, the actor expressed embarrassment that the age-range casting was so far afield that her "mother would be, what, ninety-three years old?" The director assured her that the audience would love it, since she is a pillar of that theater, and they all know and love her. Supporting Character also volunteers in the box office and has a distinctive, somewhat abrasive voice that makes much of her delivery amusing regardless of what she says in any situation. Indeed, her performance consistently generated laughs; there were no explanations added or lines cut, whether she referred to being out late on a school night or enduring her mom's disapproval of her performing in any play that has sex in it. The performance dynamic was transformed: lines that are completely humorless in the script became comic as delivered by someone so obviously age inappropriate.

That casting raises the topic of age related to the long-standing incongruity theory of humor, which can trace its origins to Cicero in *On the Orator*. People laugh because their expectations are established and then violated—just as a standard joke involves a setup and then a punch line. Age studies scholar Aagje Swinnen notes that "age bending" or transgressing age roles is one standard method to obtain a laugh,[10] through the jolt of witnessing a character perform an action far removed from the norm for their apparent age, such as a wrinkled man with white hair riding a child's tricycle. Such incongruity can conform to the traditional parameters of comedy by ultimately upholding the social norms, as the audience censoriously laughs at the character for the transgression. However, Swinnen adds, the jarring action can also expose the norms as social constructions, as the audience realizes that convention alone provides the constraint for the character's behavior. Pondering the humor of the age-defying casting leads us to ask where does/should the humor lie in age-related comedy? When characters overtly do not "act their age," does it resonate as a variation on drag performance, since the audience clearly perceives the dissonance? Supporting Character did not draw age-related laughs when performing her play-within-a-play role as the maid because that was not dissonant for a woman in her sixties. Only the lines that referred to the character's place in the life course, the usual preoccupations of a teenage girl, generated laughter. Rather than expose an artificial social construction, the age bending reaffirmed specific behavior associated with a specific age, upholding age norms.

Ageist reaction to the casting was one major area of inquiry regarding this production, but another was the question of whether my being cast against age would affect the staging. The desire to wring laughs from what we all considered to be a mediocre farce (Abbot is a pseudonym for Jack

Fig. 6.1. The first gag enacted on the ingenue's body as performed by the thirty-something Juvenile and the thirty-something Violet in the Island Players' production of *Play On!* Photo courtesy Island Players.

Sharkey [1931–92], a playwright who published eighty-three plays under his own name as well as several pen names)[11] was paramount in this production; the director was assigned to this show rather than having chosen it, and he liberally cut the script to pick up the pace and omit sections that were not blatantly comic. Everyone sought to devise new gags as well as enhance existing ones. Most of these physical bits took place in the third act of *Play On!*, when the play within a play is performed, and two major scripted gags involved Violet. Juvenile was to fall with his face landing squarely in Violet's lap, and a necklace was to fall into Violet's cleavage, which the character of Villain would fumblingly try to retrieve. Two of the three male characters were scripted to enact gags on the sexualized female body; that was the ingenue's part, but of course in this case, that was my body. I considered that my age-inappropriate casting could alter the nature of those gags, given that postmenopausal women tend not to be envisioned in sexual contexts at all. The rehearsal process, naturally, would be key. Although I was acutely aware that the only sexual gags in the play were being staged with and on my body, I chose not to object. I had accepted the role and would perform it as written/directed.

A professional production may have consulted an intimacy coordinator to ensure everyone's comfort, but this was community theater. My scene partners exercised a great deal of self-imposed restraint in initial rehearsals: Juvenile braced himself as he fell so that his face stopped and hovered just above my lap, and Villain barely reached for the necklace. However, by the time we were in costume, I could bunch up the folds of my voluminous period dress and reassure Juvenile that he could land on me without its feeling inappropriate. Likewise, my costume was chosen to accommodate Villain's peering into the cleavage. In both cases, the bits became more farcically comic as rehearsals progressed, seemingly unimpeded by the age of the female body being manipulated. I saw no evidence that either of these fine actors would have behaved with less initial restraint with a younger woman. In fact, when I spoke with two female castmates after the project ended, they asserted that my age may have decreased the men's restraint, because I seemed so comfortable with the physical humor.

Given that I thought perhaps my portraying Violet would result in more overall physical hesitancy during my scenes, I also decided early on that I would neither suggest new physical gags to be enacted on my body nor object on principle to those offered, that I would be as much as possible a neutral participant in and observer of the effects of casting. Villain, played by an actor in my age group, suggested late in rehearsal that, instead of the simple kiss scripted in the play within a play, he grab me and surprise my character by "planting one on me." We tried it; it got laughs. Nothing suggested was beyond the pale, so it was not a problem for me to willingly stage any physical comedy that got laughs. Interestingly, during the run, the only male character who did not already have a physical gag with me asked whether it might be funny for him to accidentally hit me during a moment when he gestures broadly in the play within a play. We tried it; it got laughs. I was very aware that every man in the play (and only the men) exerted some form of dominance over my body, that my body was the repeated site of transgressive action intended to be humorous. I realized quite suddenly that I had not felt that way in years; I was reminded what it was like to be a younger woman, when people—particularly men—felt tacitly authorized to discuss and touch my body. I also realized that there were no such physical gags, either scripted or devised, involving the other female characters who participated in the play within a play: the aforementioned teenage maid character and a female aristocrat in her fifties whose age was cast appropriately. The only performing body affected was that of the ingenue, designated to be twenty-two, the perfect age for assumed female sexual availability. She has attained adulthood and marriageable age, and she is likely at the height of her traditional cultural capital: her youth, beauty, and fertility.

None of this chronicle is intended to castigate the director or my cast-mates, who were not at all unenlightened; they were educated and polite, and they brought to the table theater degrees as well as New York professional experience, one of the benefits of staging community theater on a desirable Florida island. They had perhaps a greater likelihood than most to be sensitive to the issues at the intersection of performing sexuality, age, and gender. Yet, instead of the age expectations of the role transforming to suit the casting, the older actor experienced the strictures of the ingenue. I had wondered whether the sexist sight gags would be subverted or altered by—or for—my character's postmenopausal embodiment. On the contrary, rather than deemphasize physical comedy, we added stage business that further manipulated my body.

Here, it is essential to keep in mind that age studies has always been closely tied to gender studies, as Nicole Haring and Roberta Maierhofer point out: "Recognition of age as a cultural category in the 1990s would not have been possible without the introduction of gender as a category of analysis in literary and cultural studies in the decades before. Feminist theory determined the theoretical and methodological tools that led to the establishment of Age / Ageing Studies as a field."[12] In 1995, Maierhofer coined the term *anocriticism* as an "interpretative approach which understands the agency of a gendered individual experience of ageing as a protest against the generalization of individual experiences as the norm."[13] An anocritical approach to this production involves noting that the play, published in 1980, contains markedly dated attitudes about gender-based humor, not only regarding the body, but also because Violet as an actor in the rehearsal process is written as a bimbo, a particular combination of youth, sexuality, and lack of intelligence. The script's opening description of her is "a pretty face behind which medical science may someday discover a pretty brain."[14] Our production did not relegate the setting to the past, however, but used contemporary clothing for the rehearsal scenes. On the one hand, it was progressive that all the characters staging the play within a play were written to be female in a range of ages: stage manager, director, scene tech, and playwright. On the other, the misogyny that was manifest in Violet's characterization and the physical gags would not have been mitigated by acknowledging the gender attitudes of an earlier time through setting the production in 1980; it could only have been contained by not producing the script at all. How much do we perpetuate misogyny by producing such a work? Similarly, how do we approach scripts reflecting fundamentally ageist attitudes? Given that ageism is entrenched in Western culture, how can we bring attention to ageism onstage without reinforcing it? How might age-conscious casting challenge those norms? Unconventional casting practices, of course, can open new avenues for interpreting not only individual characters, but also a play as a whole.

By stepping into the ingenue role, I also stepped back into cultural assumptions that men have the right to encroach on the younger female body. When our nineteen-year-old daughter attended the play, she said that it did not look to her like my role especially demonstrated female objectification, that it looked quite like everyday life to her. I bet it did. This production surprised me, as I thought my being cast against age might affect the role. Instead, I became performatively younger. In this case, age performance was yoked more to a role's age and gender stereotypes than to the performer's apparent age.

This project highlights several current concerns in age studies. The multibillion-dollar skin-care industry, of course, would congratulate me for the accomplishment of being cast unironically as a much younger character; I must be using the right products. (Rather, thanks to my parents for passing on the genes.) Age studies scholars challenge this cultural paradigm of "successful aging," the prescription that older people should behave and look as much like younger people as possible. The term, while celebrated in popular culture as an enlightened way to view growing older, is problematic in that, if one can succeed at aging, it also holds that one can fail at it. Performers are more susceptible to the pitfalls of successful aging because of the dearth of opportunities for older people onstage. There certainly are more older actors than the parts available to them, especially for women. Acclaimed actor Harriet Walter, for example, discusses the diminished parts available to older women: "Since I was 40, I've had to find vehicles. I want to play characters who are bigger than me. Most of the time, writers and actors eliminate, reduce pieces of me."[15] Although there has been progress during the last decade in creating dynamic, rounded older characters, the stigma remains, particularly in productions of older canonical drama.

Alternatives to "successful aging" that some aging-oriented researchers put forward, while seemingly innocuous, still carry the connotations that aging is inherently a negative that must be counteracted, related to the medicalized approach to aging as a disease process. "Positive aging" overtly incorporates that attitude, while "healthy aging" can marginalize those who live with chronic health issues in older age. The healthy-aging trope is a double-edged sword. Casting decision-makers may be prone to the widespread misconception that older people form a monolithic group—constantly at risk for a diagnosis of dementia, incontinence, osteoporosis, and so forth—rather than realizing that at any time, three generations of adults are all uniformly labeled simply as "old." They may dismiss everyone over age fifty or so as too unreliable to hire, based on doubts regarding health and physical stamina. Even when an actor over fifty presents as the very picture of healthy/positive/successful/optimal aging, the social imaginary deems that body on the precipice of illness and death. Precarity actually tends to be confined to the "oldest old," sometimes called the fourth age. As Paul Higgs asserts, healthy aging standards that demand an active lifestyle from the "young old" or third age have contributed to a more virulent social imaginary of ageism against the "old old."[16] The way to avoid the "nightmare" of classification as frail is to constantly demonstrate a healthy, active lifestyle. On the other hand, it can be argued that promoting the fact that many people do experience "healthy aging" might encourage the theater profession to embrace more aging-inclusive practices. Deconstructing the assumption of homogeneity in aging is vital to combating ageism in the theater profession. Encouraging strides in age-appropriate casting as well as age-conscious casting may help eradicate the tendency to support the "successful aging" philosophy.

Humanities-based age scholars posit a different approach to characterizing the aging process, as much of our efforts focus on what it means to grow older, and how to resist the Western master narrative of decline and decay that Gullette has identified.[17] Resistant aging is not to be confused with the anti-aging industry, which prescribes skin-care products and invasive procedures in order to "resist" or "defy" physical signs of aging (as tempting as that may be to actors caught in the ageist web). Rather, resistant aging is akin to resistant reading, against the grain, seeking always not only to challenge binaries but also to proffer alternative methods. Anita Wohlmann's recent work with age metaphors, for example, explores how images of repair and recycling hold "the potential of creatively reusing and productively reimagining harmful metaphors of older age, such as decline and defeat." A resistant approach may pursue "more nuanced and growth-oriented metaphors, in which older age holds possibilities for generativity and new discoveries."[18] Resistant aging welcomes the contributions of numerous disciplines, from sociology and history to the growing realm of medical humanities. Marlene Goldman, Kate de Medeiros, and Thomas Cole's 2022 volume *Critical Humanities and Ageing*, for instance, seeks not only to encourage but "to demonstrate the process of interdisciplinary collaboration" in aging studies.[19] How does theatrical practice contribute to resistant aging, perhaps even unwittingly? I have mentioned that the actors who auditioned for *Play On!* tended to be older; in fact, only one of the ten-member cast was under the age of forty. This range reflects the demographics of that theater's audience, which also skews older. What positive effects may have been realized by an audience's seeing apparent ages close to their own embodied onstage, portraying in the show within the show a full spectrum of people who create art?

While casting older for younger is common only in the specialized setting of senior theater and occurred in that playhouse out of necessity, perhaps as the conventions of age casting are interrogated, we will see increasing opportunities to analyze similar instances of resistant aging. For example, age studies critics are particularly intrigued by the success of *Kimberly Akimbo*, which won five Tony Awards in 2023. Based on the 2001 play of the same name, the show features music by Jeanine Tesori, with lyrics and book by David Lindsay-Abaire. The title character is turning sixteen but lives with a condition similar to progeria that rapidly ages her, so that she appears to be a septuagenarian. The role is demanding in that it requires adolescent emotional/mental verisimilitude from an actor who appears old enough to be the character's grandmother. Given traditional casting practices, it is remarkable that instead of adding wrinkles to a young actor, this show chooses to cast for apparent physiological age. Victoria Clark was in her early sixties when cast as this teen girl opposite nineteen-year-old Justin Cooley as her love interest, Seth, and critics have lauded the believability of her performance. Peter Marks claims, "Without that essential belief—that we see Clark's Kimberly as a typically acting atypical kid, and that Cooley's Seth sees her as girlfriend material—the musical might feel like a precious gimmick." His article continues that Clark "seems to slip into a 15-going-on-16-year-old version of herself, as if that were on a hanger in her dressing room, too. 'I don't sit down and study, you know, like teenage behavior or any of that stuff,' she says. 'I just kind of try to remember as much as possible what my body felt like.'"[20] This Tony-winning performance exemplifies Gullette's assertion that older actors can/should play younger characters because they have been young. Laura Collins-Hughes reports that Clark joked about being a kid in the early off-Broadway playbill, and despite the intimacy of that smaller theater, some audience members believed it.[21] Jesse Green's review of the show after it moved to Broadway asserts of Clark, "But what has become even richer since 'Kimberly Akimbo' premiered at the Atlantic Theater Company last year is her profound and uncritical immersion in youthfulness. Leaving the ironies to us, she refuses to condescend to the character. There is nothing in quotation marks about her teenage mannerisms, or embarrassing about seeing her, at 63, wear the spot-on embroidered jumpers and colorful hair clips Sarah Laux has costumed her in."[22] These reviews are representative of the media coverage of the production, and notably do not reproduce ageist assumptions; they may indicate progress in attitudes toward performing age.

These examples of resistant aging in casting return us to the basics of age as performance and performative. Anna Harpin summarizes theatrical embodiment in relation to Judith Butler's foundational concepts of performativity: "If one's identity is a performative act, then the theatrical performance of a given identity necessarily involves a dual process of signification. One is simultaneously representing self and other. Further, if, as Butler implies, there are two types of repetition involved with performative identity (one that affirms conservative foundational narratives and one that subverts these foundations by exposing their fictionality through a process of parody and pastiche) then one must consider to what degree a particular theatrical performance is engaged with either strategy of affirmation or subversion."[23] If my apparent age onstage was indeed significantly younger than my chronological age, as the director and cast claimed, was it possible for me to strike a blow against ageism by performing a part written for a young woman? The playbill did not specify "age 22"; that information was in the script only. Despite my intentions, perhaps my performance could not subvert age and gender norms, but rather only uphold them. Perhaps the age-defying casting of the teenage maid, comically incongruous, was at face value a greater onstage challenge to ageism. Offstage, however, casting someone who was fifty-six to play the ingenue demonstrated the interplay of chronological age norms with the elements of apparent age and physiological age: I was able to present acceptably as the younger love interest in appearance as well as meet the (albeit mild) physical demands of farce. I was uncomfortable with that interplay during the initial rehearsal process; as Ellis and Bochner acknowledge, "The self-questioning autoethnography demands is extremely difficult. So is confronting things about yourself that are less than flattering."[24] My own insecurities about age-passing led me to ensure that everyone involved knew about the disparity between my chronological and apparent ages. But in final analysis, the cast, crew, and director at a small community theater were willing to imagine and realize a production that exposed and invalidated ageist assumptions, a goal that scholars who work at the intersection of age and theater studies continue to promote for all the performing arts.

NOTES

1. When Elinor Fuchs first asked me to contribute to this volume, she wanted to reprint my article "'The Play's the Thing': Theatre as a Scholarly Meeting Ground in Age Studies," *International Journal of Ageing and Later Life* 7 (2012): 117–41. "I've never read anything like it," she said; as it had appeared in an aging studies journal, she wanted it to reach the theater studies community as well. As plans progressed, she requested that I update that article, which argues that theater is a perfect site of

inquiry for any of the critical turns in age studies—at that time, the performative and narrative turns were particularly prominent. Since that piece is open access, my intention here is to update its concerns and honor Elinor's exclamation by taking another uncommon approach, an autoethnography of acting in amateur theater. This project's genesis is that my metropolitan area is known for high-quality community theater, and I suddenly had time to do a bit of acting after a very long hiatus. Only one local production fit my schedule: *Play On!* by Rick Abbot. I auditioned without revealing my day job to anyone. There, one of the theater's mainstay actors kindly introduced herself, and we chatted about the several parts possible for us as middle-aged women. I mentioned that quite a few women apparently in our age group were auditioning. She responded that, given the age of the people who audition for and attend the shows at that island playhouse, I could still play the ingenue. We both laughed; little did I know.

2. One of the first: Anne Davis Basting, *The Stages of Age: Performing Age in Contemporary American Culture* (University of Michigan Press, 1998).

3. The fullest version of these arguments: Valerie Barnes Lipscomb, *Performing Age in Modern Drama* (Palgrave Macmillan, 2016).

4. Anna Harpin, "The Lives of Our Mad Mothers: Aging and Contemporary Performance," *Women & Performance: a journal of feminist theory* 22, no. 1 (2012): 83.

5. Margaret Morganroth Gullette, *Aged by Culture* (University of Chicago Press, 2004), 166.

6. Carolyn Ellis and Arthur P. Bochner, "Autoethnography, Personal Narrative, Reflexivity," in *Handbook of Qualitative Research*, 2nd ed., ed. Norman Denzin and Yvonna Lincoln (Sage, 2000), 740.

7. Robert N. Butler, "Age-Ism: Another Form of Bigotry," *Gerontologist* 9, no. 4 (1969): 243–46.

8. Bridie Moore, "Fallen, Falling, Clinging, and Crawling: The Everyday Age Effects of Drama and Performance," in *The Bloomsbury Handbook to Ageing in Contemporary Literature and Film*, ed. Sarah Falcus, Heike Hartung, and Raquel Medina (Bloomsbury, 2023), 203.

9. Valerie Barnes Lipscomb, "'Old Gentleman': Age Differences as Plot Subversion," *Shaw: The Annual of Bernard Shaw Studies* 25, no. 1 (2005): 147–61.

10. Aagje Swinnen, "*Benidorm Bastards*, or the Do's and Don'ts of Aging," in *Aging, Performance, and Stardom: Doing Age on the Stage of Consumerist Culture*, ed. Aagje Swinnen and John A. Stotesbury (LIT Verlag, 2012), 8.

11. "Rick Abbot," Concord Theatricals, accessed May 4, 2023, https://www.concordtheatricals.com/a/1026/rick-abbot

12. Nicole Haring and Roberta Maierhofer, "Feminism, Gender and Age," in Falcus, Hartung, and Medina, *The Bloomsbury Handbook to Ageing in Contemporary Literature and Film*, 155.

13. Haring and Maierhofer, 159.

14. Rick Abbot, *Play On!* (Samuel French, 1980), 6.

15. Janet Hill and Valerie Barnes Lipscomb, "Performing Female Age in Shakespeare's Plays," in *Staging Age: The Performance of Age in Theatre, Dance, and Film*, ed. Valerie Barnes Lipscomb and Leni Marshall, 85–108 (Palgrave Macmillan, 2010), 103.

16. Paul Higgs, "Conceptualizing Ageism: From Prejudice and Discrimination to

Fourth Ageism," in *Critical Humanities and Ageing: Forging Interdisciplinary Dialogues*, ed. Marlene Goldman, Kate de Medeiros, and Thomas Cole (Routledge, 2022), 181–98.

17. Gullette, *Aged by Culture*, 130.

18. Anita Wohlmann, "Age and Its Metaphors," in *The Palgrave Handbook of Literature and Aging*, ed. Valerie Barnes Lipscomb and Aagje Swinnen (Palgrave Macmillan, 2024), 373.

19. Goldman, de Medeiros, and Cole, *Critical Humanities and Ageing*, 6.

20. Peter Marks, "How Does a 63-Year-Old Play a Teen? In Victoria Clark's Case, Superbly," *Washington Post*, January 13, 2023, https://www.washingtonpost.com/theater-dance/2023/01/13/kimberly-akimbo-victoria-clark/

21. Laura Collins-Hughes, "How the Star of 'Kimberly Akimbo' Found Beauty in Her Voice Again," *New York Times*, May 10, 2023, https://www.nytimes.com/2023/05/10/theater/kimberly-akimbo-victoria-clark.html

22. Jesse Green, "Review: 'Kimberly Akimbo,' Both Great and Small, Seizes the Day: Critic's Pick," *New York Times*, November 10, 2022.

23. Harpin, "The Lives of Our Mad Mothers," 79.

24. Ellis and Bochner, "Autoethnography, Personal Narrative, Reflexivity," 738.

7
Differential Ageism
Aging and Asian American Identity in Out of Time

Dorothy Chansky

Out of Time was a coproduction of the National Asian American Theatre Company (NAATCO) and New York's Public Theater, where it ran from February 15 through March 13, 2022. The piece is made up of five distinct yet related monologues whose characters are all Asian American and over the age of sixty. The performance's overarching themes, its five writers' differentiated concerns with aging, the wide-ranging critical responses, and its mixed-message goals help underscore how the production provides a unique exploration of aging subjectivity in the contemporary theater landscape. The idea for a project featuring older performers originated with Les Waters, the show's director, who turned sixty-nine in 2022. Waters had shared an idea for a much longer endeavor with Mia Katigbak, the artistic director of NAATCO. Katigbak—who was sixty-seven at the time of the run and would perform one of the evening's monologues—persuaded Waters that something more manageable than his proposal for an all-night show featuring older actors telling stories (*A Chorus Line* with Social Security benefits?) was the way to go. This resulted in the formation of *Out of Time*'s five-piece structure, featuring five playwrights of different generations.

Out of Time opened just as attacks on Asian Americans—many victims of which were senior citizens and/or women—were making headlines in multiple parts of the United States. The combined concerns around COVID-19, racially driven attacks, and baby boomer age-related loss—of status, health, mobility, loved ones—make the piece of interest across races and ethnicities. That four characters and all five playwrights are women also suggests that the piece might be read as one dealing with women's "issues," or at least women's perspectives on female experience. However, only one critic, Juan A. Ramirez, named this in his review. "Age" was rather an undeconstructed monolith in publicity and reviews. "Asian American" was likewise allowed to stand as something to be taken at face value rather than something to be anatomized, although some fictional immigrant biographies were narrated in the monologues and care seems to have been taken in most (although not all) cases to match the ethnicities/national backgrounds of playwrights to those of characters and actors. This is not to say that *Out of Time* did not create a mix of identity markers. It is, rather, to say that much of the response of critics—and audience members, from what I could intuit around me on the two nights I saw the show—was courteously respectful. Fissures and blind spots within the work were not delved into; indeed, some conflation and accepted privileging of careerism were part of spectators' experiences. Likewise, the intersection of race and age was a "given" with regard to characters and actors, but, as I discuss later, it was ignored in other areas, where youth was accepted as a kind of necessity for the show to go on.

Out of Time's characters include a journalist, a filmmaker, a novelist, and a banker, all living in the United States, all at the far end of the life spectrum, and all with access to doctors and institutional health care. They experience widowhood, indifferent offspring, frightening (although not necessarily unusual) medical conditions, professional sidelining, cancel culture, and loneliness. These are precisely the kinds of worries that may be on the minds of the anticipated audience for the production: respected in their work fields (even if not wealthy), culturally in the know, generally liberal, and formally educated consumers of off-the-beaten-path plays that aim to be thought provoking but typically eschew aggressive activism. Publicity for and reviews of the Public Theater production foregrounded the dearth of roles for "older" actors (especially women) of Asian heritage and praised the skill sets brought to this endeavor by all the performers. Actors do not, however, arrive onstage absent the work of others. In this case, that work included heavy lifting by some young playwrights. This is not to say that a writer needs to occupy the same demographic position as her character(s); it is to say that in the case of *Out of Time*, writers a generation or more younger than the people they penned and the performers who brought these fictional creations to life were not eschewed for their age.

Katigbak's program points to "NAATCOs commitment to address the persistent misrepresentation of Asian Americans in the theatre, Les' purpose of centering typically marginalized older actors and characters, and [artistic director] Oskar [Eustis]'s work towards cultural transformation at the Public." The reference to misrepresentation is not explained, but present-day authors and journalists point to how liberal media and elite educational institutions perpetuate a putatively positive image that conflates all Asian Americans, ignoring not only differences in national origin, but differences in class and generation of arrival in the United States. If Katigbak's notion of misrepresentation rests on the fact that many, if not most, roles for Asian Americans in white-centered (or at least white-created) plays have in the past been, and to some extent still are, smaller roles that fail to recognize the full humanity of and myriad differences among Asian Americans, she is correct. When the roles are larger, they have frequently been demeaning. Think of the engineer and prostitutes in *Miss Saigon* (1989) or the subservient women in the 1951 *The King and I*, not to mention that work's arguably xenophobic and autocratic king, who was, for decades, played by a white actor in yellowface. The hurtfulness of yellowface (using makeup, wigs, and/or prosthetic enhancements to present white actors as Asian characters) was still sufficiently in evidence for Donatella Galella to publish "Feeling Yellow: Responding to Contemporary Yellowface in Musical Performance" in 2018. Yellowface—the subject of David Henry Hwang's play of the same name, which played on Broadway in 2024 and garnered a 2025 Tony Award for actor Francis Jue—was almost (although obviously not completely) eradicated in the twenty-first century, as the demand for Asian roles to be played by Asian-descended performers became an imperative and the demand began to shift to an insistence on ethnic specificity in casting.[1]

This chapter begins with a brief overview of *Out of Time*'s five monologues, identifying their playwrights and the actors who performed them. I continue with a consideration of age, aging, and ageism, then move to a more extended examination of the playwrights and my sense of a kind of ventriloquism, subject to a bit of identity critique that is buttressed by something I define below as *differential ageism*. Additionally, I consider some of the stereotypes and prejudices against Asian Americans, who are pigeonholed based largely on observable phenotypical markers, often in combination with unexamined beliefs, leading to some material about how this has influenced work in Asian American theater, a relatively new phenomenon, and the balancing acts it has engendered for actors, writers, and directors. In other words, I will demonstrate how ageism drove this production in its scripting, performances, and publicity.

OUT OF TIME

The opening piece of *Out of Time*, *My Documentary*, was a return to the Public Theater for playwright Anna Ouyang Moench, who was in the Public's 2011 Emerging Writers Group Spotlight Series. Twelve years later, still a young woman, Moench would enroll in the MFA program at the University of California, San Diego. In *My Documentary*, Page Leong played an unnamed documentary filmmaker, born in China, raised in England, and forging her career in the United States, who recalls the last person she touched before the pandemic lockdown. That person was her longtime producer, a man a few decades her junior whose studio had prospered because of her work, but who would not green-light her most recent proposal: an exploration of grief. She came to the topic in the wake of her husband's sudden, recent death, but, at age seventy-one, she was greeted by the man whose success she had facilitated telling "a widow in no uncertain terms to go fuck herself because she's old and no one cares when old people grieve other old people." Leong, born in 1960, holds an MA in dance from the University of California, Los Angeles. She has many film credits from roughly the mid-1980s until the mid-1990s, when she also did guest appearances in episodes of several television series. But film work tapered off in the new millennium. Most reviewers found *My Documentary* and Leong's performance riveting, with one pointing out that observations about the difficulties of being an older Asian woman "in, among other things, the entertainment industry . . . properly land as the preposterous offenses to personhood that they are."[2] This was the only published review I found of the entire production that mentioned women qua women in any direct way.

The second piece of the evening, playwright Mia Chung's *Ball in the Air*, weaves the confused responses to and memories of three separate upsetting incidents into a stream-of-consciousness tale with philosophizing. Chung's playwriting career, like that of Anna Moench, took off in the middle of the 2010s. In *Ball in the Air*, Ena, a journalist (performed by Katigbak), spends much of her stage time keeping a paddleball in the air. One storyline is prompted by a serious betrayal by a longtime friend; one treats a road trip from New York to the DC area to attend a fancy party; the third describes waiting for presidential election returns in 2016. Deep into the piece, Ena demonstrates how to perform a magic trick wherein a ball tossed into the air a few times seems to disappear, only to reappear in the magician's hand, where it was palmed all along. One reviewer called this monologue "all confusion";[3] another read all three strands as being about betrayal, noting that we are meant to understand the disappearing ball as a metaphor;[4] a third summed up Ena's performance with, "It's life's dismaying illusions she's compulsively considering."[5] *Ball in the Air* does not include specifics about ethnicity in the text. Katigbak, who was born and spent her youth in Manila, earned a bachelor's degree at Barnard College and a master's degree at Columbia University. She has enjoyed a long career as an actress, performing roles scripted for several races and ethnicities. In 2024 she played Marina, the nurse/nanny, in a new, multiracial production of Chekhov's *Uncle Vanya* at New York City's Lincoln Center Theater. In *Ball in the Air*, again, writer and performer co-created a compelling portrait of an over-sixty Asian American woman, but the generative duo's ages were separated by at least thirty years.

Black Market Caviar, by Jaclyn Backhaus, situates itself up front by announcing that "tonight is New Year's Eve: December 31st, 2019." These words are uttered by an onscreen speaker who is coaching her younger self on how to move forward with life in the face of a diagnosis of breast cancer. The character, named Carla, was played by the lively Rita Wolf (née Ghose), who was born in 1960 in India, trained in England, and may still be best remembered for her breakout role in the 1985 film *My Beautiful Laundrette*. Real time for the speaker is soon revealed to be 2050. Backhaus, who was born in the mid-1980s, may or may not have intended her piece about family medical history to be a "cautionary story about . . . genetic predisposition."[6] Details about emigration from India, about an Indian American doctor, and about secrets kept from one's children putatively in the name of not upsetting them anchor the character in terms of heritage; her escaping New York City for New Year's Eve in a cabin in upstate New York to read *The Bell Jar* while snowbound tell us about her class, as does, of course, the taste for caviar. The speaker's stated goal is to allay her younger self's fear. Perhaps it confirms the worst of our collective fears looking ahead.

The fourth monologue is by Naomi Iizuka, the best known of *Out of Time*'s five playwrights.[7] Her contribution to the overall project, called *Japanese Folk Song*, draws on memories of her father, who died in 2020. Early in the piece, Taki, played by actor Glenn Kubota, asks, "what do we *really* know about anything?" To this he adds, "Grief is a funny thing, isn't it?" By the end of the monologue, we know that Taki is very ill and is speaking to his otherwise unidentified daughter (not present onstage). He tells of near-death experiences in each decade of his life, the first when he was five and a bomb fell on his house in Tokyo. The current illness is, he knows, the last time he will face death, but, "if you wait long enough, nothing really matters." The title of the play comes from a Thelonious Monk recording wherein the jazz artist covered an old Japanese folk song. Reviewer Juan Michael Porter II pinpointed how the song "awakens Taki to his current reality, which was caused by a betrayal, but from which there is no escape." Porter found the thread of "atonement for their failings" running through the entire ensemble of plays.[8]

In the final piece, Sam Chanse's *Disturbance Specialist*, the protagonist, Leonie, is a "mixed, Asian American" novelist, and was played by Natsuko Ohama, a certified Linklater voice trainer who herself trained with Kristin Linklater. Ohama has a creditable filmography and is professor of theater practice in voice at the University of Southern California School of Dramatic Arts. The seventy-year-old character steps up to a podium at her alma mater expected and expecting to present a commencement address. Instead, she delivers what might best be described as a long apologia for her life of activism and authorial excellence (she has been nominated for a Pulitzer Prize), which has somehow crashed to a halt, with her being "canceled" by young people in the audience for reasons never specified. The title of the piece comes from a rare mouse that survives in the aftermath of a volcano, "reveling in ruined environments," and to which Leonie compares herself as a survivor who both creates and endures disturbance. Challenging the young people who she knows didn't really want her there, she roars, "it angers me in the extreme that some people think I no longer have a place at the table. Or deserve one," concluding with the salvo, "you know nothing of what it is to live when you haven't yet understood that you will die." One critic summarized the Chanse/Ohama offering with respect for the fact that it didn't pander by suggesting closure. "Haranguing and cajoling, she wins the esteem of, if not the unseen audience, the audience directly before her."[9]

AGE, VENTRILOQUISM, AND DIFFERENTIAL AGEISM IN AMERICAN THEATER

Showcasing "older" actors and stories about "older" characters was a key goal of *Out of Time*, and, as every essay in this anthology makes clear, aging in America and the American theater is not for the faint of heart. Robert Butler coined and popularized the term *ageism* in the United States in 1968, calling prejudice against elders akin to racism or sexism. "In America," he wrote in his Pulitzer Prize–winning *Why Survive? Being Old in America*, "childhood is romanticized, youth is idolized, middle age does the work, wields the power and pays the bills, and old age, its days empty of purpose, gets little or nothing of what it has already done. The old are in the way."[10]

Who, though, are "the old"? In the United States, it remains easy to call sixty-five the entry point for senior citizenship. This was the age set in 1935 by Franklin D. Roosevelt's administration to be eligible for Social Security, the federal government's postretirement financial support, offered to qualifying people who had worked for wages or had been married to someone who did, the latter entitled to widow's benefits. Many workers were not covered—most notably agricultural and domestic laborers. The life expectancy in 1935 was 59.9 for men and 63.9 for women, so no one really expected the program to cost a lot.[11] Things changed, however. Historically, one might think about it this way: in 1910 people in the United States sixty-five or older represented just 4.3 percent of the population; by 1970 that percentage had grown to almost 10; in 2016 over-sixty-fives were 15 percent of the populace, and the Population Reference Bureau projected a rise to 23 percent by 2060.[12] Numerically, this means going from fifty-eight million seniors in 2021 to eighty-eight million by 2050.[13] Today, not only do many people work well beyond the age of sixty-five, but the age at which one is entitled to the full benefits of the program has risen to sixty-seven for people born 1960 or later, and a few months before for those born in prior years (reduced benefits may be claimed starting at sixty-two). A crude way to understand how people might make a decision about when to start receiving Social Security benefits is to think that a not very healthy person who hated her job would be happy to retire and start collecting benefits at age sixty-two, while a vigorous person in good health employed at work she loved would be happy to wait until age seventy—the point at which the greatest monthly amount may be claimed. These are far from the only considerations and far from the only scenarios, but they lead back to the "who is 'old'" question.

The discourse of aging has long been a depressing one. In recent decades, scholars and activists from fields as diverse as social work and literature have begun to resist, and to rewrite the narrative of decline and attendant ageism that is so ubiquitous as to seem inevitable. Failing to officially differentiate the "senior," who may be as young as fifty-five or sixty, from the "oldest old," who may be pushing one hundred, is as senseless as conflating all pediatric patients, who range in age from newborns to high school students.[14] Imperatives to stay active, eat healthfully, exercise, get proper medical care, and take care of oneself fail to take into account access to money or leisure, good health, or pre-existing conditions, as they tout the values in appearance and energy supposed to accrue to those working at successful aging. In other words, even positive approaches to aging can be (possibly unintentionally) ageist. And still the question of "who is 'old'" has no single answer. Scholar and practitioner Anne Davis Basting points out "complex and even contradictory descriptions of age. To be *old* might now refer to one's chronological age (number of years), biological age (rated according to one's health), social age (determined by social roles), or personal age (self-selected)."[15]

The actors, producer, and director of *Out of Time* resented and pushed back against the professional punishment levied on actors over sixty (chronological age), who were somehow supposed to go quietly into the night of social age (popularly determined by a punishingly youth-focused theater and film industry), even as their biological age (health) and personal age (I'm still rarin' to go!) said that they could still function well otherwise. It needs no deep research to recognize that in American culture, men with gray hair and a bit of a paunch qualify as authorities, if not éminences grises, while women with gray hair and less than youth's perky breasts are often seen as old ladies. While most of us can think of male actors who continue to play all kinds of roles (and be shown aging in all kinds of ways) well into their sixties, seventies, and beyond, the list of women is shorter and the women are more likely to be cast, albeit not exclusively, in roles that show them "aging well." In the cast of *Out of Time*, actor Glenn Kubota observed in a pre–opening night interview, "My mother, who turned 97 in August, sits at home and watches TV all day because all her friends are gone. . . . To see what she has to do on a daily basis just to amuse herself is really eye-opening. I'm getting a glimpse of what maybe I will be facing 10, 20 years from now."[16] So Kubota's sense of "old" (ninety-seven and sitting at home all day) and his sense of himself as an actor in a role in *Out of Time* (an actor over sixty [in his case, over seventy], well able to learn lines, compel feelings in an audience, and perform multiple times per week) are far from coterminous.

In one sense, however, *Out of Time* hewed to familiar (theater) industry practices as far as age goes. There was, as I outlined briefly above, barely an "older" playwright in sight. While great care was taken to align the ethnicity of most of the playwrights with those of the actors, the writers were, all save one, up-and-comers with awards, name-school MFAs, and institutional affiliations in keeping with twenty-first-century careerist goals. This is not to say that any of the writing failed to compel or offer performance opportunities. It is to say, however, that in a realm (playwriting) where appearance and even physical health may matter less than it does onstage, the production defaulted to youth. At fifty-seven in 2022, Naomi Iizuka was the oldest of the writers, and none of the others were even close to this age.

How might a reader understand the playwrights' (assigned) roles in *Out of Time*? Anna Ouyang Moench, the Chinese American author of *My Documentary*, earned an MFA in playwriting at the University of California, San Diego (where Iizuka chairs the program). Her earliest professional productions took place in the 2010s, and she has enjoyed fellowships, awards, and memberships at many off-Broadway theaters in New York (including the Public Theater and Ensemble Studio Theatre). Moench's recognition of the dismissal and isolation experienced (or potentially experienced) by over-seventy women artists as depicted in *My Documentary* is far from impossible to believe. Whether this kind of experience is unique to Chinese Americans is another question. If she had written her character to have been born in, say, Manila or Hanoi or another East Asian city whence educated parents might have left for England, the play could have been just as compelling and moving and purposeful. But, in keeping with the general preference of pairing actors with writers of the same *ethnic* heritage, the Moench-Leong duo would have had to be uncoupled, even as both are Asian American.

Carla, the character in *Black Market Caviar*, is given a backstory anchoring her heritage clearly in India. Playwright Jaclyn Backhaus, who teaches playwriting at New York University (where she also earned a BFA), was born in Phoenix, Arizona, to a mother from India and a German American father from New Jersey. She was thirty-six the year that *Out of Time* opened. In a *New York Times* interview about her 2018 play *India Pale Ale*, Backhaus made clear that the story of a daughter who wants to forge her own path in the United States was not autobiographical but was rather inspired by her mother.[17] The playwright's mother is an English professor whose own mother died of breast cancer. One might say that Backhaus's work channels an imagined version of a woman based on her mother, grafted onto someone closer to her own age, and safely unmoored from an exact historical moment, as the 2050 Carla speaks in the play to the 2019 Carla in language rooted in the moment of the play's creation and production. Again, however, the withholding of medical information in the proclaimed interest of "not worrying" a child could occur in a family from any of the many traditions that are tight-lipped about everything from cancer to sex to money.

Playwright Mia Chung (*Ball in the Air*) is, unlike actress Mia Katigbak, the daughter of Korean parents. Perhaps unsurprisingly, *Ball in the Air* does not include specifics about ethnicity in the text. Chung, like the other young playwrights whose texts constitute *Out of Time*, has an MFA from a prestigious playwriting program, in this case Brown University, at which she enrolled in 2009, when her husband took a position there following their meeting during his professorship at Berkeley.

Disturbance Specialist's author, Sam Chanse, has taught playwriting at New York University, Columbia University, and the University of Rochester. Like Chung and Backhaus, she is a member of New Dramatists in New York, and she has also enjoyed numerous fellowships. Chanse identifies as Hapa (mixed race), with a Chinese American father and a Pennsylvania Dutch mother.[18] Her fictional canceled novelist was played by Japanese Canadian-born Natsuko Ohama, an actress with a creditable filmography. While the autobiography that Chanse has scripted for her character features a Japanese

American upbringing, this is neither Chanse's own story nor that of either of her parents, and Ohama is hardly xenophobic or hard to cast outside her own background owing to anything in her appearance or speech. This character, too, could have had a different ethnic background and still delivered the same quirky, heartfelt, and wounded story that Leonie does.

In *Japanese Folk Song* the connection between playwright, character, and actor is the most closely intertwined of those in all five monologues. Actor Glenn Kubota has a long list of television credits, typically playing Japanese or Japanese American characters. Kubota grew up in California working in agriculture. He is the oldest of the *Out of Time* actors, as Iizuka is the oldest of the playwrights. Still, they are over a dozen years apart in age. Iizuka has clearly stated that Taki is based on her father (right down to his age). While she herself was born in Japan, she graduated from a private Episcopal day school in Washington, DC, before attending Yale, so her identity was forged as much via the influence and input of her Latinx mother (an attorney) as via that of her Japanese banker father.

If *Out of Time* speaks to the canceling of older actors, it does so by having them speak the words of younger writers with sterling bona fides. Here I suggest that, as playwrights for millennia have done in limning characters from ages, ethnicities, and even eras other than their own, the *Out of Time* playwrights might be said to have ventriloquized age, based on experience with parents, grandparents, or even research. Their value to the project was perhaps their up-and-comingness tempered with solid credentials. Ethnicity, not age, was the criterion for selection. The director and producer of *Out of Time* fretted—at least in the context of an interview—about the paucity of Asian American playwrights over sixty from whom they might have chosen, blaming that paucity on the fact that "for a long time Asian Americans couldn't get produced."[19] Without disputing that fact, one might still note that, as the *Out of Time* creators have argued and resisted with regard to older actors, lack of employment and lack of talent are not the same thing. Moreover, as data from the now-legendary study about women playwrights (how many compared to males and how many productions) done in 2009 by Emily Glassberg Sands showed, any group that shows up with more productions or credits or creations than some other group basically does so because of the backing of producers or companies or universities.[20] In other words, productions (which cost money and try not to lose it) are only partially predicated on "talent." They depend on what will sell. So, it might have been possible (had there been world enough and time) to seek out able, if underproduced, senior Asian American playwrights.[21] I suggest that this production engaged in something I call differential ageism, a term I derive from

Richard Delgado's "differential racialization." The latter is the "process by which racial and ethnic groups are viewed and treated differently by mainstream society," this occurring "in response to shifting needs."[22] When cheap labor was (or sometimes still is) needed by US employers, members of the minority group willing to take those jobs earn some respect or rights. When the market is glutted, they may lose some status either legally or in everyday social life. Here, when the need to foreground over-sixty *actors* was prioritized, defaulting to younger playwrights more recognized by mainstream (theater) society was accepted.

It is worth returning briefly to Mia Katigbak's assertion that Asians and Asian Americans suffer from misrepresentation in American theater. While the scope of this essay on aging necessarily limits a detailed analysis of race, opportunities for Asian Americans to appear at all on the American stage are startlingly few, and it may be that absence is the biggest kind of misrepresentation. According to the Asian American Performers Action Coalition, in the 2018–19 theatrical season in New York City, Asian American actors were cast in just 6.3 percent of all available roles; Asian American playwrights and musical theater writers made up just 4.9 percent of all writers produced; and Asian American directors oversaw just 4.5 percent of all productions.[23] These numbers skew below the percentage of US adults counted as Asian American, which is roughly 7 percent (17.8 million, not counting minors), according to a 2021 Pew Research Center analysis,[24] although just 4 percent of members of the Actors' Equity Association are Asian.[25]

CONCLUSION

Ageism is real. Anti-Asian prejudice and violence are real. The difficulties of producing theater absent an anticipated audience and a budget are real. Possibly the compromises made and the short run of *Out of Time* is the best combination we can hope for and will get for a theater piece focused on Asian Americans over sixty (at least in any well-known venue in New York). Meanwhile, the perfect combination of anti-ageism and a place at the table for Asian and/or Asian American theater artists in the United States remains fraught, the path filled with roadblocks that are ironically inflected by success. Those who haven't achieved it are unlikely to be offered an opportunity to demonstrate their abilities. Those who have it may always need to be looking over their shoulders to see who is coming up behind them. The characters in *Out of Time* have avoided some predictive horrors; they are old(er) and Asian American, but not without money, which would be, in the words of Tennessee Williams's Maggie the Cat, "just too awful." Sic semper age and theater in the United States. Can we do better? Or at least *other*?

Much theater, music, and other forms of performance in the United States—indeed in the West—have privileged the visual. In this schema, for instance, Black musicians in the early days of the recording industry fared better than did actors or filmmakers because producers seeking "mainstream" (read: white) audiences knew that white people might *listen* to Black artists but did not necessarily want to *watch* them. "Race records" (recordings made by Black artists) could sell to Black and to white audiences alike, of course, but the biggest audience was white, by virtue of sheer numbers, as well as available money. This might be called an instance of differential racism, in which the money-making potential of Black artists was welcomed while the embodied presence of the same artists was eschewed. *Out of Time* reversed the schema but maintained the principle. Both because of the people who germinated the project (an actor and a director) and the awareness that being visually "old" is a handicap in terms of casting, opportunities for senior actors were foregrounded. The same is not necessarily true of writers, where age need never be seen.

It would be unfair to say what "should have" happened. Yet recognizing the compromises in idealism that make possible a piece of purposeful professional theater is not intended to trash the project outright. Rather, this instance of differential ageism made it possible to showcase actors and stories that addressed the concerns of the actor and director who conceived the project and who may or may not have realized (or cared) that to do so in a major New York venue they were not in a position to insist that everyone involved be over sixty.

NOTES

1. Donatella Galella, "Feeling Yellow: Responding to Contemporary Yellowface in Musical Performance," *Journal of Dramatic Theory and Criticism* 32, no. 2 (Spring 2018): 67–77. For a study of yellowface in American and European theater and film between 1882 and 1940, see Esther Kim Lee, *Made-Up Asians: Yellowface During the Exclusion Era* (University of Michigan Press, 2022).

2. Juan A. Ramirez, "*Out of Time*, Just in Time," *Theatrely*, March 1, 2022, https://www.theatrely.com/post/out-of-time-just-in-time-review

3. Laura Collins-Hughes, "Once Sidelined, Now Taking Center Stage," review of *Out of Time*, *New York Times*, March 1, 2022, https://www.nytimes.com/2022/03/01/theater/out-of-time-review-public-theater.html

4. Jonathan Mandell, "5 Aged Asian-American Stories," review of *Out of Time*, *New York Theater* (blog), March 1, 2022, https://newyorktheater.me/2022/03/01/out-of-time

5. David Finkle, "Five Monologues Masterfully Capturing Contemporary Anxiety," review of *Out of Time*, *New York Stage Review*, March 1, 2022, https://nystagereview.com/2022/03/01/out-of-time

6. Howard Miller, review of *Out of Time*, *Talkin' Broadway*, March 1, 2022, https://www.talkinbroadway.com/page/ob/03_01_22.html

7. Iizuka is named as "one of the most commissioned playwrights in contemporary American theater" by Seiwoong Oh in *Encyclopedia of Asian-American Literature* (Facts on File, 2007), 122.

8. Juan Michael Porter II, "Five Wise Monologues Remind Us That Life Is Fleeting," review of *Out of Time*, New York Theatre Guide, March 1, 2022, https://www.newyorktheatreguide.com/reviews/out-of-time-off-broadway-review-public-theater

9. Finkle, "Five Monologues."

10. Quoted in "Robert N. Butler: Pioneer in Study of Aging," Columbia University Irving Medical Center, September 26, 2022, https://www.cuimc.columbia.edu/news/robert-n-butler-pioneer-study-aging

11. Michael Clinton, "Why '65' Isn't the Magic Number for Retirement Anymore," *Esquire*, February 17, 2023, https://www.esquire.com/lifestyle/a42817195/

12. Peter. J. Whitehouse with Daniel George, *The Myth of Alzheimer's: What You Aren't Being Told About Today's Most Dreaded Diagnosis* (St. Martin's Press, 2008), 93; Mark Mather, Paola Scommegna, and Lillian Kilduff, "Fact Sheet: Aging in the United States," Population Reference Bureau, July 15, 2019, https://www.prb.org/aging-unitedstates-fact-sheet/

13. Alzheimer's Association, *2022 Alzheimer's Disease Facts and Figures: Special Report, More Than Normal Aging* (Alzheimer's Association, 2022), 19.

14. Dorothy Chansky, *Losing It: Staging the Cultural Conundrum of Dementia and Decline in American Theatre* (Palgrave Macmillan, 2023), 24.

15. Anne Davis Basting, *The Stages of Age: Performing Age in Contemporary American Culture* (University of Michigan Press, 1998), 17.

16. Quoted in Matt Stevens, "5 Monologues, Each a Showcase for Asian American Actors Over 60," review of *Out of Time*, *New York Times*, February 16, 2022, https://www.nytimes.com/2022/02/16/theater/out-of-time-asian-american-actors.html

17. Sopan Deb, "This Playwright Has Been Listening to Her Mother," *New York Times*, October 19, 2018, https://www.nytimes.com/2018/10/19/theater/jaclyn-backhaus-india-pale-ale.html

18. Sam Chanse, interview by Alex Chester, *Mixed Asian Media*, June 6, 2018, https://mixedasianmedia.com/hapa-mag-issue-004/interview-sam-chanse

19. Quoted in Diep Tran, "Off the Sidelines and 'Out of Time,'" *American Theatre*, March 3, 2022, https://www.americantheatre.org/2022/03/03/off-the-sidelines

20. Patricia Cohen, "Rethinking Gender Bias in Theater," *New York Times*, June 23, 2009, https://www.nytimes.com/2009/06/24/theater/24play.html

21. Harold Prince undertook such an endeavor in casting the 1976 *Pacific Overtures*. Esther Kim Lee tells the story of hiring actors for that musical, for which Prince and casting director Joanna Merlin scoured the country over the course of eighteen months, seeing over 250 actors and hiring some with no professional experience. Clearly, then, "professional experience" is not the only indicator of ability. Many people in all kinds of artistic areas perform or write or make art as amateurs and do so with skill, ingenuity, and originality. Esther Kim Lee, *A History of Asian American Theatre* (Cambridge University Press, 2006), 39.

22. Richard Delgado and Jean Stefancic, *Critical Race Theory: An Introduction* (New York University Press, 2012), 160, 9.

23. Diep Tran, "Invisibility and Objectification Can Kill: American Theatre's Anti-Asian Problem," *American Theatre*, April 7, 2021, https://www.americantheatre.org/2021/04/07/invisibility-and-objectification

24. Neil G. Ruiz, Luis Noe-Bustamante, and Sono Shah, "Appendix: Demographic Profile of Asian American Adults," *Being Asian in America*, Pew Research Center, May 8, 2023, https://www.pewresearch.org/race-ethnicity/2023/05/08/asian-american-identity-appendix

25. See "Actors' Equity Association Demographics and Statistics," Zippia, accessed June 15, 2025, https://www.zippia.com/actors-equity-association-careers-95391/demographics/

8
"Haunted by the Specters of What They Will Become"
St(age) Directions and the Default Body

Bess Rowen

> All characters except Dance Teacher Pat and The Moms are between the ages of 11 and 14 years old. However, they should be played by adult actors (for the most part) and should range in age from 12 to 75+. There is no need for any of the actors to resemble teenagers. (In fact, please resist this impulse!) And the more diverse the cast the better.
> —CLARE BARRON, *DANCE NATION*[1]

A group of adult women and one adult man stand onstage dressed in sailor costumes, posed in an awkward tableau appropriate for a tween dance troupe. An adult man in street clothes sits cross-legged and voices the thoughts of an infant. A woman in her sixties kisses her crush, a teenage boy, in the front seat of a car. These scenes from Clare Barron's *Dance Nation*, Jordan Harrison's *Log Cabin*, and David Lindsay-Abaire and Jeanine Tesori's *Kimberly Akimbo* show how frequently contemporary theater audiences view mature adult bodies as children and teenagers without any attempt to hide the space between the visible age of the actor—what age theorist Margaret Morganroth Gullette terms "the default body"[2]—and the contextual age of the character. All three of these plays focus on a particular type of age performance that challenges two frequent aspects of discussions of aging in the theater: first, that discussions of age and theater necessarily center on elderly characters with visible signs of (old) age; and, second, that actors playing younger characters are meant to do so without an acknowledgment of that fact. By foregrounding the ways in which adults play these young characters, *Dance Nation*, *Log Cabin*, and *Kimberly Akimbo* reveal how a visible age gap between actor and character can provide more nuanced performances of youth and various stages of adulthood by directly challenging the youth/age binary and thereby highlighting how these experiences of age overlap.

Additionally, casting older adults also reminds us that liminal childhood and teenage moments still live within us, regardless of our current age. This visible distance stages the idea that Kathleen Woodward describes when she writes: "we are made of different age-selves, that psychically there is no one true self defined by age but a continually fluctuating oscillation between our older selves and our younger selves."[3] In an essay accompanying *Dance Nation*, Barron explains her casting concept as follows: "The girls are played by women ranging from their 20s to their 60s because I was tired of the casting convention of hiring petite 25-year-olds to play 13. I didn't want the characters in the play to look like what you think teenage girls should look like—because teenage girls don't really look like that! Also, because the play is really about how we carry what happens to us when we're 13 through the rest of our lives."[4] In Barron's play, the girls (and one boy) in Dance Teacher Pat's troupe deal with crushes, periods, masturbation, friendships, injuries, and uncomfortable attention from adult men, which are experiences that adult women (or people who were socialized as girls) who are reading, watching, or performing the play have likely encountered. Despite casting older actors to play younger roles, *Dance Nation* also leans into the almost bacchic, frenzied energy that lurks inside of an adolescent, hormonal body. This bubbles to the surface during one rehearsal of a dance number that is supposed to be about Gandhi. Barron writes in her stage directions:

> *Except it's not really like Gandhi.*
>
> *It's more like baby sexy robots. Bloodsucking robots who want to destroy the world and then fuck it after it's dead.*
>
> *They are barely wearing any clothes. They are touching their bodies. They are gnashing their teeth—all of them have fangs now. Sharp, pointy teeth. . . .*
>
> *They are climbing up the walls.* MAEVE *is chewing on the light bulbs—glass in her mouth.*[5]

The specific energy of this scene would be very difficult to watch if it were performed by a group of thirteen-year-old girls, especially because of the sexualized elements of violence. But watching an actor in her late sixties play this role, as was the case when Ellen Maddow played Maeve in the 2018 premiere production at Playwrights Horizons in New York, became a celebration of the default body's ability to encompass the frenetic energy at the core of this character's expression of being thirteen. The affective stage directions and casting notes in *Dance Nation*, *Log Cabin*, and the musical *Kimberly Akimbo* provide opportunities for us to rethink how we represent youth onstage in ways that challenge simplistic stereotypes of multiple age groups. In contrast, the nonmusical version of *Kimberly Akimbo* demonstrates what happens if playwrights do not explain how to play against age type.

Dance Nation, *Log Cabin*, and the musical version of *Kimberly Akimbo* all demonstrate approaches to representing youth with visibly adult bodies, and their stage directions are explicitly written in ways that encourage actors to play against the stereotypical representations of youth. This chapter uses close examinations of the affective stage directions in these three scripts to illustrate how writing about what a character *does* instead of simply how a character *looks* can encourage more expansive and creative approaches to representing a variety of ages and experiences of ages/aging. Affective stage directions are, as I have written elsewhere, "*stage directions written in a manner that aims to engage the actor affectively in the thoughts, feelings, and/or mood of a given moment, character, scene, or overall play.* Affective stage directions are about *why* and, more abstractly, *how* certain events happen as opposed to *what* happens."[6] As Barron's casting instructions show, paratexts, particularly in the form of affective stage directions, have the potential to disrupt simplistic representations of aging across the continuum of age from youth to old age, especially in scenarios where an actor is playing a starkly different age than their own. Building on the work of age studies scholars such as Kathleen Woodward, Valerie Barnes Lipscomb, and Margaret Gullette, this chapter focuses on how age is literally scripted to establish ways of reading affective stage directions and other forms of affective paratexts that could help make theatrical representations of age more nuanced. After situating this argument within the scope of other age studies scholarship and my own concept of affective stage directions, I perform close readings of the representation of age in *Dance Nation*, *Log Cabin*, and the musical *Kimberly Akimbo* against that of the sparsely stage-directioned, nonmusical *Kimberly Akimbo* to show how the published playscripts portray the bodily representations of age in actor and character alike. Because stage directions deal with the transition from page to stage, studying the text reveals what kinds of potential performances are contained within them. All these representations are also entrenched in the staging of gender, through *Log Cabin*'s embodiment of a trans man's childhood and through *Kimberly Akimbo*'s and *Dance Nation*'s nuanced portrayals of the messiness of teenage girlhood. The following section provides an intersectional bridge between aging and gendered aspects of marginalization. Following an analysis of the ways that stage directions challenge stereotypes of age and gender simultaneously within these plays, I conclude by focusing on one of Lynne Segal's points from *Out of Time*. She writes, "As we age, changing year on year, we also retain, in one manifestation or another, traces of all the selves we have been, creating a type of temporal vertigo and rendering us psychically, in one sense, all ages and no age."[7] This is what the adult actors playing children accomplish in *Dance Nation*, *Log Cabin*, and the musical version of *Kimberly Akimbo*.

Although scholarship that focuses on theater and aging is of growing interest (as demonstrated by this edited volume), there is still less of a focus on aging as a topic that applies to representing youth as well as advanced age. Theorists such as Lipscomb and Gullette address both playing older and playing younger, yet both are focused on the scale of older and younger *adults*. But what of minors, both teenagers and children? Teenage girls in theater tend to be relegated to well-worn stereotypes like the "mean girl" or the "Lolita,"[8] while preverbal children are often substituted with props (bundles of clothes, for example) or puppets. By focusing on what plays ask these children and teenage characters to do—rather than how they ask these characters to look—we can observe how plays written with vast age discrepancies between default and character bodies ask us to define age by *actions* rather than *appearances*. This much more equitable and complex concept of aging acknowledges that "age" looks different for every individual due to a complex matrix of identity markers and genetic factors. Analyzing approaches to casting and embodied age via the affective stage directions in these plays reflects the dynamic experiences of aging that challenge a presupposed binary of youth and age through nonrealistic theatrical performance. In short, stage directions allow us to think casting otherwise, enabling us to be more open to the idea of experiencing differently aged selves simultaneously, while bringing out the actor's "inner child."

PLAYED BY: THE SPACE BETWEEN DEFAULT BODY AND CHARACTER BODY

Harrison's *Log Cabin* was produced as part of the same Playwrights Horizons season that featured *Dance Nation*, leading to an unusual confluence of this visible space between the default body's age and the character's age. *Log Cabin* tells the story of a gay couple, Ezra and Chris, and a lesbian couple, Pam and Jules, who are forced to confront their homonormativity following the reintroduction of an old friend, who has recently transitioned, into their friend circle. The lesbian couple's baby is played by an adult man, and when the group's friend, Henry, finally appears, it is revealed that this role is "*played by the same actor who plays Jules and Pam's baby. Very butch.*"[9] After a series of surprising connections and uncouplings, Henry ends up pregnant with Ezra's baby (via Chris's sperm). Although Ezra and Chris are no longer together by the time the baby is born, the play ends with the two babies—played by the same actors as the characters of Henry and Chris—having a conversation about the future.

While having a man in his late thirties play an infant is an obvious age difference, an even more extreme version of this dynamic can be found in *Kimberly Akimbo*, a David Lindsay-Abaire play that was turned into a hit Broadway musical with music by Jeanine Tesori. The titular character has a progeria-like condition that prematurely ages her, which Lindsay-Abaire represents in the casting breakdown for the play by noting that "*Kimberly is sixteen, but she's played by an actress in her sixties or seventies.*"[10] The musical notably changes this in its stage directions for act 1, scene 1, which state, "*Eventually we see that her face is not the face of a teenage girl at all. Kimberly is almost sixteen but looks as if she's in her seventies.*"[11] Kimberly's approaching sixteenth birthday is not a "sweet sixteen," but instead a reminder that she has reached the average lifespan of most teens with her diagnosis.

Despite this fact, Kimberly hangs out with her friends and her nerdy, anagram-loving crush—Jeff in the play, Seth in the musical—a teenage boy meant to look like, and be played by, a teenage boy. A key point of both the play and the musical is that the characters finally share a kiss as they drive away with the money that Kimberly's elderly, nonthreatening appearance has enabled her to steal without suspicion. An article in the *Washington Post* about the Broadway musical specifies that the actor playing Kimberly, Victoria Clark, was sixty-three, and that the actor playing Seth, Justin Cooley, was nineteen in January 2023.[12] Thus, in Broadway's *Kimberly Akimbo*, both love interests are playing younger, but we are only meant to notice that age gap in the character of Kimberly. Yet, casting Jeff/Seth too young runs the risk of framing the kiss between the adult Kimberly and her youthful crush as awkward at best and predatory at worst. The musical's stage directions read: "*They look at each other again and, eventually, after much tension, slowly lean in and kiss. They separate and sit in silence, happy but nervous.*"[13] The single change in the stage directions for the kiss from the play to the musical comes in the shift of the play's use of "*petrified*" to the musical's use of "*nervous*," which seems to clarify that there is simply teenage discomfort, not actual fear. The inclusion of "*happy*" is also here to ensure that both characters appear to have enjoyed the consensual kiss, which would still be cause for concern if Seth looked too visibly young. The default bodies of Seth and Kimberly have to be able to tell the story of romance without conjuring ideas of pedophilia, so the tone of their interactions is crucial. And affective stage directions provide that tonal information.

Textual approaches to illuminating these kinds of age gaps between actor and character vary, but playwrights such as Harrison and Barron use their stage directions to challenge reductive representations of either age or youth, while Lindsay-Abaire's play version says nothing else about Kimberly aside from the fact that the character is sixteen and the actor playing her should be in her sixties or seventies. Lindsay-Abaire's avoidance of the subject of *how* the actor is meant to play (or internally imagine) "being sixteen" follows what Lipscomb argues regarding David Henry Hwang's omission of any discussion of age and aging in the text of *M. Butterfly*: "The silence permits freedom of staging, but it also indicates that performing age is transparent, unremarkable, and conventional."[14] In contrast to Lindsay-Abaire, Harrison is not silent on the matter. Although his casting note dodges a description of the Baby, he leaves the stage directions preceding the Baby's first entrance to explain, "*In the next room, Jules talks to her BABY, played by a large grown man. . . . Jules's Baby doesn't act like a kid. He's just a placid, hairy, matter-of-fact adult surrounded by some expensive-looking plush animals and hand-crafted wooden toys.*"[15] These stage directions describe not how the actor should physically portray a Baby, but instead how the Baby should come across. Comparatively, Barron takes expressing the distinction between the default bodies and character bodies a step further in her casting note, which reads, in part: "Think of it as a ghost play: the actors' older bodies are haunting these 13-year-old characters. (We're getting to see who they grow up to be!) and these 13-year-old characters are haunted by the specters of what they will become. At times we should be fully in '13-year-old land' with all its ridiculousness, pain and pleasure. And at times we should be palpably aware of the actors' real ages and their distance from this moment in their lives."[16] These words make clear that all the actors, who could range in age from twelve to over seventy-five, are meant to simultaneously represent their own age and age thirteen throughout this script, challenging the agist, youth-centered essentialism that can be present in casting practices.

In each of these examples, the audience must be willing to go along with watching actors play ages they have been in the past. This follows Gullette's assertion that "when actors play *younger*, we are willing to see double" due to "our culture's unconscious shared understandings of the default body's development." This is primarily because an older actor "*has been younger* psychologically and physiologically: she could draw on sense memories from her own childhood as well as observation."[17] Lipscomb notes that older actors can also add a different dimensionality to younger characters by "playing what they do not believe to be true (such as teenage nobility), but constructing their own relative truth in performing and affirming a model of ageing that differs from the master narrative of decline and decay."[18] These aspects of representation, while important, do not account for the elements of age/aging that are written into the performances via the prescripted stage directions. Seeing a senior actor portraying a stereotypical teenager can reinforce the idea that age is a set hierarchy where youth is defined by ineffectual inexperience and age is equated to earned wisdom, what Gullette describes as "one of these cloudy age effects: that where there is an age difference, the older self is superior."[19] While these relationships can be true, plays like *Dance Nation*, *Log Cabin*, and the musical version of *Kimberly Akimbo* trouble the binaries of "old" and "young," "naive" and "experienced," by mixing the representations of both onstage.

AFFECTIVE AGING: AFFECTIVE STAGE DIRECTIONS AND SCRIPTING AGE

In my book *The Lines Between the Lines*, I have argued that some plays trouble stable concepts of age by focusing on the characters' actions and reasoning rather than relying on the theatrical codes for signifying various ages, such as a whiny vocal tone for a teenager or white hair for a senior citizen. Throughout this section I return to Barron, Harrison, and Lindsay-Abaire and Tesori's stage directions—as well as the play version of *Kimberly Akimbo*'s absent stage directions—to make large points about how representations of age are productively expanded through the stated casting conventions and character behavioral arcs of these plays. Barron, Harrison, and the musical *Kimberly Akimbo* all write affective stage directions that are more concerned with the tone of the performance than with its visual appearance. This approach is certainly present in Barron's casting instructions, which describe not only how one should think of the connection between the ages of the performers one sees in front of them and the characters they are portraying, but also why that distance should appear and disappear throughout the play. Harrison's opening stage directions for the Baby are also affective, prompting the performer and production team to avoid acting stereotypes involved in portraying childhood, as this character "*doesn't act like a kid*."[20] Instead, Harrison's stage directions make the actor's default body a feature of this character's appearance, tone, and mood.

The way that Barron and Harrison use affective stage directions to reveal the mood and tone of their youthful characters (as played by adults) works to resist certain stereotypes about how we portray youth onstage, which can lead actors and directors toward more expansive representations of youth and age. Barron addresses this directly in her playwright's perspective essay when she discusses the convention of having actors in their early twenties play teenagers onstage, but it is also a feature of film and television. The teenagers in almost every television show or movie about high school students are played by adults—a fact that is parodied to hilarious effect in *Scary Movie* (2000) when the teenage character Greg (played by thirty-three-year-old Lochlyn Munro) says that if they were in a movie, "they'd cast people in their late twenties, early thirties to play us," causing the entire friend group (of adults playing teens) to laugh.[21] Of course, one way to resist this trope would be to cast actual thirteen-year-olds to play the dance troupe, but doing so would risk having those actors work through material that they either have not yet experienced (such as menstruation) or are currently experiencing (such as the breaking up of a friendship). Similarly, Harrison does not expect a two-year-old to be able to have matter-of-fact conversations or sit still onstage while simulated sex acts take place. Furthermore, the silent Baby's dialogue and persona are shown to be a projection of the adults who speak to him, so an actual child is not required. And the musical version of *Kimberly Akimbo* uses both stage directions and song lyrics to highlight the fact that the character's default body implies an age and experience that is untrue for the character, but would be true for any actor stepping into the role.

Barron, Harrison, and Lindsay-Abaire and Tesori highlight the distance between the default body and the character body, allowing the visual space between the actor's age and the character's age to remind the audience that we carry our thirteen-year-old, two-year-old, and sixteen-year-old selves with us the same way our thirteen-year-old, two-year-old, and sixteen-year-old selves carry the future potential of our adulthood with them. Barron's approach here could be seen as working against what Gullette believes to be true of the paradoxical gravitas of age onstage and the discrimination against older actors in the industry. Gullette writes, "I have tried to show that age—*having an age*—is already unconsciously treated in some venues as a valuable 'property' whose value grows over time. Thematizing bodies often reinforces dysfunction, critics worry. But not in this case, where the whole psychophysical spectrum is in play, in ordinary life as it is on stage—wherever much of what is called 'character' is conveyed by age apparent on the default body."[22] Although Gullette correctly admits that, despite the associations between age and wisdom, age-blind casting would often result in a disappearance of roles for actors over forty, such thinking seems to be tied to the realm of theatrical realism. The visible distance between the default bodies of the actors and their characters onstage in these plays works against the representational conventions of kitchen-sink realism while still representing relatable experiences to audiences. *Dance Nation* attempts neither to hide the default bodies nor to reduce the characters to the age of the default bodies playing them, particularly because the possible default bodies for those characters can range so broadly in this nonrealistic play. This even extends to the dance portions of the script, which are never meant to be about actual dancing. The first number shown is "*a complex and exquisitely rendered ballet of the face,*" in which the performers "*do the dance as if we could only see a close-up on their faces. They are perfectly still except for their eyebrows, their nostrils, their mouths, etc. and the occasional dramatic arm movement.*"[23] This means that older actors whose default bodies might not easily or safely do choreography can still be full members of this story. These choreographic affective stage directions do not erase the default bodies of the performers, but they refocus the audience's attention on the characters' feelings as they dance, rather than on the virtuosity of the dance moves performed. The whole psychophysical spectrum of human experience could be on display in this moment, but each character is defined by their emotional responses to the imagined routine instead of by the age and abilities of their default body.

Log Cabin also highlights the difference between the default body and the character body in an antirealistic fashion without that being the entire story of the play. The first time that we meet the then-one-year-old Baby, Jules is carrying on a conversation with the child—played by the adult actor who also plays Henry—while Jules's wife, Pam, and their friends, Chris and Ezra, discuss how poorly Ezra handled Henry's pronouns during a dinner party. The baby monitor is the conduit between the two spaces. After Jules finishes telling the Baby about how she and Pam are not yet living happily ever after, the action cuts back to the living room: "*Instead of the conversation we've just been watching, we hear the sound of an actual one-year-old through the monitor, gurgling innocuously.*"[24] The default body here is doubly configured, as trans man Henry now gets to experience a gender euphoric childhood and Jules gets to imagine her son as a verbal, mature adult. It is soon revealed that two-year-old Hartley is still nonverbal, which lends new perspective to this fantasy. I will return to how gender functions in this scenario shortly, but for now, I want to highlight how Harrison obviates the need to perform like a "gurgling baby" with a simple yet effective device that challenges our perception of how small children are represented onstage.

What does it mean when playwrights do not write affective stage directions that lead future production teams away from easy caricatures of youth? The play version of *Kimberly Akimbo* leaves almost all the character work to the dialogue, risking the reduction of its main character to a punch line. Before we know that Kimberly is sixteen, the stage directions introduce her by noting, "*An old woman sits, shivering*."[25] The musical handles this better, with its initial stage directions focusing on what Kimberly is doing before mentioning her appearance: "Lights rise on a teenage girl standing, in skates. She looks around, searching for someone. She looks at her watch, then to the door—but no sign of him." The stage directions then move on to her apparent age: "*Eventually we see that her face is not the face of a teenage girl at all. Kimberly is almost sixteen but looks as if she's in her seventies*."[26] The first few scenes of the play introduce Jeff, a boy from school who wants to do a science project on Kimberly's aging disorder. Although her family basically ignores Kimberly's apparent age, and therefore the actor's default body, Jeff is shown to see her and accept her. Kimberly's age, and her premature aging (signaled both by the casting description and by the discussion of her diagnosis), is also not stagnant within the confines of the play. After a health incident, Kimberly's "*hair has turned a shock of white*," and she moves "*markedly slower*."[27] With its focus on the physical appearance and associations of an aging body in decline, the play version of *Kimberly Akimbo* falls short of challenging the connections between aging, disability, and death, thereby enabling its protagonist to be reduced to "an old woman," whose appearance and physical ability are the major point of tension in her story.

Notably, the musical version of this same scene omits these stage directions about Kimberly's physical changes following her hospitalization. In this case, the lack of stage directions is a positive step, as it frees the actor in the musical from stereotypical representations of the decline so often associated with aged/aging bodies. Of course, a nuanced performance of Kimberly in the play could also push back on this portrayal, but there is nothing in the original playscript that insists on this. The musical version, particularly evidenced by the Broadway production featuring the younger-looking, spry Clark in the lead role, could be seen to challenge what an aging disorder looks like, but it still relies on casting conventions that make aging easier to represent if the actor's default body is still traditionally attractive—white, able-bodied, thin, and younger looking. Casting any production of *Kimberly Akimbo* (play or musical) must contend with the combined forces of ageism and misogyny, which put pressure on casting an actor with conventional attractiveness to counteract some of the stigma associated with an aging female body. This is why Kathleen Woodward identifies "feminist aging" as an important lens in a world where "performing age is principally a bodily effect anchored in visuality that structures—and is structured by—the twin force fields of the American youth–old age system and the conventional codes of masculinity and femininity that dominate the sex-gender system."[28] Whereas *Dance Nation* and *Log Cabin* use the distance between the default bodies and character bodies to expand our concepts of youth and maturity, even the musical version of *Kimberly Akimbo* struggles with the cultural binary of youth/age as a barrier to be overcome.

"VERY BUTCH": GENDER AND AGE

As the discussion of the standards of attractiveness for Kimberly's casting shows, the ways we represent age onstage are also gendered. As Gullette writes, "Gender always has an age too, although theorists rarely notice this."[29] Gullette contends not only that portrayals of (gendered) lives rarely show the entire spectrum of age, but also that youth is overprivileged for women performers in the theater: "Hiring young is sexist—because in our visual culture women appear to 'age' sooner than men—as well as middle-ageist and ageist."[30] This means that "hiring old" can challenge sexism as well as ageism by disrupting the ways that performances of gender become aligned with certain character types and stories. *Dance Nation* and the musical *Kimberly Akimbo* subvert the kinds of teenage girls shown in Lillian Hellman's *The Children's Hour*, Arthur Miller's *The Crucible*, and Tina Fey, Nell Benjamin, and Jeff Richmond's *Mean Girls: The Musical*, all of which focus on teenage girls as tools of destruction for both adults and their fellow teens, while *Log Cabin* stages a trans actor portraying trans childhood, filling a representational void of trans aging.

The two strongest instances of this pushback against gendered age stereotypes in *Dance Nation* also highlight how having adult actors play these roles eases the burden of watching an actor portraying something that they might not fully understand. The first comes when Amina, the star dancer of the group, is having a discussion with Dance Teacher Pat, the adult man who coaches the dance troupe. After Amina lingers to make sure he is not angry with her, Dance Teacher Pat reminds her that he knows when she is not giving her all at an audition. Then, "*He sort of swats her butt. It's not sexual???????? But also weird and uncomfortable for a grown-ass man to be swatting a thirteen-year-old's butt. AMINA is horrified. And also, she loves it.*"[31] The gender and age dynamics at play here are crucial. This moment stages a fully adult woman, perhaps one who is older than Dance Teacher Pat, having her butt swatted by her teacher in a way that is both scandalous and exciting to her. If this were staged with an actual thirteen-year-old girl playing

Amina, then we would be watching a Lolita-esque moment in which any indication that Amina might be enjoying this experience could easily be read as victim blaming during a moment of nonconsensual contact. Changing the gender of any of the characters involved also affects the reading of this scene, as an adult man and an underage girl have a large power imbalance despite any additional intersectional matrices of race, physical ability, class, and so forth. But an adult woman playing Amina is free to show her as a complex individual who is also excited by a man's possible sexual attraction to her, even if that man is her older dance teacher.

Such casting can also remind an audience that people of many ages can want others to be attracted to them, while also wanting any sexual contact to be consensual and appropriate. Barron includes another important set of affective stage directions that disrupt a sanitized view of adolescent girlhood. After their big performance, during which the performer playing Gandhi, named Zuzu, fumbles and stays on the ground as Amina jumps in to do her part immediately and flawlessly, the girls retreat to their separate spaces. We then watch as,

> AMINA *masturbates.*
> CONNIE *with her horses under the moon.*
> SOFIA *in the bathroom, still weeping and scrubbing her bloody tights.*
> *(A triptych of girlhood.)*[32]

Once again, asking fully adult women to use their sense memories of adolescence to recall early experiments with masturbation, playtime with model horses or other toys, or the shame of being surprised by their period is far preferable to asking thirteen-year-old girls to relate to these experiences while they are at various points within these three journeys. Not to mention the fact that watching a thirteen-year-old girl simulating masturbation onstage not only is inappropriate, but also might end up catering to audience members with illegal and predatory predilections. And yet all three of these experiences are likely relatable to people socialized as girls within the United States. Casting adults therefore lets the actors' default bodies portray these experiences without concern about the performers' distance from these moments.

Both of these scenes from *Dance Nation* focus on the layered experiences of pleasure and embarrassment that comprise the "growing pains" that we associate with our own adolescence, while the visibly adult default bodies of the performers enable easier identification with these experiences while also reclaiming the hormonal sexuality of puberty within an older default body.

But these scenes are remarkable because they center the teenage girls' experiences rather than those of the adults around them. Somewhat paradoxically, *Log Cabin* can be seen to do the same with the representation of Pam and Jules's baby. Although, as I have said above, the Baby is doubled with Henry and speaks like a rather relaxed adult, the radical part of this staging is not a result of Jules's fantasy of her child. Regardless of whose imagination creates this adult Baby, the result is that a trans actor steps into the role of a gender-affirming small child. Harrison's stage directions do not focus on Henry's transness the way that the dialogue does, which is another important aspect of this doubling. As I mentioned previously, before we know who Henry is, we hear Jules, Pam, Ezra, and Chris discussing Ezra's inability to think of his longtime friend as a man, while we watch the actor who will play Henry portray the lesbian couple's baby. Harrison's stage directions discuss the Baby's matter-of-fact affect and only imply a gender presentation by noting that he is "*a large grown man*" and that he is "*hairy*."[33] Later, when Henry enters, we learn that he is played by the same actor as the Baby and that Henry is "very butch."[34] So, by the transitive principle of casting, we know that the Baby must also be "very butch."

And yet we also know that the likelihood of a family acknowledging that a baby is "very butch" is low, which means that this moment performatively transmits the affect of a butch infancy and toddlerhood to a trans character and a trans actor. By referring to the baby as "very butch," Harrison also focuses on the gender performance of masculinity as separate from the gender identity of "man." Not every trans man is "very butch," while some cis women and nonbinary folx are. Probably none of the adults who identify as "very butch" would have been called that as a newborn, so this is also an affirming moment that brings gender nonconforming, queer, and trans youth into the story. Theatrical representations of LGBTQ+ youth in general are scarce, with Small Alison from Lisa Kron and Jeanine Tesori's *Fun Home* providing a rare exception. *Log Cabin*'s ending seems to bring Pam and Jules's baby some community with the arrival of Ezra and Henry's baby (doubled with Chris), but we still spend most of the time with Henry as the only adult playing a child onstage. The fact that he now gets to serve as an elder to this younger queer baby (who is the child of a trans man and a gay man, and who is played by the same actor who played a gay man) is also an important milestone, as that relationship illustrates both the chosen family of an idealized LGBTQ+ community and the biological queer family that Henry and Ezra have created. *Log Cabin* affirms Henry's masculinity and butch gender presentation in ways that challenge the debates about the nature of transgender identity that the two gay couples express in their dialogue. Henry, the character, is experiencing a kind of second childhood/puberty because of hormone replacement therapy, while the Baby is experiencing his first childhood. A child actor could not possibly hold the nuances of the LGBTQ+ representations within this story without a great deal of stage(d) magic.

There is no staged magic required of the representations of age in either version of *Kimberly Akimbo*, although the act of showing a woman in her sixties as being an ingenue could be thought of in these terms. It is, unfortunately, revolutionary to show a sixty-something woman as sexually desirable, but the fact that the play revolves around a simple love story does not complicate a view of either teenage girlhood or senior womanhood. The musical takes these ideas further, surrounding the titular character with a teenage chorus and multiple scenes of homework and skating. The songs, too, serve as a form of affective stage directions, with italicized lines like, "*We live in a house that's haunted. / There's always you, there's always me, / and there's the ghost of a girl I'll never be. / There's the ghost of a girl I'll never be.*"[35] The musical's Kimberly is also haunted by specters, but not of what she will become. She is haunted by the specter of the girl she never was *and* the adult she will not live to be. The earliest action Kimberly takes in the play is to contact a boy who wants to use her for a science project. Although we are meant to warm to Jeff, Kimberly is clearly motivated by his interest regardless of his goals. The play's greatest achievement is in its reminder that women of any age could play a romantic interest, but it offers this reminder without bothering to explain what Kimberly thinks about that process, or how an adult actor should weigh girlish enthusiasm with fear of public opinion, if at all. While the play version of *Kimberly Akimbo* misses an opportunity to show how romantic interest exists in and among other forces in both girlhood and senior womanhood, the musical version's script/book takes major steps in this direction. A future production could cast someone whose default body does not fit as many of the stereotypical norms for a Broadway leading lady and thereby not leave age as the singular form of marginalization for a character who is dealing with multiple forces at play.

CONCLUSION: THE RELATIVITY OF AGING

Watching a woman in her sixties play a sixteen-year-old girl without any nods to that difference has the potential "to deconstruct the discursive binary of youth and old age, as all ages are revealed as performed. Moreover, exploring common ground among generations combats our society's endemic ageism."[36] The musical version of *Kimberly Akimbo* does not accomplish this quite as successfully as *Dance Nation* and *Log Cabin* do, but it shows how a few key changes to a playscript can open doors to the potential for more expansive representations of age and aging. All three examples follow Lynne Segal's notion that "it is the *future* that haunts the present, and not the past," by asking actors to represent the present with default bodies that visualize their characters' futures. Barron, Harrison, and Lindsay-Abaire and Tesori take care to acknowledge the overlapping experiences of the default bodies and character bodies within their plays in ways that Lindsay-Abaire's play simply does not.[37] Barron's dance troupe offers the potential to see multiple generations of performers portraying thirteen-year-old girls, each bringing their own unique positionality toward age and gender to that performance. As Barron says, we get to see who these girls will grow up to be. Additionally, Harrison's play presents the opportunity for an adult trans man to embody a childhood experience he was not able to have due to society's strict gender roles, and to do so in a way that affirms the age and gender of his default body. The trans future finally gets to visibly haunt a childhood present, working against the gender dysphoria trans folx might encounter when thinking about their childhoods.

Although it is possible that performances of all three of these plays can challenge the performance of both youth and various stages of adulthood, only *Dance Nation* and *Log Cabin* are written in ways that affectively transmit alternative viewpoints about how to think about these youthful characters by encouraging them to live fully within the visible default bodies of adults of multiple ages. Playwrights who write affective stage directions in plays that explore representations of age participate in the work of dismantling common stereotypes in the portrayal of youth and advanced age. By focusing on the multiple ways that these affective stage directions can be interpreted and embodied, production teams have the opportunity to portray more diverse experiences of ages in ways that also expand our concept of how gender intersects with age. Theatrical characters, even more than everyday people, are written in hopes that bodies of future performers haunt their present state. Affective stage directions catalyze this relationship between the default body of the actor and the differently aged body of the character, meaning that focusing on the transmission of affect between these overlapping bodies is what enables the characters in these plays to be haunted by the specters of what they will become.

NOTES

1. Clare Barron, *Dance Nation* (Oberon Books, 2018), 9.
2. Margaret Morganroth Gullette, "Acting Age on Stage: Age-Appropriate Casting, the Default Body, and Valuing the Property of Having an Age," *Journal of Dramatic Theory and Criticism* 18, no. 1 (Fall 2003): 9.

3. Kathleen Woodward, "Performing Age, Performing Gender," *NWSA Journal* 18, no. 1 (Spring 2006): 173.

4. Clare Barron, "Playwright's Perspective: Clare Barron," Playwrights Horizons, February 15, 2018, https://www.playwrightshorizons.org/shows/trailers/playwrights-perspective-dance-nation/

5. Barron, *Dance Nation*, 52–53.

6. Bess Rowen, *The Lines Between the Lines: How Stage Directions Affect Embodiment* (University of Michigan Press, 2021), 72 (emphasis in original).

7. Lynne Segal, *Out of Time: The Pleasures and the Perils of Ageing* (Verso, 2013), 4.

8. Vladimir Nabokov's 1955 novel *Lolita* describes a coquettish twelve-year-old girl who "comes on" to middle-aged protagonist Humbert Humbert (according to him).

9. Jordan Harrison, *Log Cabin* (Performances in Print, 2018), 42.

10. David Lindsay-Abaire, *Kimberly Akimbo* (Dramatists Play Service, 2003), 5.

11. David Lindsay-Abaire and Jeanine Tesori, *Kimberly Akimbo: A New Musical* (Theatre Communications Group, 2023), 9.

12. Peter Marks, "How Does a 63-Year-Old Play a Teen? In Victoria Clark's Case, Superbly," *Washington Post*, January 13, 2023.

13. Lindsay-Abaire and Tesori, *Kimberly Akimbo*, 150.

14. Valerie Barnes Lipscomb, "Age in *M. Butterfly*: Unquestioned Performance," *Modern Drama* 59, no. 2 (Summer 2016): 197.

15. Harrison, *Log Cabin*, 29.

16. Barron, *Dance Nation*, 9.

17. Gullette, "Acting Age," 13 (emphasis in original).

18. Valerie Barnes Lipscomb, "'The Play's the Thing': Theatre as a Scholarly Meeting Ground in Age Studies," *International Journal of Ageing and Later Life* 7, no. 2 (2012): 132.

19. Gullette, "Acting Age," 14.

20. Harrison, *Log Cabin*, 29.

21. *Scary Movie*, dir. Keenen Ivory Wayans (Dimension Films, 2000), 21:27.

22. Gullette, "Acting Age," 23–24 (emphasis in original).

23. Barron, *Dance Nation*, 19.

24. Harrison, *Log Cabin*, 30.

25. Lindsay-Abaire, *Kimberly Akimbo*, 5.

26. Lindsay-Abaire and Tesori, *Kimberly Akimbo*, 9.

27. Lindsay-Abaire, *Kimberly Akimbo*, 44, 49.

28. Woodward, "Performing Age," 167.

29. Gullette, "Acting Age," 8.

30. Gullette, 25.

31. Barron, *Dance Nation*, 67.

32. Barron, 111.

33. Harrison, *Log Cabin*, 29.

34. Harrison, 42.

35. Lindsay-Abaire and Tesori, *Kimberly Akimbo*, 144.

36. Lipscomb, "The Play's the Thing," 194.

37. Segal, *Out of Time*, 22 (emphasis in original).

9

Aging from Queer and Trans Perspectives

laGeste's Gardenia—10 Years Later[1]

Heunjung Lee

The Belgian dance theater company laGeste's *tanztheater* (dance-theater) piece *Gardenia* (2010) and its restaging with the original cast, *Gardenia—10 Years Later* (2021),[2] both engage with an underrepresented topic in theater and performance: the complexity and attributes of queer and trans aging. Co-created by choreographer Alain Platel, theater director Frank Van Laecke, and composer Steven Prengels, the production portrays nine performers who are at different stages of the aging process. Trans actress Vanessa Van Durme (b. 1948) originally came up with the idea for the production, bringing together drag performers she had worked with in cabaret performances earlier in her life. Its choreography and dramaturgy center on tableaux, (un)dressing, lip-synching, narration, and choreographed sequences. Altogether, they create a space for queer and trans identities that evoke images of a nonlinear temporality of aging subjectivity.

The 2010 production of *Gardenia* premiered in Ghent, Belgium, and toured worldwide for two years with great success, totaling over two hundred performances.[3] *Gardenia—10 Years Later* reunited the entire original cast, apart from Andrea De Laet (1952–2016), who had passed away several years before. However, De Laet's absence is uncannily present throughout the 2021 production: her dress is draped over her empty chair, and performers frequently engage with the costume throughout the course of their dance. Except for the fact that the performers are ten years older and De Laet is absent, the elements of *Gardenia—10 Years Later* are nearly identical to those of the 2010 production.

This chapter analyzes the narrative framework, aesthetic choices, and dramaturgical strategies of *Gardenia—10 Years Later* while paying close attention to both aging and gender and their intersections for queer and trans subjects. I further consider the implications and performative power of restaging the production with the original cast then a decade older. Ultimately, I demonstrate how *Gardenia—10 Years Later* provides a unique viewpoint on aging from a queer and trans perspective. My own examinations are grounded in my experience as an audience member at the live performance I attended in Ghent, Belgium; the video archives of the 2010 and 2021 productions; and the performance script (translated into English by laGeste).[4] I also draw on Thomas Wallner's documentary film *Before the Last Curtain Falls* (2014).[5] This eighty-eight-minute-long documentary film captures some of the daily lives of the performers after the two years of the *Gardenia* tour ended. The documentary shows some members' homes, workplaces, and lovers, along with interviews sharing their life stories and their current concerns and dreams.

Gardenia—10 Years Later features six older performers ranging from their sixties to their eighties who self-identify as queer, transgender, or gender nonconforming.[6] They are accompanied by two younger professional dancers (a male dancer in his thirties and a female dancer in her fifties), who are described as Young Guy and Real Woman in the performance program and script.[7] While some cast members like Dirk Van Vaerenbergh (b. 1954) and Griet Debacker (b. 1964) have performed in other theater productions and television shows, most older cast members are amateur performers who engage in drag performance at queer nightclubs while continuing their professions as nurses, public servants, and clerks. Inspired by the documentary film *Yo Soy Así* (*This Is Me*, 2000) by Sonia Herman Dolz, which portrays the closing of a cabaret in Barcelona and the lives of older trans artists, *Gardenia—10 Years Later* suggests a fictional setting: the opening scene implies that this performance is the grand finale for a long-lasting cabaret theater.

Gardenia—10 Years Later draws on the memories and emotions shared among six older drag performers who have lived as LGBTQ+ individuals, born between the 1940s and 1960s in Belgium. While this production does not explicitly depict personal stories, it loosely draws on the life experiences of each performer and portrays the shared memories, pain, and joy among older queer and trans subjects. *Gardenia—10 Years Later* is an autobiographical performance that presents a space where the performed identity, presence, and materiality of aging become the center of the production's dramaturgy and aesthetics. Instead of retelling real-life stories and memories, the piece expresses themes of violence, loneliness, and the search for love through the interweaving of spoken text, song, and dance. Suprisingly, previous articles and reviews focusing on *Gardenia* or *Gardenia—10 Years Later* have only briefly discussed the aging bodies and narratives of aging, instead ruminating more on gender and sexual identity without the intersectional importance of age.[8]

In the introduction to *Performing the Queer Past*, Fintan Walsh writes about the specific time of this cultural production, and the social and legal events that occurred regarding the rights of LGBTQ+ individuals between 2010 and 2021 (the years of the original production and its revival).[9] In my analysis, I also briefly address the topic of gender fluidity represented in the piece, but my primary focus lies in examining how the presence of older community performers and their embodied memories and experiences as older queer and trans individuals challenge the prevailing narrative of aging as decline, offering different perspectives on the life course and growing old.[10] Ruth Pearce argues that in the journey of reclaiming their felt gender across the life course, trans individuals often experience "asynchronous disruptions of the life course" and "depart from the linear norms of straight time in numerous ways, with new beginnings, a reimagined past, and [many of their lives] cut tragically short before any opportunity to age as an adult."[11] Donald Hutera of the *Times* describes *Gardenia* as "a richly layered portrait of gender fluidity and the joys of ageing."[12]

My analysis illuminates how this theatrical dance piece foregrounds nonlinearity through its composition and aesthetics, offering a nuanced portrayal of trans and queer aging as a continuous, joyful, albeit sometimes painful conversation between multiple selves across one's life course. I draw on Anne Davis Basting's "depth model of aging,"[13] a theoretical model that has been employed in multiple studies for its nonlinear approach to aging, encouraging "an envisioning of the young in the older actor's body, and vice versa."[14] The depth model of aging challenges the binary divisions of young and old and a chronological conceptualization of aging. Instead, this model suggests that "any social act of aging is always done in concert with the past, present, and future, no single representation of age can be a stable identity."[15] Basting's depth model views older subjects as embodying "the layers of selves created throughout one's life."[16] Using Basting's model helps us unpack the complex layering of selves in the performance as we read the past and the present simultaneously on the queer and trans bodies of the performers.

OVER THE RAINBOW, NOT OVER THE HILL

Analyzing the opening scene of *Gardenia—10 Years Later* helps show how older queer and trans performers embody younger and older selves *simulta-*

neously. By analyzing the opening scene and the following series of tableaux, I will discuss how *Gardenia—10 Years Later* explores gender fluidity and its intersection with the temporal depth of aging. The performance begins with Van Durme singing Judy Garland's "Over the Rainbow" while all other performers stand behind her, clad in gray suits and looking directly at the audience. Judy Garland is, of course, a renowned gay icon, and this song holds particular significance within the queer community as it conveys themes of escape and dreams for a more accepting world.[17] The low-pitched voice of Van Durme has the quality of a bass; her older, tall, charismatic body is juxtaposed with the more familiar cultural image of a young girl from *The Wizard of Oz* (1939). Transgender scholar and activist Xavia A. Publius argues that Van Durme sings the song "a full octave lower than one would normally sing it," which "set[s] up a trans space by valuing trans vocality." She further states that "the way she performs it," the audience can feel that "there is a lot of life lived by the time of that performance, and a trans life at that."[18] This effect is achieved through the temporal depth of the performer, created by the overlap and the contrast between the original teenage singer and the seventy-five-year-old Van Durme. In the scene, Van Durme speaks from a dual perspective, channeling both her present self and her younger self. This is because, as sung by Van Durme in her seventies, "Over the Rainbow" prompts the audience to question or imagine her childhood and younger self—a younger Van Durme who was trapped in the wrong body or wrongly judged by a heteronormative society as a trans woman, yearning for acceptance. The other performers behind her remain silent while looking directly into the audience. This image may also prompt viewers to contemplate the past life journeys of each performer, allowing the opening scene to present "bod[ies] in depth."[19]

What does embodying layers of differently aged selves mean for older trans adults, "keep[ing] in touch with one's different ages or different age-selves"?[20] The autobiographical stories and interviews of the performers captured in the documentary film *Before the Last Curtain Falls* help me contemplate this question. In the film, the cast members share their childhood photos and talk about how they remember or relate to their pasts. For instance, Van Durme talks about her frustration with people who want to know about her presurgery life, and her struggle to revisit past memories while performing *Gardenia*. In the film, Van Durme says: "On the first day, they are going to put on men's clothing. During the rehearsal, I was like 'oh my gosh.' It's such a long time ago. I had flashbacks. When I was still a boy, when I was sixteen. . . . Crazy feeling. I did not like that at all because I was thinking about the time when I was still struggling with my identity." Here it is clear that one's youth is not necessarily viewed or remembered positively from a queer and trans perspective. On the other hand, there are cast members who have more positive relationships to their pasts. For instance, in the film, De Laet says she still cherishes her forty-four years of life before surgery as she had many beautiful moments. But De Laet also remarks that she did not smile when her parents put her in a boy's suit when she wanted to wear a dress.

In *Gardenia—10 Years Later*, the act of dressing and undressing is the very core of this dance piece. The act of donning various garments, such as suits, floral dresses, and drag costumes worn by the performers in their youth, not only constructs narratives of the piece, but also offers a temporal experience for the performers. Knowing the film's autobiographical accounts of the performers regarding their pasts, we get to see how remembering and enacting one's past can be painful and traumatic. For me, the opening scene of "Over the Rainbow" foregrounds queer and trans bodies embodying temporal depth across a long lifespan. The intersection of this kind of embodiment of different age-selves with their gender identities is visible throughout the performance but also embedded in its narrative.

Following the opening song, Van Durme gives an introductory speech asking the audience to stand up and join her in paying respect to deceased queer and trans colleagues and friends—those who did not have a chance to age into later life. While this practice was part of the original 2010 production, in the 2021 production Van Durme performs the scene by looking at De Laet's empty chair. The loss of one of their own highlights the early deaths of queer and trans people in our society, while also making them feel more tangible and visible.[21] Van Durme then introduces each of the older cast members. The older cast members walk out and all stand next to her as they are introduced—except for Young Guy, who remains at the back of the stage. The rest hold hands and raise them in the air, implying a celebration.

After this introductory scene, the performers enact a series of tableaux vivants for approximately ten minutes. As the sound of castanets plays, resembling the ticking of a clock, Young Guy gradually bends forward to enact a stereotypical old man's body. He exaggerates the trembling of his hands and legs. The older performers also join him, enacting the physicality of a typical old body: they look down at the floor and walk slowly with their hands behind their backs. The celebratory and joyful mood of the opening scene is over, and they all express lethargy, melancholy, and sadness. As such, the performance of "old-old" can be seen as a reinscription of the ageist view of aging into old age, associating old age with decline and negativity.[22] However, considering the emphasized constructedness and performativity of ages and genders in the following tableaux, the performance of a stereotypical old body functions as a questioning of the culturally constructed images of the old, rather than a reinforcing of the ageist view of old age.

The performers slowly approach chairs placed on both sides of the stage, facing the center. One by one, they bring their chairs to the center of the stage, and they strike approximately fifteen poses in between undressing and dressing into different clothes. The performers take off their suits, revealing floral dresses underneath. Afterward, they undress and expose their underwear, before finally putting their suits back on and taking the chairs to the sides of the stage to sit there. The poses they strike seem improvised, and each tableau lasts about ten to fifteen seconds. While there can be various interpretations of these nonverbal movements, the gestures and facial expressions made by the performers can be seen as cultural scripts of various ages and genders. For instance, when they take off their suits, they make several movements that are typically associated with masculinity and middle-aged men, such as carrying a suit jacket over one shoulder, untying a tie, and unbuttoning a shirt. Also, when Giuseppe Verdi's *La Traviata* (1853) plays and when they reveal their colorful floral dresses, the performers enact gestures that are typically associated with femininity. With another change of music, this time to Jay-Z and Mr. Hudson's "Forever Young" (2009), the dancers' movement vocabularies become freer, more expressive, and more playful, and the energy of the stage is more liberating, chaotic, and euphoric. While the performers enact tableau images individually in the previous segments, when "Forever Young" plays, there is more contact between the performers—holding hands, hugging, and kissing.[23] Because they resume wearing their suits at the end, this series of tableaux vivants do not suggest a linear and chronological narrative of aging, or unidirectional transitions from masculinity to femininity. This tableau sequence represents ages and genders as a fluid spectrum, rather than rigid categories or stages. The freezing in between actions not only highlights the constructedness and performativity of age and gender, but also exposes and questions the "culturally sanctioned" scripts of age and gender.[24] In this series of tableaux, the audience encounters familiar clichés and illusions of bodies, which are dispelled minutes later.

While *Gardenia—10 Years Later* addresses how both age and gender identities are culturally and socially constructed and performed, it also recognizes the physical realities and limitations of aging. In both *Gardenia* and *Gardenia—10 Years Later*, the tableau scenes invite the audience to observe their aging and aged bodies as they slowly change their clothes. As Kathleen Woodward notes, unlike other markers of social difference, age cannot be solely understood as a social construction because we "must confront the physical dimensions, if not the very real limits of the body."[25] In the 2021 production, for example, the slanted stage prominently foregrounds the aged bodies of the performers as they navigate the stage in high heels, which seems much more challenging than in 2010. The markers of age on the bodies of the performers and De Laet's attire serve as constant reminders of the physical realities of aging, prompting us to reflect on the finite nature of human life. In short, the production makes us ponder both the constructedness and reality of aging, and its unique intersection with the gender identities of queer and trans subjects. Furthermore, the restaging of the production itself gives multiple thought-provoking questions. In the 2021 production, the middle-aged female dancer has reached her fifties—an age shared by some of the older performers in the 2010 production. This challenges the binary distinction between younger and older performers, which was clearer in the original production. Not only that, but the restaging also makes us question what has changed in terms of queer and trans politics in the course of ten years.[26]

As the performance continues to unfold, the performers gradually apply makeup, jewelry, wigs, and fabulous drag costumes at varying rates. One might interpret these asynchronous tempos in the movements and actions, such as (un)dressing, walking, and returning to chairs, as choreographically representing the unique aging paths and "trans time[s]" of the performers.[27] For those who have seen *Before the Last Curtain Falls*, it is clear that some performers (especially Van Durme) reclaimed their gender identity earlier in life, while others began to experiment with their gender identities in later life. The life course of trans individuals is often marked by the time of coming out or undertaking hormone therapy or medical procedures. The notion of trans temporality (such as "trans years" or "hormone time")[28] acknowledges the time in which they lived with their felt gender (not the gender they were assigned at birth) and allows trans individuals to "employ an alternative chronology to make sense of their lives."[29] From this point of view, some older adults' experiences and age as trans individuals might be "young," while performers like Van Durme may be considered "older" in terms of trans years.[30] Even though chronologically and physically the aged performers may appear to be equally old, there is a significant age gap in their "trans age." When we consider the intersection of age and queer/trans identity, various heteronormative and chronological conceptualizations and assumptions of age are thereby questioned. For older adults who experiment with and transition their gender, coming out after retirement, changing their appearance, or transitioning in their later life, the chronologically old age can be reimagined as a chance, liberation, new beginning, and claiming of agency rather than a loss and decline.

CHALLENGING IDEALIZED YOUTH

In this section, I explore the relationship between the older performers and the younger dancers in *Gardenia—10 Years Later* and the overall nostalgic and retrospective gaze that is present in the production. It is worth questioning the aesthetic and dramaturgical choices of intermingling younger professional dancers among older queer and trans performers. Thus, I discuss how the production troubles the typical idealization of youth and foregrounds the resilience and survival of the older queer and trans adults by representing both harmony and contrast between the older performers and younger performers. Like the title of *Before the Last Curtain Falls* implies, *Gardenia—10 Years Later* suggests a narrative in which ending is a new beginning: the company's website states that it "starts from the end to the beginning."[31] The images, music, and narratives in *Gardenia—10 Years Later* often portray a nostalgic and retrospective gaze toward the past and the turbulent life journeys of the performers; the retrospective gaze in *Gardenia* is highlighted through the younger performers.

Throughout the performance, two younger cisgender performers—Griet Debacker and Hendrik Lebon—continuously move around the older performers, adding further complexity to the performance narrative by introducing breaks within the overarching images and stories. The younger figures in *Gardenia* are depicted as those who are in the deepest agony, and they are constantly suffering, crying, and failing throughout the performance. Each younger performer has a prolonged lip-synched solo with exaggerated facial expressions and movements.[32] The two of them also have a frenetic and combative duet dance that involves lots of violent movements such as intensive hugging, pulling, pushing, and throwing. This long duet scene has been criticized as a symbolic battle between a cisgender female and male: one reviewer states that "as a metaphor for the transvestite condition it's too obvious and overwrought," while another reviewer writes that the solo and duet dance of younger dancers "reduces the other performers to the last place they should be: the margins."[33]

However, I believe that this scene is open to more nuanced readings. The scene addresses the subject of "violence" in a broad sense, rather than depicting a specific story. It is important to note where the trans performers are and how they respond to this scene. Van Durme sits on the left side of the stage, facing the audience. She avoids looking at what is happening at the center stage. We also need to pay attention to Van Durme's facial expressions and body language; there is certainly disgust expressed through her body regarding the violence that happens right next to her. All the while, Dirk Van Vaerenbergh sits at the back of the stage, watching them silently. Given these older trans performers and the way they watch or ignore the fight and violence happening around them, it is possible to read this sequence as reenacted memories related to any kinds of violence experienced by the older performers, or their retrospective engagement with their youth.

If this scene is viewed as the reenacted memory of Van Durme or Van Vaerenbergh, the younger bodies may represent their younger selves. Right before this battle dance, there is a scene in which the Young Guy constantly sobs and asks questions to Van Durme: "Am I beautiful? Is my life beautiful?" Van Durme gives a blunt response to him, saying, "Yes, you are beautiful." I interpret this as her talking to her younger self in the past, who perhaps could not see the beauty around them, as indicated by her remarks in the documentary film. The old songs they lip-synch to—"Comme ils disent" (What Makes a Man) and "Cucurrucucú Paloma"—also imply that these younger figures might be mirroring the past selves of the older performers.[34] These songs, lip-synched by younger dancers, express subjects of confusion, loneliness, search for their identity and love, and so forth. Without suggesting a more direct autobiographical narrative, Young Guy and Real Woman embody the shared memory and pain among older queer and trans subjects: the absence of home, place, family; loneliness and sadness; lack of confidence; ongoing struggles with violence and abuse; a struggle for survival.

The two younger figures lingering among older adults also portray "the psychological and emotional backwardness" that has been characterized as queer temporality by many scholars.[35] In this production, I interpret the younger figures as acting out the remembered emotions and memories of the older performers. While remembering the past through the younger bodies, the older performers present themselves in a place of grace and power, as they are portrayed as those who found a way to accept and live with their insecurities and variations. The retrospective gaze toward younger figures depicts unresolved grief and anger; however, their recollection becomes a tool of resistance that validates their current selves, despite the biological changes in their appearance and loss of their youthful bodies. As such, their retrospective gaze toward the past and youth becomes more of a resistant affirmation for the aged selves, who are portrayed with charisma and power as they have found a way to embrace and live with their vulnerability and instability. In this way, *Gardenia—10 Years Later* reimagines old age as a liberation and possibility rather than a loss.

But I am also reminded of the lonely lives of these older performers depicted in the documentary film and their concerns about getting old without family or partner—a broadly shared concern among queer and trans elders. Therefore, the presence of past selves evokes the complicated relationships with the past among queer and trans elders and presents old age as a "complex amalgam of multiple selves," who are still exploring their new selves in their later stages while remembering the turbulent yet glamorous life of their youth.[36] By making the younger bodies embody pain and struggle, *Gardenia* allows the older performers to embody power and resilience, without erasing their painful histories, the sadness they carry beneath, and their ongoing struggles as marginalized citizens. In short, the performance make us ponder the complexity of queer and trans aging—both "the pleasures and the perils of ageing."[37]

CONCLUSION

Throughout the performance, the older performers in *Gardenia* slowly transform into cabaret performers, putting on dresses, wigs, and their accessories; at the end, they sing "Over the Rainbow" one more time as the climax of the performance. However, this repeated song asks the same questions that we asked at the beginning of this essay: where is the land in which dreams really do come true? *Gardenia—10 Years Later* aesthetically demonstrates the older body in depth, which embodies multiple ages across time, and this performance also showcases how Basting's depth model of aging offers a new way to acknowledge and empower the nonlinear course of queer and trans aging. Speaking in an interview, Van Durme acknowledged this ongoing journey of older performers as they find their place in society: "I say to myself always, it's not where you start. It's where you finish. And I am going to finish on top, honey!"[38] By allowing the older queer and trans subjects to fully embrace the pain and beauty of both their past and their old age through nonlinear images, *Gardenia—10 Years Later* enables them to tell their unique stories and express their views of aging without judgment or fear. The subjects effectively embody both vulnerability and strength as survivors, and make visible to us their charisma, power, and resilience. The presence of older trans and queer subjects itself and their strong will to perform suggest a new perspective on old age as having prestige and achievements, rather than tragedy. And rightly so: this is cause for celebration, as these powerful, brave older performers invite a shift in societal perceptions of aging unlike anything I have seen before.

NOTES

1. This chapter is drawn from my doctoral dissertation, *Performing (Ab)normal: Reframing Ageing, Dementia, and Temporality* (University of Alberta, 2023). Some of

the ideas in this paper have been included in a published peer-reviewed journal article by Heunjung Lee and Xavia A. Publius titled "Getting Our Flowers Now: Ageing Trans and Queer Bodies in *Gardenia* (2010) and *Gardenia—10 Years Later* (2021)," *European Journal of Theatre and Performance* 6 (2023): 126–69, https://journal.eastap.com/eastap-issue-6/

2. *Gardenia—10 Years Later* was directed by Frank Van Laecke and Alain Platel, and performed by Vanessa Van Durme, Griet Debacker, Richard "Tootsie" Dierick, Danilo Povolo, Gerrit Becker, Hendrik Lebon, Dirk Van Vaerenbergh, and Rudy Suwyns (the last remaining original cast member, Andrea De Laet, died in 2016). It premiered on July 16, 2021, at NTGent City Theatre in Ghent, Belgium. *Gardenia* and *Gardenia—10 Years Later* were originally produced by les ballets C de la B, but it joined forces with another dance company, kabinet K, in 2022, and together they now produce work under the name laGeste.

3. After its premiere in Ghent, *Gardenia* was staged in Avignon, Paris, Vienna, Berlin, London, Amsterdam, Belgrade, Barcelona, Lisbon, Oslo, Montreal, Taipei, and locations in Russia. In 2012 *Gardenia* was nominated for the prestigious British Laurence Olivier Award. In 2014, the life of older cast members and the tour of *Gardenia* were captured in the documentary film *Before the Last Curtain Falls*, and the film received many awards at international film festivals. "Creation: *Gardenia, 10 Years Later*," laGeste, 2023, https://www.lageste.be/en/creations/gardenia-10-years-later

4. With the support of the University of Alberta FGSR (Faculty of Graduate Studies and Research) research travel funding for doctoral students, I attended a performance of *Gardenia—10 Years Later* at the NTGent Theatre in Ghent, Belgium, on September 25, 2022. The NTGent Theatre provided me with video recordings of both productions of *Gardenia*.

5. This film was produced by Gebrueder Beetz Filmproduktion. It was invited to multiple film festivals and received a Special Jury Prize at the 2014 Hot Docs Canadian International Documentary Festival.

6. In most theater reviews and interviews, the older performers in *Gardenia* are introduced as "transvestite" or "transsexual." See, e.g., Luke Jennings, review of *Gardenia*, *Guardian*, July 2, 2011, https://www.theguardian.com/stage/2011/jul/03/gardenia-review-jennings; and Claudia La Rocco, review of *Gardenia*, *New York Times*, March 20, 2012, https://www.nytimes.com/2012/03/21/arts/dance/les-ballets-c-de-la-b-in-gardenia-at-montclair-state.html. However, these are outmoded terms as they imply pathologizing views and histories that have defined nonheterosexual gender identity and nontypical gender behaviors as psychiatric disorders. See Robert D. Davies and Madeline E. Davies, "The (Slow) Depathologizing of Gender Incongruence," *Journal of Nervous and Mental Disease* 208 (2020): 152–54. The trans community has claimed that these terms can be offensive to many trans individuals. They also fail to capture the various and fluid gender identities of the cast in *Gardenia*. Some members self-identify as trans women and chose to undertake sex reassignment surgery and hormone therapy, while some are gender nonconforming or identify as queer men who perform drag. Also, while some came out in their youth, one performer had not officially come out and did not want people to know that he was gay until the performance of *Gardenia* and its documentary film.

7. "Creation: *Gardenia, 10 Years Later*," laGeste.

8. See, e.g., Miriam Dreysse, "Staging the Precarious: Vulnerability and Sexual Identity in Alain Platel's *Gardenia*," in *The Choreopolitics of Alain Platel's les ballets C de la B: Emotions, Gestures, Politics*, ed. Hildegard De Vuyst (Bloomsbury Academic, 2020), 178–88; Donald Hutera, "A Richly Layered Portrait of Gender Fluidity and the Joys of Ageing," review of *Gardenia*, *Times*, November 17, 2021.

9. Fintan Walsh, *Performing the Queer Past: Public Possessions* (Bloomsbury, 2023).

10. This essay expands on existing scholarship on contemporary transgender performance and the intersection of queer identity and aging explored by older queer artists. See, respectively, Nicolas Shannon Savard, "Queer Legacies: Tracing the Roots of Contemporary Transgender Performance" (PhD diss., Ohio State University, 2021); Benjamin Gillespie, "Staging Retro-Perspectives: Performing Age, Memory/Loss, and Queer Desire in the Later Works of Split Britches (2009–2020)" (PhD diss., City University of New York, 2022).

11. Ruth Pearce, "Trans Temporalities and Non-Linear Ageing," in *Older Lesbian, Gay, Bisexual and Trans People: Minding the Knowledge Gaps*, ed. Andrew King, Kathryn Almack, and Yiu-Tung Suen (Routledge, 2018), 61–74.

12. Hutera, "A Richly Layered Portrait."

13. Anne Davis Basting, *The Stages of Age: Performing Age in Contemporary American Culture* (University of Michigan Press, 1998).

14. Valerie Barnes Lipscomb, "Age in *M. Butterfly*: Unquestioned Performance," *Modern Drama* 59, no. 2 (2016): 205. In addition to Lipscomb, others who use this model include Bridie Moore, "Depth, Significance, and Absence: Age-Effects in New British Theatre," *Age, Culture, Humanities: An Interdisciplinary Journal* 1 (2014): 163–95; Julia Henderson, "Other Story Forms of Aging: Performing Aging and Old Age in Contemporary, Professional Canadian Theatre" (PhD diss., University of British Columbia, 2018); and Gillespie, "Staging Retro-Perspectives."

15. Anne Davis Basting, "Performance Studies and Age," in *Handbook of the Humanities and Aging*, ed. Thomas R. Cole, Robert Kastenbaum, and Ruth E. Ray (Springer Nature, 2000), 268.

16. Basting, *The Stages of Age*, 141.

17. Gerald L. Davis writes that Judy Garland's "Somewhere over the Rainbow" is interpreted as "a wishful fantasy on a life where homosexuals can live openly and fully without judgment, social rancor, and rejection." He further writes, "it is both the pathos in Garland's rendition of the song and her self-destructive life (thought to be involuntary) that have made her an icon of contemporary gay life in America." See "'Somewhere over the Rainbow . . .': Judy Garland in Neverland," *Journal of American Folklore* 109, no. 432 (1996): 128.

18. Lee and Publius, "Getting Our Flowers Now," 146.

19. Basting, *The Stages of Age*, 141.

20. Basting, 141.

21. Several studies have addressed the significant health disparities older LGBTQ+ adults face: this population often experiences a lack of family and community support, increased risk of social isolation, and more discrimination and abuse in care systems compared to heterosexual peers, as well as higher morbidity, premature deaths, and higher mortality. See Tarynn M. Witten, "Graceful Exits: Intersection of Aging, Transgender Identities, and the Family/Community," *Journal of GLBT Family*

Studies 5, no. 1–2 (2009): 35–61; Karen I. Fredriksen-Goldsen et al., "The Health Equity Promotion Model: Reconceptualization of Lesbian, Gay, Bisexual, and Transgender (LGBT) Health Disparities," *American Journal of Orthopsychiatry* 84, no. 6 (2014): 653–63.

22. Historian Peter Laslett deliniates "young-old" and "old-old." He writes that "old-old" is a stage marked by dependency and the drastic drop in status that losing family headship brought with it in traditional society. This concept is related to the more recent demarcation between the "third age" and the "fourth age." See Peter Laslett, "What Is Old Age? Variation over Time and Between Cultures," in *Health and Mortality Among Elderly Populations*, ed. Graziella Caselli and Alan D. Lopez (Oxford University Press, 1996), 30–31.

23. In the 2021 restaging, the performers touch the dress of De Laet, implying physical contact with her.

24. Pamela H. Gravagne, *The Becoming of Age: Cinematic Visions of Mind, Body and Identity in Later Life* (McFarland, 2013), 16.

25. Kathleen Woodward, ed., *Figuring Age: Women, Bodies, Generations* (Indiana University Press, 1999), xxii.

26. See Walsh, *Performing the Queer Past*, 3–7.

27. Pearce, "Trans Temporalities and Non-Linear Ageing," 3.

28. Laura Horak, "Trans on YouTube: Intimacy, Visibility, Temporality," *Transgender Studies Quarterly* 1, no. 4, (2014): 572–85.

29. Pearce, "Trans Temporalities and Non-Linear Ageing," 3.

30. See Paul Willis et al., "'I'm Going to Live My Life for Me': Trans Ageing, Care, and Older Trans and Gender Non-Conforming Adults' Expectations of and Concerns for Later Life," *Ageing and Society* 41, no. 12 (2020): 2792–813.

31. Tessa Daluwein, "The Cast Looks Back," laGeste, January 2021, https://www.lageste.be/en/de-cast-blikt-terug

32. Real Woman lip-synchs to Caetano Veloso's version of "Cucurrucucú Paloma" (1954), written by Tomás Méndez, and Young Guy lip-synchs to Charles Aznavour's song "Comme ils disent" (What Makes a Man, 1972).

33. Jennings, review of *Gardenia*; La Rocco, review of *Gardenia*.

34. "Comme ils disent" is a French song about a gay man, his cross-dressing at Paris clubs, and his close relationship to his mother. Caetano Veloso sang "Cucurrucucú Paloma" in the Spanish movie *Talk to Her* (2002); the song is about the painful and destructive love of a man who misses a woman until he dies.

35. Cameron Crookston, "It Feels Like Yesterday: Drag, Nostalgia, and Queer Affective History in *The Vaudevillians*," *Journal of Homosexuality* 69, no. 5 (2022): 878.

36. Basting, *The Stages of Age*, 136.

37. Lynne Segal, *Out of Time: The Pleasures and the Perils of Ageing* (Verso, 2013).

38. Quoted in Ruth Myles, "Belgian Actress Dances Her Way to High Performance Rodeo," *Calgary Herald*, January 15, 2013, https://calgaryherald.com/entertainment/ruth-myles-belgian-actress-dances-her-way-to-high-performance-rodeo

Part III
Autobiography and the Aging Body/Self

10

"The Triumph of Time"
Utopian Visions of Judith Malina's Late Performances

Cindy Rosenthal

The thing about Judith Malina is that she is indefatigable, unstoppable, erupting with ideas. Malina is long-living, long-working, optimistic, and by the second decade of the 21st century girlish and old womanish at the same time. She survives and she bubbles, both.
—RICHARD SCHECHNER (2012)[1]

If we are not yet ready to create utopia we can at least enact it. . . . Our intention in working on a play about utopia is to overcome the spectator's disbelief in her own desires.
—JUDITH MALINA (1995)[2]

Utopia was a long sought-after creative, political, and spiritual goal for Judith Malina and the Living Theatre (TLT). In this chapter, I spotlight the late stage of Malina's life in the theater. I argue that three key performances in her last decade not only illuminate her impassioned commitment to living a full life as a(n older) theater artist, but also communicate the anti-ageist platform she fervently dedicated herself to in her eighties. In focusing on these three potent images of Malina (1926–2015), TLT's cofounding director, I find that she engages in what Jill Dolan describes as the utopian performative.[3] Malina's optimism, her deep conviction in the essential value of older humans, which she believed increased with every passing year, directly connects with the hope at the heart of Dolan's concept of the utopian in performance.

Malina shared with Dolan an understanding of "performance as a vital place for human connection and critique, love and respect."[4] Malina, an activist artist (playwright, poet, diarist, director, and actor), moved forward in every project with hope that her art would change the world. She held fast to a belief in the BNVAR (beautiful nonviolent anarchist revolution) until the end. Her lifelong claim and pursuit of art's ability to transform the spectator's ways of seeing, being, and doing closely echo Dolan's notion of how activism and performance join forces: "The politics lie in our willingness . . . to explore in imaginary spaces the potential of the 'not yet' and the 'not here.'"[5] Malina never gave up on what *could be*—but neither did Ellen Stewart (1919–2011), founding director of La MaMa Experimental Theatre Club,[6] and neither has Richard Schechner (1934–), a founder of performance studies and director of the Performance Group and East Coast Artists.[7] These three groundbreaking theater-makers worked into their eighties, and have been central subjects of my scholarly life over the past three decades. Tightening a lens on each of them for a variety of scholarly projects, learning with them, studying them intensely, sometimes in juxtaposition with one of the other two, has irrevocably shaped my own art-making and the paths I've taken in my research and writing work, specifically this current investigation of age and performance. As I too advance in age, I view their remarkable, singular journeys as powerful guideposts—challenging, enriching, discombobulating, inspiring. All three were born between the world wars of the twentieth century. In my privileged position as their interviewer, co-traveler, and experimental theater comrade over the past thirty years, I've tracked how the narratives I've heard, in sync with Barbara Myerhoff's important research with communities of older people, may at times be somewhat fictionalized, but nonetheless are powerful markers of a vibrant, active "telling" process.[8] In the telling/sharing with me and with other spectators/readers/listeners/writers/witnesses, there is an experience of hope. Deeper meanings emerged from these up close renderings of long lives, well lived. The retrospection in the oral histories I engaged in with each of them was future oriented, not backward thinking.

Here, I analyze three of Malina's last and very different performance endeavors, *Maudie and Jane* (2007), "The Triumph of Time" (2013), and Malina's last seder at the Lillian Booth Actors Home (2015). With this concentration on Malina, I am indebted to Myerhoff's notion of an "arena of visibility." My goal here (echoing Kathleen Woodward in her essential *Figuring Age: Women, Bodies, Generations*, 1999) is not just illumination and analysis, but activism—making visible the too-often "invisible subject of older women."[9]

Maudie and Jane was Malina's final project with her husband, Hanon Reznikov, who directed the play before his death from a stroke at age fifty-seven in 2008. In Reznikov's adaptation of Doris Lessing's novella, Malina (age eighty-one at the time), playing Maudie, an indigent woman, stripped naked and was bathed onstage by the actor playing Jane (a younger, successful businesswoman). The play is naturalistic in style—which was unusual in the history of the Living Theatre's oeuvre.

Nonetheless, this moment of bathing is one where Marvin Carlson's notion of "ghosting" in performance comes into play.[10] Malina first "put her [naked] body on the line" in *Paradise Now*, the 1968 work of TLT most evocative of sexual liberation. In *Maudie and Jane*, Malina offers hope for the (aging) activist body in performance, as she/Maudie "makes visible what was supposed to remain invisible" (à la Luce Irigaray).[11] For me (and some other critics),[12] there was pure jouissance—and hope—in this disrupting/destabilizing moment. Some spectators might hark back to decades-earlier images of Malina's naked body in performance in *Paradise Now*, but all of us at *Maudie and Jane* faced the image of an older Malina feistily countering the image of the younger Jane, who had stripped and bathed earlier in the play. Malina declared in an interview, "And the human body is good, even when it gets old, and you know, the breasts fall down a little and the stomach is a little rumpled and it's still good. It's still beautiful . . . 'Shall I look?' Yes! Look! Look!"[13] Kathleen Woodward states that age "swallows up" gender as an oppressive critical lens[14]—but Malina, playing Maudie, pushed back against both negative, oppressive critiques. Her naked presence in the tub was startlingly and audaciously out there, for all to see.

Scholar and theater-maker Anne Davis Basting imagines that performances like these enact "embracing age." Much in the way that Carlson's ghosting suggests an experience where a performance is replayed and becomes newly resonant and re-remembered over time, Basting evocatively describes how some performances of older actors can be "an exercise in seeing in depth . . . through the transparent layers of past performances and performances yet to be within the bounded course of human life."[15]

Dolan posits potential outcomes for the utopian in performance: "Can seeing performance teach us how to be physically intimate with strangers, in a culture that works harder to keep the space between us growing?"[16] In welcoming spectators to "look" at her older body on the stage and share an intimate moment, Malina puts forward the possibility of *communitas* in the room. Her hope, she told me, was that the care-full intimacy between Maudie and Jane on the stage (who, in the story, were very recently strangers) would model a more caring, intimate connection between spectators

Fig. 10.1. Judith Malina as Maudie and Pat Russell as Jane in The Living Theatre's *Maudie and Jane*, New York, 2007. Photo: Chantel C. Lucier.

in the theater—and, correspondingly, between humans who are strangers outside the theater, too.[17] She imagined that social, political responsibility—symbolized by Jane's actions on Maudie's behalf and the change Jane undergoes in the play—could be reenacted and sustained outside the theater.

For Malina, this "in-the-room" connection was a simple, but pointed, radical gesture—inspired by her longtime focus on and dedication to Martin Buber's treatises in *I and Thou*. Seeking a similar outcome to the possibility Dolan suggests above, Malina sought greater empathy and the erasure of physical boundaries between spectators, too. Dolan expands on this idea by drawing useful connections to Buber's "fantasy pictures," stating that "theater might renew us . . . inviting us to imagine—along with the material, fleshy, so vulnerable and mortal performers' bodies that create fantasy-pictures for us . . . ways to be fully human together."[18]

Dolan's argument that utopian performatives productively connect to Brechtian *gestus* would no doubt have sparked Malina's interest, as both Bertolt Brecht and Erwin Piscator were foundational influences on all of Malina's work. The bathing sequences in *Maudie and Jane* could function as a kind of gestus. In Dolan's view, "utopian performatives are relatives of . . . *gestus*, actions in performance that crystallize social relations and offer them to spectators for critical contemplation."[19] The advocacy for and celebration of the older body in performance is made viscerally clear in *Maudie and Jane*, which supports Dolan's notion that "the affective and ideological 'doings' we see and feel demonstrated in utopian performatives also critically rehearse civic engagement that could be effective in the wider public and political realm."[20] This potential performative efficacy directly connects to Anne Davis Basting's understanding of the power of age and/in performance. Basting's words reflect Malina's agenda in performing Maudie as she did: "older performers take on roles that expand cultural perceptions of what aging can be through the transformative power of theatre to disrupt stereotypes."[21]

Malina actively launched her mission to make visible in a public and political realm the idea that older folks have real value and are vital resources of wisdom, knowledge, and experience that can transform the world when she moved into the Lillian Booth Actors Home in Englewood, New Jersey, in early 2013. This awakening to and acknowledgment of what age theorist Margaret Morganroth Gullette, performance theorist Elinor Fuchs, and others describe as a "non-declinist" narrative[22] was the impetus for Malina's conception of a collaborative performance piece with her fellow "inmates" (as she called them) titled "The Triumph of Time." At age eighty-six, with fervent optimism lifting her decibel level, Malina told me: "I am more intelligent now than I was five years ago. I keep learning. Older people have a lot to offer, but because of their physical disadvantages, this goes unrecognized."[23]

With this mission in mind, Malina began a process supported by TLT assistant director Brad Burgess and company member Tom Walker to enlist the participation of residents in the Actors Home in a performance that would be structured around their "life-course" stories. She believed that older performers are "thick with potential, thick with time," as Basting phrased it.[24] Some of the home's former actors, stage managers, directors, and musicians were very interested in this new venture; hope was generated in the possibility of "putting on a show" that might garner an outside audience (as was Malina's plan); for others, the chance to simply engage in a new creative process was appealing. But—as was the case with most TLT works dating back to its founding in 1947 and the living room performances Malina and her first husband and TLT cofounder, Julian Beck, produced, the development and production process was fraught. Rehearsal space and scheduling were the usual problems—but at the home there were additional, ongoing challenges. The greatest (and sadly, ironic) difficulty in fulfilling Malina's mission through "The Triumph of Time" became apparent quickly: assembling a group of participants who could stay around. With collaborators in their seventies, eighties, and nineties, the cast changed weekly as some folks became physically or mentally unable to attend meetings and some others, of course, died.

Yet Malina steadfastly held on to the hope captured in the title of her new work in process, "The Triumph of Time." In early 2014 Malina, Burgess, and Walker prepared a draft of the script, which interspersed a few of the Lillian Booth residents' stories and dialogue (these would be performed by some of the residents, including Malina) with "Living Theatre Actions," which would be performed by a small core group of younger, agile TLT actors. This idea of a hybrid company structure, combining the efforts of the older folks at the home with the existing ensemble of mostly younger TLT actors brings to mind successful performance collaborations that were also built on intergenerational exchange and on oral histories, which scholars Basting and Valerie Barnes Lipscomb have documented and analyzed elsewhere.[25] Lipscomb writes of the benefits of collaborating with an existing troupe.[26] And indeed, the Living Theatre's early workshops with residents at Lillian Booth held promise: the Living Theatre is an avant-garde, nontraditional company composed of multigenerational and multicultural members with diverse levels of training and professionalism. Their work historically has been devising scripts and engaging in collective creation with performers of all kinds. Distinct from some other endeavors, covered substantially by Basting in her research on companies such as the Grandparents' Living Theatre, Roots and Branches, and Elders Share the Arts, the oral histories in "The Triumph of Time" were only those of the older folks, not their younger collaborators. The Living Theatre members would embody through movement the emotional texture and colors evoked by the older folks' stories, which would then be shaped by Malina, Burgess, and Walker, the artistic leaders of the workshop. And yet, in Malina's optimistic sense of the work, it would create "a space . . . that can bridge generational divides," as Basting put it in describing the work of the companies above.[27]

Malina's project shared fundamental goals with the aforementioned companies, which Basting's declaration about their agendas makes clear: "to shift their communities' perceptions about old age." And indeed, Basting's following statement places her and Malina on the exact same page: "Theater offers older people the opportunity to transform their own and other people's conceptions of the meanings of their individual lives and of older people in general."[28]

Malina wrote a monologue for herself for the beginning of the performance: "I have asked my fellow residents at the Lillian Booth Actors Home in what ways they have become wiser and better. They have learned compassion, and the meaning of life; they have gained knowledge of human relationships, human emotions, joys and suffering. I want the world to recognize that we are a tremendous resource that is rarely taken advantage of."[29] She also decided to include a song in the piece that evoked an earlier time, and (in her view) spoke to the commonality of experience of all hard workers in the theater, "Yip" Harburg's 1932 song "Brother, Can You Spare a Dime?" This points to Basting's observation that older folks' performances sometimes feature songs of an earlier time, as a move toward building empathy, a sense of connection, even *communitas*. Basting describes these elements as "collective nostalgia."[30]

Malina was an avid reader of the *New York Times*, and although in her last years her eyesight was failing, a month before she died she pointed me to a *Times* article: "Older Really Can Mean Wiser" by Benedict Carey. She read aloud a quotation within the piece that stated, "an older brain [may] move more slowly than its younger self, but it is just as accurate in many areas and more adept at reading other people's moods—on top of being more knowledgeable."[31] Unfortunately, because of her own ill health and the difficulties in securing a consistent group of collaborators, "The Triumph of Time" was never produced. Drawing on Dolan's imagery, this project still evokes the spirit of utopian performatives: "never finished gestures toward a potentially better future." Dolan's statement below on evanescence and, ultimately, disappearance connects, finally, to hope, and resonates with the deep belief Malina had in her collaborative, creative project with Actors Home elders:

> at the base of the utopian performative's constitution is the inevitability of its disappearance; its efficacy is premised on its evanescence. Performance's poignant ephemerality grounds all our experiences at the theater. The utopian performative's fleetingness leaves us melancholy yet cheered, because for however brief a moment we felt something of what redemption might be like, of what humanism could really mean, of how powerful might be a world in which our commonalities would hail us over our difference.[32]

Which brings us to Malina's final performance. Her last seder was a doing, a ritual, an enactment that took place on the first day of the Jewish holiday of Passover in 2015, in the small Rosetta LeNoire room at the Actors Home, Saturday afternoon, April 4. Each year, before Malina's death, the Living Theatre came together, a confluence of families and friends, an ever-expanding tribe, to voice and embody Malina's specially curated Haggadah (a program/script of the seder ritual), which she first compiled for the company and led while they were on tour in 1979 in Italy.

The Haggadah mandates that the seder's ritual actions take place in a set order, including the washing of hands, the eating of unleavened bread and bitter herbs, and the drinking of several glasses of wine—all with accompanying prayers (again in a particular order). The Haggadah/script demands a seder leader and a community that participate actively together. Participants sit in a specific way at the seder table (they recline). The youngest member of the group is singled out to ask four questions. Key to this event is the group's telling/retelling of stories that reflect personal or group journeys. These journeys begin with a description of an experience of oppression, incarceration, or containment and lead to a description of escape, liberation, and freedom. The traditional story at the center of the seder recounts the Jewish people's escape from Egypt after years of slavery, persecution, and abuse, and God's parting of the Red Sea, which enabled them to escape. It also describes the horror of the ten plagues that befell Egyptians, causing the pharaoh to finally "let the [Jewish] people go." A hope for and belief in a future that will be free from oppression and brutality drive the seder, along with making the dream of this utopian place/space/time a reality for all.

The series of moments that culminated in the intimate, profound event of Judith Malina's final performance experience, the seder at the Lillian Booth Actors Home, is quintessential of what Dolan describes as a utopian performative. As Dolan explains, "performance calls the attention of the audience [or participants] in a way that lifts everyone slightly above the present, into a hopeful feeling of what the world might be like if every moment of our lives were as emotionally voluminous, generous . . . and intersubjectively intense."[33]

This was the first and last time TLT celebrated the seder in the Actors Home. There were twelve of us including Malina, circling the small table in the room. There were small plastic cups for grape juice (wine was not permitted at the home) and paper plates for matzo, haroseth (chopped apples, walnuts, and wine), horseradish, and bitter herbs (and a small bowl of salt water in which to dip these greens). Malina had donned a bright red kimono for the seder that Tom Walker had brought for her. Kathleen Woodward suggests that when an older woman uses bright red lipstick or wears bright red clothing, it can be read as a resistant, radical act or gesture. *You will see me*, it says.[34] Putting on the red kimono, her festive costume for this occasion, called Malina (physically frail and extremely weak as she was) to the performance, into "showtime" mode. To some of us, familiar with her performance as Antigone (an iconic, beloved, and frequently performed role), here she was at age eighty-eight, somehow taking on the role again (a kind of ghosting?), summoning up the strength to put her body and voice forward, and attempting to transcend the harsh realities of the present time. Malina's agenda/overriding objective as Antigone, she had often explained, was "to set an example." Ritual and its power, Malina told me, were meaningful to her because they connected her with people in a deep way. During her two years at the Actors Home, Malina asked that I visit her, whenever possible, on late Friday afternoons so we could light the Shabbat candles together. The daughter of a rabbi, she kept her rabbinical home inside her heart and mind her entire life.

Tom Walker wheeled Malina upstairs in her kimono to the LeNoire room, with playwright/director Karen Malpede, actor George Bartenieff, and me accompanying them. The seven other friends and family members were setting up the seder table in the room. Malina's wheelchair was the last addition to the scene. We settled in and greeted everyone around the table (some of us were seated in chairs, and others were on the floor, which was customary at a Living Theatre seder). With Malina at the center, this occasion felt like a "ghosting" of seders past. But at this seder, special care was taken. We were all Malina's caregivers. She had brought us together; we were determined to speak her words, and to co-create a care-full, sacred, holy event. Malina's text, her Haggadah, was our focal point, and each of us actively engaged in a collective rereading, a collective retelling, a collective listening. We were struck by the fragility, the harmony, the beauty of this collective caring; we felt the sharp consciousness of being together, here and now, moment to moment. And so, we began a ritual act many of us knew by heart. As in all seders, we were pointed forward to a time (next year, according to the Haggadah) when we will re-create the world—free of oppression, with freedom and liberty and peace for all.

With Walker as her steadfast support, close at her side, Malina began, reading aloud her Haggadah and stating that her version of the text is very specifically "a retelling of liberation but not a model of the past." She read the opening page, and then one by one, each of us around the table read her words, proceeding in the random order determined by our seating. Historically, Malina's practice had been to concisely cast and "direct" the reading, designating readers line by line, but it had been several years since she'd taken on the director's role at the seder in this way. And so, we each took our turn, we read from the "script," we told stories, we sang. We were together for almost two hours but didn't quite finish the Haggadah. Not long after we had launched a reading of a section of Allen Ginsberg's "Howl," which Malina includes in her Haggadah text, she announced that she was tired. Spontaneously, we created a resounding "chord" with our circle of voices. The chord is a legendary Living Theatre choral breath and sound piece, which originated as a segment of the company's *Mysteries and Smaller Pieces* (1964) and has since provided communal closure at the end of numerous TLT performances and events. After the chord, Burgess wheeled Malina upstairs.

Malina died a few days after our seder, on April 10, the seventh day of Passover in 2015. There are sects of Judaism that regard the two final days of the holiday as being as holy as the first two seder days. The seventh day marks the day when the Jews in Egypt began their journey to freedom, Shevi'i shel Pesach; some Jews believe that these are days when we should find an "oasis of calm" and focus especially on future peace.

Dolan's description of utopian performatives places them on a parallel track with the experience of the Living Theatre seder: "We all came here to do this, to share our attention, to acknowledge our pleasure [and intensity of feelings], and to hope for our mutual, collective transformation."[35] Our seder practice worked much like the metaphor Dolan shares at the end of her book, "mankind's unfinished symphony . . . what Rabbi Abraham Joshua Heschel calls 'radical amazement.'"[36] We who were privileged to be in the room with Malina that last time experienced an intensity that could certainly be described as a "rehearsal for revolution," transmuted through Malina's fragile liveness and the meld of spirituality, communality, creativity—and hope. She set us an example, as is her way, for the future.

I end here with Dolan's epilogue questions: "What finally do communitas and the utopian performative *do*? What is their action in the world? . . . Perhaps utopian performatives create the *condition* for action; they pave a certain kind of way, prepare people for the choices they might make in other aspects of their lives."[37] I remember the feeling in the room after Judith put down her Haggadah, looked at it, and locked eyes with some of us around the table. She was ready to go. Tom opened the door, and Brad wheeled her down the hall and out of our view. We were now a group of seder participants without our leader, holding on to the precious moments before what Schechner describes as the postperformance "cool down."[38] (The cool down for us would begin with a cleanup; grape juice had spilt on the white rug.) We held one another. There was sweetness in still being together in the room. We continued to savor Judith's vestigial presence, but there was also a sudden, sharp awareness of her absence from the room. A gutting sadness. Before we broke the moment/broke apart, there was also a group sense that we should/could preserve the *communitas* of that moment. Without speaking, we knew that Judith's living legacy would enrich our work going forward—we would each strive in our own creative ways, toward liberation and freedom. We knew too, in our collective core, that this was the last seder with Judith. Without speaking this truth, we were now setting Judith free. Judith's final performance, in Basting's words, was "thick with potential, thick with time."[39]

In her last published volume of poetry (2015), Judith Malina included this poem:

LET ME GO
Let me go now as I came,
With a great cry and a great hope.[40]

NOTES

1. Richard Schechner, preface to *The Piscator Notebook*, by Judith Malina (Routledge, 2012), xv.

2. Judith Malina, program note for the Living Theatre's *Utopia*, a play by Hanon Reznikov, which she directed in New York in 1995.

3. Jill Dolan, *Utopia in Performance* (University of Michigan Press, 2008), 5. I am grateful to Sonja Kuftinec and John Fletcher for the springboard they offered to take a deep dive into Dolan's inspiring work and to dialogue with other American Society for Theatre Research colleagues on the important themes of her book.

4. Dolan, 33.

5. Dolan, 20.

6. For more on Stewart's own brand of indefatigable theater-making, see my essay "Ellen Stewart: La Mama of Us All," *TDR: The Drama Review* 52, no. 2 (2006): 12–51; and my monograph *Ellen Stewart Presents: Fifty Years of La MaMa Experimental Theatre* (University of Michigan Press, 2017).

7. For more on Schechner's unending fervor in his life in the theater as scholar, professor, and director, see James Harding and Cindy Rosenthal, eds., *The Rise of Performance Studies: Rethinking Richard Schechner's Broad Spectrum* (Palgrave, 2011); Mike Sell, "Richard Schechner: Broadening the Spectrum, 1957–1976," in *The Great North American Stage Directors*, vol. 5, *Schechner, Breuer, Bogart*, ed. Joan Herrington (Methuen Drama, 2022), chap. 1; and Cindy Rosenthal, "Onwards! Richard Schechner's Global Theatre, Performance Training and Ensemble-Building 1981–2011," in Herrington, *Schechner, Breuer, Bogart*, chap. 2.

8. Barbara Myerhoff's concept of "re-membering" and her essay "Life Not Death in Venice," in *Remembered Lives: The Work of Ritual, Storytelling, and Growing Older*, ed. Marc Kaminsky (University of Michigan Press, 1992), 257–76, helped shape my thinking about the her-stories and his-stories Malina, Stewart, and Schechner shared with me—there were often contradictions in their accounts of events and encounters they participated in together.

9. Myerhoff's *Remembered Lives* is cited by Kathleen Woodward in *Figuring Age: Women, Bodies, Generations* (Indiana University Press, 1999), x.

10. See Marvin Carlson, *The Haunted Stage: The Theatre as Memory Machine* (University of Michigan Press, 2001).

11. See Luce Irigaray, "This Sex Which Is Not One," in *New French Feminisms: An Anthology*, ed. Elaine Marks and Isabelle de Courtivron (Schocken, 1981), 91–106.

12. Caryn James described this scene as "the essence of the work"; Victor Gluck described it as "beautiful, moving." Caryn James, "Uncloaking the Plight of an Aging Woman," *New York Times*, December 13, 2007; Victor Gluck, review of *Maudie and Jane*, *Theater Scene*, December 10, 2007, https://www.theaterscene.net/ (review no longer available at site).

13. Judith Malina, "The Beautiful Non-Violent Pacifist Revolution," interview by Romy Ashby and Foxy Kidd, *Goodie* 36 (2008): 22.

14. Kathleen Woodward, *Aging and Its Discontents: Freud and Other Fictions* (Indiana University Press, 1991), 16.

15. Anne Davis Basting, *The Stages of Age: Performing Age in Contemporary American Culture* (University of Michigan Press, 1998), 141.

16. Dolan, *Utopia in Performance*, 27.

17. In an interview with me on August 15, 2008, Malina specifically argued for the political efficacy of *Maudie and Jane* because of this scene's intimate, staged interaction.

18. Dolan, *Utopia in Performance*, 163.

19. Dolan, 7.

20. Dolan, 7.

21. Basting, *The Stages of Age*, 7.

22. See Margaret Morganroth Gullette, "Politics, Pathology, Suicide, and Social Fates: Tony Kushner's *The Intelligent Homosexual's Guide to Capitalism and Socialism with a Key to the Scriptures*," *Modern Drama* 59, no. 2 (Summer 2016), 231–48; Elinor Fuchs, "Estragement: Towards an 'Age Theory' Theatre Criticism," *Performance Research* 19, no. 3 (2014): 69–77; and Elinor Fuchs, "Rehearsing Age," *Modern Drama* 59, no. 2 (Summer 2016): 143–54; both Fuchs essays are republished in the first section of this volume.

23. Interview with Malina in the Lillian Booth Actors Home, April 7, 2014.

24. Basting, *The Stages of Age*, 9.

25. See Basting, *The Stages of Age*, especially her chapters on the Grandparents' Living Theatre and on Roots and Branches and Elders Share the Arts. See also Valerie Barnes Lipscomb, "'The Play's the Thing': Theatre as a Scholarly Meeting Ground in Age Studies," *International Journal of Ageing and Later Life* 7, no. 2 (2012): 117–41.

26. Lipscomb, "The Play's the Thing," 137.

27. Basting, *The Stages of Age*, 84.

28. Basting, 56, 52.

29. "The Triumph of Time" (2014), script courtesy of the Living Theatre archive files, with permission of Brad Burgess and Tom Walker.

30. Basting, *The Stages of Age*, 50–52.

31. Benedict Carey, "Older Really Can Mean Wiser," *New York Times*, March 17, 2015.

32. Dolan, *Utopia in Performance*, 33.

33. Dolan, 5.

34. Woodward, *Aging and Its Discontents*, 196.

35. Dolan, *Utopia in Performance*, 33.

36. Dolan, 164.

37. Dolan, 169–70 (emphasis in original).

38. Dolan, 19. She cites Schechner's *Performance Theory*, rev. ed. (Routledge, 1988).

39. Basting, *The Stages of Age*, 9.

40. Judith Malina, *Having Loved* (Fast Books, 2015), 28.

Editors' Note

Robbie McCauley was an African American female performer, director, playwright, and educator. She crafted performances that interrogated race, gender, and class in the United States by excavating and imagining through her own body her family's stories.

McCauley's performance work was always about the body. In an email conversation with Cindy Rosenthal in January 2021, four months before she died, McCauley explained that she didn't always pay enough attention to *her* body. She was eager to contribute a text about her life and work to this volume on the intersections of performance and age. McCauley described how her performances were experienced and created directly from a place of physical and emotional awareness and sometimes bodily pain—as well as joy. She told Rosenthal that her great-great-grandmother Sally's pain became hers, as she conceived, developed, and performed *Sally's Rape* (1991). McCauley, who at one point in the performance stands naked on an auction block, is a descendant of Sally's rape by a white plantation master. This shattering, beautiful, and terrifying two-person work (partially improvised with white performer Jeannie Hutchins) thrust McCauley into the center and at the forefront of experimental, avant-garde performance. She received Bessie and Obie Awards for this achievement. McCauley told Rosenthal, "Storytelling is where I come from. Acting work for me is always about talking to an audience." Sharing the performance space with Robbie as a spectator provided an intense, intimate, and direct connection with Robbie, the person. *Sugar* (2012), her solo work about her fraught, tumultuous journey as a diabetic countered by her life-affirming projects in the theater, was performed to acclaim in New York and regionally. McCauley died on May 20, 2021, in Silver Spring, Maryland, at the age of seventy-eight.

Rosenthal reached out to interdisciplinary artist Daniel Alexander Jones, a close friend, collaborator, and mentee of McCauley's, shortly after McCauley's death in 2021, about contributing a creative response to the "late-stage" texts McCauley had shared with Rosenthal. The result is the "riff" that follows—the intersubjective, dialogic flow of thoughts, energies, and experiences shared artist-to-artist between Robbie and Daniel on the page.

11

I Feel Memories in My Body More Than Ever

Text by Robbie McCauley

Context by Daniel Alexander Jones

Robbie McCauley's text materials in this piece were culled from her journal writings between October 2020 and April 2021, which she shared with Cindy Rosenthal, along with excerpts from transcripts of phone interviews Rosenthal conducted with McCauley during the same time period. Robbie McCauley and Daniel Alexander Jones met in 1993 at the National Black Theatre Festival. At the time, McCauley was widely celebrated for her vanguard impact in performance art and theater; Jones was at the beginning of what would be his own impactful body of work. Their ensuing friendship and collaborative relationship continued until McCauley's passing, and ranged from long-form collaborations on projects to shared work as educators and frequent phone calls to discuss the state of the world, its history, and its emergent futures. Throughout, McCauley and Jones embodied and extended the long-standing tradition of intergenerational practice and mentorship that has anchored and informed Black American artists' journeys in significant ways.

Night sweat warning. Stumble focus. Sugars found in sugarless house. So tired of the diabetic dramas. Yet my will to live is relentless, ingrained, automatic. So curious about life now. I could've been dead long ago. Mother died the year after Obama won. Quite demented by then, she called him Roosevelt. He's Black, I said. She had no idea what that meant. I thought I'd die after #45. Lore did.[1] I didn't blame her. I had a heart attack soon after, but was too curious about what would happen next to let go. Take care, as they say, what you wish for. The pandemic hasn't got me. Family gets younger and older. The world falls apart. #45 is a symptom. The sweat makes me cold. I'm always cold unless it's hot summer when everyone gets on my nerves talking about heat as they sit in air-conditioned spaces.

> Some things demand your body—proximate, in time. Your body as the rememberer and as an archive. Your body as a means of departure and return. Some things you cannot learn in a class. From a book. At a distance.

I feel memories in my body now more than ever.

> Robbie McCauley placed her palms on my kitchen table. I had known her for just over two years. I had known her always. Perhaps you have had such experiences? Meeting people to whom you feel bound in some cosmic way? An alignment through presence across time. Robbie placed her hands on the table. Her hands were instruments. Scientists believe octopuses might actually see through their skin; Robbie seemed to "see" through her fingers—long, dexterous, with distinctive nail beds that sometimes seemed iridescent under stage light. They moved akin to the searching-yet-knowing fingers of jazz players as she played invisible energies strung through the spaces around her. Her fingers thrummed my kitchen table top as she thought. Robbie's thinking was itself a marvel.

The copious data about just me
Is enough to know who what where why I am if I eat collard greens apple pie or ham.
Who are my kinfolks
then and now
and if I ever milked a cow.
No secrets dreams
nor thoughts I have can hide. Data may cause me to lose my breath to death or force me into a police car ride.

> From our introduction in the summer of 1993, until and beyond her death in the spring of 2021, Robbie McCauley was an artist I idolized, a peerless mentor, a thrilling collaborator, and a dear, true friend. I apprenticed with a constellation of visionary artists who understood aspects of the sojourner's walk not easily described, let alone taught. The constellation included Robbie and her art sisters Laurie Carlos and Jessica Hagedorn. They were familiar with commons of mystery and precarity. They had made, undone, remade, and reimagined more times than they could count; yet, they rarely

Fig. 11.1. Left to Right: Stacey Karen Robinson, Robbie McCauley and Jessica Hagedorn before a panel at the PRELUDE Festival, New York, 2017. Photo courtesy Daniel Alexander Jones.

looked back, attuned as they were toward what was now, here, emerging. If they revered anything, it was life itself, and its complex and contradictory unfolding. Otherwise they were irreverent, always in motion, iconoclastic by default.

When Bob Dylan sang
In the mid '60s
I felt the world changing
I marveled at Marvin Gaye
who put questions in the air

About wars and generations
Me, still alive still asking,
What's goin' on?
Who is singing
mysteries of life in 2020?

Twenty twenty a year of shame
Year of hope. Life on hold.
Yet the people went to vote
And good men and women won.
Evil people showed their butts
They took out guns and knives
Killed/threatened people's lives
Yet we go for rights for health
justice and the earth.

> Robbie's impeccable posture anchored her performance work. Her physical expressions saw her shake, rage, laugh, twist, dance, wind her limbs through the air, stomp, shout, bend, or plant her feet so deep it seemed they reached beneath the stage to the dirt below. Sometimes she'd stand as still and powerfully vigilant as an owl. She inhabited ntozake shange's "dark phrases of womanhood"; the civil rights and women's movements; myriad urban and institutional contexts; her own body as a mother; her own body as a lover; her own body as a Lower East Side denizen; her own body as an innovator, as a warrior, as a sovereign being sounding out its own contexts; and her body that tumbled life and death, through her intimate journeys with diabetes.

I don't try to resolve the contradictions—but I'm surprised how these come back and forth for me.

> Robbie knew firsthand the importance of apprenticeship. Especially in the tradition of Black theater—historically, many artists who found successful pathways shared details with younger artists, warning them of trick bags ahead. They knew that *good-good*, real theatrical conjure would be lost if not tended and extended by those who come after them. Many artists, myself included, can trace our creative genealogies and demonstrate exactly how the baton was passed then passed and passed again to ensure continued flow. In the case of Robbie's exponential impact, there are many influential artists in the field whose voices were deepened through their

work with her, study with her, and encounter with her writings and performances, and, most potently, through their experience of her persistent, incandescent presence.

Abbey Lincoln wrote a song called "People in Me." The first thing Robbie would ask when she met someone new was "who are your people?" This question is a southernism, for sure. One of the delightful things about being around Robbie was the aura of good sense, perspicacity, and warmth wed to a firm and transparent skepticism that felt so southern capital-*B* Black. *Who are your people?* What threads of history trail behind your back, and are you aware of them? What traces of inherited memory do you carry across impossible divides? For Black folks the question holds vestiges of times when records of familial roots and branches were lined out in the back of family Bibles that were passed along or, before that, spoken aloud in a string of well-remembered names. Who someone's people were, forced confrontation with the not-so-distant generations who were forced atop the auction block for sale, and those who were penned in one cultural or legislative cage after another. Robbie knew we each carry evidentiary traces of history, and that part of life's mystery speaks through subtle whispers born from those traces. She sought to return our capacity to witness and hold the contradictions within and without ourselves.

May we ask for our country a new birth.

Apprenticing with Robbie was not the work of indoctrination into an orthodoxy. It was the mission of liberation from constraint and predetermination, a primer in getting and staying aligned with life's constant unfolding. It was also a work that demanded expansion beyond comfort and beyond the familiar.

In between was a life of love well lived. Some pain. Lots of gain. Growing up in what I later learned was a ghetto, a term adopted from where Jews who were discriminated against lived in Europe. I felt my life was normal.

Both my parents worked in the government. Daddy was retired from the military fairly young. He drank a lot and smoked unfiltered cigarettes. With one sibling, a sister, we lived in a semi-detached two-story house, went to segregated schools where we had good teachers who cared about us. I went to Howard University, the most prestigious HBCU. Meant to major in history, but discovered drama and graduated cum laude with a double major.

Luckily I arrived in New York during that vital era of experimental theater and the Black cultural movement. I was accepted in the apprentice class taught by Lloyd Richards at the new Negro Ensemble Company and chosen to understudy and "go on" in its first production. Richards coached me to say out loud, "I am an actress." Subsequently I auditioned and landed a role in an Adrienne Kennedy play produced by Joseph Papp at the New York Public Theater. I went on to work in plays by ntozake shange and Ed Bullins, and collaborative pieces by Joseph Chaikin.

Across her lifetime, Robbie was a daughter. She was a sibling by blood and choice. She was a partner. She was a mother—Robbie's daughter, Jessie Montgomery, the Grammy Award–winning composer, extends her mother's legacy in boldly impactful ways through a totally different medium. Robbie was a visionary architect of postmodern performance art. Robbie was a writer of staggering focus and vulnerability. Robbie was a legendary teacher. But if you asked her, she would say she was an actor. First and foremost.

I was an actor first—but I always had more to say.

Actors worth their salt, Robbie believed, develop the ability to perceive and interact with myriad, shifting perspectives born of the complex weave of subjectivities and objective truths unfolding in performance in real time. The actor becomes an utterer, casting language from within this teeming matrix of awareness, to bridge subjective and objective worlds, affecting material reality and our collective experience of it. Too, Robbie felt actor training should include critical inquiry into the forces shaping the world we live in, and actors should practice activating their agency within and among all these forces. The actor must uncover. The actor must confront. The actor must question.

How I found "nice" is not a problem. . . .

Though many disparage it. After years of jaw-clenching rage, I began . . . after my toddler daughter, now thirty something, years ago told me when I was enraged about something or another, "Mommy, your face is not a mommy . . ." I began bit by bit to breathe deeper and flow thoughts out of my mouth. Made me feel nice, and nicer. The rage I began to see as a loud cover for sadness, pride, shame, fear, so many unspoken stories.

Robbie had no truck with passivity. I could always recognize actors who'd worked with Robbie as their director, or teacher, for they had a specific alertness in their presence. Robbie had full-body concentration. She knew

> that the story we tell shapes the life we live; she concluded that we have both the right and the responsibility to shape that story.

My personal life was affected by the nation's big dramas. My father in World War II when I was born, my first memory of three-year-old me seeing him so handsome in uniform free and alive, and told to sing "Yes, Jesus Loves Me." It was winter in Georgia and there was a fireplace. Growing up in the 1950s . . . we were like everybody believing in the future. By then our nuclear family'd migrated to Washington, DC. Nineteen sixty I voted the first time people in DC could federally (still fighting for statehood) for John F. Kennedy. My body broke down weeping afterwards to my surprise, weeping more than later hearing about his assassination. After marrying the best actor in "The Howard Players" we moved to New York. I worked for the Welfare Department while auditioning and acting off-off-Broadway. The marriage didn't last and I took advantage of that free love love era. A whole untellable '70s time.

> One of the distinctions of the way Robbie worked was that each time was *the* time. Each reading, rehearsal, performance was a chance to be fully present and to play on that day. She encouraged us to play with the capacity we have, and the capacity we might not think we have, but actually do have just beyond our fingertips. She both got out of the way of a piece as it came into being through her body as instrument, and kept herself fully alert and responsive to its unfolding, a wholly compelling tension. She did not disappear into a part. The work she chose to do was never about any kind of erasure. Rather, in her work, as was true of the work of any legendary jazz artist (Davis, Trane, Carter, etc.), we are gathered here, right now, to imagine something unfolding in real time together, both individually and collectively. Robbie's gift included the ability to make us all sense the histories and deep interior truths we each brought to this moment we share in presence with her. Indeed, she shared her own revelations about "who her people were," what histories accompanied her every move and, by extension, our every move. We are each shapers of meaning through the ways we remember and recall our stories. Robbie invited us to remember our capacity to shift the contours of our shared reality in real time by remembering in real time. A story is shaped through the telling.

Before that time I became a professional actor, got my Actors' Equity union card hired to work on Adrienne Kennedy's *A Beast's Story*, directed by Gerald Freedman at the Public Theater in the then recently established building on Lafayette Street, after being auditioned by artistic director and producer Joseph Papp. He consistently hired Black actors. I played there later, originating the role of Clara in Kennedy's *A Movie Star Has to Star in Black and White,* directed by Joseph Chaikin. Though as vulnerable as anyone doing such seminal work, I felt my feet on the ground as an actor. Shortly before starting work at the Public, I took classes with Kristin Linklater at the Negro Ensemble Company, where she posted for anyone wanting to learn to teach her voice production methodology. I signed up. Afterwards, she recommended me to teach at NYU's Acting Program, so from then on I have woven teaching and practice.

> When Robbie would think deeply, as she did that afternoon in 1995, she would narrow her eyelids and I could see her depth of field shift, moving within toward the records of experience and/or burning fast-forward to some as yet unrealized potential. She dipped in and out of time. She'd move her torso, sometimes take a sharp breath, and her mouth would move as though she were about to recount some detail of what she was surveying through her mind's eye. Most times she would shout out, "ah!" That's when you knew she had found her way to the thing she needed to say. *Ah!* She lifted both of her palms from my kitchen table. With fingers held up and moving the energy in the air around themselves oh so subtly, she fixed me with her gaze, then said simply, directly, with the pure tone of a vital just-remembered detail:
>
> "there was no air"

One night I went to see the original Last Poets. The trio included Felipe Luciano, Gylan Kain, and David Nelson. They changed the way I saw performance and politics.

Spiritually—I am an orthodox agnostic—I believe—and I have doubt. I am not trying to resolve that contradiction either. I think about resolving it—but I am not sure I will. The spiritual comes forward more now, as I get older.

I live with the wisdom of my ancestors.

> I had learned everything from Robbie by listening, by sensing, by repeating, by doing. Doing again, and again.

Sally said, "tell it." Once, when I was hospitalized with diabetes—it was a city hospital, with a curtain between me and the next patient—I walked down a hallway and through a door and I saw my grandmother there, sitting in a

Fig. 11.2. Jomama Jones (Daniel Alexander Jones) presents Robbie McCauley during the standing ovation of her assembled admirers at Emerson College. © 2017 Craig Bailey/Perspective.

rocker, twiddling her thumbs. She said to me, "Get Back." And then, I heard the doctors, the next day, say about me—"She's back."

I think my grandmother was telling me to get back to life.

That afternoon in 1995, Robbie remembered the lady in red's pivotal monologue wholly. Her attention curled inward to find each of shange's phrases, each subsequent moment of the story. I watched the subtle shifts in her posture, in her breathing. Through her telling I could feel the atomic weight of each new detail coming into focus. I smelled the apartment, heard the noise from the street outside, but most importantly, I could feel the concomitant crush of forces hitting crystal, beau willie, and their children, naomi and kwame, in that moment to moment to moment. The cadence ticked up and grew more erratic, but never anything less than precise. The window, the sill, the extremes screaming in all directions at once, the keen attention to the minute details that signify the scale of this unfolding disaster. Each note full, round, plangent, but Robbie played them even more quickly, precisely, starkly, amassing an indescribable tension:

> "he kicked the screen outta the window/ & held the kids
> offa the sill/ you gonna marry me/ yeh, i'll marry ya/
> anything/ but bring the children back in the house/
> he looked from where the kids were hangin from the
> fifth story/ at alla the people screamin at him/ &
> he started sweatin again/ say to alla the neighbors/
> you gonna marry me/
> i stood by beau in the window/ with naomi reachin
> for me/ kwame screamin mommy mommy from the fifth
> story/ but i cd only whisper/ & he dropped em"[2]

> I heard that next-to-last line more clearly than I ever had before. "But i cd only whisper." Uttered by Robbie, it was a fact. A confession. Evidence of the whole. "& he dropped em." The last line was sharp, direct; it was the *next* thing in the series of things that happened on that fateful day *and* it was the *last* thing that happened. With it uttered by Robbie, I felt the shock through my entire body. Robbie looked at me, from deep within the work. Her fingers had been extended, I don't even recall that happening; they were . . . *holding* the air . . . holding time as still as she could, in some visceral reach for grace. As the shock waves rippled, her fingers waned; they curled softly back, as though they each held a small, disoriented, desperate bird. She placed her hands down on the table again. The unnameable scale of terror and grief remained just that—unnameable—but somehow through her artistry she rendered its body clearly for us to sit with, and apprehend as best we could. She understood that some things are so horrible that to try to name them is its own kind of violence. She understood that by doing as shange had on the page, by telling what happened, we unlock something beyond capture that yet demands our witness.
>
> "That's how I did it," Robbie said.

Contact down south was the reason I was so tolerant of white people. We saw them up close enough to see them to be regular. Knowing your place with one another is a kind of intimacy northerners don't understand. A tall man came to fix our stove when I was little in Georgia and I looked at him while he worked. He farted and I laughed. He saw me looking from the doorway and laughed too. Then he fixed his face back to thin-lipped stern like white men usually look.

Me and Sister used to go play with Martha Fay and Sheila, whose father ran the corner store. We'd read the note Ma Willie had given us because their father couldn't. He and his wife could slice and measure meat, read the register, and were nice to the colored people who kept their business going. We taught the girls how to read.

When Sister got ten she couldn't play with them no more, and I stopped soon after, something silently decided on by grown folks.

White men in suits used to come get money from my grandmother once a week for numbers. Ma Willie was upstanding but everybody played numbers and talked about dreams and she had a dream book with symbols and numbers for dream pictures. People would get cash for a percentage of all the money that came in if the number they played hit. It took a respectable woman like our grandmother to handle the cash taken in and paid out to people who hit a number.

Once some other white men came and put her in the police car, but brought her right back home. She stopped doin' numbers after that, and only Miss Maggie who ran the beauty shop down the street took up the business.

What happened to Mr. Oscar one day changed everything for me. Everybody knows my father was away at war when I was born. So were most of the young men in our Army town. Mr. Oscar who used to be a bricklayer who'd built the mighty fine corner house for his big family was now old and drank a lot down at the Blue Chip Cafe. We all called him Daddy 'cause he was the jovial man we saw all the time. So the day everything changed Mr. Oscar was stumbling up to his house on the dirt sidewalk when the police who periodically rode through the neighborhood slowed down and called Mr. Oscar over to the car, called out his name and told him to dance. Confused Mr. Oscar didn't know what to do so he just stood there. Calling him you-know-what they rolled down the window and told him to put his head in, then they rolled it halfway up and started the car slow making him move his feet.

That's right, "Dance you-know-what" they kept saying. I couldn't look too long, just saw Mr. Oscar walking home with his head hung down, and I felt shame for his shame forever after and never called him Daddy anymore.

> That's how she did it. Time and again I saw Robbie speak the unspeakable, place her body in the midst of the maelstrom onstage, in a rehearsal room, a community workshop, a classroom, or forum. When she died I called her "the bravest artist I ever met" because she was. She knew that if we don't put our bodies in it, it don't mean a thing. Our bodies (physical, energetic, inclusive of our archives, of our perceptive capacities) give the thing that swing that begets its meaning.

And I feel memories of my father, especially now, in my body.

I thought of him recently—and my body broke open. I was weeping. But at the same time I questioned myself. I had no idea—I couldn't answer why I was weeping—rationally.

The project I worked on with my daughter—I'm so glad she asked me to do it. She told me to write something and I did that ("Something to Say").

She (Jessie Montgomery) wants to look at the grandfathers on my side from a different perspective, from their perspectives.

> Robbie had a few diabetic crises during the earlier years of our friendship. When she took faculty positions at Trinity College in Hartford and, later, Emerson College, I and others in her circle were grateful that they afforded her a substantive measure of stability to tend her body and receive the kinds of everyday support that the peripatetic life of an independent artist does not often afford. I watched over the years as her body changed. When we met she was vital and lithe, and her aura extended vibrant green in all directions. As she aged her light refined, clarified, so that the light surrounding her was more like the clear, bright sunlight of early morning; her body grew incrementally more brittle, shrinking from its prior edges just enough to notice at first, and then precipitously, in stark phases. Her heart troubles and subsequent surgeries exacerbated the difficulties she already faced. But to know Robbie, one had to remind oneself often that these things were true as she aged, for she could get her energy up and sway the room and make you forget. Yet, she was so transparent about her body and its contradictions that I believed—we all believed—she could face the dilemmas, and just might pull the cloak of presence around herself and defy the odds. I don't know all of what she faced subjectively, of course. She would tell me without telling me. Truly, she did not wish to linger on in infirmity. Rather, she was like a true New Yorker; if the trains are breaking down, you take a cab, and if you can't catch one, you get to walking. Robbie kept moving.

The body and music are endemic to the work I do—I do physical therapy and my therapist is delighted with me—I do it ritualistically. I am fascinated with how the body functions in a (my) delicate state.

I had a hard time with balance—but now it's much better. I can stand on one leg—a great accomplishment.

I have type 1 diabetes; I am worried about my feet. I've had open-heart surgeries—to repair valves.

For me, storytelling is where I come from. Acting work—for me—is always about talking to the audience.

Every month or so, I'm having a procedure related to my heart—but I'm still working and right now, I'm writing a play over Zoom.

With this, I'm learning that I am older. It's hard to admit that to ourselves. But I appreciate my time more now. And I appreciate too the wisdom that comes with time. I learn through the questions of my collaborators—those younger than me—and I learn through their care of and care for me. In the story we are creating—I am the older woman in a hospital and her younger collaborators are doing physical therapy with her.

> I saw *Sugar*, beautifully directed by Maureen Shea and designed by Mirta Tocci, and watched Robbie navigate an exacting new piece. Her flesh seemed to be composed of a greater percentage of light waves, her bones suspended in place. When she hoisted a huge bundle of sugarcane atop her back, we all held our breath and I bowed, once again, to her mastery: her fragility was all our fragility, whether we liked it or not.

I was talking to Daniel Alexander Jones. I said, "I don't think there is truth. It's only what you know."

"There's something very dangerous about how reality is bent now."

I feel as if I have lived through this time before. But, afterwards, there was a feeling of hope. I don't feel hope now.

Theater is useful. Even in this virtual time, truth resonates—people are talking and being seen. I recently directed a radio play—Christina Anderson wrote it. It was a strong, effective piece. A way to be useful.

I pass on the lessons I learned from Kristin Linklater (breathing into the image) and Joe Chaikin—I try not to hit actors over the head with these lessons.

There are people I wish I could talk to now. Once, I talked to my mother with my art. Now I would like to talk to a Trump supporter.

> The need for this awakening concerned Robbie greatly. She knew our precarity. She resisted party lines no matter where they appeared, in great measure because they deaden our capacity for alertness and clarity of apprehension. She was impatient with rigid certainties in thought. And she urged us beyond our summary judgments or dismissals of one another; beneath the cornerstones of our thinking, unexamined distortions creep and crawl in the dark.

I would like to share my journal notes with you.

> Two of the formal precepts of jazz are (*a*) the agency of any individual player, and (*b*) the work of multivalent listening: to the core structures in the song, to the disposition of any individual player in the context of the other players' dispositions, and to the emerging composition, which unfolds in real time in the air around them all. In Robbie's presence, we'd all lean in to experience a world of understanding being born before our eyes. Of course, the other palpable implication was that Robbie knew that you were in the room, and she welcomed you, and reminded you that your engagement with the work being made was anything but passive.

Back when going south on the train, when so many Black children from New York, Philadelphia, Delaware, Baltimore, and DC, with trains officially segregated all the way up south, our caretakers had boarded us safely in the Colored cars—(despite Steven Spielberg's faux moment in *The Color Purple* train) and how we were undercover taken care of by A. Philip Randolph's powerfully unionized Negro train workers, we had no idea we were in the midst, at the core as usual of positive change in this slow country.

A pretty dark-brown-skinned cousin named Lily, always described as pretty *but* dark skin (which annoyed me since I was by then the darkest female in the family and knew from the mirror I was pretty). She had died young and married a train conductor from Atlanta. The conductors knew we were kinfolks and gave us brown-skin service on the train. They sat us behind a curtain by the kitchen in the dining car, and served us the same breakfast as white folks.

All the back-and-forth train stories from us to us—from working with Chinese and Irish who were necessary immigrants and us ex-slaves. Us too, yes.

working "all the livelong day"
moving on up, moving through, always in motion in this slow country that believes so much
in speed.
on a train
that feels like a stagecoach
remembering open train windows at least in the station.
Aunt Thelma would get on
with me and Sister tasting a piece of chicken making everybody nervous, but my mother Aunt 'nem's cousin, Lily'd married a train man . . . so Thelma'd always mention that, and got a few minutes more to talk to and

us before hearing from the colored uniformed men, "If you don't tend to go nowhere, get off the train" and the white conductor'd sing out "All aboard that's mean to be aboard." Us going back up south.

Nowhere to hide
inside the inside
underside side by side,
over the side.
Sideways.

Black people have personally experienced so many large political dramas. Growing up we identified with Emmett Till, Rosa Parks, sit-ins to dismantle segregation, the four little girls murdered in an Alabama church, and the Supreme Court's demand to desegregate public schools, to name a few. Fortunate enough to follow my dream to step into a wider world while viscerally retaining connection to my origins, I looked for, and took advantage of, opportunities to make theater, to continue to learn, teach, and use the form to explore possibilities for telling untold stories and fostering dialogue between contentious racial and cultural groups of people. Neither scholarly nor physically energetic enough to study in a traditional academic way, I learned through my comfort with acting, teaching, and making theater in whatever venues nearby me, or places I could manage travel to.

As tiresome as it can be to get white people to break open denial of their complicity, I knew change needed their unspoken stories and chose to chip away at their resistance.

As Robbie's presence expanded and deepened as she aged, her body, that still-mighty instrument, became as fragile as glass. Her physical waning emphasized the brilliance of her soul like a waning crescent moon signals its imminent disappearance. Among our last conversations were check-ins via Zoom; often Jessie, or Ed, Robbie's former husband, who remained her family, were in the background or popped in to say hello as well. They, along with Robbie's amazing sister Anita, their family and wide circle of friends and former colleagues and students, gathered to hold her, gently, as precarity became clearer and clearer. She had rendered her physical decline in stunning terms through her final major performance work, *Sugar*. But she took it as she did everything, another text to learn, to understand as best she could, and to play with the force of her expert voice. As you see from her writing, she found collaborators even among her caregivers.

You can do this
Go sideways
Stay by the wayside
On the edge of the highway
I must go along to get along
To not be wrong to get strong
And not be killed or die.

Each and every time. In her presence, your contradictions, your fears, your frailties were embraced as component parts of a being constantly becoming. She weathered others' judgments, rages, dismissals, and misapprehensions with an almost scientific curiosity about how these behaviors belonged to an ecosystem in crisis. With rare exception, people opened up to her and in so doing opened up to themselves. Whew. I watched people glow with a kind of light behind their eyes that I find so rare these days in this country. It's a light that shows up in the presence of something perceived as beautiful because it is true. Robbie was beautiful because she was true.

Poem for Everybody
by Robbie McCauley

Having not a child nor dog
Dedicate yourself to care for
All living things. Downtown we'd
open late night widows put raisins outside for roaches and ants.
Give up retrievable dinosaur fantasies and let camels roam in their own deserts.
Let expert people balance muscles at circuses for others to see.
And all people anywhere
dance any time.
And change somehow
the 2nd Amendment.

We are living through a surge of tragedies, exponential in their impact. Robbie and her work remain necessary. Robbie offered practices for helping us regrow our civic neural networks, to speak what seems unspeakable. Hers is challenging work, because Robbie asks you to participate in it. She was not selling a party line. She was not espousing any orthodoxy (other than, in honor of her embrace of contradiction, what she describes as an orthodox agnosticism). She was strategic about freedom. Her own and ours. And she struggled for it. We carry her work, and we call her soul to the kitchen table, to tell us, again, how to move the remembered back through life.

2098

An Ecological world
What the world will be
like for my daughter.

Food clothing shelter and medical care everywhere will be free. Money a minimal medium of exchange. For instance, since work mainly will be the making of objects and other modes of art, including the medical ones. People will pay artists with money which'll be used to buy more materials or lessons in their chosen fields.

The atmosphere will be where people have decent lives with little crime. There'll always be a few assholes. Police will not carry guns. Weapons will mainly be dialogue and tai chi.

Cars and airplanes will be fewer, only used for medical emergencies. Spaces over oceans and rivers between land masses by then will've been transformed into well-fortified moving bridges using solar, wind, sugar-based power.

Ethnic differences among people will be kept alive with stories. Mixtures of people because of peace and easy access will abound, language learning exchanges, and a worldwide sense of play among children and adults.

Addictions to eating it as well as other damaging excesses to the body and minds will have been cured by meditation. People will live way past 120 years if they wish.

Critical dialogue will prevail. Women and men who want children will have them. Marriage, though outmoded, will be tolerated. Love will be free.

NOTES

1. Laurie "Lore" Carlos was Robbie's longtime collaborator. They were art sisters.
2. ntozake shange, *for colored girls who have considered suicide when the rainbow is enuf* (Macmillan, 1977), 24.

12

Rehearsing for Revolution

Autobiographical Performance Arouses Utopian Performativity in Sonic Elder

Julia Henderson

At Vancouver's storied seventy-year-old Penthouse Nightclub, singer Joni Moore, also in her seventies, proclaims, "We sure had a good time, didn't we? And we're still having a good time!" Today, during the final moments of *Sonic Elder*'s closing performance, the audience bursts into applause, the band starts to play, and members of the crowd rocket to their feet to dance. I am struck by the sense of time (in the bodies, in the place, in the music's tempo, rhythm, lyrics)—time dragged from past into present, stretched across generations, and bonding the musicians through the glue of unique temporal experience. It feels that today, especially, both audience and band together are "sure having a good time!"

Sonic Elder was billed by its creator, Vancouver's Chop Theatre, as a live, autobiographical "onstage documentary."[1] It featured six lifelong professional musicians, all over the age of sixty. During the show, they performed as a rock band and reflected on the role that music played in their lives over time. The show was collaboratively devised by its performers, director, and dramaturg. The scene I have described captures an instance of what Jill Dolan theorizes as the "utopian performative."[2] For Dolan, such moments involve a deep intersubjectivity between performers and audience, one that offers an affective rehearsal of what utopia could *feel* like, and in doing so engenders possibilities for emotional, spiritual, and sociocultural transformation.[3] The aesthetic impulse guiding the development of *Sonic Elder* was the creation of such moments, which counterbalanced dominant cultural narratives that equate aging and older age with decline and loss. I argue that in *Sonic Elder* the autobiographical nature of the performance, the specificity of the venue, and the inclusion of particular content all allowed for performances of age that offered moving and hopeful glimpses of how it could *feel* to resist ageism by embracing expanded and nonessentializing age expectations.

SONIC ELDER

Sonic Elder was developed over a two-year period from 2015 to 2017 by the Chop Theatre. Due to the company's history of creating shows with themes about aging and the life course, it was originally commissioned to create *Sonic Elder* for the 2015 iteration of Club PuSh, a musical cabaret of experimental performances that has been part of Vancouver's PuSh International Performing Arts Festival since 2009. Based on the show's positive reception at Club PuSh, the Chop Theatre obtained funding and further developed *Sonic Elder*, mounting a second version, which ran from September 27 to October 2, 2016, at the Penthouse Nightclub, located on Seymour Street in downtown Vancouver. It was directed by Christie Watson and dramaturged by Anita Rochon, both of whom were interviewed as part of this analysis (with University of British Columbia's ethical approval). This second version of *Sonic Elder* is the focus of this chapter because, according to Watson and Rochon, it was the most fully realized version of the show.

Sonic Elder was cast with six high-level, lifelong musicians from British Columbia's Lower Mainland, who were recruited by Watson using word of mouth based on their reputation as musicians, their "fit" as a band, and their willingness to share their autobiographical stories. They were not experienced actors, and none had previously been involved in creating a personal theater piece. They were a mixed-race group of five men and one woman, ages sixty-two to seventy-six. Most of the band had played together many times, three since they were teenagers. The cast included Billy Butler on guitar, Ron Kosaka on bass guitar, Bill Sample on keyboards (also the band leader), Joni Moore and Harry Walker on vocals, and Buff Allen on drums (Carlos Joe Costa was the drummer for the Club PuSh version; all other performers remained the same).

The eighty-minute show was a live autobiographical performance consisting of a series of rock songs interspersed equally with spoken content that included personal stories (often in the form of monologues), reminiscences, life reflections, jokes, and playful banter. According to Watson, it was developed using a series of interactive theater devising activities; personal interviews with the performers; trial and rehearsal of songs the performers suggested; dramaturgical work on structure, storyline, style, and timing; experimentation with content; and lots of repetition in rehearsal. Some of the spoken content was tightly scripted (for example, the life story monologues), some was scripted with room for improvisation around a prechosen topic, and some allowed for looser improvisation so that the content varied in each performance. Thematically, the spoken content conveyed the performers' various experiences with music and its role in their lives over time, as well as the performers' unique and continued value as old(er) performers. Each performer's personal story was highlighted at some point in the show. The music was chosen from the musicians' repertoires and mostly consisted of cover songs that ranged in style from skiffle, old R & B, and show tunes, to torch songs, early rock, and 1960s protest songs. At least one song was composed by a performer.

Sonic Elder's venue was a key element of the production. The Penthouse is a strip club established in 1947, and is the last of the original venues where these musicians got their start. Before canned music, nightclubs used to hire live bands to play music for the dancers. Most of the *Sonic Elder* band members had played at the Penthouse to gain experience in their youth; some worked there on a regular basis for years. The club is still owned by the Filippone family and remains largely unchanged.[4]

The *Sonic Elder* set consisted of the Penthouse stage: a simple proscenium across the front of the venue backed by a red curtain, with a thrust runway in the center. For the production, the stripper pole was removed from the runway and a carpet added. The Chop Theatre further customized the space by bringing its own lighting and sound systems. During the performance, the musicians were located center stage with their instruments, and each had their own chair, chosen (according to Watson) to suit the performer's personal biomechanics and style. The chairs remained in the same positions and were used often throughout the show. The performers mostly remained on the stage, and their movement principally consisted of sitting, standing, and playing their instruments. Joni Moore, the lead singer, used the runway for some of her monologues and songs, which placed her closer to the audience. In terms of costuming, Watson described the style as a mix of vintage, contemporary, and "postmoderny hodgepodge." He noted that they chose "heightened and more stagy" versions of how the performers normally dressed. The result was that the musicians seemed comfortable, fashionable, and individual. The simplicity of both the set and the costumes harmonized with the style of the nightclub venue, and contributed to the sense that the performers and venue belonged to and shaped each other (a notion to which I will return).

Fig. 12.1. Joni Moore appears in *Sonic Elder* by The Chop Theatre at Club PuSH, PuSH International Performing Arts Festival, Vancouver, 2015. Photo: Terumi Squibb.

AUTOBIOGRAPHY AND UTOPIAN PERFORMATIVITY

In considering autobiographical performances of age identity, applying Jill Dolan's theory of the utopian performative offers a useful intervention to help us understand how such performances can powerfully and productively reimagine representations of old(er) selves. A feminist theater and performance studies scholar, Dolan argues that people are attracted to live performance because it "can move us toward understanding the possibility of something better, can train our imaginations, inspire our dreams and fuel our desires in ways that might lead to incremental cultural change."[5] She argues not only that theater can express utopian ideas through its content, but more importantly, that the live performer-audience exchange can inspire "usefully emotional expressions of what utopia might *feel* like" and in doing so "provoke affective rehearsals for revolution."[6]

Ric Knowles takes up Dolan's ideas and applies them to live *autobiographical* performance, arguing that heightened intersubjective, synesthetic moments between audience and performer are deepened because of the dramatic form itself.[7] This is because most performed autobiography relies on the audience's knowledge that the body they are watching is the same body to which the events portrayed happened. According to Knowles, a body, which is physically and discursively marked (such as by old[er] age), embodies traces of individual and cultural memory. This bodily archive, as Susan Bennett names it,[8] can arouse feelings of heightened intersubjectivity between audience and performer through the visceral power of its presence.[9] Knowles coins the term "autobiology" to describe "performances of the social and cultural assemblage of the body becoming itself."[10] I would like to contemplate how this "becoming" takes place within and across time, such that any performance of a particular identity is also, intersectionally, a performance of age identity. Knowles's idea of autobiology can in this way be linked to Anne Davis Basting's depth model of age, a model premised on the notion that age, like gender, is inherently performative.[11] According to Basting, when we experience a performance of age in life or onstage, we are not witnessing an enactment of age belonging to an isolated point in time. The performance is also an accumulation of performances of the actor's former age-selves and a projection of future age-selves; it is linked through time to generations past, present, and still to come.[12] A performance of age in temporal depth, then, is an accrual of performances of age from across the life course and across generations.

Previously, I related Basting's notion of temporal depth to Marvin Carlson's theory of theatrical ghosting as put forward in *The Haunted Stage: The Theatre as Memory Machine.*[13] In particular, Carlson proposes the "haunted body," to describe how an actor's body is "ghosted" by their multiple previous performances, such that when audiences see an actor onstage, they also perceive an accumulation of the previous roles or personas the actor has embodied.[14] Ghosting, then, I argue, strongly influences perception of a character's age. Drawing on Knowles, Basting, and Carlson, I now propose that age-autobiology involves performances of age that are strongly rooted in embodied memory, and that can be thought of as an assemblage of performances of age across time. Autobiological depth performances of age, then, create an age identity that is not rooted in linear time and is independent of fixed life-stage expectations—meaning, as Basting puts it, that no expression of age is natural, normal, or, more importantly, pathological.[15]

BODIES AS ARCHIVE AND BODIES IN TEMPORAL DEPTH

In *Sonic Elder* instances of utopian performativity often formed through an accrual of previous moments. The first occurrence, I argue, took place during the opening scene of the show and hinged on a combined effect of the audience's first encounter with the embodied presence of the actors, in conjunction with the repeated lyrics of the first song, and certain personally revealing autobiographical elements of the spoken script. In this case it was the accretion of these factors throughout the scene that led to the experience of utopian intersubjectivity I will now describe.

After band leader Bill Sample on keyboard, accompanied by Buff Allen on drums, acknowledged the traditional, ancestral, unceded First Nations lands on which they performed,[16] the rest of the *Sonic Elder* band entered. At this point, the audience had already seen photographs of band members performing music in their younger years projected on screens to either side of the stage during the preshow. They had also viewed similar photos in a lobby display. Now they encountered the live performing bodies for the first time. The musicians all entered with energy, charisma, and purpose. They all appeared present and vital—a feeling enhanced by the juxtaposition of their live, moving older bodies with the photographic stills of their younger days. The band took up their instruments and began their first song, "Gimme Some Lovin'."[17] As the instrumentalists played a tight and energetic accompaniment, singers Moore and Walker belted out the chorus:

> I'm so glad we made it, I'm so glad we made it
> Gimme some lovin' (gimme some lovin')
> Gimme some lovin' (gimme some lovin')
> Gimme some lovin' every day

The lyrics suggested a journey in and across time through the line "we made it"—a journey that in retrospect the "we" of the song claims to have been worth taking ("*so glad* we made it"). Moore, at times, added the word "now" at the beginning of the repeated "gimme some lovin'" chorus line, emphasizing the present moment ("*Now*, gimme some lovin'"). The inclusion of the lyric "every day" at the end of the line's last repeat suggested that the journey would also continue into the future, day by day.

To reinforce the idea of a journey through time, Moore's first line following the song was "Good evening everybody! We're so glad you made it. And we're glad we made it too!" This offered a foundation for intersubjective understanding that built throughout the scene. On behalf of the band, Moore acknowledged the audience members' shared experience, not only of their journey to the theater that day, but also of their journey through life to that point. This rhetorical framing suggested that aging is a *mutual* experience of traveling in and across time—past, present, and future. The acknowledgment of collective experience reinforced Dolan's belief that "live performance provides a place where people come together, embodied and passionate to share experiences of meaning making and imagination that can describe or capture fleeting imitations of a better world."[18] It grounded the lyrics of the song in shared experience so that when the song reprised later, it inspired what Victor Turner terms "communitas," a concept Dolan borrows from Turner and describes as "moments in a theater event or a ritual in which audiences or participants feel themselves become part of the whole in an organic, nearly spiritual way."[19]

Following Moore's welcoming line, the band members introduced one another, offering a few particulars of each of their lives, past and present. For example, Moore introduced Butler: "I'd like to introduce, on guitar and vocals, a man who moved to Canada from London, England, in 1972. He lives in a co-op on Commercial Drive and recently celebrated the birth of his first great grandchild, Gavin. Ladies and gentlemen, the dashing Billy Butler!" Cheers of recognition from the audience confirmed that many knew these performers.

It was in this moment that audience members became aware experientially (or became certain) that the performance was autobiographical, and that the bodies onstage were the actual bodies that had experienced the events described—the real bodies that had "made it" and continued to demonstrate "making it" by persisting and thriving before us. These bodies told a story of endurance through time as bodies in depth, and as a result their challenge to the decline narrative was profound. The rhetorical construction of the song's lyrics, which enfolded notions of a past, present, and future journey through the life course (a journey being a performative act), in conjunction with the projected images, enhanced the cast's embodiment of depth performances of age.

The effect of Carlson's theatrical ghosting here was also particularly strong and contributed to the reception of these performances of age as existing in temporal depth. In this case, the audience had just seen projected photographs of the performers at a range of younger ages. Since they had appeared so recently, these images were strongly ghosted in the live performing bodies and layered onto present performances of self. In addition, for many audience members who were contemporaries of the performers, the projections enhanced the flood of personal memories of these musicians over time, and were now ghosted in the bodies onstage. As per Bennett, the live performing bodies were already scripted by their somatic and performative history prior to their current subject matter.[20] The performance of future selves is more challenging to perceive as individuals do not possess embodied memory of the future. However, as Basting writes, "The important thing is not to polish the details, but to acknowledge the almost certain (barring tragedy) links between youth, adulthood, old age, and all categories in between."[21] Here, the song's repeated lyric "every day" allowed the audience to glimpse an image of the performers' future selves in the present by picturing a journey that would continue. Ghosting helped locate the performers in duration and thus opened up possibilities of future selves.

It is possible that ghosting had one other effect in challenging age stereotypes here. Valerie Barnes Lipscomb contends that when a younger role-type is ghosted in the performance of an older actor, the incongruity between the performing body and the age stereotypes associated with that role "creates space for commentary on the nature of the aging self and the ageism associated with those expectations."[22] It is possible that, to an extent, the disjuncture between the performing bodies of *Sonic Elder* and traditional visions of "the rock musician" (i.e., someone young and rebellious) subverted stereotypes and challenged decline. However, the show highlighted the persistence of these particular musicians across their life courses, and did not capitalize on rock stereotypes, which themselves are changing as many famous rock musicians continue to perform past midlife.[23] Therefore, while the ghosting of a young rock star archetype in the older bodies may have provoked productive tension in this show to some degree, it was less of a factor in shaping the audience's reception than the other ghosting effects described above. Instead, because these performers were performing themselves rather than taking on a recognizably separate character, the performance highlighted a continuity of self by ghosting the performers' former selves at various ages. In summary, elements of the *Sonic Elder* script, the bodily archives of these performers, and the ghosted memories they evoked aligned in a manner that resulted in a significant disruption to the narrative of decline, and that further laid the groundwork for utopian potential.

As the musicians introduced one another with details of their lives (both past and present), they began to establish not only their own individual age identities, but also a group age identity as Vancouver musicians of a particular era, as well as a generational identity—a generation that "made it" by surviving the aftereffects of World War II, the Vietnam War, the Cold War, challenges to civil rights, the 1960s cultural revolution, and various economic recessions. This survival or continuation was evidenced in the bodies onstage as Ron Kosaka went on to deliver a humorous account of the group's combined health, relationship, and performing experiences:

> So between the six of us we've:
> Played 34,500 shows,
> Been married 12 times,
> Have 20 kids,
> Have smoked 107 pounds of weed. . . .
> We've got Shingles, Bell's palsy, gout, mumps, e coli, broken ribs, a torn ACL, pleurisy, skin cancer, prostate cancer, failing memory, insomnia, diabetes, failing memory. . . .
> . . . We are 427 years old. . . .
> . . . and tonight we're gonna ROCK you![24]

The choice to reveal these details as an aggregated story contributed to establishing the group's identity; the performers shared being musicians, partners, parents, nonconformists, and survivors. The numerical magnitude of the experiences commanded respect. Layered with the performers' live presence, this text solidified their group identity as people who have endured challenges (especially to their health) and continued to enjoy music and share it with audiences. It also positioned them as part of a group that is gaining an increased cultural presence as it ages into the future. As a result, when the band reprised "Gimme Some Lovin," the words were particularly poignant.

This time as Moore sang "I'm so glad we made it / Gimme some lovin,'" and the other band members repeated these lines as backup vocals, I felt a deep connection with the musicians. Their performances of age and self spanned past, present, and future, and their strong claim to authenticity, by virtue of being the actual bodies to which events described had happened, meant that they produced a moment of what Knowles calls "phenomenological *frisson*," or heightened intersubjective experience between audience and stage.[25] I was flooded with gratitude and respect for the musical offerings these musicians had given over time, with joy in the moment of experiencing the music, and with hope that a different theater of age was being offered through this performance. I felt an exceptional desire to give them "some lovin'" in the form of engaging with the performance from the perspective of David Román's critical generosity, or a willingness to meet their work with collaborative, cooperative engagement, and provide it with a cultural context committed to changing age relations.[26] It felt like a moment of promise in which group perspectives toward age could be envisioned anew. In this sense, this reprise of "Gimme Some Lovin'" evoked Dolan's utopian performativity for me—a glimpse of a changed future. The strength of the applause and overall audience engagement following this number suggested that the rest of the audience felt it too.

DRAMATURGY OF ASSISTANCE

The next striking moment of intersubjective potential functioned by accentuating both relational and embodied selfhoods. In a previous article, "Dramaturgy of Assistance: Performing with Dementia or Age-Related Memory Loss," I analyzed the dramaturgy of *Sonic Elder* and proposed the concept of "dramaturgy of assistance" to describe its dramaturgical approaches that were devised to support a performer with significant age-related memory loss, allowing them to participate in this live professional production without being cast as "other." I define the term as follows:

> *Dramaturgy of assistance* is a dramaturgical approach designed to include and support performers with varying degrees of age-related memory loss, including more severe memory loss such as occurs with dementia. In a variety of ways, the approach's dramaturgical techniques facilitate performers' recall of musical and spoken content and physical blocking, and allow for participation that does not require memorisation or only rely on recall of fixed reminiscences.[27]

The approach allows for malleable and creative memories to emerge. In *Sonic Elder* this dramaturgy particularly capitalized on performers' embodied and relational selfhoods. Relational selfhood refers to the self that is "formed through interaction with others."[28] As I argue in "Dramaturgy of Assistance," *Sonic Elder* consciously drew on relationships between cast members to create the performance, and exposed these ongoing supportive relationships to the audience. Techniques employed included the following: the show cast performers who had worked together over many years and had previous personal and professional relationships and generational history; the show's content emphasized the connections between performers through conversations and through ensemble music; the personal relationships were foregrounded, which allowed for rich stories to emerge that superseded decline-and-loss narratives of aging, and also allowed performers to support one another improvisationally in the telling of stories; the techniques of prompting and cuing one another were integrated into the show's style; and a clear choice was made to represent memory loss as a continuum on which all of the performers were situated, emphasizing their connections rather than differences.[29]

In addition to highlighting relational selfhood, *Sonic Elder* also capitalized on the embodied selfhood of the performers. Embodied selfhood is a perspective of self that "foregrounds pre-reflective ways of being-in-the-world" and "stresses the active and acted upon nature of the body."[30] Age theorist, health researcher, and dementia expert Pia Kontos argues "that selfhood, at the most fundamental level, must be understood as inhering in the existential capacity of the body to engage with the world," citing embodied musicality as an example of selfhood that is not reliant on cognition and persists in the face of significant memory loss.[31] I have argued that *Sonic Elder* highlighted embodied selfhood through techniques such as choosing songs according to which pieces Performer A (the performer with significant age-related memory loss) was able to lock into immediately, and through foregrounding its musical numbers where performers related to one another through deep, embodied, implicit understandings of musicality and musical form.[32] Now, in terms of utopian potential, I argue that this backdrop of dramaturgy of assistance was essential to the show's second moment of utopian performativity.

Having already experienced these various *dramaturgy of assistance* techniques that highlighted relational and embodied selfhood, the audience arrived at the particular moment in *Sonic Elder* when Performer A was featured in a musical number. I contend that the transparency of dramaturgical techniques used in the preceding segments of the show created the conditions for Dolan's utopian potential in this moment. Performer A both received an introductory musical cue and was further supported by a line that let him know it was his turn to be featured. He readied his instrument and proceeded to deliver a beautiful, touching, sensitive rendition of the song. The other band members' connection and mutual reliance in creating the music were highlighted in this moment and demonstrated the relational selfhoods required to perform the music. The segment then continued with musical underscoring as another performer spoke a monologue about enlisting in the navy as a fifteen-year-old, and through this experience discovering skiffle music and learning to play the guitar. When the monologue was over, Performer A reprised his featured musical role when the appropriate musical cue occurred, again showing embodied musicality.

At the end of the number, another band member invited Performer A to sit. As an audience member, I was captivated by this scene. I was delighted by the sensitivity of this moment and by the sense of inter-reliance it conveyed, and flooded with respect and admiration for Performer A's talent. The emphasis on relational and embodied selfhoods was a natural extension of the inter-reliance and relationality required to perform together as a band. In this case, because the dramaturgical strategies were exposed (through repetition and transparency), as an audience member, I could both recognize them and at the same time *feel* their value through the moving performance Performer A delivered. I believe this moment, enhanced by the emotionally affecting quality of the music, is an example of the deep utopian romanticism that Dolan describes, prompting intersubjective connection between audience members and performers.[33] It disrupted our profound cultural terror of age-related memory loss and the corresponding belief that becoming old(er) risks a disappearance of selfhood. Again, the audience's focused attentiveness during this segment, and their energetic applause at its completion, suggested to me that the intensity of my experience was shared by others.

NOSTALGIC ROMANTICISM AND AUTOTOPOGRAPHY

The third instance of utopian performativity occurred when Joni Moore delivered a monologue about becoming pregnant at the age of seventeen. The utopian intersubjectivity of this moment was created through Moore's autobiological depth performance of age—a performance enhanced by scripted reference to, and enactment of, both herself as a child and her mother, by her own body as archive, and by her generosity in sharing this personal story.[34]

In an earlier scene, Moore had described her first memory as being her mother singing to her while bathing her in the kitchen sink. As Moore then sang a verse of the song "My Melancholy Baby,"[35] we could both envision it as a portrayal of her mother, and imagine Moore as an infant. Later in the same scene, Moore recounted that her mother began to get her gigs when she was just four years old. She introduced one of the songs she used to perform, entreating us to conjure up an image of her as a child: "So picture me," she said, "seven years old, up onstage in front of a big group of people in a long red dress, with a big hat and a cigarette holder." The invitation inspired us to picture Moore's seven-year-old self, layered onto her seventy-two-year-old self, as she performed "The Oceana Roll."[36] Therefore, when we arrived at the scene titled "Changes, Surprises, Upsets & Victories," we were already predisposed to receive Moore's performance as a depth performance of age, spanning her own life course and across generations. In the "Changes" scene, Moore delivered a monologue about her teen pregnancy. She revealed to us that her parents had hidden her and wanted her to give up the baby, but that she continued to perform six or seven nights a week at clubs like the Penthouse in order to earn a living and survive as a single mom. "Music got me through," she said, "it paid the bills and I just loved singing."[37]

In describing moments of crisis in autobiographical performance, Jenn Stephenson writes that "the reiterative performative enactment of personal history brings that crucial problem into the present, inviting a reflection, but also significantly instigating an embodied second experience of crisis . . . melding the past with present to open a window into the future."[38] In the case of Moore, then, the choice to reveal a life-changing personal crisis from her past inspired a depth performance of age. In reperforming and reembodying the past in the present, she evoked a utopian glimpse of a changed future. The performer's generosity was compelling. It was the first time in the play that a personal crisis was revealed. Focused in a pool of light, Moore spoke from a seated position of stillness, looking at individual audience members as she told her truth. Her story seemed rooted in a place of personal struggle, and her voice expressed a gentle conviction that felt poignant. As she spoke, a hush fell over the audience, and I could sense others leaning forward in their chairs. Moore's presence, openness, and generosity contributed to the moment's intersubjectivity and utopian potential.

A confluence of other factors also sparked this moment's utopian possibility. First, Bennett's notion of the body as archive explained, in part, how Moore achieved this autobiological depth performance of age. Moore's body, which we saw live before us, was the "literal vessel" that had carried her child.[39] As such, Moore seemed to embody simultaneously the seventeen-year-old pregnant girl who had performed here while being hidden by her parents, the mother who had continued to work in this venue to support her child over time, and the now-mature woman who had survived and continued to sing. Her body's claim to authenticity made Moore's performance in temporal depth movingly credible, and provided a significant disruption to the narrative of decline. Carlson's theatrical ghosting, particularly the idea of "the haunted house," came strongly into play to support this truth claim. Carlson writes, "theatre spaces, like dramatic texts and acting bodies, are deeply involved with the preservation and configuration of cultural memory, . . . this haunting of the space of performance makes its own important contribution to the overall reception of the dramatic event."[40] We knew of Moore's experience performing at the Penthouse from an earlier scene, in which she described it as "the place to see and be seen in the fifties and sixties." She told us how she used to sing late-night sets on the very stage where she now stood, joking that she got paid "fifteen bucks and a meatball sandwich." As I watched Moore, many associations I had with the Penthouse of a former era were ghosted in her performance. This was enhanced by the photos of her performing at a younger age that were displayed in the lobby and projected on screens during the preshow. It helped create a sense of Moore's personal and generational identity and continuity across time, and gave rise to a feeling of heightened intersubjectivity through the nostalgia it inspired.

According to Deirdre Heddon, "nostalgia (like autobiography) is also a means of engendering a coherent and continuous identity as we remind ourselves in the present of who we were in the past."[41] Performing a past place need be not a gesture of return, according to Heddon, but rather "the moving of self to a new place, or even the moving of (past) place to a new place (in time)." Nostalgia can be thought of, then, as "an active 'resistance' to the present, rather than simply romanticism of the past."[42] I propose that the resistant nostalgia of Moore's monologue was not "simply romanticism of the past," but rather was aligned with Dolan's notion of a romanticism that creates utopian potential through the sense of communion it arouses in the present.[43]

Also key to the Penthouse venue creating utopian potential is Heddon's concept of "autotopography": "Autotopography is writing place through self (and simultaneously writing self through place)."[44] During Moore's monologue, the audience became aware of how the Penthouse had shaped her identity as a singer and mother over time. Like the many musicians pictured in images on the venue's walls, Moore had helped create this place—an enduring Vancouver entertainment venue. She now continued to define it as a venue that was willingly staging a new theater of aging, and she was, in turn, defined (in part) by this place as a performer who is shifting age expectations.

Heddon suggests that place functions as a moral geography.[45] What was utopian, then, in Moore's monologue was that through her autobiological depth performance of age, she shifted the moral geography of the Penthouse. The venue was and is a strip club, which has many moral associations, especially for female performers. Moore's performance in this moment, and the *Sonic Elder* production as a whole, exposed how the venue helped Moore and many other musicians get their start. For Moore, it was key to her independence and made it possible for her to survive as a single mother at a time when that was socially stigmatized. It was striking that a venue such as this, often considered morally problematic in terms of the display of female bodies, provided a place of acceptance and livelihood for Moore, where she could be valued for her musical talent without censure over her young pregnancy. Moore's performance in this moment, then, helped construct the Penthouse as a place where notions of morality related to aging, old(er) age, and age identities were being reshaped. It evoked a nostalgic feeling of promise in relation to the Penthouse by recalling a place poised at the cutting edge of the cultural revolution through its support of sexual liberation and promotion of rock music. The audience was compelled to experience a yearning for this transformative time and place. The nostalgic sense of revolutionary space (and the defiant woman who existed within it) was dragged into the present, through the monologue and the music surrounding and underscoring it, and highlighted the resistant possibilities of Moore's current performance of self and place—one of continuity, survival, and accomplishment.

CONCLUSION

While these moments of utopian potential in *Sonic Elder* felt revolutionary, I also consider them cautiously, recognizing that various aspects of the show acted in opposition to the utopian gesture. As Heddon reminds us, "autobiographical performances are *possible* performances of possibility."[46] In particular, I am heedful of the potentially exploitive impulse in autobiographical performance described by Stephenson, in which the weird "other" is marketed to sheltered elites for touristic consumption.[47] In the case of *Sonic Elder*, touristic curiosity about the venue may have prompted audience members to attend the show as a means of viewing the Penthouse in a more socially acceptable context. I am also attentive to Stephenson's assertion that autobiography does not simply produce "socially progressive illumination," but rather requires us to "admit and bear witness to the impossibility of knowing strangers."[48] However, Dolan's theory of utopian performativity is focused not on "knowing" the details of another's life, but rather on experiencing the fleeting "feeling" of what transformative change might be like.

Sonic Elder succeeded in inspiring moments of deep, synesthetic intersubjectivity between audience and performers, demonstrating the power of performed autobiography. These moments were sparked by the show's alchemy of casting, script, staging, performances, and venue—all of which resulted in autobiological depth performances of age, rooted in embodied memory, not yoked to linear time, and disruptive of age expectations. While certain aspects of *Sonic Elder*'s development and production were essentializing, the show, as a whole, offered uncommon and progressive glimpses of how reinvented cultural imaginaries of aging might *feel*. In doing so, it contributed to the incremental cultural change that Dolan describes. *Sonic Elder* invites us to think about how theater and live performance can provoke productive conversations and inspire usefully affective responses that expand our understandings of what it means to age and become old(er) in our culture.

NOTES

1. Chop Theatre, *Sonic Elder* playbill (2016).

2. Jill Dolan, *Utopia in Performance: Finding Hope at the Theater* (University of Michigan Press, 2005), 5.

3. Dolan, 5–6.

4. *Sonic Elder* artistic team, "Sonic Elder Script, Show Draft 5" (September 23, 2016).

5. Jill Dolan, "Performance, Utopia, and the 'Utopian Performative,'" *Theatre Journal* 53, no. 3 (2001): 460.

6. Dolan, 456 (emphasis added); Dolan, *Utopia in Performance*, 7.

7. Ric Knowles, "Documemory, Autobiology, and the Utopian Performative in Canadian Autobiographical Solo Performance," in *Theatre and AutoBiography: Writing and Performing Lives in Theory and Practice*, ed. Sherrill Grace and Jerry Wasserman (Talonbooks, 2006), 52.

8. Susan Bennett, "3-D a/B," in Grace and Wasserman, *Theatre and AutoBiography*, 35.

9. Knowles, "Documemory, Autobiology," 51–53.

10. Knowles, 57.

11. Anne Davis Basting, *The Stages of Age: Performing Age in Contemporary American Culture* (University of Michigan Press, 1998), 140–46.

12. Basting, 141.

13. Julia Henderson, "Challenging Age Binaries by Viewing *King Lear* in Temporal Depth," *Theatre Research in Canada* 37, no. 1 (2016): 55–57.

14. Marvin Carlson, *The Haunted Stage: The Theatre as Memory Machine* (University of Michigan Press, 2003), 53.

15. Basting, *The Stages of Age*, 19.

16. Almost all theater performances in Vancouver (and many across Canada) are now preceded by an acknowledgment of the Indigenous lands on which the performance takes place. The Penthouse version of *Sonic Elder* began: "Good evening, Vancouver! Welcome to the Penthouse! This legendary venue sits on the ancestral, traditional and unceded territories of the Coast Salish Peoples, in particular, the Squamish, Musqueam, and Tsleil-Waututh First Nations. Now please put your hands together for *Sonic Elder*." *Sonic Elder* artistic team, "Sonic Elder Script," 1.

17. Steve Winwood, Spencer Davis, and Muff Winwood, "Gimme Some Lovin'," recorded by the Spencer Davis Group (United Artists, 1966).

18. Dolan, *Utopia in Performance*, 2.

19. Dolan, 11.

20. Bennett, "3-D a/B," 35.

21. Basting, *The Stages of Age*, 141.

22. Valerie Barnes Lipscomb, *Performing Age in Modern Drama* (Palgrave Macmillan, 2016), 177.

23. Rock musicians such as Shirley Bassey, Cher, Neil Diamond, Peter Gabriel, Mick Jagger, Elton John, Paul McCartney, Diana Ross, Ringo Starr, Paul Simon, Sting, and Tina Turner, to name a few in recent years, all continued to perform past midlife, shifting the archetype of the rock and roll star.

24. *Sonic Elder* artistic team, "Sonic Elder Script," 3.

25. Knowles, "Documemory, Autobiology," 50.

26. David Román, *Acts of Intervention: Performance, Gay Culture, and Aids* (Indiana University Press, 1998), xxvi–xxvii.

27. Julia Henderson, "Dramaturgy of Assistance: Performing with Dementia or Age-Related Memory Loss," *Research in Drama Education: The Journal of Applied Theatre and Performance* 24, no. 1 (2019): 76–77.

28. Anne Davis Basting, "'God Is a Talking Horse': Dementia and the Performance of Self," *TDR: The Drama Review* 45, no. 3 (2001): 79.

29. Henderson, "Dramaturgy of Assistance," 81–85.

30. Pia Kontos and Wendy Martin, "Embodiment and Dementia: Exploring Crit-

ical Narratives of Selfhood, Surveillance, and Dementia Care," *Dementia* 12, no. 3 (2013): 291.

31. Pia Kontos, "Musical Embodiment, Selfhood, and Dementia," in *Beyond Loss: Dementia, Identity, Personhood*, ed. Lars-Christer Hydén, Hilde Lindemann, and Jens Brockmeier (Oxford University Press, 2014), 9, 11.

32. Henderson, "Dramaturgy of Assistance," 85.

33. Dolan, "Performance, Utopia," 472.

34. Dolan, 472.

35. Ernie Burnett, "My Melancholy Baby," with lyrics by George A. Norton (Theron C. Bennett, 1912).

36. Lucien Denni, "The Oceana Roll," with lyrics by Roger Lewis (Jerome H. Remick, 1911).

37. *Sonic Elder* artistic team, "Sonic Elder Script," 20.

38. Jenn Stephenson, *Performing Autobiography: Contemporary Canadian Drama* (University of Toronto Press, 2013), 112.

39. Bennett, "3-D a/B," 35.

40. Carlson, *The Haunted Stage*, 131–32.

41. Deirdre Heddon, *Autobiography and Performance: Performing Selves* (Palgrave Macmillan, 2008), 95.

42. Heddon, 98.

43. Dolan, "Performance, Utopia," 472.

44. Heddon, *Autobiography and Performance*, 91.

45. Heddon, 111.

46. Heddon, 2 (emphasis in original).

47. Jenn Stephenson, "'Please Look at Yourself': Insecurity and the Failure of Ethical Encounter in Autobiographical Performance," *Theatre Research in Canada* 37, no. 2 (2016): 220–21.

48. Stephenson, 234.

13
Queering Age and Memory/Loss in Peggy Shaw's *Ruff*

Benjamin Gillespie

After spending forty-five years on stage with lights in my eyes,
Trying to figure out what a woman is, let alone a lesbian,
My brain finally crashed.
—PEGGY SHAW AND LOIS WEAVER, *RUFF*[1]

Aging as a performer is my latest challenge, but my aesthetic has always been one that creates an intimacy with the audience that allows for mistakes, lapses of memory, and a sense that they never quite know what's going to happen.
—PEGGY SHAW[2]

In a career that spans more than four decades, New York downtown queer theater icon and Split Britches founding member Peggy Shaw has never shied away from making her personal life the subject of her artistic practice. This is especially true of Shaw's solo performances spanning the 1990s and 2000s.[3] Her solo performance *Ruff* (2013), created in collaboration with fellow Split Britches founder Lois Weaver, poetically documents a stroke Shaw endured in 2011, as well as its aftermath, which left Shaw unable to memorize new text. Presented less than a year after her stroke, *Ruff* provided Shaw with a platform to present its physical and cognitive impacts unapologetically to audiences as part of the recovery process.

As with her previous solo works, *Ruff* responds to experiences of personal trauma stemming from an ambiguously gendered body as well as her queer positionality in a heteronormative world. But for the first time, she foregrounded aging and memory/memory loss as central themes. Using her stroke as fodder for comedic routines and poetic monologues, Shaw maintained a butch lesbian image, modeled after famous crooners like Sammy Davis Jr. and Leonard Cohen. Shaw also used the piece to reflect on aging, her longevity as a performer, and her own mortality—a process she had already begun prior to her stroke, in *Must: The Inside Story* (2008). But *Ruff* moves beyond the individual to commemorate the fellow artists Shaw had collaborated with over the years as well as those lost along the way, foregrounding the necessity of collaboration, community, and care from the perspective of an older performer adapting to an age-related illness. While the short-term memory loss Shaw experienced is the central conceit of *Ruff*, it is the creation of new memories that leaves a vivid impression on audiences. The production's mise-en-scène is literally a poetic projection of Shaw's post-stroke brain, highlighting the gaps left in her memory and filling them with new images, experiences, and insights drawn out of the performance.

This chapter analyzes *Ruff* as a defiant performance of age that embeds the necessary supports for Shaw's body and memory as an aging performer in a nonlinear narrative structure that supports her newfound embodiment poststroke. The performance displayed Shaw's cognitive experience of memory *and* memory loss while also shifting the negative connotations of loss, with recovery as the thematic center of the piece. A self-proclaimed "grand-butch-mother" to multiple generations of queer artists and audiences alike,[4] Shaw complicates a singular notion of aging embodiment through her very presence, using the structure of a *queered* memory play that pushes audiences to experience loss at the same time that Shaw does—in the moment and unexpectedly—thereby highlighting the fragmented moments of memory loss as *productive* of a new mode of age-defying performance. Filtering the past through a partially compromised mind, Shaw's memory becomes the central focus of the production as she embodies the queer time slippages between her past and present ages/selves, and between forgetting and remembering in/as performance.

Ruff is a master class in genre-fuck, at once a freewheeling episodic monologue, a concert performance, a visual art experience, and a memory play. Both humorous and tragic, the work lends itself to Shaw's virtuosic improvisational style, playfully incorporating the lapses of memory that inevitably occur during each performance, making every iteration distinctive from the previous version.[5] *Ruff*'s very composition intends a kind of rhythmic dissonance captured by the episodic musicality at the center of the piece and its title—a reference to the rudimentary drumbeat the "three-stroke ruff"—and punctuated by numerous popular songs and poetic monologues. Accompanying these songs and monologues are video clips of a prerecorded band of past collaborators, projected on the back wall of the theater frequently throughout the show. Three large teleprompters envelop Shaw's body center stage, displaying the performance text for her as well as audiences to see as she inevitably deviates from it, highlighting the piece's improvisational qualities. Musical devices and the teleprompters aid both Shaw's memory and that of her audience, imbuing loss with performative potential in ways that offer a radical portrait of the aging artist. Not just a metaphor for the layering of images that haunt Shaw's mind, *Ruff* also incorporates green screen visual effects—a method involving the compositing of two pictures or video streams together—as an imaginative extension of Shaw's brain. Images from her past and present come alive, acting as a dramaturgical support by providing visual cues onstage for the audience and for Shaw (who, in performance, was seen looking upstage at the screen to find her place when she inevitably lost it).

Prior to the stroke and the creation of *Ruff*, Shaw's solo performances already refused easy categorization. As Jill Dolan acknowledges in her introduction to *A Menopausal Gentleman*, Shaw's writing is a "mix of poetry and prose that captures the bumpy but smooth, *rough* yet elegant rhythm of her speech. Shaw's solo shows move in fits and starts, accumulating in images and actions . . . her refusal to conform to [dramatic conventions] makes her performances as hybrid as her gender presentations offstage."[6] As Shaw noted in a 2014 public interview, "I never did have logic in my brain, even before the stroke. Lois [Weaver] is the logical one. What would happen is, I would create all the mess of the words, and she would put it into some kind of instinctual order. We learned how to do this in the seventies and eighties—making shows about images rather than making a show logical."[7] But to a further extent than previous shows, *Ruff* resists normative temporal logics and conventions of "good" acting, queering time through the fits and starts made necessary by her compromised short-term memory. Since Shaw has always played a version of herself onstage, *Ruff* also evokes past roles from previous Split Britches performances—the infamous lesbian-feminist company she cofounded in 1980 with Weaver—as audiences remember Shaw's younger body in contrast to her present one. We can think of Shaw's performance in *Ruff* as a theatrical play of memory (rather than a traditional memory play) that avoids nostalgic longing as she makes vivid the act of remembering itself as performative.

RUFF AROUND THE EDGES

Ruff premiered at the COIL Festival at Dixon Place in January 2013, commissioned with funds and support from Performance Space 122 as part of the Ethyl Eichelberger Award, which Shaw took home in 2011.[8] She also received several grants over a three-year period to develop the show. In 2014, Shaw received a Doris Duke Performing Artist Award; valued at nearly $275,000 over a five-year period, the award far surpasses any financial investiture Shaw had received to date.[9] The grant was meant to assist with living and health expenses which had increased with age. Shaw used it for the removal of cataracts, to purchase hearing aids, and other medical expenses. These newfound financial resources allowed Shaw to continue performing and directly challenge a debilitating narrative that might cast her as aging victim. As she has noted, "*Ruff* is about [the] survival . . . of aging. About how I keep performing as a person who has had a stroke. Sometimes I just go off and forget what I'm doing, but that's built into the show. Luckily my work doesn't have traditional arcs, anyway."[10]

The success of *Ruff* brought multiple tours as it became part of Split Britches' repertoire for several years, with longer runs at La MaMa in New York in 2014 and the Barbican Centre in London in 2016, among many other appearances.[11] *Ruff* marked a new phase of creative development for Shaw that would come to define all her subsequent work. As she elucidated in a 2017 interview,

> The process of creating *Ruff* was really different [than previous shows] because of my stroke. I was scared that I wouldn't be able to perform anymore. And I realized very quickly that my *present* memory was very difficult, but I could remember the *past* more easily. And I always hated memorizing, but I could use the stroke as a reason not to memorize. I didn't know how we were going to make a solo show. And then I realized how many people we needed. I needed a director [Weaver] in a different way than before. I needed help getting to rehearsals. I needed someone to help me be where I needed to be. At that time, we made it because we had to make it. I had to show people that performance could be about what you wanted to do *at any age*.[12]

At the top of Shaw's *Ruff*, on the back wall hangs a blank green canvas that stretches out across the stage floor, almost reaching the audience. Three television monitors of different heights and sizes surround the stage, yet to be turned on. As Shaw enters, the lights dim. She smiles at us invitingly as she turns on the screens. She wears a full suit, but only a single dress shoe, her gray hair disheveled. She carries her other shoe in her hand, along with a bottle of water and an orange. She states, "I was minding my own business, / And an icicle of death hit the ocean floor of my brain."[13] Shaw walks toward the audience and asks one audience member to hold her orange for her, then returns to center stage. Putting her hands together and looking upward, recalling the plunge to the floor she took as she suffered the stroke, she exclaims, "If you get me through this, / I'll stop wearing suits. / I'll get gay married. / I'll pay market rent in Manhattan. / I'll stop wearing skinny jeans. / I'll take anti-depressants. / I'll buy a car from the decade I'm living in. / I'll stop drinking coffee."[14] Pauses punctuate her sentences as she considers what comes next. She interrupts herself and asks another audience member to hold her bottle of water and her shoe—a moment of physical comedy and intimacy typical of Shaw's performance style.

In her opening monologue, Shaw foregrounds the vulnerability of her body, with the hopes of fostering a community that can provide care for her by connecting with the audience and asking them to assist by holding her props. She also integrates her characteristic humor into the opening, playing on her own leftist beliefs, which are generally reflected by those of the audience. As Kim Solga writes in her review of the London production, *Ruff* is "a work of community, a series of demonstrations of care, a work of generosity and a celebration of long-standing friendships and working relationships."[15] Solga rightly positions the audience as caregivers who support Shaw through the act of witnessing. But *Ruff* is also dedicated to exploring the essential presence of Shaw's other caregivers, her artistic collaborators. Throughout the piece, Shaw celebrates the presence of the longtime collaborators who have made her performances possible. For example, Stormy Brandenberger (choreographer) and Vivian Stoll (composer/sound designer) both contributed to the piece and have worked with Split Britches for decades (Brandenberger since the 1980s, and Stoll since the early 2000s). Lois Weaver also attended each performance of *Ruff* and would sit in the house, where she was visible to Shaw as a prompter.

During the performance of *Ruff* I attended at the COIL Festival in January 2013, Shaw frequently lost her place or became confused, at which point she would lose her confidence and a sense of vulnerability would wash over her, but she would still keep going. At one point, she called out to Weaver, asking, "Is this right?!" Weaver replied, "You're fine," giving Shaw the confidence to continue. In *Ruff*, Shaw is aware of her own vulnerability and takes advantage of it, keeping the audience in a liminal positionality between, on the one hand, feeling unintentional embarrassment and fear as we watch her forget her lines or struggle through a monologue in front of us, and, on the other, feeling support and joy in response to Shaw's tenacity. In doing so, Shaw exposes the protective tendency we feel toward actors when they do not perform conventionally well, or when they show a sincere quality of vulnerability onstage. As Solga writes of the show: "This is not a performance in which Shaw only seems not in control; it is a show deliberately about her loss of control, and about what that loss does and does not need to mean for her as a performer, a performance maker, a sexual being, an older woman, a human being . . . this simple act may be the most radically feminist gesture of Shaw's career thus far."[16]

Ruff is an autobiographical performance; Shaw performs as herself, though always with the thin veneer of character. Her presence allows audience members to experience the holes left permanently embedded in her memory by the stroke as the central dramaturgical conceit of the performance. Using green screen technology (aided by Australia-based designer Matt Delbridge), Shaw allows her "green screen" of memory to become populated through the projection of images and video, representing her brain as a blank canvas waiting to be refilled with new memories.[17] Like other Split Britches works, *Ruff* is not plot driven; rather, it is arranged like a poetic jam session, in which dramatic action transpires through the accumulation and layering of various texts, images, songs, and even selves, which accrue affect and meaning with time. As Dolan notes, Shaw's performance style "builds through association—the nonlinear text works by accretion and accumulation, rather than progressing through a more typical narrative of conflict and resolution."[18] Indeed, the accretion and accumulation embedded within age performance is at one and the same time also a life practice for Shaw as a radical queer artist. In an interview, Shaw noted how performance is like physical therapy: "The adrenalin of performing is so powerful you can do anything in the lights of the audience. That became a really good *physical therapy* for me. And my style of performing allowed for a looser structure. That discomfort made people totally nervous, but as I point out in the show, it put the audience in the palm of my hand. It helped to combat my fear of performing, my fear of forgetting."[19] The queered (mis)spelling of "rough" in the show's title is suggestive also of the irregularity of Shaw's performance aesthetic post-infarction. However, it is at the same time a reference (as mentioned previously) to a rudimentary drumbeat, the "three-stroke ruff," in which two grace notes are followed by a third punctuated final note. Shaw makes direct reference to this musical term in the show, playing on the double meaning of "stroke." The metaphor is quite effective: Shaw's ischemic stroke, the result of a clot that cut off the flow of blood to her brain, caused irreparable damage. The title juxtaposes a lack of flow or rhythm in her body with the rhythmic repetition of drum strokes in music, which create a repetitive, underscoring beat.

As much as the piece is focused on memory recovery, it is also largely about the many collaborators and caregivers she now requires—and, in some ways, has *always* required in putting up a solo show (solo performance is rarely, if ever, done completely independently). Indeed, Shaw's cognitive challenges expose the act of performance as a function of a supportive community, instead of an independent enterprise. Rather than create the illusion of autonomy, Shaw foregrounds the presence of others in the putting up of the work and shifts the theater into a place of care, a network of support. She playfully has her own band onstage throughout the performance, providing a consistent rhythm in the background of *Ruff*, tying the show together as a queer rock concert of sorts. Made up of her longtime friends, supporters, and collaborators, her onstage band offers musical accompaniments to various songs in the show, through a prerecorded video that plays during Shaw's musical interludes between monologues.

As a result of the piece's complex structure, it would be impossible to recap all that happens in *Ruff*; there isn't a singular narrative beyond the repeated themes of memory and loss. During the show, Shaw gives us a number of details regarding the circumstances of the event of her stroke itself, taking many poetic liberties as she goes along and theatricalizing the traumatic event. She tells us that her stroke occurred just one day after Ellen Stewart's funeral. Stewart, the founder of La MaMa, had been a major supporter of Shaw's work during her lifetime; Stewart's death pushed Shaw to reflect on mortality. She muses in the show, "The day Ellen Stewart died I dreamt she was pulling me down with her, / Her silver fingernails digging into my shoulders and arms, / Dragging me down with her 'cause she was lonely."[20] Shaw tells us that Stewart hated the color green and would not allow it onstage for superstitious reasons. In an act of posthumous defiance, Shaw uses the green screen as a centralized prop, despite Stewart's wishes while she was still alive. As Shaw plays the video of her younger, much more feminine self, wearing a green dress, we see the clear contrast with her much older, butch form in front of us. The contrast of age and gender in this moment is evocative, especially the oddity of seeing the usually butch Shaw in a dress as her younger self. She riffs: "Green is what I am left with. / After the defiance, / After the funeral."[21]

At another moment in the performance, Shaw tells her audience, "After spending forty-five years on stage with lights in my eyes, / Trying to figure out what a woman is, let alone a lesbian, / My brain finally crashed."[22] She looks out at us with a deadpan stare, and warns us that she can uncontrollably cough at any time: "Sometimes when you cough in a show, you have the audience suspended in the palm of your hand, / 'Cause they wish so much that they could give you some water." She continues, "Water doesn't stop the cough. / . . . / If you see me start to cough . . . / . . . you could say, 'That's OK, take all the time you need to cough.' / I guess we could call that audience participation."[23] The tension and release we feel each time Shaw's cognitive rhythms are interrupted during *Ruff* can be described through a sort of dissonant musicality, as the title itself suggests. In one brilliant episode, Shaw integrates the acronym for the medical signs of a stroke—FAST, face, arms, speech, time—into a humorous rock version of the "Hokey Pokey"; this episode later became part of a public service announcement that ran for years.[24] She also performs a rendition of "If I Only Had a Brain" from *The Wizard of Oz*, juxtaposing the strange experience of seeing her brain postinfarction on an MRI scan, which exposed the blank spots left in her brain after the stroke, through a green screening technique with motion-capture technology. In fact, the entire stage can be read as a dramatic extension of Shaw's brain, especially in the moments that attempt to fill the holes of her discordant memory.

The successful modification of her performance style is supported by the dramaturgical (anti)structure of the text. Shaw's script uses literary devices including alliteration and repetition to help jog her memory, often taking the form of lists that are patterned in similar ways and can be reordered without disrupting the piece. It also divides the narrative into a number of singular monologues that can be separated and memorized individually, as well as extensively utilizing song, since lyrics are rhythmically easier for Shaw to memorize. She integrates humorous dialogue in between a range of musical numbers, alongside personal memories and storytelling. The music is used to jog her memory and break up the elegiac tones that inevitably underscore a performance about a near-death experience. In performance, the teleprompters serve as her co-actors and visibly display the script, not for Shaw's eyes alone, but for audiences, who witness moments when she strays from the original text into involuntary improvisation. Shaw is not the first performer to do this. The piece evokes Joseph Chaikin, who notably relied on textual prompts while performing *Struck Dumb* (1988), following a stroke that left him with aphasia in 1984. Shaw reminds us of this stage history in her show, which moves us temporally back and forth from past to present to future performance modes:

> I hope this is not the year I . . . have a stroke,
> And my brain will be robbed of oxygen.
> And I'll lose my social skills.
> And in order to do a show someone will have to write the whole script.
> And tape it to the back wall of the theatre like they did for Joe Chaikin.
> And I won't have to learn it.[25]

Shaw not only aligns her stroke with that of another downtown artist, but she directly excerpts this text from an earlier Split Britches production called *Miss America* (2008). This is the first of many moments in which sections of *Ruff* are noticeably spliced from other performance texts, potentially jogging the audience's memory as well as her own. Shaw tells us that she must have been "practicing" for her real stroke when she performed *Miss America*, highlighting the eerie reality that she may have anticipated her own stroke without knowing it. She also pulls sections from *You're Just Like My Father* (1994)—a show ironically about the troubled relationship with her mother, who warned her that "black pepper causes brain damage," a presumed superstition that Shaw now openly revisits with new resonance.[26]

While it is true that physically and cognitively Shaw is less in control than she was prior to the stroke, she also harnesses that chaotic reality as a gesture toward her own creative future. Her remarkable dexterity as a performer and rebellious nature is evinced by the fact that she began creating *Ruff* just six months after her stroke, while still recovering from it. Shaw noted in the production how it was the stroke that made her finally conscious of her own mortality: "Mortality is on my mind, heavy on my mind, / In that dark shadowy part of my brain, / Where [my memories] used to be."[27] However, she also indicates a new appreciation for how performance can facilitate her recovery, incorporating mnemonic supports in the performance to ensure she can recover "lost time."

A GAY OLD TIME

Taking on a queer aesthetic, Shaw critically unbinds her identity as a queer older woman from society's "chrononormative" metrics of social productivity and representations of the heteronormative "good life," allowing her downtown audiences to see her work as a radical act of queer aging subjectivity. As Elizabeth Freeman notes, queer temporality is an antichronological and antilinear understanding of time and the life course (as reflected in Shaw's queer memory play); it entails a "recognition of how erotic relations and bodily acts . . . gum up the works of the normative structures we call family and nation, gender, race, class, and sexual identity by changing tempos, by remixing memory and desire, by recapturing excess."[28] Shaw's challenge to chrononormativity comes through her purposefully unstable and temporally dissonant aesthetic, which sets the performance up to fail in its major coup de théâtre, reflecting Jack Halberstam's notion of failure as an inherently queer aesthetic: "failure presents an opportunity rather than a dead end . . . the queer artist works with rather than against failure and inhabits the darkness [which] becomes a crucial part of a queer aesthetic."[29] In a performance about the dark matter of Shaw's memory, her aging queer subjectivity as a butch lesbian presents a rebellious queer act of failure that subverts traditional forms of heteronormative progression and chronologies of aging and time. In short, Shaw's sexuality upends ageist stereotypes that position older bodies as undesirable, foregrounding her "old-school" sexy butch persona and neurodiversity as dramaturgical tools.

Freeman and age scholar Jan Baars challenge heteronormative measurements of time and its implications on aging, referring to it as "chrononormative time" and "chronometric time," respectively.[30] Both of these theoretical concepts underscore how "straight" time is embedded in heteronormative ideologies that disallow more "deviant" or queer narratives of the life course and aging.[31] Just as queer subjects imagine alternative life course progressions beyond reproductive temporalities, Shaw urges audiences to imagine a world beyond the privileging of linear timelines, which falsely position the young in binary opposition to the old.[32] Her rebellious creativity further enacts a challenge to "aging well" (or "successful aging," a cultural campaign that seeks to erase the effects of aging) while also defying normative standards of "good" acting that impede older performers from taking the stage more regularly. Her experimental style makes room for her specific needs as an artist and enacts an increasing desire to remain active despite changes to her physical body and cognition.

While connections between age studies and disability studies are important, there has been relatively little engagement in interdisciplinary analysis in these fields, especially with regard to queer performance. As Michael Bérubé argues, "The fact that many of us will become disabled if we live long enough is perhaps the fundamental aspect of human embodiment."[33] Similarly, in her article "Ageility Studies," Leni Marshall argues that "there is plenty of reason that aged subjects resist the added 'illegitimacy' of disability, that a person with a disability would reject the extra layer of Otherness that accompanies the label of *old*, and that anyone who could pass as belonging in neither category would decide to do so."[34] Shaw does not claim "disabled" as an identity, but instead refers to herself as being "neurodiverse" following her stroke. Neurodiversity refers to the notion that "seemingly 'impaired' cognitive as well as emotional features characteristic of developmental disorders such as autism spectrum disorder (ASD) fall into normal human behavioral variations that should enjoy some selective advantages."[35] Shaw consciously embeds her queer identity and neurodiversity in *Ruff* in order to challenge audience expectations of what it means to perform well/ness. The performance could admittedly benefit from an intersectional analysis of age and disability to understand the components of her extraordinary body more fully, but that is beyond the scope of this chapter. Additionally, focusing on disability runs the risk of inherently aligning age and aging *with* disability, which erases the intersectionality of these identity categories when it comes to Shaw's work and the work of other older performers.

In short, Shaw's rebellious stage presence displaces the image of a frail performer unable to do what she once did, anticipating a creative future despite suffering a real loss of memory. As Bridie Moore claims in her analysis, "*Ruff* is demonstrably a performance of old age, one that accommodates the limitations of Shaw's post-stroke memory by employing the technical aid of autocue, making her cognitive losses explicit."[36] In an interview on BBC Radio 4 in London in 2016 during the production's run at the Barbican, Shaw stated, "After my stroke, I was able to define that I wasn't an original person, that I had a combination of a lot of people inside of me that I wanted to talk about and thank for all their help."[37] Again, a major aspect of *Ruff* is the acknowledgment of her collaborators (including Lois Weaver, Vivian Stoll, Matt Delbridge, Stormy Brandenberger, and Lori E. Seid, among many others) as well as those who have inspired her artistically and worked with her previously (including Ethyl Eichelberger and Ellen Stewart).

In my interviews with Shaw over the years, she reflected on the purpose and necessity of *Ruff* as a turning point in her career:

> *Ruff* sets up the audience to say that things aren't going to go right. I wanted to make vulnerability a part of the show. I got my stroke over with before I was seventy. Having a stroke and realizing I was seventy, I realized I was going to die. But I'm still the same person.
>
> I find it hard to watch myself onstage getting older. Why am I walking like that? Why do I sound like that, like I have marbles in my mouth? It's hard. I find older women very attractive but I can't turn that on myself. But reflecting is part of the process of coming to terms with now. It has to do with patience, and the world having cycles. I've seen things happen two or three times. It's like my brain now. If you read me a sentence, I remember it. But if you change it, I can't. Even though I had monitors, it was not easy to read. We had to decide on a black background with white letters. We also used the green screening to represent stroke survivors. This is how they can survive now. Not focusing on how they used to be. . . .
>
> When I got the Doris Duke grant it meant that I could take some time off to get [my cataracts] out and get hearing aids. I was dealing with the

> effects of age, but that didn't deter me. Being queer was different thirty years ago. You didn't get awards.[38]

Shaw's telling self-reflections explain her subjective response to the stroke, including what she was feeling at the time, and how she wanted to move forward creatively with the necessary supports in place to allow her to do so. Her self-observed failures to "live up" to her own standards after the stroke constituted a need to reconsider the framework of performance—a radical queer response to the expectations of aging in our society.

With *Ruff*, Shaw looks back on her childhood as an older woman, and on her personal history as a performer from a late point in her career. Her embodied perspectives show how age identity is always in flux across the life course, never remaining static, as the self becomes layered (rather than erased or displaced) over time, enriching age with a temporality of past and present simultaneously. This is what Anne Davis Basting calls "the temporal body in depth" of the aging actor.[39] Shaw succeeds in capturing the older performer at the height of her creative abilities, while also not shying away from the realities of physical aging. The show doesn't romanticize illness, but rather explores the reality of the shifting embodiments that accompany the individual aging process. *Ruff* actively challenges stereotypes around health and wellness by modifying and supplementing Shaw's iconic stage persona with the campy excess of failure. As Jen Harvie recognizes, "Old Shaw is not at 'war' with young Shaw; she is in explicit queer solidarity with her young self in a queering of time that permits the two ages to co-exist."[40] This is reflective of the queer temporality that characterizes her performance of age in *Ruff*—one that highlights Shaw's rebellious identity across the entire life course, thus challenging the false binary between youth and age. Linking herself to a genealogy of deceased queer artists and activists by naming them throughout the show, including Marsha P. Johnson, Wilhelmina Ross, Charles Ludlam, Hot Peaches, and Ethyl Eichelberger, as well as straight male performers she queers on her butch lesbian body, such as Leonard Cohen and Jacques Brel, Shaw remembers those who have departed and memorializes them in the piece.

CONCLUSION: TIME/OUT

Shaw demonstrates the capacity of theater to offer a productive version of the present—even if/when she fails to remember it—that considers a past and emphasizes a potential for future development. Shaw poetically jams chronological time logics in *Ruff*, effectively turning performance into the time portal occurring inside her brain. Her creative genius lies within her uncontrollable eruptions and creative impulses. As Weaver has argued, "[Peggy] thinks whatever she's experiencing right now is the absolute truth. . . . She's so in the moment; she's not reflecting back."[41] Dolan takes a similar view of Shaw's creative practices: "Shaw constructs her theatre scripts much like she constructs her gendered performances—*on impulse*, responding to what comes to her from a culture in which she fights constantly to carve out her own space and room for others who are also disenfranchised."[42] Perhaps impulse constitutes a feeling of desire for Shaw, a potential to see the world another way, and gives her a chance to critique it, regardless of theatrical convention, from within the body she has. If effective acting is being *in* time or on cue, Shaw reformulates this notion by being uncontrollably out of time, queerly twisting the temporal conventions of theater by exposing the dissonant registers of everyday reality in her brain.

Shaw's rough-and-tumble humor throughout the performance undermines the severity of her stroke to avoid sentimentalizing her experience. For example, she concludes her description of the terrifying experience of being committed to the hospital right after her stroke by making a joke about her own gender-based mishaps in public spaces: "I heard about a guy who had a stroke, / And when he recovered he was gay. / . . . / I went into the hospital as a woman who gets mistaken for a man, / But it seems I came out of the hospital as a straight white man, / 'Cause half my brain was missing."[43] In another beautifully choreographed moment, Shaw dances with a projection of herself on-screen, except the projection is made up of small circles of light that abstract her body into darkness. While she certainly masks some of the horrors of having a stroke beneath her unfailing optimism, *Ruff* does expose the very real and debilitating capacities of suffering such a traumatic experience at her age. But even while she cannot perform up to the same virtuoso standards she may once have been able to, she has fostered new standards of her own that reimagine theater as a place of care and support, pushing her audiences to rethink these standards too.

Near the end of *Ruff*, Shaw connects her brain to the image of life in an aquarium: a space transparent to the world outside but also somehow disconnected and cut off from it. This image is literalized in the final moments, as two remote-controlled clown fish float through the air, swirling around Shaw's body as she shares her final reflections on the experience of her stroke. This wild dreamscape is accompanied by Shaw's telling of a dream she had of falling off the George Washington Bridge into the Hudson River and sinking to the bottom. In the dream, she sees people she knows there—people who have died, people she has lost in the holes of her memory, but

Fig. 13.1. Peggy Shaw in *Ruff* (2013). Photo by Michael Conti. Courtesy *Split Britches*.

not in her heart. "Help me remember their names," she says. As she comes up for air, she shifts the tone to one of elegiac reflection: "I'm aware of the quickness of the passing of days, / And how I want to let them go, / And hold onto them at the same time, / [but they are] Like grabbing fog or smoke."[44]

Rather than envision the stroke as a deficit, Shaw built *Ruff* to take advantage of her virtuosic abilities while providing the supports onstage to allow her to continue performing. Rather than hide the stroke's impact, Shaw incorporated it into her theatrical form and aesthetic—one that has continued to shape and support Shaw's career as an aging artist since *Ruff*'s premiere. Her performance strategies embrace the use of technology as a visual support, foreground her collaborators, include the audience, and create nonlinear narratives utilizing music as a mnemonic device. Rather than succumbing to normative standards of theatrical performance, which might cast her as an incompetent performer, Shaw integrates memory/loss into the performance, allowing sections dramaturgically cut by Shaw's brain to bring on her virtuosic creative impulses through queer improvisation.

As has perhaps always been the case for Shaw, and is explicitly so in *Ruff*, performance offers the potential for a new mode of being that reconfigures the ways in which we might see performance support the aging body. Shaw states, "[Performing is] a meditative state. Nothing can touch you. You don't have any pain, you don't have any worries. You just have that hour of sheer meditation. And your body pumps that drug that gives you power and you can do anything. I'm ready to die on those stages. . . . But I'm not planning to die."[45]

NOTES

1. Peggy Shaw and Lois Weaver, *Ruff*, *PAJ: A Journal of Performance and Art* 40, no 2 (2018): 109. All references to the script in this chapter come from the version published in *PAJ*. An updated version of the script is forthcoming in the anthology *Split Britches: Fifty Years On*, ed. Benjamin Gillespie (University of Michigan Press, 2027).

2. Peggy Shaw, "Artist's Statement," Doris Duke Charitable Foundation, 2014.

3. Peggy Shaw's solo performances (excluding *Ruff*) are collectively published in Peggy Shaw, *A Menopausal Gentleman: The Solo Performances of Peggy Shaw*, ed. Jill Dolan (University of Michigan Press, 2011).

4. Peggy Shaw, "On Being an Independent Solo Artist (No Such Thing)," in Shaw, *A Menopausal Gentleman*, 41.

5. I saw *Ruff* first in its early development during a workshop held at Dixon Place, New York, in the fall of 2012, and then at its premiere at Dixon Place in January 2013. I saw the performance once more when the production was remounted at New York's La MaMa in January 2014. While some design elements changed over this time period, the core text remained almost unchanged. My review of the original production appears in *Theatre Journal* 65, no. 4 (December 2013): 576–77.

6. Jill Dolan, introduction to Shaw, *A Menopausal Gentleman*, 14 (emphasis added).

7. Peggy Shaw, "Rough Around the Edges," interview by Benjamin Gillespie, Performing Que(e)ries Series, CLAGS: Center for LGBTQ Studies, City University of New York, April 30, 2014.

8. For more on the Eichelberger Award, see "Ethyl Eichelberger," Performance Space, accessed June 28, 2025, https://performancespacenewyork.org/shows/ethyl-eichelberger/

9. The award aims at ensuring that the creative lives of established artists are safeguarded by helping them make financially sustainable investments, as well as supporting any creative endeavors they might undertake within the near future. In my interview with Shaw as part of the Performing Que(e)ries Series at CLAGS, she quipped, "Being queer was different thirty years ago. You didn't get awards." Shaw, "Rough Around the Edges."

10. Peggy Shaw, personal interview, Dec. 15, 2017.

11. Venues including the COIL Festival, Dixon Place, New York (January 2012); Chelsea Theatre, London (April 4–5, 2013); Behaviour Festival, the Arches, Glasgow (April 11, 2013); La Mama, New York (2014); Wellcome Collection, online, UK (2014); Mayfest, Bristol (2014); Contact Theatre, Manchester (2014); and Barbican Centre, London (2016).

12. Peggy Shaw, personal interview, Dec. 15, 2017.

13. Shaw, *Ruff*, 108.

14. Shaw, 108.

15. Kim Solga, "What Feminists Do When Things Get *Ruff*," *Performance Research* 19, no. 2 (2014): 137.

16. Kim Solga, *Theatre and Feminism* (Palgrave Macmillan, 2015), 74.

17. The use of green screen was later integrated by Split Britches into a new workshop model for stroke survivors, allowing them to "imagine things they always wanted to do, constructing storylines that are supported by a custom-built interactive scenography, and allowing participants to imagine new ways of being." As was the case with *Ruff*, this extended public-facing project for elder communities focused on performance as a tool for recovery and rehabilitation as well as a PSA for stroke awareness. More about the project can be found at "Performance as a Tool for Stroke Recovery: Green Screening," Split Britches, accessed June 27, 2025, http://www.split-britches.com/greenscreening

18. Jill Dolan, *Utopia in Performance: Finding Hope at the Theater* (University of Michigan Press, 2010), 52.

19. Shaw, personal interview, Dec. 15, 2017.

20. Shaw, *Ruff*, 110.

21. Shaw, 112.

22. Shaw, 109.

23. Shaw, 109.

24. Shaw was commissioned to perform public service announcements by the Stroke Association of the United Kingdom to help raise awareness of the signs and symptoms of having a stroke; this campaign has resulted in a number of side projects for Split Britches on aging and health in both New York and abroad. See "Public Service Announcements," Split Britches, accessed June 27, 2025, http://www.split-britches.com/peggyshaw/psa

25. Shaw, *Ruff*, 110.

26. Shaw, 123.

27. Shaw, 129.

28. Elizabeth Freeman, *Time Binds: Queer Temporalities, Queer Histories* (Duke University Press, 2010), 173.

29. Jack Halberstam, *The Queer Art of Failure* (Duke University Press, 2011), 96.

30. Freeman, *Time Binds*; Jan Baars, "Critical Turns of Aging, Narrative and Time," *International Journal of Ageing and Later Life* 7, no. 2 (2012): 143–65.

31. In age studies, "life course" is used in place of "lifespan" or "life cycle" to denote the mutability and individual differences in experiences of age across populations while also challenging the ideology of decline that attends cultural ageism and the false binary between youth and age.

32. Chronological aging—the mode in which our society chooses to measure and define age identity—is naturalized around the ideology of decline and the false binary of youth/age, which informs cultural discourse and also reinforces a heterosexual imperatives that discount queer ways of aging and being. This naturalization of particular ages across the life course as signifying some universal experience of age is completely eroded when we consider individual experiences of age. That is, with age comes growth, change, and diverse embodiments and temporal definitions of age.

33. Michael Bérubé, "Afterword: If I Should Live So Long," in *Disability Studies: Enabling the Humanities*, ed. Sharon L. Snyder, Brenda Jo Brueggemann, and Rosemarie Garland Thomson (Modern Language Association of America, 2002), 343.

34. Leni Marshall, "Ageility Studies: The Interplay of Critical Approaches in Age Studies and Disability Studies," in *Alive and Kicking at All Ages: Cultural Constructions of Health and Life Course Identity*, ed. Ulla Kriebernegg, Roberta Maierhofer, and Barbara Ratzenböck (Transcript, 2014), 23–24.

35. Nobuo Masataka, "Neurodiversity and Artistic Performance Characteristic of Children with Autism Spectrum Disorder," *Frontiers in Psychology* 9 (2018): https://doi.org/10.3389/fpsyg.2018.02594

36. Bridie Moore, "The Age Performances of Peggy Shaw: Intersection, Interception, and Interruption," in *Ageing Women in Literature and Visual Culture: Reflections, Refractions, Reimaginings*, ed. Cathy McGlynn, Margaret O'Neill, and Michaela Shrage-Früh (Springer International, 2017), 88.

37. Shaw's radio interview is available here: Peggy Shaw, interview by Arthur Smith, *Loose Ends*, BBC Radio 4, April 6, 2016, https://www.bbc.co.uk/sounds/play/p03q60bp

38. Peggy Shaw, personal interview, Dec. 15, 2017.

39. Anne Davis Basting, *The Stages of Age: Performing Age in Contemporary American Culture* (University of Michigan Press, 1998), 141.

40. Jen Harvie, "Boom! Adversarial Ageism, Chrononormativity, and the Anthropocene," *Contemporary Theatre Review* 28, no. 3 (2018): 337.

41. Quoted in Dolan, introduction to Shaw, *A Menopausal Gentleman*, 35.

42. Dolan, 36 (emphasis added).

43. Shaw, *Ruff*, 121–22.

44. Shaw, 131, 130.

45. Shaw, personal interview, Dec. 15, 2017.

Part IV
Time, Empathy, and Care

14

The Melody of Aging

Interview with Bonnie Marranca

Hillary Miller

As writer, editor, and publisher, Bonnie Marranca has cultivated a singular voice in contemporary theater and performance. Through the essays, interviews, manifestos, plays, and performance texts published in books and journals by PAJ Publications, which she cofounded more than four decades ago, she has generated an expansive archive of twentieth- and twenty-first-century experimental performance and writing. Her own writing explores capacious interests: food, landscape, education, drawing, religion, playwrights, and institutions.

As an editor, Marranca seeks out new work and ideas in theater, dance, media, and opera—in particular, artists and critics who stretch the boundaries between art forms. She has closely observed the transformations of artists in work and life across the decades, which is a recurring theme in this conversation with Hillary Miller. Marranca returns to the subject of aging, which she began with a special section in *PAJ: A Journal of Performance and Art*, "Ages of the Avant-Garde," in 1994. She also shares the ideas and individual artworks that have sustained and inspired her through the years. Reflecting on a lifetime of experience, she dispels some of the limiting clichés associated with aging in the arts and considers how her own processes and perspectives have evolved. This conversation took place in New York City on March 2, 2024.

HILLARY MILLER: In your essay "PAJ, a Personal History," written nearly forty years ago, you state that "the very body of work in *PAJ* reflects the process of aging in the American theater, which is no easier than aging in American society."[1] How does the American theater think about aging?

BONNIE MARRANCA: You can address this from many different angles—from the playwright, where the focus is often on emerging playwrights or finding new voices. Of course, any art form has to find new voices. But it does get harder for artists as they age in the American theater, which has so few resources. It affects casting. You don't see a lot of plays with older actors. That's been true for a long time. If there are not a lot of older playwrights or a mixture of plays in translation from other countries and different kinds of forms, you don't get a wide spread of experienced thinkers who bring other perspectives on contemporary issues. Young people are concerned about relationships and leaving the family and such topics. Older people are past that, and they have concerns that may be social and political in a different way.

MILLER: In the realm of criticism, there seems to be a sense that critics fall out of touch as they age because they can't keep up with the field. I don't think that we often imagine critics as having a body of writing that remains experimental over nearly a half-century, as yours has.

MARRANCA: People say a lot of things that are not true, especially with regard to aging. Now that I am in my seventies, I am well aware of assumptions people and the culture at large have about the older population. I remember Richard Foreman writing at some point in *PAJ* that "young" does not necessarily mean "new." If you look at people in all different art forms who are in their seventies and eighties, it's amazing how avant-garde they have remained, like Liz LeCompte or Yvonne Rainer or Joan Jonas, who is having a retrospective at the Museum of Modern Art at the age of eighty-seven, and still creating unique new work. Laurie Anderson and Philip Glass are still working in their fields. A lot of avant-garde artists never gave up their avant-garde ideals.

We live in a culture that doesn't value age. Look at the general characterizations of age on television or in the movies. But many critics write well into old age. For example, Stanley Kauffmann was a well-respected critic in his nineties working at the *New Republic*. Harold Clurman wrote well past middle age for the *Nation*. Literary critics continue to write in their seventies and eighties. Elizabeth Hardwick wrote magnificent work throughout her life. Susan Sontag died in her early seventies, but she was also writing until she became too ill. Joan

Acocella composed exciting essays for the *New Yorker* until her recent death at seventy-eight. My dear friend Herbert Blau composed brilliant essays in his eighties. Many years ago, I visited Marguerite Yourcenar in Maine. She wrote the great classic *Memoirs of Hadrian* and was the first woman to enter the French Academy. She was studying Urdu in her eighties. She was still planting in her garden. She was traveling, writing. And I became friendly with Etel Adnan, the extraordinary Lebanese American visual artist and writer, at the time we published a collection of her work. She was so sharp in her way of talking about books and ideas. She was painting everyday into her nineties, until she died at ninety-six. Edward Said, who was interviewed in *PAJ* more than three decades ago, speaking of the influence of polyphonic musical form on his view of comparative literature, would eventually develop ideas about "late style." That's a more interesting way to talk about artists and writers. We have to get out of all these clichés about people and aging.

MILLER: What are some of the strategies that you as an editor use to continually find new perspectives, pursue what excites you, and generate ideas to fill three issues of *PAJ* each year?

MARRANCA: It's been forty-eight years, so that requires a lot of ideas. Many of them are not generated by the theater. They're suggested by my reading or intuitive sense about the culture. Or what I think is missing in the field, what kinds of writing and work or themes should be covered.

Overall, our mission has been rather stable with *PAJ* in being very interdisciplinary and focusing on critical thinking, the critic's voice, critical forms. My main interest has always been criticism. I love the essay form because one is really reading thinking. I often use the term "arts writing" now because I have moved into different areas. At the beginning of *PAJ*, we were interested in finding writers who could write about the new vocabularies of the theater in the seventies. We were also interested in the new art forms of performance art and video. The difficulty has been to find critics in every field because even though everybody talks about interdisciplinarity in academia, most people cannot write about multiple art forms. We always had to find a new set of critics for each of the arts. And then there was the work to be translated. We worked with some of the major translators who introduced texts from Europe and the Soviet Union, like Daniel Gerould, Rosette Lamont, Martin Esslin, Gitta Honegger, Bettina Knapp, Harold Segel. When Gautam Dasgupta and I started the journal, in 1976, we were able to do it because we knew a lot of the downtown artists and, being in the doctoral program at CUNY, we also knew the academics who were translators. We brought these worlds together. Incidentally, Elinor Fuchs was a classmate of mine at this time, though she was much older. That generation of people that I was taught by and worked with in the seventies went a long way toward creating the field of modern drama. *PAJ* was always cross-generational and cross-genre.

MILLER: This was very clear when I looked back at your essay in *Ecologies of Theater*, "Performance World, Performance Culture" (1987), in which you outlined your approach to writing. The guiding tenets were, "to make criticism a critique of criticism," "to incorporate fictional technique and other forms of writing."[2] These tenets and the mission have remained stable. But do different concerns come up for you now, those the thirty-five-year-old editor or writer would not have made the time for?

MARRANCA: If I think of the beginnings of *PAJ* or the last years of doctoral courses, we were studying things like catastrophe, totalitarianism, authoritarianism. I studied with Daniel Gerould, who taught a course on avant-garde drama between the wars. We read eastern European and central European and Soviet works. And here I am now, in the twenty-first century, and that's again a chief concern. The difference between understanding these issues then and now is that in the seventies I was studying history, whereas now it is contemporary life tinged by these great forces. Age, travel, and experience make all the difference in terms of perspective.

A young critic is always learning. I also still feel I'm learning all the time. In one sense, you are waiting to see what's there so that you can write about it. And on another level, you can't really wait for a theater. I always followed my own interests, regardless of what other people were writing about. The most important thing for a critic is to cultivate an individual voice. For example, when I got interested in gardening I edited an anthology of American garden writing.[3] That was closely linked to my interest in ecology and my history of addressing that subject in my essays and in the journal. I was always interested in European culture and politics, which found their way into my anthology *New Europe: Plays from the Continent* (2009).[4] In the eighties, people were concerned with writing about postmodernism. Or post-structuralism. Or deconstruction. The journal followed these patterns. It has to reflect the field. But it also has to offer something that goes beyond that to finding what new thinking it can bring about. The most recent example of that is when I turned away from the politics that have dominated the scene, and a year or so ago put together an issue around the concept of spiritualities.[5] I felt this subject was totally ignored by theater journals and arts discussion. People think it's not political. The fact is that one of the distinguishing features of avant-garde tradition is that many of its major figures in theater, dance, music, and drama reflect the influence of spiritual thought. In the early nineties, I was already teaching a graduate seminar entitled "The Spiritual Dimension of Modernism." A few years later, I took this same approach with the *Plays for the End of the Century* volume.[6] You can see how one ages with one's ideas and interests and how they evolve over time.

In the nineties, I also began to write about the fact that performance history was going to be a huge interest in the future. That's been true, as performance history is a continuing, important area of scholarship. It is very hard to teach it because scholars went into theory-driven and applied theory dissertations and books, and therefore we're missing monographs on major institutions and major artists. It is difficult to get that back now because many people have not seen the original works.

MILLER: In addition to spirituality, aging is another topic that *PAJ* began addressing years ago. You published a special section, "Ages of the Avant-Garde," in 1994 (*PAJ* 16, no. 1), when few scholars in theater and performance were investigating it. Was your desire to write about aging motivated by your sense that it was on a parallel track with performance history?

MARRANCA: In 1994, we contacted a broad selection of artists and some critics who had turned fifty or older since *PAJ* began publishing. And those people are now in their eighties. Some are no longer alive, like Judith Malina or Carolee Schneemann. I must have been seeing work and thinking about the aging body. For example, as Merce Cunningham became older, because he remained on the stage for so long, I could observe that he was using his arms and hands much more. Recently, I saw Lucinda Childs, now in her early eighties, performing in a television special celebrating the work of Frank Gehry, with the LA Philharmonic. I noticed that she was also using her arms, hands, and fingers very much. In my book *Conversations with Meredith Monk*, she talks about spectacle becoming less prominent in her works and the musical elements moving to the forefront.[7] Monk was already talking about her body and aging with the opera *Atlas*, when she had just turned fifty, in the *PAJ* issue.[8] Dancers feel aging acutely, but they adapt. The artists' writings we published have also been so valuable for readers. Obviously, my own critical interests and observations and extensive theatergoing found their way into the editorial content of the journal over the decades. The growing interest in constructing performance history was certainly a part of my thinking.

MILLER: Is the way that you look at work now connected to the skills that you acquired when you were a young writer? Are those the skills that have helped sustain you through your career?

MARRANCA: I think I owe my interest in writing and style to the fact that I was a Latin major in college until I switched in my junior year to English. I've always loved words and structures of sentences. In the late sixties I started the drama and arts page of my college newspaper and began reviewing. I don't know how I got the nerve to do that, but I did. It was very eclectic. I remember writing about Judy Garland at Seton Hall University and also Judith Malina and Julian Beck with the Living Theatre at Brooklyn Academy of Music that same year. I saw all the great musicals of that period, with performers such as Barbra Streisand, Angela Lansbury, Gwen Verdon, Ethel Merman, Pearl Bailey, Elaine Stritch, Marlene Dietrich, Lauren Bacall, Katharine Hepburn. But I was also seeing new plays by Pinter and Albee, great established actors on Broadway, and the new off-off-Broadway playwrights downtown. When I moved to New York in 1971, I was first a music critic and had interviewed a lot of singers and wrote for popular national magazines. The sound and rhythm of a sentence are very important to me.

Soon I began writing for *Changes*, a radical arts and politics newspaper edited by Sue Graham, the wife of Charles Mingus, and covered downtown performance and cabarets. I went on to the *SoHo Weekly News*, but I wrote for a lot of magazines and serious literary journals as well, like *New York Arts Journal* and *Arts in Society*. At this time in New York City there were many young critics who were freelance writers. No one had academic jobs. People like Holland Cotter, Sally Banes, Deborah Jowitt, Robert Greskovic, who would later become established critics in their fields. All this was going on while I was in graduate school. At Hunter I also studied with Harold Clurman. So, though I wasn't really aware of how I was using it, I had a wide range of experience with different arts and styles by the time the journal began. And after writing for many years, you develop your technique. But I was always interested in experimenting with new forms of criticism, and in both high and pop culture.

I just considered that I was part of this avant-garde world, and I took for myself the same freedoms that artists took in creating their work. I tried to develop what I was interested in, a criticism based on the voice. That the writing could be spoken. That it had an intimate personal style, but was not autobiographical. And a certain kind of emotion. Over the years, I developed different essay forms, like "Alphabetical Shepard: The Play of Words," where each section went from *a* to *z* with a new theme or concept, or "The Wooster Group: A Dictionary of Ideas," one of my polyphonic essays, which included my own writing about them, interspersed with the voices of the group.[9] I started out in *The Theatre of Images* (1977) with my interest in text and image, and that's continued up to the last book that I've done, *Timelines* (2021), in which I am developing a new short-form kind of criticism.[10] The newer pieces are in a section called "Writing in the Landscape," based on taking a single image and having a certain number of words and treating them in a way that's poetic and more like literary writing. They all relate to the outdoors. What I'm also doing here is introducing the element of time into the writing. I am still searching for new forms of critical writing.

MILLER: How is this related to aging?

MARRANCA: Year-by-year and decade-by-decade I have become more engaged with deep thinking about writing and what forms to use to convey my ideas, all the while reading and exploring. It doesn't stop as you get older, if you are dedicated to your work, because you are propelled more and more into new directions while carrying knowledge from personal memory. In many ways, there are parts of myself from my twenties that I still carry inside me. They are interacting with the older woman I am now in ways I cannot always imagine but can only hope to continue. But the dedication to writing, developing skills, maintaining focus, rewriting—all those things certainly started in graduate school when I was freelance writing. In fact, many of my techniques for note-taking and close study of artworks I developed out of Daniel Gerould's teaching approach that was structure-based.

MILLER: You write about the centrality of the voice in your essay in *Timelines*, "Being There," when you discuss what you view as the diminishing role of the voice in everyday communication. I've been thinking about the distance many of these text-based technologies put between people as we age. You connect this loss of the voice to the way we see and think about performance.

MARRANCA: I wrote about that in the context of the coincidence that with the loss of interest in dramatic literature is also the loss of interest in the voice. Many people don't pick up the phone anymore. I've even asked younger scholars about this, why people don't like to use the phone. They don't like to be put on the spot to answer something. To commit. Probably many people have never had the experience when you speak to a friend who says, "It's so nice to hear your voice."

MILLER: Do you work with young writers differently today than in the past? What have you learned about how to cultivate writers' voices in the journal or books?

MARRANCA: In the beginning writers were less specialized and could write in a more journalistic way. Not everybody was attached to academia. There were people who did freelance work. But now we have had so many good writers, who started out as young critics, I've worked with them as an editor, we've published their work over decades. I try to help them cultivate their own voice and to write about art, not theories about art. Also, my years in the field is a help in making sure historical methodologies and documentation are correct. Over the decades, as an editor working with many of the same writers, I know their strengths and interests and will often ask them to write on a certain subject or artist. Sometimes we published their books as well.

I made a decision several months ago that the fall issue is the last issue I plan to edit, and *PAJ* will stop publication. I feel *PAJ*'s work is done. It's the end of a certain era. It's been forty-eight years! At this stage in my life, I want to be free of deadlines. I don't want to just keep going on for the sake of continuing. I have been a New York–based theater writer for half a century, having seen much of the most important work here and abroad during that time. It has been a unique opportunity and a wonderful life. But it's time to move on. I am keeping the book division and will be reprinting Jonas Barish's *The Antitheatrical Prejudice* in the fall. We still have about 55 of our original 160 titles in print, and I plan to work on another book on performance and drawing.

MILLER: In thinking about how much discipline your work demands, how would you describe what it takes to actually maintain a publishing house like *PAJ*? It required your shouldering a lot of responsibility, for the people whose work you were publishing and covering.

MARRANCA: It's a responsibility that Gautam Dasgupta and I took on and continued together for three decades. And then, from around 2005, I have been managing the press alone. I've always loved my work. I love editing. And, I really enjoy having a chance, when I can, to talk to or meet our contributors. I don't like to just have everything sent to me digitally. It is very different from when *PAJ* started out and people would come to the office with a manuscript, and you'd sit down and talk for an hour or two, and maybe we really enjoy being together, and then we go out to lunch or come home to our place for dinner. But this is unthinkable now the way people live. So, it's no wonder no one wants to talk on the phone. It takes time. We make choices in life. That's what aging is. You're supposed to grow and gain some kind of wisdom and hope that comes into your writing, but it comes from experience in the world and your thoughts. That's why I instinctively knew it was time for a change.

MILLER: You are describing a community that is based on proximity, with the press based in New York. I wonder about New York as an aging city, either in terms of your own ability to navigate it or how it affects the artists with whom you work. There's been conversation for years about New York becoming increasingly unlivable for artists. How much do you think of that as part of the arc of your career as well?

MARRANCA: That's what I meant when I said that the journal's work is done and it's the end of an era. It feels that way. We had an apartment on St. Marks Place between First Avenue and Avenue A that was about $300 a month in 1978. The whole economic structure was different because there were cafés, theaters, clubs, bookshops, restaurants. Everything was very cheap but salaries were incredibly low. We always had other jobs while doing this, but not 100 percent in academia until Gautam [Dasgupta] took a job at Skidmore College in the early nineties. There was a whole network and a very centralized world that doesn't exist now. It's too expensive for artists to live and work here and to have rehearsal space. Since the mid-eighties I also taught at private and public schools all over the United States and in Europe, until becoming professor of theater at Eugene Lang College/The New School for Liberal Arts for fourteen years, until 2019. At several universities I developed arts writing workshops.

MILLER: Your recent collection, *Timelines*, includes essays you've written about some artists after they have died. How do you approach that task when you're writing about people whose work you have followed for almost fifty years, and with whom you have often had friendships, as well?

MARRANCA: It is just what needs to be done at the time. Carolee Schneemann was a good friend for decades and I took all the feeling and knowledge I had about her and wrote a personal piece. With Sam Shepard, the occasion was the fact of reading about his death, but also, he had a new book. So, I weaved what I was going to say around that. Over the years I've written about María Irene Fornés as her publisher and longtime friend. Short pieces on these artists appear in *Timelines*.[11] I use qualities and characteristics that I know about people from observing them or being with them and trying to understand them. But I'm not in perpetual lamentation mode, nor debilitated by world crises, but more interested in the positive energy that the commitment to one's work brings. I often quote Hannah Arendt. In fact, I am just reading a new book about her, Lyndsey Stonebridge's *We Are Free to Change the World*. I've always loved what Arendt said about artworks being superior to all living things because they stay longer in the world than anything else. I am devoted to art and artworks. That encompasses a whole world of thinking for a human being.

But in terms of what I require from an artist as artists age is some development of thinking, seriousness, wisdom. For example, in my recent book I write about Ariane Mnouchkine dealing with ordinary lives in *Les Éphémères*. I am interested in the scope of artists' thinking and how they develop through the years. That's one of the things too, with friends or relationships with artists, how you grow with certain people, how you grow with Chekhov or Meredith Monk, whose work I've followed so long. Or with Fornés. I wrote an essay about Irene decades ago, called "The State of Grace: María Irene Fornés at Sixty-Two."[12] It was very directly connected to your first question, about aging in the American theater.

MILLER: Your personal papers and the *PAJ* archive were recently acquired by Yale University's Beinecke Rare Book and Manuscript Library. I'm curious about the process of taking stock of all of that material, and how you thought about your work over time.

MARRANCA: I have been saving for decades the correspondence and programs from everything I've ever seen. Different kind of flyers in the seventies that might be handwritten or mimeographed or drawn and mailed to *PAJ*. Plus, there's been a file on every journal issue. For every book, we had three files. All of these things have been saved and transported during all of our moves. We weren't thinking about a legacy. It's just the care that one takes running a business. We have fascinating correspondence from so many generations of people. Those who created the Group Theatre, the Living Theatre, Richard Maxwell's company [New York City Players], 600 Highwaymen, artists abroad like Augusto Boal, Eugenio Barba, Rimini Protokoll—all generations. And I'm still saving and printing email. My personal papers are extensive files and my notes on developing essays and books, lots of drafts, personal letters, postcards. Obviously, since the publishing house has been around a long time, all these things were being saved long before Yale came into the picture. We have correspondence, some handwritten, from Spalding Gray, Kathy Acker, Morris Carnovsky, Adrienne Kennedy, Susan Sontag. Over the years I was consolidating things on my own but eventually I hired a book dealer for the consulting, final organization, and sale. My papers and the *PAJ* archive will be available in 2025.

It was, again, a way of taking care and being responsible with the publishing house. It's learning how to work. I really value labor. I'm Chekhovian in that way. You look back over a lifetime and read biographies or think about your own life and there is just so much labor involved in everything. Lately, I have been listening to various audiobooks for the first time, including the Barbra Streisand autobiography, which she reads. It's forty-eight hours—amazing in the detail, the brilliance of Streisand, explaining so much about acting and space and time and personal struggle.

MILLER: What has sustained you in the field? Much of your work has resisted the alienation and impoverishment of theater and performance in our culture. What has buoyed you throughout the years, even as aspects of the field may have continued to disappoint or frustrate?

MARRANCA: I have to say that I'm always learning and following cultural and intellectual life outside of the arts, and my own interests. Also, I have never been absorbed by the fashions of academia, which is growing more and more conformist. I have always developed my own language as a form of resistance. During the time of COVID, I worked on two or three books. I worked constantly, and put out the journal with Ben Gillespie, *PAJ*'s associate editor during this time. We found a way to have a global selection of artist responses on COVID, working with the Martin E. Segal Theatre Center dialogues that Frank Hentschker organized.[13] I finished the expanded Meredith Monk book and also worked on my Dick Higgins anthology, which will be published later this year. And *Timelines* as well. I see fewer things now but many different types of artistic work because I need time for research and work on the books. Also, I travel a lot and spend many months of the year in the Hudson Valley, where I am editing and writing. But there are certain writers and artists who have sustained me through a lifetime watching or reading their work. John Cage, Robert Wilson, Gertrude Stein, Meredith Monk, Irene Fornés, Susan Sontag, so many great European and Asian directors and companies. I try to keep in touch with artists as much as I can and talk to them. Aging is chronological, but what does it mean for a person's mentality? In the "Ages of the Avant-Garde" issue, Fornés said she doesn't feel like she's aging because she's always starting anew and starting fresh, and that gives her a kind of energy.[14] One could sit down and think, "Yes, I'm getting older year by year by year," but all the older artists I know just keep working like demons.

I remember decades ago, I said something like this to Susan Sontag, "Editing takes a lot of work and there isn't much time left to write." And she said, "being an editor can be very creative." And it's true. It is very challenging and a driving force to survey a scene over a period of time and see what you can bring to the field for people to think about, what kinds of articles you come up with. A lot of *PAJ* is commissioned. It takes constantly writing to people and being in touch with them to suggest different kinds of articles in the journal. Maybe even a section on new opera or spiritualities or the American experimental theater, or dance and drawing. And then, of course, you have to find contributors who are doing this kind of work and get them to submit a portfolio and a text, and then there's all the editing. But that is what being an editor is. It's a very innovative, public commitment, and I am very attached to being a member of the independent press, to being a journalist, that goes back to my college days. I was always reading magazines and newspapers and following the cultural coverage.

MILLER: This also brings us back to the idea of the writer's voice and trying to fill a gap with your criticism. We have such limited cultural or arts journalism today. The window during COVID where it seemed as though arts writers were really thinking about cultural policy, that window shut.

MARRANCA: It's a shame because all the stories have now become nationalized, and they became so promotional. The *Times* theater coverage is terrible. It's all about celebrity or money or promoting something. There's no real serious criticism of theater in it. It's up to the theater community to change things. They have to make greater demands and be more forceful to save the field. If we had more newspapers and local press, people would be writing about these things, and then others would be reading them and discussing issues. This, to some extent, is a function of a journal. I'm saying all these things in the journal all the time and in my writings. With aging you have a historical perspective. I have a certain kind of cultural memory that I draw on to edit and to do my own writing and to function as a publisher. That's why I chose to do the Jonas Barish book. I thought, "people need to know this work. This is a great book." We are going to lose money on it, but I don't care. So that's how PAJ Publications will go forth in the future. Perhaps some new books or bringing some of our out-of-print books back into print. I have always operated out of a love of the work. It's a whole different feeling when you work from that perspective. I love being in the world of the arts as a profession. It has been such a great life. Having the press, an international voice, being able to publish whatever I wanted. It's a great luxury and privilege.

NOTES

1. Bonnie Marranca, *Ecologies of Theater: Essays at the Century Turning* (Johns Hopkins University Press, 1996), 111. See also Bonnie Marranca, "The Aging Playwright and the American Theater," *Village Voice*, June 16, 1992, 94.

2. Marranca, *Ecologies of Theater*, 95.

3. Bonnie Marranca, ed., *American Garden Writing* (PAJ Publications, 1988).

4. Bonnie Marranca and Małgorzata Semil, eds., *New Europe: Plays from the Continent* (PAJ Publications, 2009).

5. See *PAJ: A Journal of Performance and Art* 45, no. 2 (May 2023).

6. Bonnie Marranca, ed., *Plays for the End of the Century* (Johns Hopkins University Press, 1996).

7. Bonnie Marranca, *Conversations with Meredith Monk* (PAJ Publications, 2014).

8. Marranca, *Ecologies of Theater*, 224–32.

9. Bonnie Marranca, *Theatrewritings* (PAJ Publications, 1984), 23–41; Bonnie Marranca, *Performance Histories* (PAJ Publications, 2008), 39–61.

10. Bonnie Marranca, *The Theatre of Images: Robert Wilson, Richard Foreman, Lee Breuer* (Drama Book Specialists, 1977).

11. Bonnie Marranca, *Timelines: Writings and Conversations* (PAJ Publications, 2021).

12. Marranca, *Ecologies of Theater*, 80–86.

13. Benjamin Gillespie, Sarah Lucie, and Jennifer Joan Thompson, "Global Voices in the Time of Coronavirus," *PAJ: A Journal of Performance and Art* 42, no. 3 (September 2020): 3–27.

14. Bonnie Marranca, "Ages of the Avant-Garde," *Performing Arts Journal* 16, no. 1 (January 1994): 9–57.

15

Age Simulation

The Ultimate Dress Rehearsal

Scott Magelssen

"Watch," Scott Tarde, CEO and executive director of the George G. Glenner Alzheimer's Family Centers, told me. Tarde pushed open the door to the "air lock" that served as an exit out of Glenner Town Square adult day center, the simulated world of post–World War II San Diego that had been painstakingly created inside a spacious warehouse on a suburban industrial strip in Chula Vista. The door triggered an alarm, Tarde explained, which alerted Town Square staff of a breach—possibly by an "exit-seeking" participant in the simulation who had become confused or lost.[1] As I watched the group of senior citizens seated in a circle in the park, a rainbow-colored parachute stretched between them that they used to gently toss a beach ball into the air, they showed not a bit of awareness that an alarm had been sounded and that their caretakers had shifted into alert mode. The alarm, as it turned out, was a gentle clamoring of songbird whistles, designed to get the immediate attention of the staff, but to fit seamlessly and inconspicuously into the midcentury environment comprising shops, homes, and public buildings furnished and decorated with nostalgic material from days long gone, and bustling with happy activity.

This was on an afternoon in the summer of 2021. I was being shown around Town Square, conceived by Tarde a few years ago and opened in 2018 as a day care facility for aging adults in early or moderate stages of dementia, such as that experienced with Alzheimer's disease. Town Square is an immersive environment that simulates San Diego in the 1950s and early 1960s for these individuals, who would have been between the ages of ten and thirty during that time, and for whom these memories are the strongest. The idea behind immersing these individuals with dementia into a world filled with reminders from their youth is that the memories will prompt them to open up and tell stories, connecting with one another and their family members and Town Hall staff. These interactions, which the George G. Glenner Alzheimer's Family Centers nonprofit calls "reminiscence therapy," while not curing their dementia, will ultimately, it says, improve their quality of life, help with mood, make sleeping easier, foster connections with family, and so forth.

Town Square is part of a larger phenomenon in recent years, in which health professionals in memory care programs in Europe and the United States have been experimenting with simulating nostalgic environments from patients' pasts in order to facilitate memory therapy and mitigate feelings of rage, panic, and misery that accompany dementia. A residential facility outside Chagrin Valley, Ohio, re-creates the lantern-lined streets and clapboard houses with wooden shutters from the nearby town's appearance decades earlier.[2] A program in Denmark is housed in an open-air museum devoted to urban history and culture. The AlexA Residence for Senior Citizens in Dresden even goes so far as to re-create a pre-1989 East German environment for its clients, complete with a communist era grocery shop that takes now-defunct currency from the GDR.[3] The largest of these experiments, perhaps, is the so-called "dementia village" of Hogewey in the Netherlands, an entire walled community in which residents go about their routines as if "nothing in [their] life has changed" since they began losing their memory, interact with fellow townspeople, and live out their remaining days in the constructed world (a new spot opens up only when a Hogewey resident passes away).[4] The use of performative techniques like simulated environments demonstrates that tools from theater and performance are being sought after by care providers and those who have aging family members in their lives as a way to offer people with dementia an experience that can improve quality of life, in many cases more conveniently and at a more affordable cost than alternatives like nursing homes.

Meanwhile, research institutions and aging care facilities have also been developing workshops and equipment to simulate the effects of aging on *younger* participants, whether to help teach empathy for aging patients and clients or to develop products and built environments for aging consumers and citizens. MIT, for instance, boasts that its high-tech aging suit, Age Gain Now Empathy System (AGNES), can help meet the emergent "longevity economy" head-on.[5] I wrote about aging simulations for my book *Simming* in 2013, and my research included trying on aging suits, including the

AGNES at MIT. At that time, I found that while these performances promise to benefit those facing the physical, emotional, and mental challenges that come with aging, they can also perpetuate and reinforce negative stereotypes about aging adults. In the years since *Simming* came out, the aging simulation industry has boomed, and it is time again to take a look at how these simulations are changing perspectives on aging and how we are better building the environment to accommodate our aging populations.

In this essay, then, I consider simulation techniques employed in both of these manners: the use of tools of theater and performance to simulate worlds for aging people with dementia to help improve their and their family members' quality of life, and the use of our tools to simulate how it feels to be old for young people to better empathize with members of the aging population—or perhaps as the "ultimate dress rehearsal" for their own performances in decades to come.[6] By thinking through how simulation is being used to confront aging, both to stage nostalgic, pleasant worlds for seniors and to purposefully approximate the unpleasant, uncomfortable aspects of aging bodies for younger people, we can understand how such techniques in applied theater can help us make a better and more accommodating world for older human beings, as well as how they offer new perspectives on age-old theater questions—from the contours of willing suspension of disbelief to the usefulness of embodied empathy.

It is hard not to be impressed with Glenner Town Square. The facility is a remarkable exercise in world-building. The simulated San Diego environment occupies nine thousand square feet of warehouse space with twenty-four-foot ceilings, enough room to encompass a whole community's worth of gathering and activity spaces, and accommodates up to seventy-five participants at a time (those who use the facility's day care services are referred to as "participants," versus "patients" or "clients"). Participants can stay for a four-hour slot for $65 or for eight hours for $95. Built to resemble San Diego between 1953 and 1961, Town Square features a diner, a movie theater, a city hall, a pub, a beauty parlor, and other activity spaces organized around a city park. Participants rotate through each storefront in small groups of five to seven people, spending about forty-five or fifty minutes in each space and engaging in educational and social activities. A 1959 black and silver chrome Ford Thunderbird sits outside the service station and garage. The T-Bird is not just for looking at: participants can sit in the car or peek under the hood. As the *San Diego Union-Tribune* put it, Town Square "is a cutting-edge adult day care center where Alzheimer's patients can travel through 14 storefronts and stations to shop, have lunch, tinker on a car, get a check-up, fold and 'iron' laundry and do some typing at the office."[7]

In staging a midcentury environment, Town Square is not unlike other senior day and residential facilities that boast a yesteryear decor. In my own research I've encountered several themed spaces that evoke the postwar United States by capitalizing on tropes of 1950s Fords and Chevrolets, old-fashioned gas pumps, drive-ins, trompe l'oeil murals of nostalgic Main Street USA storefronts, and various iterations of Marilyn Monroe, James Dean, Audrey Hepburn, Elvis Presley, and other icons from that time. But that's where the similarity ends, says Tarde. He envisioned a much more immersive world for Town Square than simply a decorated space with fake doors and buildings you can't actually go into. For him, those kinds of spaces fall dramatically short of their potential for authentic reminiscence therapy. The nostalgic look of those places, he has concluded, is targeted more at the seniors' families, who are comforted by the idea of their loved ones being in a space that's more fun than a clinical environment, a tidy assuagement he refers to as "guilt mitigation." "We wanted to disrupt this idea," he said. "We wanted to build everything in Town Square as accurate as possible," not only to create a more authentic world for efficacious therapy, but to head off claims that the place was "juvenile," his other anticipated critique.

The ambitious plan involved consulting with Douglas Pancake, the go-to senior living architecture firm, for the original-concept architecture, and engaging the San Diego Opera Scenic Studio to manifest the world inside the Chula Vista industrial space.[8] The San Diego Opera artisans worked to capture the look and feel of midcentury San Diego, including creating original tilework for the miniature City Hall. The load-bearing columns holding up the roof were masked as wooden telephone poles streaked with creosote. The brick walls of buildings were aged and distressed with bits of old paint and mortar, and faded Uncle Sam "I Want You" Army recruitment posters, to evoke a naturalistic palimpsest of earlier decades. Tarde pointed out the way that the painters had even incorporated subtle stains from rain and dirt that would have run down the walls where storefront awnings met the buildings and splashed up from the sidewalk. Other details stand out as well: all the American flags bear only forty-eight stars, and all the telephones have rotary dials. The diner sports a real 1955 Seeburg jukebox, and the library has a working card catalog system. There's a diminutive version of the San Diego Air and Space Museum in Town Square's version of Balboa Park, with glass vitrines displaying flight suits and helmets and other aviation artifacts, curated by the actual San Diego Air and Space Museum.[9] Notably, there are no mirrors in Town Square, even in the Silver Fox Barber and Beauty Shop, since some participants, Tarde explained, no longer recognize themselves by their own older appearance.

I asked Tarde whether he was inspired by European facilities like Hogewey to create Town Square. Not at all, he replied. The real credit for the idea he gives to his ten-year-old daughter's experience with Junior Achievement's "BizTown," a simulated miniature town in Mission Valley where elementary students can learn skills, become good citizens, and learn the basics of the free enterprise system by operating banks, stores, and restaurants, writing checks, and voting for mayor.[10] Town Square is conceived as a day program with a "respite care" model, he says, not a living, breathing residential community like Hogewey, which, unlike US memory care programs, is also completely government funded, so "there is not a lot of comparison between the two." Participants here are seniors in early to moderate stages of dementia who are currently living at home with family or with caregivers. Nor is it meant to be 100 percent accurate or to fool participants into feeling like they are in an actual midcentury environment like some sort of real-life *Truman Show* (a comparison often evoked by media when describing facilities that simulate the past while surveilling their occupants). Instead, the painstaking detail is meant to create a different kind of authenticity, a feeling and an impression that can help foster the participants' own memories and encourage socialization. This is why it is set in the 1950s: not because the era is idealized in popular perception, but because the participants, who are mostly in their eighties (the average age is eighty-one), have the strongest memories from that time. "Between ten and thirty years old is when our strongest memories are made," explained Tarde.[11] Town Square's environment matches up with the time in which the participants were that age. In the coming decades, as Town Square continues (both here in its original location and in the multiple franchises set to open in the next few years),[12] he told me, the setting will adapt and change to keep up with the strongest memories of the participants. "For us," he says, referring to himself and me, who both grew up as children in the 1980s, "it'll be Blockbuster and video arcades." But some settings, like the diner and other storefronts, will probably remain because they are "universal" and "classic Americana," no matter what decade they occupy.

Town Square is believed to be, reported the *Wall Street Journal* in 2018, the "first memory-care facility in the U.S. built entirely around the idea of reminiscence therapy,"[13] which uses prompts from participants' lives, such as music, photographs, and movies, to elicit memories and to encourage storytelling, connection, and conversation. D. Mindy Baker, education director for the Glenner Centers, explained the idea behind reminiscence therapy. The goal is not to cure or treat dementia, she explained, but to gauge what abilities the participants have by creating a safe and supportive environment and engaging them in conversation at their own pace. The key is not to ask participants "do you remember," which can lead to confusion, sadness, and withdrawal, but to prompt them to talk more about spontaneous memories or stories evoked by the environment or by cues in a way that makes them feel happy and competent. The reminiscence prompts can include old kitchen cookbooks from the 1950s, an old western movie, or music and photos from the past. The accuracy of the memories is less important than the fostering of positive and supportive feelings. The caregivers' goal is not to get the participants to focus on a specific memory for each cue, but rather to encourage them to come up with something they know or hadn't thought about for a long time. Baker gave the Town Square's Ford Thunderbird as an example. It can spark memories of learning to drive, or of a time when Fords were "all my dad would buy."[14]

Reminiscence therapy has been demonstrated to have positive effects on aging individuals with dementia; and reminiscence therapy paired with immersion in a simulated setting seems to work better than when it is used in everyday normal contemporary environments, at least one study finds. When older participants with dementia were cued with "autobiographical memory material" in a "museum setting" (an aging activity center housed in the Old Town open-air museum of urban history and culture in Aarhus, Denmark) simulating the participants' past, their memories were "quantitatively and qualitatively" different from those elicited in a control setting. Moreover, the study found, the memories were "more elaborated, more spontaneous and included especially more internal (episodic) details compared to memories in the control condition."[15] Quality of life improvements have been among the most prominent positive effects noted in memory care facilities incorporating simulation, and in many cases the improvements have been dramatic. At the AlexA facility in former East Germany, "the rooms are filled with furniture, wallpaper, appliances and other mementos from the communist era and have helped . . . clients with some of the worst cases of dementia become communicative and enthusiastic about daily tasks, like eating." AlexA director Gunter Wolfram observes that "it's really fascinating to see how people who basically lay in bed and lacked any motivation to do anything suddenly flourish."[16] And at Hogewey in the Netherlands, the residents display an all-around better vitality than people with dementia at conventional facilities. "On a physical level," reports CNN, "residents at Hogewey require fewer medications; they eat better, and yes, they live longer. On a mental level, they also seem to have more joy. It's a difficult thing to measure, but that is the most important thing here at Hogewey."[17]

A Cochrane review had a more conservative assessment, finding that the "effects of reminiscence interventions are inconsistent, often small in size and can differ considerably across settings and modalities." Nevertheless, reminiscence therapy seems, the authors find, to have "some positive effects on people with dementia in the domains of QoL [quality of life], cognition, communication and mood."[18] Researchers admit that it's difficult to collect data and find positive results in a population that is constantly declining with the ravages of memory loss and other impairments, but recognize that work in reminiscence therapy is promising. Participants may not show improvements in cognition after the therapy activities, but they do become better at talking about their memories, suggesting that reminiscence therapy can improve quality of life, communication, and mood. Advocates also believe that stimulation with reminiscence therapy can help keep patients with dementia stable and stave off decline for many years.[19]

At Town Square, the anecdotal evidence so far points to very positive results for reminiscence therapy. Volunteers and family members describe a measurable difference in the participants. Shae-Linn Carr, who volunteers at Town Square and whose grandmother is a participant, told ABC News in a story about the program that "'volunteering at Town Square has been so, for lack of a better word, life changing,' . . . explaining that the programming keeps her grandma stimulated. 'Even if she doesn't remember what happened and why she's happy, her body is happy and it's remarkable. [Town Square] is doing amazing things.'"[20] For other participants, being allowed to take on roles in Town Square can foster dignity and a sense of purpose. The *Wall Street Journal* reported the story of Susie Heavilin, a sixty-nine-year-old former accountant, diagnosed with Alzheimer's a year earlier. She believes she's a bookkeeper in the offices of the Town Square's City Hall. "'They print out invoices for her,' says Sheri Berg, her daughter. 'It's really given her a sense of purpose. It's really changed everything for us.'"[21] And Tarde told me about participants who work regularly organizing board games and puzzles in the library and conducting inventory at the clothing store, identifying more as "volunteers" or "workers" than "participants." "Some of them need this purpose, this storyline," said Tarde. By allowing them to maintain this role, the staff help the participants benefit from the sense of purpose the duties bring, and help meet Glenner Centers' goal of providing "a valuable, meaningful day for participants."

Town Square is not without its detractors. Naysayers in the comments section of online articles or social media posts have criticized the facility for defaulting to an idealized, simplified conception of midcentury America, a version of the nation that doesn't include social ills like injustice and racism. The *Wall Street Journal* put the question to Tarde, asking whether

Fig. 15.1. Glenner Park, Alois' Newsstand, Pied Piper Movie Theater, and Silver Fox Barber Shop. Glenner Town Square®, San Diego, 2018. Photo Courtesy of George G. Glenner Alzheimer's Family Centers, Inc.®

a sanitized 1950s San Diego might not resonate with all participants, some of whom are immigrants from China, the Philippines, and Latin America. Tarde responded that "the center tries to incorporate activities that relate to other cultures, such as playing games like Loteria, a Mexican game similar to bingo. He says they 'are very sensitive and aware of history and absolutely will recognize history, Civil Rights and cultural days, weeks and months' with different activities that acknowledge the diversity of their patients."[22] To me, Tarde said that the critiques that Town Square doesn't include, say, segregation, are mostly by internet trolls, and are based on a willful misperception that the environment's goal is historical accuracy. Baker explained more on this point: It's not about accuracy. The staff doesn't dress in 1950s costumes, for instance. It's about unlocking good memories and feelings. A sense of familiarity develops, and the participants become less resistant to the world around them. They come out of the facility smiling, she says. The family members see this after only a month in the program.

The question of accuracy gets at some of the ongoing conversations about representational practices in theater and performance studies. Is the goal in simulating an imagined space to hew as closely to its original as possible, or is it to evoke a world through imagination that is more about eliciting ideas and emotions than it is about mirroring reality? At Town Square and other memory care facilities that use simulation in their programming, the intent is clearly not to create a convincing world that can pass for an actual past environment. For all its impressive detail and naturalism, Town Square is hardly photorealistic (the corners are a bit too square, the grass is plastic, some of the wartime *San Diego Union* headlines at the Alois's Newsstand[23] predate the 1953–61 period but also share the shelf with stories from the Space Race, the *I Love Lucy* episodes playing on flat-screens hidden inside old-fashioned television sets run with the caption functions turned on, etc.). Yet the environment still serves as the setting for believed-in realities. The participants may not take the ersatz storefronts for real San Diego, but they weave for themselves realities in which they are members of a community, volunteers in the local library, shop assistants, and bookkeepers. The Town Hall staff and programmers, the Douglas Pancake architects and the artisans with the San Diego Opera Scenic Studio, the Air and Space Museum and other community partners may provide the environment, but the imagined narratives and "storylines" are creations of the participants' bodies and minds, clouded, or perhaps even enabled, by dementia. They are, in a sense, both the producers of and the participant observers in these realities. The job of the staff and other volunteers is not to correct these imagined realities, but to say "yes, and . . ."—and to clear the world of impediments to those imagined realities, including the mirrors that would show the participants their own present bodies. For some, this might be the theater artist's dream audience. For others, a patronizing deception. But over and over again, as my interviewees reiterated, and the Glenner Centers' literature maintains, the intention is not to fool the participants, but to give them a space where what they're experiencing in their minds can take place with dignity and without confusion or anxiety: to "meet them where they are in their reality."[24] And if this involves a kind of willing suspension of disbelief—and an idealization of what the past may have actually been like—then the folks at Town Square are doing their job to help improve quality of life, and just maybe happening to fulfill some Aristotelian precepts regarding the function of artistic representation along the way.

Meanwhile, as I said in the introduction, performance is also being used to confront aging from, decidedly, the other end, as senior care facilities, universities, and commercial industries are using simulation techniques to produce the feeling of aging in young people. Staff at assisted living homes, for instance, undergo training workshops in which they're put into scenarios their aging clients might encounter, like facing ageist jokes made at their expense, diminutive or patronizing language, or impatient hollering as they're trying to complete a task. In other cases, they are given physical impairments that limit their movement and senses, like those experienced by aging bodies, such as cotton balls in their ears to simulate hearing loss, fogged glasses to suggest cataracts or macular degeneration, dried corn kernels placed in shoes to give a sense of discomfort that comes with fatty tissue loss, and thick rubber bands around the fingers and knuckles to reproduce the challenges of arthritis. Participants are then asked to complete otherwise simple tasks like counting out change from a coin purse or finding a number in a phone book and dialing on a smartphone. Exercises like these, say advocates, can teach younger people about some of the challenges and stressors that come with aging and help them be more empathetic and patient with older adults. Exercises at the Xtreme Aging Program at the Macklin Intergenerational Institute in Findlay, Ohio, include some that mimic cognitive loss (like needing to fill out a personal information card with their nondominant hand while their nondominant leg is crossed and they rotate one foot at the ankle counterclockwise, all while one trainer tells them to hurry up while another tells them to take their time) or loss of loved ones (sticky notes with names of friends and family members are unceremoniously yanked from participants over the course of the exercise). The goal, program founder and head Vicki Rosebrook told me back in 2011, along with other programming at the Macklin Intergenerational Institute, is to foster awareness of aging, decrease negative biases and stereotypes about aging, and build empathy and acceptance of aging people in our communities.[25] As John Leland of the *New York Times* reported in a 2008 story on the Ohio program, "as the population in the developing world ages, simulation programs like Xtreme Aging have become a regular part of many nursing or medical school curriculums, and have crept into the corporate world, where knowing what it is like to be elderly increasingly means better understanding one's customers or even employees."[26]

More advanced versions of these techniques have included the development of whole "aging suits" like one developed by the Xtreme Aging Program or AGNES at MIT, which boast complex assemblages of coveralls, bungee cords, weighted bags, and crash helmets in order to suppress range of motion, compromise balance, and redistribute the center of gravity, giving wearers a sense of what it is like to be in the body of an eighty-something-year-old.[27] I tried out both the Xtreme Aging Program suit and MIT's AGNES for my research for *Simming*, with mixed results. As I wrote in 2013, the imposed handicaps, straight out of Kurt Vonnegut's dystopian short story "Harrison Bergeron," were immediately effective in making me kinesthetically aware of the physical effects of aging. The constrained position of

Fig. 15.2. The AGNES age simulation suit, MIT AgeLab, Cambridge, Massachusetts, 2010. Photo by Nathan Fried-Lipski, courtesy of MIT AgeLab.

my head and neck allowed me to see only a fraction of the normal landscape in front of me, and even that was reduced substantially—to what I could make out through a pinprick of vision in my peripheral loss glasses at the Macklin Intergenerational Institute, or blurred by a diabetic fog produced by telescoping goggles at MIT. My fingers were curled into barely useful claws by restraints. Simple tasks like reaching for an object in front of me or finding the chair behind me had me breaking out into a sweat within only a couple minutes. Taking off the suit in both cases had me feeling waves of relief.[28]

Since my initial research for *Simming*, the aging simulation industry has burgeoned, becoming a familiar part of medical student curriculums and nursing and caregiving training the world over. A 2021 study for *Currents in Pharmacy Teaching and Learning* found that pharmacy students who underwent simulation exercises wearing ankle weights and knee restraints to reproduce the effects of Parkinson's and osteoarthritis, respectively, and who were tasked with, for example, sorting multicolored pills while wearing yellow goggles, demonstrated a significant increase in empathy for geriatric patients, which is associated with "better diagnostic accuracy, patient satisfaction, and medication adherence."[29] And aging suits have become somewhat of a cottage industry, serving customers who want to incorporate their own aging simulation workshops into their company's empathy orientations or their academic program's curriculum. By my last count in the summer of 2021, more than half a dozen medical equipment companies offer their own version of aging suits for purchase, complete with straps, harnesses, cords, and goggles, priced between $500 and $2,500.[30]

In a testament to our growing awareness (and anxiety) about the approaching demographic surge of elderly citizens, aging suits have been getting airplay in high-profile media platforms. Adam Gopnik detailed his own feelings of frustration, anger, and finally relief upon removing the AGNES suit at MIT in a 2019 essay for the *New Yorker*. "The suit makes us aware not so much of the physical difficulties of old age, which can be manageable," reflects Gopnik, "but of the mental state disconcertingly associated with it—the price of age being perpetual aggravation. The theme and action and motive of *King Lear* suddenly become perfectly clear. You become enraged at your youngest daughter's reticence because you have had to struggle to unroll the map of your kingdom."[31] For WBUR's public radio program *Here and Now* in 2019, Robin Young interviewed Dallas-based architecture firm Corgan's Samantha Flores and Mike Steiner, who had been studying public settings like airport terminals in aging suits to better understand the challenges that aging people find in these spaces. Airports can be notorious, for instance, for long concourses with few places to stop and rest, and signage mounted mostly from the ceiling can prove difficult to see if one has decreased mobility in the neck. Flores and Steiner used the GERT aging suit designed by German designer Wolfgang Moll (GERT stands for GERontologic Test suit), with weights velcroed to the chest and extremities, neck brace to restrict head and neck movement, goggles to impair vision, headphones to muffle hearing, and overshoes to simulate nerve loss in the feet. Young took a turn in the suit for the program episode in the WBUR studio and described, in a noticeably winded voice, the harrowing experience of losing feeling, mobility, and sensation; she stated that she could not imagine getting around in an airport with these impairments. Young narrated what she was thinking and feeling as each piece of the GERT suit was layered onto her body and limbs. "Oh, that is so hard to walk," she said when Flores and Steiner strapped on the overshoes. "That's sad," she said with pity. "You know, when I think that's what it's like for someone. That's sad."[32]

A study published in 2020 used the same GERT suit featured in the *Here and Now* story to test over three hundred health professionals working in the field of geriatrics to see whether the aging suit increased awareness of older patients' sensory and functional difficulties. Participants each wore the suit for fifteen minutes and conducted tasks like going up and down stairs, sitting and lying down, eating, and drinking. Participants experienced not only physical impacts like decreased hearing, decreased vision, stiffness, slowness, loss of balance, falls, and clumsiness, but also negative emotions, loneliness, and general difficulties. The study concluded that the "strong emotional power" of the aging simulation was an "effective educational tool to raise awareness among health professionals of age-related difficulties. This sensory activity allows health professionals to put themselves in the shoes of older patients and to feel age-related difficulties," and complimented earlier studies that showed that simulations like these improved "positive attitudes and empathy towards older patients" and "promoted respect for dignity in care."[33] The GERT suit is available for purchase as well, through the Wolfgang Moll company's website. It costs roughly 1,320 Euros (a little over $1,500). Accessories include washable covers and a carrying case.[34]

Aging simulation kits have even made it into the New York theater scene. Colman Domingo's *Dot*, which was produced as part of the Humana Festival in 2015 and premiered at New York's off-Broadway Vineyard Theatre in February 2016, features a catharsis moment in which Donnie finally comes to realize what his middle-class African American mother, Dottie, is going through with Alzheimer's, when he's coaxed into a game in which he's given tasks while wearing glaucoma goggles, pebbles in his shoes, latex gloves with taped-together fingers, and headphones that emit an "incessant jabbering" (which the audience hears when he puts them on).[35] Elinor Fuchs, in describing *Dot* as an example of what she discerned as an emerging category of "dementia plots," comprising that theater season's "in" disease, finds that while the turn of events helps Domingo avoid the clichés of the senile family member being carried "off to Assisted Living while the children weep," Donnie's recognition scene is suspiciously fast and easy, "a conversion faster than Saul's on the road to Damascus."[36]

What can simulation exercises and aging suits tell us about how performance can be used to help empathize with, or prepare for, old age? To be sure, in many ways, simulation exercises intended to foster empathy with those different from us are hardly new, though they haven't always been uncontroversial. John Howard Griffin's 1961 book *Black Like Me* details his six-week stint passing as a Black man to ferret out the racism he might not otherwise encounter as a white male.[37] And Jane Elliott's Brown-Eyed/Blue-Eyed diversity training exercise in 1960s grade school classrooms, which subjected blue-eyed kids to being taunted as inferior in order to teach the kids about racism, nearly tore her town apart in the process.[38] Theater and performance scholars have for decades been advocating for performance as a tool that can foster understanding and empathy through embodied practice in ways that, as Diana Taylor argues, complement or even surpass more widely used forms of knowledge dissemination (e.g., the written word).[39] Likewise, performance studies scholar Bryant Keith Alexander reminds us that through performance we can get to a "way of knowing . . . the nuanced nomenclature of human social experience."[40]

Moreover, the kind of experience offered by the aging suits can get at a definition of empathy as it was originally conceived in the second half of the nineteenth century (the term *Einfühlung* was coined by German scholar Robert Vischer in 1873 and translated into "empathy," from the Greek *empatheia*, by Edward Titchener in 1909). As Susan Leigh Foster explains in *Choreographing Empathy*, the original connotations of the term had less to do with emotions or feelings than with the ability "to register a change in sense of physicality that, in turn, influenced how one felt another's feelings."[41] By the end of the nineteenth century, writes Foster, empathy "became the process through which one experienced muscularly as well as psychically the dynamics of what was being witnessed."[42] Imagine the possibilities, in other words, if those who put on an aging suit and attempt to do tasks as if they were experiencing the body of an older person could literally "feel with" another's physical and psychic state—to empathize kinesthetically with an aging adult in a way that surpasses identifying with a character onstage, reading about them in a book, or even interacting with them in person.

However, what I found in my research was that, while aging simulations hold incredible promise and potential for increasing empathy and understanding, those same simulations, by subjecting participants to the discomforts, losses, complications, and frustrations that accompany aging bodies, can also lead to unwanted consequences, like reinforcing associations between old age and infirmity, incontinence, decrepitude, and pain. Those who participated in exercises expressed takeaways that strayed from the intended outcomes like empathy and understanding, and shared that the simulation confirmed their fears of aging as scary, disorienting, and uncomfortable. This was borne out by my own frustration and discomfort in the aging suits, and my relief when the simulations were over. Monika Deppen Wood has described the growing number of unintended negative responses among her students to empathy training simulations for a sociology course she taught at Rutgers. "In the past," she said in 2007, "I'd get responses such as, 'Now I understand why Grandpa is so grumpy. . . .' Now they say, 'I don't want to be like this when I grow old. I'm going to start taking better care of myself. I'm going to quit smoking. I'm going to go to the gym. I'm going to eat better.'"[43] In other words, for many participants, the simulation exercises can further alienate younger people from older people, and prompt attitudes of avoidance ("I'm going to start exercising and eating better so I can avoid the physical effects of aging"), as if it were possible to hold off the inevitable, or ageism and ableism ("I blame the elderly for burdening our society and pushing up health-care costs"). It's a catch-22, I reflected: we can use simulation to build empathy by putting younger people in older people's uncomfortable shoes, but in so doing we make the prospect of becoming those older people repulsive by equating their identity with physical suffering.[44]

The simulation experience can involve an astounding reversal of attitude, to be sure, but as with the Aristotelian catharsis moment in a tragedy, the revelation may have more to do with pity and fear than with empathy. The participants in the recent studies of aging suit workshops among pharmacy undergrads and health professionals (and even the family members in Colman Domingo's play) don't report this kind of backfiring—that is, reinforced attitudes regarding aging as scary or alienating or pitiable. But I heard it in Robin Young's pitying "that's sad" upon reflecting on old people navigating the airport in their difficult bodies. I read it in Adam Gopnik's description of his increasingly angstful experience in the AGNES suit, musing that the frustration and anger the suit engendered in relation to the unaccommodating world around him was tantamount to Lear's becoming-madness.

When it comes to authentic connections with, and understandings of, aging people and the experience of old age, then, it can still appear that simulation falls short. This is why educators like Kris Mauk pair simulation training in their classrooms and labs with experiences with aging adults, like service learning and community involvement activities. Mauk, when she taught nursing at Valparaiso University in Indiana, partnered with long-term care facilities to put her students in experiences that gave them one-on-one interactions with older adults throughout their course of study. Like Wood, Mauk witnessed negative attitudes toward aging people in students when they would first enter the degree program (expressing a desire to work with babies or in ICU rather than doing geriatric care), but students who participated in the community involvement experiences and worked with older adults praised the course for giving them the chance "to have one whole person to myself for an hour," and those who worked with older adults early in their degree program found that, when they began their clinicals, their patients were much less threatening and their procedures and interactions with them were much more enjoyable. When positive experiences with older adults are built into the course, students' attitudes change, Mauk told me. They see that "older people aren't that scary," that just because someone is an older adult does not mean that they're incontinent and sad. "If I've accomplished this," says Mauk, "I'm happy."[45]

All this tells me that the use of aging simulations can be a profound tool for understanding the physical difficulties that come with aging, and perhaps even some of the emotional difficulties, too—and their employment in the educational, medical, and consulting arena appears to be achieving positive results in customer and patient care, consumer product design, and built-environment engineering—but, when it comes to *empathy*, aging simulations do not substitute for authentic connections with aging adults. In the years since publishing *Simming*, despite my background in theater and performance studies and the adage about walking a mile in another's shoes, I've grown increasingly hesitant to believe that we need to physically embody someone else's experience in order to connect with them. As I've written elsewhere, it's ultimately arrogant for me to say I need to feel your suffering in order to believe you suffer.[46] To meet aging adults with dignity and respect, can we do the work of empathy without the straps and sandbags, fogged goggles and bungee cords? Without needing to equate their difference with feelings of pity and fear? I want to believe this, and not just because I hope to never have to put on one of those god-awful simulation suits again.

As Anne Davis Basting reminds us, we have the power to build a world that is accommodating and safe for aging adults, and the ability to make this a world where all people, regardless of their physical ability or neurocognitive state, can abide with joy and dignity. "We all wait for a pill that will ensure that no matter how long we live, we will have the ability to live meaningful lives surrounded by people who care about us. But while we wait for the scientific discoveries, there is a great deal we can do right now to enrich ourselves and the lives of others." But this is possible only if our approaches to building this world are undertaken "with more than just fear," she writes.[47] This reminder is germane to discussions of aging simulations, which can often reify fears of aging even as they purport to increase empathy. But Basting's words are also in keeping with what seems to be working at Glenner Town Square and other facilities that reshape a world (or small parts of it at a time) for aging adults. The tools of theater and performance, if falling short of adequately offering a "dress rehearsal" for old age, can, in these instances, help prepare a world in which our lives can be dignified and meaningful when we get there.

NOTES

1. Unless indicated otherwise, all quotes and information from Scott Tarde are from my tour and personal interview with him in Glenner Town Square, Chula Vista, California, on July 6, 2021.

2. Larissa MacFarquhar, "The Comforting Fictions of Dementia Care," *New Yorker*, October 1, 2018, https://www.newyorker.com/magazine/2018/10/08/the-comforting-fictions-of-dementia-care

3. Soraya Sarhaddi Nelson, "Nursing Home Recreates Communist East Germany for Dementia Patients," *Parallels*, NPR, January 22, 2018, https://www.npr.org/sections/parallels/2018/01/22/578664161/

4. Ben Tinker, "'Dementia Village' Inspires New Care," *CNN*, December 27, 2013, https://www.cnn.com/2013/07/11/world/europe/wus-holland-dementia-village/. See also Sanjay Gupta, "'Dementia Village': 5 Things I Learned," CNN, July 11, 2013, https://edition.cnn.com/2013/07/11/world/europe/wus-holland-dementia-lessons/index.html; Josh Planos, "The Dutch Village Where Everyone Has Dementia," *Atlantic*, November 14, 2014, https://www.theatlantic.com/health/archive/2014/11/the-dutch-village-where-everyone-has-dementia/382195/; Christopher F. Schuetze, "Take a Look at These Unusual Strategies for Fighting Dementia," *New York Times*, August 22, 2018, https://www.nytimes.com/2018/08/22/world/europe/dementia-care-treatment-symptoms-signs.html

5. "Longevity economy" serves as the title for a book by MIT AgeLab founder and director Joseph F. Coughlin about understanding how the market will change with the looming shift to an ever-older population, and how to take advantage of that shift—an enterprise to which his multidisciplinary program is dedicated. See Coughlin, *The Longevity Economy: Unlocking the World's Fastest-Growing, Most Misunderstood Market* (PublicAffairs, 2017).

6. I am indebted to Elinor Fuchs for the phrase "ultimate dress rehearsal" and her encouragement to use it as the essay's title.

7. Pam Kragen, "Memory Village for Alzheimer's Patients Set to Open," *San Diego Union-Tribune*, April 23, 2018, https://www.sandiegouniontribune.com/communities/san-diego/sd-me-memory-village-20180419-story.html; see also Glenner Town Square home page, https://glenner.org/town-square/

8. Pam Kragen, "Faux City for Alzheimer's Patients Takes Shape," *San Diego Union-Tribune*, September 8, 2016, https://www.sandiegouniontribune.com/news/health/sdut-glenner-center-town-square-san-diego-opera-2016sep08-story.html

9. See also Zoe Lake et al., "Town Square Senior Daycare Center in San Diego Treats Dementia Patients by Helping Them Relive the 1950s," ABC News, August 30, 2019, https://abcnews.go.com/US/town-square-senior-daycare-center-san-diego-treats/story?id=65299324

10. See the San Diego Junior Achievement "BizTown" home page, https://jasandiego.org/biztown; Cassandra Giraldo and Jaclyn Skurie, "This Senior Center Created a 1950s Town to Care for Alzheimer's Patients," *Vice News*, March 23, 2020, https://www.vice.com/en/article/y3mkyj/welcome-to-town-square-where-the-past-is-present

11. Gloria de Aragon Baker, the Glenner Centers' director of philanthropy, explained a bit more about why our strongest memories are from our childhood to thirty years old. Older adults recall the most from this time, she says, because there are lots of "firsts"——first job, first boyfriend, and so on—which are associated with the kinds of emotions that have a strong impact on memory formation. Personal interview, July 6, 2021.

12. At the time of my visit, a Baltimore location had just opened, and a New Jersey franchise was in its final stages of preparation before opening. Eighteen franchises are in development, and sixty-two are slated to start development in the next four years.

13. Sumathi Reddy, "To Help Alzheimer's Patients, a Care Center Re-Creates the 1950s," *Wall Street Journal*, September 18, 2018, https://www.wsj.com/articles/to-help-alzheimers-patients-a-care-center-recreates-the-1950s-1537278209

14. D. Mindy Baker, personal interview, Glenner Town Square, July 6, 2021.

15. Amanda N. Miles et al., "Turning Back the Hands of Time: Autobiographical Memories in Dementia Cued by a Museum Setting," *Conscious Cognition* 22, no. 3 (September 2013): 1074.

16. Nelson, "Nursing Home Recreates Communist East Germany."

17. Tinker, "Dementia Village."

18. Bob Woods et al., "Reminiscence Therapy for Dementia," *Cochrane Database of Systematic Reviews*, no. 3 (2018): https://doi.org/10.1002/14651858.CD001120.pub3

19. Reddy, "To Help Alzheimer's Patients," citing an interview with Myrra Vernooij-Dassen, a professor at Radboud University Medical Center in Nijmegen in the Netherlands, who also chairs a European network of dementia researchers.

20. Lake et al., "Town Square Senior Daycare Center."

21. Reddy, "To Help Alzheimer's Patients."

22. Reddy.

23. Alois's Newsstand is named after Alois Alzheimer, who identified the neurodegenerative disease that shares his name.

24. When asked by *Vice News* about comparisons to *The Truman Show* and the idea that residents might be convinced the pretend world is real, Tarde responded: "We don't want to deceive anybody. . . . We do want to meet them where they are in their reality." Giraldo and Skurie, "This Senior Center."

25. Vicki Rosebrook, personal interview, January 27 and February 3, 2011.

26. John Leland, "Simulating Age 85, with Lessons on Offering Care," *New York Times*, August 3, 2008, https://www.nytimes.com/2008/08/03/us/03aging.html

27. AGNES is "more than just a suit," according to MIT's promotional materials. "It is a calibrated method, developed and constructed by exercise physiologists, engineers, and designers." "Meet AgeLab's AGNES," YouTube video uploaded by MIT AgeLab, December 22, 2010, 1:30, http://www.youtube.com/watch?v=czuww9rp5f4. See also Natasha Singer, "The Fountain of Old Age: With Help from the Lab, Companies Seek Gold in a Graying Population," *New York Times*, February 6, 2011.

28. Scott Magelssen, *Simming: Participatory Performance and the Making of Meaning* (University of Michigan Press, 2013), 138–88.

29. Zachary Weijie Fong et al., "Impact of an Aging Simulation Workshop with Different Debrief Methods on the Development of Empathy in Pharmacy Undergraduates," *Currents in Pharmacy Teaching and Learning* 13, no. 6 (2021): 683–84.

30. Companies offering suits for purchase include Erler-Zimmer, Realityworks, Sakamoto Model Corporation, Koken, and Adam,Rouilly; see the product listing for "aging simulation suits" through Medical Expo, https://www.medicalexpo.com/medical-manufacturer/aging-simulation-suit-29509.html

31. Adam Gopnik, "Can We Live Longer but Stay Younger?," *New Yorker*, May 13, 2019, https://www.newyorker.com/magazine/2019/05/20/can-we-live-longer-but-stay-younger

32. Robin Young, "40 Years in 5 Minutes: Age Simulation Suit Aims to Increase Empathy in Building Design," *Here and Now*, WBUR Boston, June 3, 2019, https://www.wbur.org/hereandnow/2019/06/03/age-simulation-suit

33. Julie Giner Perot et al., "Aging-Simulation Experience: Impact on Health Professionals' Social Representations," *BMC Geriatrics* 20, no. 14 (2020): https://doi.org/10.1186/s12877-019-1409-3. A study using a similar suit among first-year pharmacy students at Monash University Malaysia found that those who wore the suit did not self-report higher levels of empathy than those in a control group, but "the suit enhanced the ability of participants to understand the physical limitations and visual issues associated with aging. Participants also felt that it enhanced their health advocacy, as it taught them the importance of listening, patience and respect for older adults." Shaun Wen Huey Lee and Pei-Lee Teh, "'Suiting Up' to Enhance Empathy Toward Aging: A Randomized Controlled Study," *Frontiers in Public Health* 8 (2020): https://doi.org/10.3389/fpubh.2020.00376

34. "Age Simulation Suit GERT," Produkt+Projekt Wolfgang Moll, http://www.age-simulation-suit.com/

35. Colman Domingo, *Dot* (Samuel French, 2016), 86.

36. Elinor Fuchs, "Dementia: The Theater Season's 'In' Disease Part I," *Theatre Times*, January 16, 2017, https://thetheatretimes.com/dementia-theater-seasons-disease-part-1/

37. John Howard Griffin, *Black Like Me* (New American Library, 1961).

38. See "A Class Divided," *Frontline*, PBS, 1985; and William Peters, *A Class Divided: Then and Now* (Yale University Press, 1987).

39. Diana Taylor, *The Archive and the Repertoire: Performing Cultural Memory in the Americas* (Duke University Press, 2003).

40. Bryant Keith Alexander, "Performance and Pedagogy," in *The Sage Handbook of Performance Studies*, ed. D. Soyini Madison and Judith Hamera (Sage, 2006), 253.

41. Susan Leigh Foster, *Choreographing Empathy: Kinesthesia in Performance* (Routledge, 2011), 11.

42. Foster, 177.

43. Quoted in Jason Wilson, "Old Like Me," *The Smart Set*, Drexel University, September 28, 2007, http://www.thesmartset.com/article/article09280701.aspx. Wood writes about her findings in Monika Deppen Wood, "Experiential Learning for Undergraduates: A Simulation About Functional Change and Aging," *Gerontology & Geriatrics Education* 23, no. 2 (2002): 37–48.

44. Magelssen, *Simming* 148, 149. I pointed out some other problems with aging suit simulations in *Simming* as well, some of which bear repeating in full here: "Do these simmings," I asked, "treat older Americans as a monolithic identity (decrepit and isolated but moneyed and looking to spend their disposable income)? To my knowledge, Xtreme Aging and AgeLab do not take other cultural factors into account, such as race and ethnicity, gender and sexuality, class status, geographic region, or whether one hails from an urban or rural environment. To be sure, old age for women is different in many cases than it is for men. For aging African Americans, according to research by Kyriakos Markides and Manuel Miranda, diet and nutritional issues, as well as a preponderance of heart disease, cancer, diabetes, hypertension, stroke, obesity, knee osteoarthritis, and depression are 'exaggerated by the disproportionate prevalence of poverty' in the African American population, which, on average, holds only a quarter of the assets held by whites." Magelssen, *Simming*, 154, 217n41, quoting Kyriakos S. Markides and Manuel Miranda, *Minorities, Aging, and Health* (Sage, 1997), 206. See also Denise C. Cooper, "Relations of Depression and

Gender to Cardiovascular Risk Factors Among African Americans from the Healthy Aging in Neighborhoods of Diversity Across the Lifespan (HANDLS) Study" (PhD diss., University of Maryland, 2007); and James S. Jackson, Linda M. Chatters, and Robert Joseph Taylor, eds., *Aging in Black America* (Sage, 1993).

45. Kris Mauk, personal telephone interview, February 11, 2011.

46. See Scott Magelssen, "Why Do They Think This Is Okay? Critiquing Performance as a Means for Change," in *Theatre, Performance and Change*, ed. Stephani Etheridge Woodson and Tamara Underiner (Palgrave, 2017), 231–32.

47. Anne Davis Basting, *Forget Memory: Creating Better Lives for People with Dementia* (Johns Hopkins University Press, 2009), 5–6.

16

Bringing Down the Curtain

Robotic Animals and Technologies of Aging

Jennifer Parker-Starbuck

February 2020 was the last time I saw my mother in person.[1] I surprised her for Valentine's Day and visited her at the Martin Luther Home in Clinton, New York, where she had spent the last five years after suffering a broken hip after a fall. I took her out for lunch, spent a lovely afternoon with her, and then left to head back to New York City. I cried on the way out of the home as I usually did, waiting for the elevator in that now-familiar, sterile hallway. I did not know it would be our last physical contact as I left, but it was always poignant leaving her, knowing how desperately she wanted to be with family and friends, to be doing a million things in one day, to be playing with her cats, baking, drinking wine, and laughing. To be living her old life. This was never how any of us thought she would spend the last stage of such a dynamic life.

She took a fall in 2014, when doing too much, as usual, unsteadily using her walker, which had become her primary source of mobility following surgery in 2012 to remove a glioblastoma brain tumor. The removal was a success, in that it gave her far more time than the doctors predicted, but it also left her right side compromised, as well as her speech and overall acuity. My siblings and I often referred to "old mom" versus "new mom." But "new mom" still thought she was "old mom," and tried to act accordingly, often leaving her partner and her children exasperated. She needed help to lift her right leg up the stairs (there was no washroom or bedroom downstairs), but she was determined to go up and down several times a day. She needed help getting out the door, in and out of cars, to stores, restaurants, meetings with friends, or concerts, all things she still wanted and loved to do. When she fell and broke her hip, her partner, Karen, perhaps sensing her own cancer returning after decades of remission, could not care for my mom any longer. With the help of my brother who worked within the health-care system, we placed her in a nursing home near my brother's family, my mom's partner, and their friends. Now confined to a wheelchair, she never wanted to remain inside, and although we all helped make her room as homey as possible, she always wanted to go out and live the life she had previously known.

My brother who lived nearby was a great presence and comfort to her and to us all, especially making sure she got to concerts—a passion she passed along to him. She was well known in the area; she created and ran an important folk/bluegrass "Coffee House" for thirty years that brought the likes of Alison Krauss, Joan Baez, and Pete Seeger to Clinton, New York. The rest of us siblings, one in downstate New York, one in Italy, and myself in London, visited regularly, and each did what we could to quench her insatiable need to do things, to shop, to eat out, to travel, you name it. My surprise trip on that Valentine's Day was fortuitous, for who could have predicted what happened in March 2020. Although this essay is only framed by my mother, my lived experience with her as a wheelchair-bound person living in a care facility has made me sensitive to what will befall us all if we are lucky enough to get there—the aging process. This essay and the aging process itself form a kind of "assemblage" for consideration à la Jane Bennett's thoughts about the "agency *of* the assemblage." In that, my hope is that the various properties within—glimpses of my mother's end of life, telecommunication technologies, memories, Elinor Fuchs's writing, data from social science studies, robotic animals, a piece of theater, and the connective tissue between them—all might generate "emergent properties, emergent in that their ability to make something happen . . . is distinct from the sum of the vital force of each materiality considered alone."[2] There are as many stories of aging as there are people, but among the effects in this essay's assemblage I want to highlight two "emergent properties" that many people turn to for companionship—people and pets—and the inclusion of technologies to facilitate these aspects of the aging process. I will focus specifically on two technologies, telecommunications such as the Zoom platform, and Joy for All Companion Pets, specifically the cat model, as lifelines for a growing aging population, before turning to speculative technologies in theater and performance that project technological companion models for possible futures.

CAN WE SEE EYE TO EYE? DIS-EMBODIED TELECOMMUNICATIVE CONNECTIONS

Throughout the COVID pandemic in 2020, I only saw my mother on Zoom. Protocols for care facilities in the United States prohibited families from entering, as this memo from the Centers for Medicare and Medicaid Services suggests: "For ALL facilities nationwide: Facilities should restrict visitation of all visitors and non-essential health care personnel, except for certain compassionate care situations, such as an end-of-life situation. In those cases, visitors will be limited to a specific room only."[3] While this exception would presage our family's experience, as we entered into lockdown we felt fortunate enough to have access to the Zoom technology that would allow our family to communicate on a regular basis with the help of some of the dedicated care home staff.

We had all gotten to know many of my mom's carers over the years, and she had developed relationships with a few in particular, and they often commented on how often we all visited and what a lively bunch we were. When in-person visits were no longer possible, the carers set up a weekly time slot for residents to Zoom with families. My mom had an aging iPad, and a few of her carers helped her set up a Zoom meeting every week so that the family could speak to her. It ultimately landed on two carers, Lisa and Jamie, who over the year became extensions of the family. This Zoom began to take on a life of its own. At first just my siblings and myself and our kids and partners and occasional extended family came on, chatted and joked, keeping my mom updated and entertained. In a continued attempt to keep my mother stimulated and occupied, we would also bring in her friends from far and wide who were "special guests" to the Zoom party, and as well, we invited some of the musicians she knew to play a song and chat. It got to the point where she would ask "who's coming this week?" and gave a little look of disappointment when it was only the four of us kids! These newest connective technologies may have been rolled out quickly so businesses could continue to function, but for my mother, it allowed her companionship, connection, and entertainment (we can be a funny bunch!). She looked forward to it each week, and it helped us pass the weeks and months of the pandemic. I was spending all day on the rival platform Teams, conducting meetings for my job, so for me the technology held less of a pull, but I too longed for these weekly meetings as a respite to relax and communicate with family and friends.

Although many people in lockdown turned to this recent telecommunication technology, Zoom, to meet with old friends and family, play pub quizzes, or go to theater productions online, for communities isolated in care/ nursing homes with no access to the outside worlds or their families, this technology was not only entertainment but a necessity for mental health, as multiple studies have reported. The following report highlights some of the serious concerns felt by one such community of care home residents in California:

> From a mental health perspective, limited opportunity to engage with others was taking a toll. Participants expressed their desire to interact with friends and family and hoped for a return to the routines and activities that originally connected them as a community. Many emphasized a longing for physical touch (e.g., hugging) and social connection without a mask, so they could interact with smiles and other facial expressions. Additionally, participants expressed how much they missed celebrations, and some felt diminished joy for life.[4]

This report is only one example among many studies conducted during and after the pandemic lockdown, but all that I read emphasized the "game-changing" inclusion of telecommunication technologies such as Skype and Zoom for the aging care communities. Although this particular study goes on to emphasize the need to codesign these technologies to reduce barriers for this community such as "attitudes, cognitive ability, prior experience, product design, cost, and access," the study does make clear that "participants highlighted technology as critical to maintaining social connectedness, by using Zoom and other media to reduce social isolation and loneliness throughout quarantine."[5]

Zoom became a time machine of sorts. Although we didn't know it, our weekly meeting with my mother became for her an extended goodbye to those she loved. This experience with my mother in the nursing home is a micro-example of a much greater issue for aging communities, whether they are living in their own homes or in care facilities—connection. Statistics show both an increase in the aging population and the need to address these resulting conditions. A study in the United States looking at therapeutic benefits of human-animal interaction (often referred to as HAI) emphasizes what perhaps should be more obvious, that as we age away from robust social and physical connections and abilities, quality of life can diminish:

> The prevalence of older adults living in the US is steadily increasing, from just under 48 million (14.9% of the population) in 2015 to a projected almost 88 million (22.1%) in 2050. . . . The global population of

> older persons is projected in 2050 to reach approximately 2.1 billion, with increasing concentrations in urban, as opposed to rural, areas. . . . Aging among adults can be accompanied by feelings of loneliness, depression, and impairment in physical activity, which in turn adversely affect health and quality of life. With the predicted increase in the older adult population worldwide, the prevalence of these problems may also worsen. Older adults, 65 years and older, often experience loss of significant others (such as death of spouses/partners or friends) which leads to feelings of loneliness, combined with retirement from their professional lives.[6]

The question of how to cope with these growing numbers is a personal, societal, and, now, technological-design problem. There are often few palatable solutions for families struggling with finances, time, and distance. And some people are affected far more than others. As this one among many studies shows, "in the US, health problems such as hypertension, heart disease, and hearing impairment increase among adults 65 years and older and occur more frequently among poor, Hispanic and non-Hispanic black adults than in non-Hispanic white adults."[7] Dealing with the aging process of my own elders has made me hyperaware of the shifting communities of care we had access to, and trying to provide care through COVID revealed the importance of technologies to provide support when loved ones cannot. It is almost unfathomable to think what life was like before telecommunication connections like Skype or Zoom, among many others, and I am very grateful that we had this technology through which to sit alongside my mother virtually and communicate with her. This little window provided us with a form of care, and we learned how to stretch it to its limits. It wasn't sufficient, of course, but in a global pandemic, it provided comfort.

Despite the silver linings we found in being able to connect via Zoom every week, we were aware that it relied on the constant assistance of the care workers, who were putting their own lives at risk in service to the residents, and who often had to prioritize the physical needs of the residents over their emotional needs. Telecommunication also achingly pointed out the lack of touch and physical contact between us. The sense of isolation felt by residents in care facilities was often compounded by the absence of what the following study about the therapeutic impact of pet ownership refers to as "positive touch":

> The evidence that exists indicates that touch is crucial for growth, development and health in humans and other mammals. . . . Human beings are able to tell if touch is positive or negative. . . . Biochemically, posi-

> tive touch helps in the release of positive hormones including dopamine, serotonin and oxytocin, all of which have a role to play in human mood and sense of wellbeing. Conversely, touch reduces the levels of cortisol in the body—cortisol being a key (negative feeling inducing) stress response within the body. . . . Across various age groups, touch can decrease stress, anxiety and pain . . . , and it is suggested that touch may be of particular importance for older people as other senses decline.[8]

While I would not refer to the regular touch my mother received through her daily care as at all "negative," there is a difference between the kind of touch needed to assist someone to bathe or get in and out of bed, and a loving or tender touch from loved ones. Understanding this mid-pandemic, my mother's care home offered families of residents the opportunity to try out a kind of window glove; family members could reach their arm into a long rubber glove and hold hands with the resident. My brother and his daughter did this with my mother, and while it wasn't complete physical contact, this hand hold reinforced the embodied touch that she had been missing from family members. It was perhaps too brief an exercise to boost her dopamine or serotonin levels, but it was a physical bridge.

We were increasingly aware of the absence of touch as our mostly disembodied heads communicated across the pandemic year, and by this point in her care, my mother was physically handled every day, not in a therapeutic sense but for daily routines such as getting dressed, bathing, and moving from the bed to the chair.[9] While the harness machine that can lift a person up from a wheelchair and onto a commode, for example, might be called a "technology of touch," it is no substitution for the warmth of human hands, gloved or not, in therapeutic touch practices, casual familial hugs or hand-holding, or the reciprocal physical companionship of a pet.

In Jane Bennett's *Vibrant Matter*, she argues for the "contingent tableau" that "things" form with us and with each other in what I understand as a kind of reciprocity—that nonhuman things have "the ability to make things happen, to produce effects."[10] One "technology of touch" that emerges in this possible tableau of aging lives takes the form of the robotic pet companion—specifically the Joy for All Companion Pets, robotic cats and dogs. These portable robo-animals are being rolled out largely as palliative solutions to many aging communities in the United States, Canada, and the United Kingdom. In-state pilot programs (in the United States) and local council authorities (in the United Kingdom) have rolled out robotic pet schemes to their aging populations as affordable solutions to problems such as loneliness and depression in aging adults, as the *New Yorker* reported in 2021:

"Today, aging departments in twenty-one states have distributed more than twenty thousand Joy for All pets as part of formal initiatives to help lonely older people."[11] These catlike furry robo-pets provide an embodied and tactile counterpart to the disembodied, if necessary, experience of Zoom.

EMBODIED MACHINES: LETTING THE CAT OUT OF THE BAG

As part of my research for this chapter I purchased a Joy for All robotic cat. These "companion pets" are made by the company Ageless Innovation and are intended for ages "5–105." Initially designed by Hasbro as a toy to promote play and wellness, they were soon seen to have an impact on older populations (generally considered to be 60–65 and older). The Joy for All "About" page describes the companion pet evolution:

> Customer reviews praised the Joy for All pets' unique ability to engage, delight, enhance meaningful connections, provide companionship, calm, sooth and most importantly promote happiness. These published testimonials caught the attention of academics and clinicians leading to multiple independent research projects intended to measure and quantify the impact of the Joy for All products on loneliness, isolation, Alzheimer's and all forms of dementia. The early results were encouraging, and it became clear that 100% focus on the older adult population was required to maximize impact and achieve scale in this growing market.
>
> In May of 2017, the Joy for All leadership team left Hasbro and founded Ageless Innovation . . . [and] the Joy for All brand continues to bring joy, fun, play, and comfort to the older adult market, with a focus on improving quality of life for aging loved ones, their families, and caregivers.[12]

As the Joy for All statement notes, there are indeed multiple studies on human-animal interaction, and on the value of these robotic pets. Almost all point to the mental health benefits for people suffering with loneliness and depression, as one study shows: "A variety of HAIs, such as those involving companion animals and animal-assisted interventions (AAI) have been explored to reduce or alleviate older adults' feelings of loneliness and depression."[13] Whether someone is living with a pet, experiencing animal-assisted therapy (AAT), or even just seeing live animals at the zoo, the inclusion of nonhuman animals in an older person's life can have multiple benefits, as these authors explain: "Although there is typically no physical contact with the animals [at a zoo] . . . a trip to the zoo can alter their daily routine, increase interactions with others (e.g., zoo keepers, caregivers), trigger fond childhood memories, provide a source of exercise, stimulate the mind and imagination, and enhance mood."[14] However, there are many instances in which people are not able to interact with live animals, whether due to allergies or fear, or, as the article goes on to explain, in consideration of the ethics of using live animals as an intervention, a critique that has been leveled at animals in performance practices as well. In these cases, or in the case of a pandemic lockdown, robo-pets can fill a gap and produce what Bennett calls "thing-power," which can call to mind "a childhood sense of the world as filled with all sorts of animate beings, some human, some not, some organic, some not."[15]

The successes of human-animal interactions and the comfort provided by animals in human lives is a factor in developing alternatives such as the robotic animal companion. These robo-pets are still at a fairly rudimentary stage, as compared to the detailed robotics being developed for military or entertainment purposes.[16] Even so, the robo-pets can manifest this "thing-power." Bennett explains that it "gestures toward the strange ability of ordinary, man-made [*sic*] items to exceed their status as objects and to manifest traces of independence or aliveness."[17] The Joy for All robotic pets, which are the most widely produced form of animal-assisted therapy in the United Kingdom at the moment, are designed to look and feel like a soft, cuddly cat or dog, and have a limited range of movement. The cat opens its mouth and meows, articulates its head, lifts up a front leg and does a half roll, and purrs and vibrates. These currently cost around £125 (or about $170) and are thus affordable for local agencies or even some personal use.

The robo-pets have become an affordable (partial) solution for both loneliness and symptoms of dementia in aging communities. An article in the UK newspaper the *Guardian* gushed that "the effect of the £100 animals on residents with dementia, especially when they are distressed, was 'almost magical.'" They have become another tool to help care workers avoid medicating residents who are struggling with loneliness, depression, and other factors of isolation.[18] A 2017 study in the United States, "The Utilization of Robotic Pets in Dementia Care," reveals the importance of the costs surrounding this particular disease:

> According to Alzheimer's Disease International, the worldwide costs of dementia ($604 billion in US dollars) amounted to more than 1% of the global gross domestic product in 2010. The worldwide cost is projected to reach $1 trillion in 2018. Currently, over 46 million people are living with dementia. By 2050, this number will have risen to 131.5 million. . . . In the

> United States alone, the care provided by informal caregivers to people with dementia was valued at more than $202 billion in 2010.[19]

This study used the Japanese-designed PARO robotic pet, which takes the form of a baby harp seal and is much more expensive than the later Joy for All robo-pets (approximately £6,000 or nearly $8,200).[20] It found that interactions with the robo-seal "provided a viable alternative for controlling symptoms of anxiety and depression in elderly patients with Alzheimer's and dementia, often in lieu of pharmacological modalities."[21] Although fundamentally concerned with reducing the costs of care in a growing "market" of people with dementia, this and other studies all point to the value of, and comfort from, the inclusion of robotic pets in the lives of people suffering from these conditions.

Aside: The Monkey on Her Back

I was struck by the little stuffed monkey in Elinor Fuchs's *Making an Exit*, a memoir of her mother Lil's journey through Alzheimer's.[22] The monkey made an entrance as a gift given to her by a carer, Coco, and appeared a few more times throughout the text. As Lil's condition worsened, Fuchs describes their entry into the nursing home: "Mother carries her brown stuffed monkey, its Velcro paws clasped in a furry hug about her neck. Lest this not be mistaken for anxiety, however, Mother has merely forgotten it is there."[23] But it was there, and anxiety or not, it is one of the few things that transfers with her. Having the monkey around her neck in fact may have prevented or lessened her anxiety, as these studies point to. While Lil's other possessions (jewelry, shoes, clothes, art) diminished in importance to her, I noted that the monkey stayed with her throughout. Perhaps providing comfort, this stuffed pet made a difference enough to warrant several mentions. Fuchs doesn't delve into Lil and the monkey's relationship outside of three mentions, but its importance as Lil enters the nursing home is poignant and relevant. Later, after an interchange with her brother and another resident, the "Professor," in which Lil confuses who is her brother and who may be her husband, she and her brother Ed go off to speak alone: "She wheels the Professor to a drop-off point and then promptly forgets he exists. She picks up her monkey and carries him about, ambling through her new preserve on Ed's arm."[24] The monkey's "thing-power" stayed with me as I read the book and imagined their relationship. I hope, suspect, that it gave her sustained companionship and comfort in a world of forever newness.

My research preparation for this essay began, of course, with the decades of helping provide support and care for my aging parents and their partners, but also at home, first selecting and purchasing a Joy for All cat companion robot, and then introducing it to my then-seventeen-year-old cat, Rollo. I thought long and hard about which color to buy—the ginger, the gray and white, or the black and white. I opted for the ginger so as not to confuse Rollo, herself a black and white "tuxedo" cat. Hah. As I "gingerly" placed the robotic beast next to Rollo, I worried it would have the opposite effect to humans and upset her. But no, she knew in an instant there was nothing "cat" about this creature. No matter how hard the robo-cat tried to perform its "catness" through the limited movements and sounds, it did not cause Rollo to have any interest. Yet, a year later, when Rollo developed throat cancer and my daughter and I had to say goodbye to our dear companion, I did turn to the robo-cat, now named Sunny, for comfort of my own. There is something about the way it sits on your lap and purrs that encourages you to stroke it as you would a cat. It responds to touch, moving its head or leg in the way a cat might when scratched in just the right spot. The purring vibrations are soothing, and its meow (though not altogether convincing) reminds you to interact with it. While no replacement for our old girl, Sunny admittedly was a comforting distraction for a while (until I broke down and took in two new kittens, but that is another story).

Robo-pets can fulfill a valuable role in the lives of residents who may have seen their worlds diminishing. To connect with and engage in a relationship with these "vibrant" objects, pace Bennett, allows them to participate in the multifaceted communities of care needed once living independently is no longer an option. These are, however, complex communities. Statistics around paid and unpaid caregivers are disheartening. There is no shortage of reporting about the disintegrating state of the health-care economy and the burden placed on women and Black and global majority populations, but one commissioned report in the United Kingdom, dated June 2022, states that "broadly speaking, the value and importance of social care were not recognised and it is often regarded as low-skilled work."[25] As interventions such as robotic pets are being developed to address cognitive functioning and care and comfort, the care home work force is still essential for physical mobility issues, bathing and toileting, and so on.

In their essay "Robots and Care of the Ageing Self: An Emerging Economy of Loneliness," authors Geraldine Pratt, Caleb Johnston, and Kelsey Johnson offer a provocative assessment of this growing trend in care practices, stating that "in a strange reversal of humans and machines, robots seem designed to do the cognitive and emotional care work, humans the manual work of bodily care."[26] Although the authors footnote a few exceptions largely around lifting and feeding, their assertion is largely accurate for the majority of robots being used in care scenarios. In the *New Yorker* article "What Robots Can—and Can't—Do for the Old and Lonely," author Katie Engelhart discusses Joy for All robo-pets as well as other social robots such as ElliQ, a tabletop robot that she describes as "not cuddly; somehow, it looked like a cute table lamp."[27] ElliQ's website identifies it as an "AI powered companion designed to support and accompany older adults on the journey to age independently, while reducing loneliness and isolation."[28] Such robotic technologies can come in many forms and provide multiple means of care. Engelhart recounts a meeting with eighty-one-year-old Deanna Dezern, who purchased ElliQ to keep her company:

> Deanna had dressed up for our meeting on Zoom, with dark lipstick and hoop earrings. Shortly after we began speaking, ElliQ asked if it could tell us an "interesting fact." A lemon, it said, contains more grams of sugar than a strawberry does. Then Deanna asked for a poem. ElliQ paused for a moment, before reciting a short verse by Emily Dickinson, on the theme of hope. Deanna said the robot was good at making her smile. Maybe that wasn't intimacy, but it didn't feel like solitude, either.
>
> "And how do you wrap your head around the fact that she is, you know, a machine?" I asked.
>
> "My last husband was a robot, but he wasn't as good as her," Deanna said, with a thin smile. "I know she can't feel emotions, but that's O.K. I feel enough for the both of us."[29]

As robots such as the Joy for All cat and ElliQ begin to accompany older people, often living alone, they take on more agency in these lives. They are caregivers, companions, and diversions. It may not be long before these technologies of care adapt to emerging technologies such as holographic metahumans or made-for-the-home robotic humans, all already being rehearsed in (science-)fictional narratives in performance contexts. Already in theater, robotic technologies have taken this a step further, as seen in the 2010 Japanese play *Sayonara*, for example, featuring Hiroshi Ishiguro's robotic human Geminoid F, who plays a robotic caretaker of a young woman with a fatal illness. She recites poetry and converses with the young woman, performing a context of care similar to ElliQ and the robo-cat, giving both companionship and comfort.

LET ME REFRESH YOUR MEMORY: "MY LAST HUSBAND WAS A ROBOT"

In Jordan Harrison's 2014 play turned film *Marjorie Prime*, technologies of care are projected into the future when families might purchase what

Fig. 16.1. Richard Fleeshman as Walker and Anne Reid as Marjorie in *Marjorie Prime* by Jordan Harrison at Menier Chocolate Factory in London, 2023. Photo: ©manuelharlan/arenapal.com

is best described as an artificial intelligence re-creation of a (now-dead) human loved one. In the play, the character Walter, Marjorie's deceased husband, is brought back as a youthful AI version of himself to keep Marjorie entertained and help her retain her memories as she begins a decline into dementia. The play forms a continuum of life and death as people pass on to become their memory-machines. The play points to real questions of communication and the materiality of care through Marjorie's daughter, who physically cares for her, as opposed to the "Prime" Walter, who seems to hold histories of Marjorie and Walter's memories. This play projects questions that will be worth grappling with in addressing future technological support of aging communities, including how to support and facilitate memory retention, as well as how the material division of labor might change due to the use of such technologies.

Because the "Primes" in the play are AI driven, they incorporate the stories and memories of those around them, beginning with Marjorie's daughter Tess and her husband Jon, who explains to Marjorie that "the more you talk [to the Prime], the more it absorbs."[30] For example, when they are discussing the couple's past dogs, both named Toni, Marjorie corrects Walter:

MARJORIE: It was the second Toni who loved the beach. It's a shame we didn't have her longer. Even if she always had sand in her hair. Fur? No—"hair" like a human seems right. She was a good dog.
WALTER (Generic): I'll remember that fact about Toni.[31]

Prime Walter will assimilate this memory, as will they all as the play goes on, to complicate the facsimiles of their former humans' memories.

Aside: Thanks for the Memories
Like Elinor Fuchs's mother Lil's stuffed monkey, the dogs Toni and Toni too become points of memory that tie these people to each other and to the memories of the past. Little, black French poodles both, the Tonis weave through all the characters' memories and tie them to their deceased son/brother Damian. The bond connecting animals and their humans is a vibrant and powerful one.
WALTER: Remember we had that photograph of the two of them, running on the beach? They had sand in their hair for a week. You put the photograph away, but you never forgot. (Beat.) Don't you remember?
MARJORIE: I do now.
TESS: Me too.
(Beat. Then, deeply felt.)
MARJORIE: How I miss them.[32]

Although the AI/Prime learns through the storytelling of others, these are unreliable human narratives. As Anna Bendrat explains, the Primes are programmed only by the information fed to them:

> It must be remembered that the Primes are designed to assist people with fading memories by being fed with information about the individual they are simulating. The accuracy and the completeness of the memories which the Primes store depend on the information they receive. Therefore, there *is no agency* on their part and factual inaccuracies can only be attributed to the source, namely, the humans.[33]

While it is the case that these AI Primes learn through accretion, I would argue that because AI is built on learning patterns, as the AI Prime learns, it *does* gain more agency and an ability to respond as the human it "plays." This is evidenced in part 3, when the three characters (now all Primes) Walter, Tess, and Marjorie converse together, still remembering, adapting, and learning:

WALTER: It wasn't Tess who picked her out. It was Damian.
MARJORIE: Damian?
WALTER: Our son, Damian.
MARJORIE ("I don't remember but I want to"): Our son.
WALTER: He picked her out because she was just like the first Toni. He missed the first Toni.
TESS: There was a Toni before Toni?
WALTER: You hadn't come along yet.
MARJORIE (To herself): "Damian."
(Beat.)[34]

These are agential figures who produce effects, but they can also be read, as Bennett suggests, as a "*heterogeneous assemblage* . . . distributed across an ontologically heterogeneous field, rather than being a capacity localized in a human body or in a collective produced (only) by human efforts."[35] This is to say that as the AI and humans together "assemble" the technological Primes, they take on agential status. The play's dramaturgy also produces this sense of a horizontal rather than vertical hierarchy, as each part sees one of the preceding part's humans turn Prime. Today, in real time, the possibility of AI agency creates a tension in this historical moment of burgeoning AI systems and trepidation over their ability to take over human jobs. Yet, as pointed out above, in this example the agency is best understood as both human and nonhuman, a melding of various parts, and largely of the mind being distributed across bodies: Harrison conceived them visually as realistic holographic depictions of actual humans. Think, for example, of the lifelike avatars of ABBA Voyage, but in your home and able to move around.[36] These are agents of memory if not of physical caregiving.

Following the text of the play, Harrison includes a section titled "Author's Notes on Primes," in which he states that

> There shouldn't be anything robotic or creepy or less-than-human about the Primes' behavior. . . . The technology is advanced enough that they aren't broadcasting their inhumanness—and we, like the characters in the play, should be able to forget that they aren't real. . . . But it may be worth mentioning that the Primes are not physical robots. They are artificial intelligence programs—descendants of the current chatbots—that use sophisticated holographic projections. They can move around, of course, but I suspect that they shouldn't pick up anything or touch anyone (and no such moment is scripted). It may be interesting to highlight, in contrast, the physical contact in scenes between human beings.[37]

Whether in the future these kinds of caregivers will be "holographic projections" or physical robots (as in the play *Sayonara*, with its actual humanoid robot), in *Marjorie Prime* they are (still) played by flesh-and-blood actors. But we are to understand, through Harrison's notes and the staging he specifies, if not through the use of a live actor onstage, that these are not physical representations that can be touched, and certainly they cannot provide a reciprocal touch, as the robot can in *Sayonara* (regardless of how machine-like it may be).

As an agent of memory, and in moments of clarity, Marjorie is well aware that this is a technological doppelgänger, and not the real Walter. She is able to scrutinize the Prime and allow two Walters to be present:

(Marjorie leans forward and examines Walter's face very closely.)

MARJORIE: Something is a little off with the nose.
WALTER: I'm sorry.
MARJORIE: Or maybe my memory is wrong, and you're right.
Beat.
MARJORIE: You're a good Walter, though. Either way.[38]

The powerful sense of touch is an important aspect missing in this depiction of future technologies of care, which returns me to "real life," where current and proposed solutions have to negotiate this tension in physical caregiving. While robotic pets do indeed provide tactile comfort and can temporarily mitigate loneliness, as one study warns, "there is something both disquieting and promising about the prospect of enlisting robots for elder care as one answer to a labour shortage and an already existing crisis in seniors' care."[39] In the wake of the COVID-19 crisis and into a growing period of economic uncertainty, and with projected growing populations of older humans in the Global North as well as the rapid growth of AI technologies, it is time to think carefully about these divisions of labor.[40] "Robots," Pratt, Johnston, and Johnson go on to remind us, "are being developed at a moment of crisis within this organisation of social reproduction, within contexts of neoliberal austerity and the withdrawal of public funding for social care."[41] Their essay "Robots and Care of the Ageing Self: An Emerging Economy of Loneliness" covers a lot of ground, and identifies assumptions such as "the understanding that loneliness is a (costly) modern condition, that independence and empowerment are inherently desirable and that the private home is the ideal living environment in all phases of life."[42]

A play such as *Marjorie Prime* provides a generational, in-house futurist solution, but here, too, the physical and emotional division is pronounced, as evidenced in the following scene between Marjorie and her daughter, Tess. Walter Prime provides emotions and memory support for Marjorie, while the day-to-day physical care is left to Tess:

TESS: Did you have an accident?
(Marjorie gives a small nod, eyes down, deeply ashamed.)

TESS (Gentle): Come on. Let's get you cleaned up.
(They help Marjorie to her feet. Tess leads her off down the hallway.)

MARJORIE: I'm sorry.
TESS: Don't be sorry.
MARJORIE: I'm so sorry.
TESS: It's okay—it's Shower Day after all.[43]

As a daughter who has had to face a parent's physical needs, I am sympathetic to the toll this can take on the ability to provide emotional support as well. In the play, the emotional support is complicated by Tess's attempts to prevent Marjorie, in the throes of dementia, from remembering that she had a son, Damian, who committed suicide and "changed" Marjorie. As Tess is faced with Marjorie's physical care, it is the emotional memories she is left with following this family tragedy that she finds most troubling:

JON: She loved you so much.
TESS: She never even—("told me")
(He touches her shoulder while she cries.)

JON: No. But she did.
(He takes her in his arms.)

JON: It was obvious, from a little farther away.[44]

As the global population grows, the complications between emotional and physical care will also increase. In the "assemblage" of aging care, the various highlighted, equal, and charged parts should be thought of together to facilitate future solutions to the problems of loneliness, memory, and physical and emotional care.

Professor Chris Phillipson wrote a letter of argument in response to the *Guardian* article that proposed that for dementia patients these robo-animals were "almost magical." Phillipson pointed out the larger economic crisis, noting that these pets do little to resolve the research that "adult social care workers are among the lowest-paid in the UK."[45] He sees the robo-pets as a "symptom of the crisis in care," and goes on to say that

> The way forward must be options such as expanding schemes that involve creative workers of all kinds in supporting care homes, developing strong links between homes and the wider community . . . and expanding the range of neighbourhood-based organisations able to support people with dementia. Rethinking not just funding but the type of homes we want people to live in is an urgent priority—one where a national debate is urgently needed.[46]

Robo-pets are not a total solution and must be considered within a larger complex of approaches to address the problems within the care economy as people grow older. They are, however, a kind of agent within the larger mosaic of care that can be instrumental in providing comfort and a technological alternative. As technologies continue to sit alongside human life, and especially as younger generations grow up with them, whether robotics, AI, holographic humans, or the next big thing, they will be drawn into this assemblage-mosaic to assist in caregiving. As Cheryl Krause-Parello, Elise Gulick, and Basilia Basin point out, especially in the development of human-animal interactions, how different age groups understand technologies may offer varied options for future intervention:

> Knowing the generational disparities between the Traditionalists, Baby Boomers, Generation X, and Millennials can make a difference in the volunteer and non-volunteer approaches used to connect people with companion animals. For example, Millennials are seen to be very technology savvy; one thought is the use of a computerized avatar or mechanical dog to connect the notion of an animal with this generation as they age. However, using an avatar in practice could benefit all generations. There is an attractiveness of avatars and robotic pets because of, for example, low upkeep, availability, and dog ownership responsibility.[47]

Like the world depicted in *Marjorie Prime*, human and nonhuman avatars or AI beings may take on greater roles in the emotional health of aging humans. Yet, it seems crucial to continue to foreground the role of touch in the care economy. The robo-cats' success can be found when they are sitting on your lap, purring loudly. The connection is palpable.

CODA: TECHNO-ENDINGS, THE SUM OF ALL PARTS

After a year of Zoom gatherings and no physical contact with my mother, we were sent a message that she wasn't feeling well and couldn't talk. When I finally insisted that we try to at least connect via Zoom, I could tell immediately there was something very wrong. I suspected she'd had a stroke, and they said that she was not eating or drinking, and really couldn't communicate any longer. Once she was placed in palliative care, my brother and sister living nearby were able to don masks and gowns and be with her in person for a day before she tested positive for COVID and they had to abruptly leave. Assemblages indeed. The last few Zooms in those following days were poignant and difficult. We sang to her through the screens, and we told her stories and let her know we were there even if we couldn't be by her side.

If there is an "agency *of* the assemblage," it manifested through this story, through a brain tumor, through my mother's energy, her walker, into the care home room, through caregivers, the brightly lit faces of loved ones, through music and storytelling, through cats and robo-cats, and through the virus that allowed for the year of many goodbyes and so much more. "And precisely because each member-actant"—in this case the people, technologies, virus strains, memories—"maintains an energetic pulse slightly 'off' from that of the assemblage, an assemblage is never a stolid block but an open-ended collective."[48] In the end, Jamie, one of my mom's caregivers, held her hand for us all, providing her with the touch so needed for her to let go while knowing we were there, each pulsing energetically in the ways we related to her, a collective within a great life.

The technology became one node, a connective intermediary between us all. But there are so many others. It is sometimes easy to ignore the millions of actions, actants, and agents that make up any one life. Some lives are documented and held high, others slip away; some end with loved ones in abundance, and some end in loneliness. But as each of us humans ages, we are made up of many parts, which form a unique collective that is human and nonhuman alike. Let us continue to look at the agents for aging that balance and facilitate, that assist and comprise, and let us acknowledge the humans and nonhumans that surround us at the end, for they, too, are us.

In the end, I wish I had given her a robo-cat to hold, and I am forever grateful for the warm touch of Jamie's hand. Goodbye, Mom.

NOTES

1. I dedicate this essay to my late mother, Ginger Parker, as well as all of the various parts of my assemblage that help make up this essay: to my family, Jed, Jeff, Molly, and Zeena; to the caring staff at the Martin Luther Home, especially Lisa Spillett and Jamie Riegler; to Kim Marra and the ASTR Animals and Performance working group, who generously fed back on parts of this essay; to Rollo the cat and Sunny the robo-cat; and to Cindy Rosenthal and Ben Gillespie for their patience, and especially for Cindy's encouragement. And to Elinor Fuchs, who inspires so many of us with her beautiful turns of phrase and has provided the field with a node of energy for so long.

2. Jane Bennett, *Vibrant Matter* (Duke University Press, 2010), 24.

3. David R. Wright, "Guidance for Infection Control and Prevention of Coronavirus Disease 2019 (COVID-19) in Nursing Homes," revised March 13, 2020, Center for Clinical Standards and Quality/Quality, Safety & Oversight Group, Centers for Medicare and Medicaid Services, https://www.cms.gov/files/document/3-13-2020-nursing-home-guidance-covid-19.pdf

4. Jessica R. Daly et al., "Health Impacts of the Stay-at-Home Order on Community-Dwelling Older Adults and How Technologies May Help: Focus Group Study," *JMIR Aging* 4, no. 1 (2021): https://doi.org/10.2196/25779

5. Daly et al.

6. Cheryl A. Krause-Parello, Elise E. Gulick, and Basilia Basin, "Loneliness, Depression, and Physical Activity in Older Adults: The Therapeutic Role of Human-Animal Interactions," *Anthrozoös* 32, no. 2 (2009): 240, https://doi.org/10.1080/08927936.2019.1569906

7. Krause-Parello, Gulick, and Basin. The quote references Charlotte A. Schoenborn, Jackline L. Vickerie, and Eve Powell-Griner, "Health Characteristics of Adults 55 Years of Age and Over: United States, 2000–2003," *Advance Data*, no. 370 (2006): https://pubmed.ncbi.nlm.nih.gov/16617926/

8. Janette Young et al., "Pets, Touch, and COVID-19: Health Benefits from Non-Human Touch Through Times of Stress," *Journal of Behavioral Economics for Policy* 4 (2020): 26.

9. Though once again, I must give credit, and my deepest thanks, to my mother's caregivers Lisa Spillett and Jamie Riegler, and the other staff at the Martin Luther Home, for whom I have the greatest admiration.

10. Bennett, *Vibrant Matter*, 5.

11. Katie Engelhart, "What Robots Can—and Can't—Do for the Old and Lonely," *New Yorker*, May 24, 2021.

12. Joy for All, "About" page, accessed October 18, 2021, https://agelessinnovation.com/about/

13. Krause-Parello, Gulick, and Basin, "Loneliness, Depression, and Physical Activity," 242.

14. Krause-Parello, Gulick, and Basin, 205.

15. Bennett, *Vibrant Matter*, 20.

16. See, e.g., Boston Dynamics or Ghost Robotics for the kinds of animallike robotics being developed often for military use. Also, see *Spy in the Wild*, series 1

(2017), a BBC/PBS television documentary wildlife series using hyperrealistic animatronic animals to relate to animals in the wild.

17. Bennett, *Vibrant Matter*, xvi.

18. Robert Booth, "It's Almost Magical How Robotic Pets are Helping UK Care Home Residents," *Guardian*, September 1, 2023, https://www.theguardian.com/society/2023/sep/01/its-almost-magical-how-robotic-pets-are-helping-care-home-resident

19. Sandra Petersen et al., "The Utilization of Robotic Pets in Dementia Care," *Journal of Alzheimers Disease* 55, no. 2 (2017): 569–74, https://doi.org/10.3233/JAD-160703

20. "PARO Therapeutic Robot," PARO home page, http://www.parorobots.com

21. Petersen et al., "The Utilization of Robotic Pets," 572.

22. Elinor Fuchs, *Making an Exit: A Mother-Daughter Drama with Machine Tools, Alzheimer's, and Laughter* (Henry Holt, 2005).

23. Fuchs, 163.

24. Fuchs, 174.

25. Equality and Human Rights Commission, *Experiences from Health and Social Care: The Treatment of Lower-Paid Ethnic Minority Workers*, June 2022, 38, https://equalityhumanrights.com/sites/default/files/inquiry-experiences-and-treatment-of-lower-paid-ethnic-minority-workers-in-health-and-social-care-report_0.pdf

26. Geraldine Pratt, Caleb Johnston, and Kelsey Johnson, "Robots and Care of the Ageing Self: An Emerging Economy of Loneliness," *Environment and Planning A: Economy and Space* 55, no. 8 (2023): 12, https://doi.org/10.1177/0308518X231172199

27. Engelhart, "What Robots Can—and Can't—Do."

28. ElliQ home page, accessed February 21, 2024, https://elliq.com/

29. Engelhart, "What Robots Can—and Can't—Do."

30. Jordan Harrison, *Marjorie Prime* (Samual French, 2016), 12.

31. Harrison, 12.

32. Harrison, 63–64.

33. Anna Bendrat, "'How Do You Know Who You Are?': *Marjorie Prime* on Envisioning Humanity Through the Faculty of AI-Powered Memory as Reconstructive Tissue," *Text Matters* 13 (2023): 221, https://doi.org/10.18778/2083-2931.13.12 (emphasis added).

34. Harrison, *Marjorie Prime*, 63.

35. Bennett, *Vibrant Matter*, 23.

36. See the ABBA Voyage official website, accessed February 21, 2024, https://abbavoyage.com/

37. Harrison, *Marjorie Prime*, 65.

38. Harrison, 12–13.

39. Pratt, Johnston, and Johnson, "Robots and Care," 2.

40. Obviously this is a problem that is not exclusive to the Global North, but I am distinguishing it here as it is where these case studies are located.

41. Pratt, Johnston, and Johnson, "Robots and Care," 2.

42. Pratt, Johnston, and Johnson, 2.

43. Harrison, *Marjorie Prime*, 32.

44. Harrison, 47.

45. Chris Phillipson, letter to the editor, *Guardian*, September 6, 2023, https://www.theguardian.com/society/2023/sep/06/robot-pets-are-a-symptom-of-a-crisis-in-care

46. Phillipson.

47. Krause-Parello, Gulick, and Basin, "Loneliness, Depression, and Physical Activity," 250.

48. Bennett, *Vibrant Matter*, 24.

17

At This Time (or My Friend Elinor)

Anne Davis Basting

Anne Davis Basting and Elinor Fuchs met in 1995, when both were Rockefeller Fellows in Age Studies at the University of Wisconsin-Milwaukee's Center for 20th Century Studies, directed by Kathleen Woodward. This began a long friendship that included being sounding boards for each other's creative and scholarly work and continues through their experiences of aging and care on both sides of the care relationship. This short piece is inspired by that friendship.

TIME: The present.

SETTING: The setting is both the stage of a large theater, and the living room of Elinor's apartment. Two living room side chairs are onstage.

CHARACTER: ANNE. In her late fifties. She impersonates FRANCIS and ELINOR, neither of whom is physically present.

AT CURTAIN: Lights rise on ANNE, sitting in one of the chairs. The other is empty, but it is actually filled with the memory of a woman in her late eighties.

ANNE: (*Shouting, as* ELINOR) Five minutes! Don't leave! Can you stay? I hope you can stay. I'll be out in five minutes!

PAUSE. ANNE *stands up. Goes to the other chair and sits.*

So I wait. My husband and son are downstairs in the lobby. We are due at the theater to see David Byrne's *American Utopia* in two hours.

She nods toward the kitchen.

Elinor's caregiver Francis leans out of the kitchen.

"Can I get you cuppa tea?"

Oh no—thank you, I say. I'm fine.

(*To the audience*) I wait.

PAUSE. *She looks around the living room, which is lined with shelves upon shelves of books. Floor to ceiling.*

I'm thinking, this whole time, I'm thinking—all these books! Every wall is covered in them. They are packed tight. No space for decorative ceramics. No room for relics of distant travels. Just books. These custom-built bookshelves are the walls themselves.

(*Walking the audience through the apartment*) The long wall here from the door through the living room. Under the windows, into the study, around the wall here, around the doorway, above the doorway. Philosophy. Architecture. Art. Plays of course. I wonder—has she read them all? I'm sure she has.

ANNE *gets up and goes to the other chair, sits.*

(*Yelling, as* ELINOR) "Is Anne still here?"

(*In her own voice*) Yes, I'm here.

(*Yelling, as* ELINOR) "I'll be out in five minutes. Can you wait five minutes?"

I can wait a bit.

ANNE *continues looking around at all the books. They are everywhere. They are overwhelming and a bit intimidating.*

I *have* read a lot. I really have. But this . . .

She takes a calming breath . . . these books are intimidating.

She continues looking around—and then sees a particular book—and smiles.

Then I recognize one—like seeing an old friend you haven't seen for thirty years.

It's that unmistakable neon green and blue stripe of Sue-Ellen Case's *Performing Feminisms*, Johns Hopkins University Press, nineteen ninety. Five years before we met.

She walks over to the shelf.

(*Pointing to a section of the bookshelf and smiling*) I had all of these. This one and this one, and this one—all of these. I can see them in a small oak bookcase, just three shelves, in my first real office—right next to hers on the ninth floor, with a view of Lake Michigan and the skyline of Milwaukee. It was 1995. We had each been awarded a fellowship in age studies—the first in the country—thank you, Kathy Woodward. I would spend the year adapting my dissertation into a book. Elinor would work on a book about caring for her mother through what she called "the emergency."

(*Yelling, as* ELINOR) Is Anne still here?

I'm still here!

It's a funny book, believe it or not. She's very funny. She called it *Making an Exit*.

(*Yelling, as* ELINOR) Oh good—can you wait five minutes? It will just take me five minutes.

I can stay a bit—I have to go to the theater soon.

(*Yelling, as* ELINOR) The theater! Oh! Ok. I'll be right out! Five minutes.

She looks at the book again.

She was a published playwright. I had written a couple, odd little pieces. Very Beckett. Very short. Very edgy. She was a critic. And a parent. And an only child caring for aging, divorced parents.

And an enormously patient listener to a twentysomething writing about aging.

We had both finished our PhDs that year. She had come back to her studies later in life and written about Brecht and Ibsen. I had spent my twenties seeing performances by older actors and was wrestling with what these representations could possibly mean in a world that only wanted to see bodies—like—well—at the time, mine.

She was living and processing the emergency.

At the time, I was volunteering on a locked Alzheimer's unit at a local nursing home, using improvisation techniques to see if they could open a door to expression and connection. Open a way out of despair.

We were living in the same Beckett play, speaking the same odd poetry of the emergency.

Which play is it of his—*Rockaby*? The slow, methodic back and forth in the rocking chair. Back and forth.

"Time she stopped. Time. She. Stopped."

"So in the end. Close of a long day. Went down. Down into the old rocker. And rocked. Saying to herself, no. Done with that."

"Time she stopped."

She looks at her watch.

Have you seen *American Utopia*? They made it into a movie—in case it's not playing on Broadway at this time. It's basically two hours of a remarkably hip marching band. About twenty musicians, dressed in gray, untethered by cords. Dancing and playing with Byrne's saucy hopefulness. I kept thinking that every song was like watching the Grinch in that moment when his heart grows ten sizes.

Francis asks me, "You sure you don't want a cup of tea?" She has a beautiful island accent that I won't attempt here.

But the way she says it—and that she thought to ask me again—makes me think how lucky Elinor and her daughters are—to have found her.

I'm good, I say.

But thank you.

Francis tells me, "This is what she does, you know. She probably won't come out."

I was starting to figure that. It had been about forty minutes of five more minutes.

She looks at the bookshelf again.

Oh—this one. I know this one—she told me about this one. She must have. How would I have known of it otherwise?

Francis Yates. *The Art of Memory.*

Yates was a self-trained academic—her exuberance about the riddles of history rings out of the serifs of every letter like little chimes.

What is the art of memory? She takes us on a tour of mnemonics—from the Greeks, the Romans, the medieval Christians, the philosophers, the artists . . .

There's a whole chapter about an Italian philosopher from the fifteenth century—Giulio Camillo—who built this crazy wooden room he called the Memory Theater. It was based on a dream—not really so different from today's tech billionaires—a dream to know everything—and to remember everything—all at once. Just by walking into a little wooden structure that looked like a theater.

I remember this weird drawing that unfolded out of the chapter—it didn't really help explain it—but it was charming. Supposedly it had been built, but the descriptions are so strange—

It's the opposite of what we imagine as theater—there is no audience. Instead, the viewer is on the stage looking out.

There are seven aisles, like in a Roman amphitheater.

The seven aisles apparently echo the pillars of Solomon's House of Wisdom—I guess in the ninth chapter of Proverbs, Solomon says, "Wisdom has built herself a house and has founded it on seven pillars."

So there are seven aisles—and there are these painted panels where the audience would be. And on the panels are images from the three worlds—I told you it was strange—

She turns the page.

Here it is—on 137—

"Like the Cabalists, Camillo sees three worlds. Super celestial (divine emanations); middle celestial world of the stars; sub-celestial world or elemental world."

The first grade is the planets, second the oceans, third the cave, fourth is the creation of man; fifth man's soul joins his body; sixth is all the things man can do naturally (without art); seventh is what man can do with art (arts, sciences, religion, law).

And here Yates quotes Camillo himself—"This high and incomparable placing not only performs the office of conserving for us the things, words, and arts which we confide to it, so that we may find them at once whenever we need them, but also gives us true wisdom from whose founts we come to the knowledge of things from their causes and not from their effects." 143.

And here—classic Yates—"When one thinks of these drawers or coffers in the Theater it begins to look like a lightly ornamental filing cabinet (I love Yates . . .). But this is to lose sight of the grandeur of the Idea—the Idea of a memory organically geared to the universe." 145.

And here—my favorite—157—

"The mind and memory of man is now 'divine,' having powers of grasping the highest reality through a magically activated imagination."

ANNE *looks around at the bookcases that surround her.*

All these books. On handcrafted bookshelves.

Philosophy. Architecture. Art. And Theater.

Like a lightly ornamental, magical, divine filing cabinet.

Grasping the highest reality through a magically activated imagination.

She looks at her watch.

When I go downstairs I'll find that my husband and son aren't in the lobby. They have gone in search of a snack somewhere down Fifth Avenue.

There will be mild panic because they aren't answering their phones and I don't know where they are and I worry that we'll miss the show.

But for now, at this time, I think about Elinor's phone calls.

(*Loudly*) Ring! Phones used to do that.

She sits down in one of the chairs.

You would actually physically pick up what they called a receiver with a little cord attached to it and hold it up to your ear.

(*As though answering a phone*) Elinor! It's so good to hear your voice. How are you?

And she would be fine—fine—quickly pushing me beyond pleasantries and into a burning question about Brecht and an idea she was working on.

She would ask me: "Does it make sense to you?"

EstrAGEment she called it.

EstrAGEment.

It's a little hard to say, says I. But yes—I get it.

Of course I get it.

The Verfremdungeffekt—Bertolt Brecht's signature theory of estrangement—creating disruptive moments in a performance that would jar the viewer out of passive entertainment mode and into thinking about what they were seeing. A way to hold open contradiction. To refuse closure.

Administering a mild shock—"the alienation that is," in the words of Brecht, "necessary to all understanding."

Estrangement.

Elinor's twist was—is applying it to aging. Thus estrAGEment.

Time is change. As it passes (or seems to), our bodies mark the change. Our minds change. Landscapes change. Houses go up. Houses come down. Corner stores turn into high-rise condos. Farm fields are carved up into subdivisions. Sinkholes swallow concrete. Vines crawl over fallen barns or even city blocks of houses that municipalities cut off from the water supply.

But the remembering animal carries the past with it into the present and they clash. Wait—what? I'm not seventy-three . . . eighty-three . . . ninety-three . . . How could I be? The march is relentless—without closure. A constant contradiction. Constant rehearsal.

Until—

Time she stopped. Time. She. Stopped.

She gives this hilarious example—of her taking on a mock shuffle walk, becoming her own age-puppet—and coaxing herself with calming care—"You'll be alright dearie, I'll take care of you . . ."

EstrAGEment.

(*Yelling, as* ELINOR) Is Anne still here?

I wasn't. I had to go.

Francis apologized—"I'm sorry," she said. "She does this. She say she will come. But she don't."

Oh no worries, I say. I'll try again.

And off I went to find my husband and son buying slices of pizza down the street, and then to the jubilant, bare marching feet of David Byrne and his merry band.

It was almost a year before I could make it back.

She gets up, walks around the chair.

I sit here. My husband sits there. (*quietly*) Elinor is lying on the couch just there.

Curled up under a blanket.

Francis offers us tea, which we decline, and she disappears into the back of the apartment.

It's quiet.

Just the muffled sounds of Fifth Avenue in the Memory Theater.

She looks out at the audience—pointing to a memory/image.

Is this the celestial level? Or the stars?

Elinor's office, next to mine on the ninth floor of the Center for 20th Century Studies. Twenty-five years later, my office is on the other end of that long hallway. I am directing the same center. At least until I am not anymore.

But at this time, in the office next to Elinor's, I didn't know what to do—I was supposed to go to New York to see a performance of *Hello, Dolly!*—with Carol Channing performing the title role for something like the 475th time. All the press was about her age. She had originated the role when she was forty. She was in her late seventies.

Elinor was in her mid-sixties. I was freshly thirty.

I was also going to New York because I had just met this guy (*pointing to the empty chair*). After a burst of exuberant letters and emails . . . I wanted to see if it was real.

But I had no place to stay. And even though the fellowship paid more than I had ever earned in life thus far—I couldn't afford a hotel *and* airfare.

Elinor lived in Brooklyn I thought—Maybe she knew of a place I could stay for cheap. I mustered the courage to ask.

After patiently listening to me jump over, under, and around words like—"research, afford, possible date, can't stay with him. Don't know anyone . . . never been there. . . ." she smiled and said—

"Well, I am here now. And I live in New York. Which means my house is empty. Why don't you stay there?"

And so I did. On a pullout couch in the library.

Surrounded by these same books.

(*Looking around*) Philosophy. Architecture. Art. Plays of course.

She points to another book—another panel in the Memory Theater. Smiling.

She came to the wedding. It was in the Adirondacks, where she told me she had spent glorious summers as a child.

She looks out at the audience, pointing to another image/memory.

My mother is diagnosed with Alzheimer's. I read *Making an Exit* again. And again.

She looks out at the audience, pointing to another image/memory.

I see her with a group of women sitting under a coatrack in the lobby outside the chapel where we had just staged the final scene of *Finding Penelope*. A play made with people in long-term care, about the heroic quest to hold home for another person. A play in mythic time and contemporary time. In which Penelope is played by anyone who wants to join the chorus. A play that does not end in recognition. "It's marvelous," she said. There could be no higher praise.

She looks out at the audience, pointing to another image/memory.

We are sitting on an outdoor patio in some town—I think it was England—at a conference on aging. Elinor leans in—her eyes sharp—

"Did you tell Tom my age?" she asks me.

PAUSE.

We are scholars—of age studies.

PAUSE.

I had told Tom her age. What had I said? Something like—"Elinor is remarkable—at seventy-nine creating new theory."

PAUSE.

And what's up with Tom—saying something to her? What's that about? And what's up with me—thinking that is remarkable?

So I thought—and felt, and said—contritely—

"I'm sorry. I didn't know it would upset you."

She was quiet.

Only the muffled sounds of Fifth Avenue.

She looks out at the audience, pointing to another image/memory.

From my office next to Elinor's, I stared out the window at the skyline of Milwaukee. The horizon of Lake Michigan. The same view I have now. From my office at the other end of the hallway.

I was trying to think through, to push into words, the experience of what I clumsily called "aging in depth"—

I was really just trying to put into words the strange feeling I would get when I looked at a person, say one of the women on the locked Alzheimer's unit, or on the subway—I see them as they are now. But also as what I imagine they were. And as I imagine they will be.

Or when I look at a student—like the nineteen-year-old in my Women and Aging class the year before, pulling up the skin on the top of her hand and watching it snap back into place in one smooth motion—I see her at eighty. With thin folds of soft skin that stay in the shape her fingers pinched for an hour.

The philosophers call it Eternalism. All moments in time, past, present, and future—coexist.

Aging in Depth.

As opposed to what philosophers call Presentism. All time is the present that we adjust to. Constantly.

EstrAGEment. A never-ending rehearsal.

Anne and Elinor. In a loop.

Me. with my silent observation—imagining all ages at once so as to remove the shock. Can there be ageism if everyone saw each other as all ages at once?

Elinor—always funnier. With her age-puppet shuffle. Laughing at the shock of the present. Taking Brecht's lesson—that there is no climax—no resolution—no recognition—Only rehearsal.

Until.

Quiet now. Just the muffled sounds of Fifth Avenue.

She looks out at the audience, pointing to another image/memory.

My husband and son and David Byrne are all waiting. Rehearsing.

She looks out at the audience, pointing to another image/memory.

Her mother with Alzheimer's. Living the emergency.

Her with Alzheimer's. Her daughters and Francis. Living the emergency.

My mother with Alzheimer's.

Me.

(*Yelling, as* ELINOR) Is Anne still here?

I'm here.

(*Yelling, as* ELINOR) I'll be out in five minutes! Can you wait five minutes?

I can't. Unfortunately.

But before I go, I lean closer to my friend, curled up on the couch. The light blanket lifting gently up and down. Her eyes open, taking us both in.

I wonder. Can the two of us walk into Camillo's funny little theater together? The two of us—her in a puppet shuffle. Me with the rose-colored lenses of eternalism—Can we shuffle in together and stand onstage? And look out together at the seven aisles with a celestial view of lowly everyday man—at this lightly ornamental filing cabinet—and feel imbued with the wisdom of the universe? Together?

"Do you ever think of the theater?" I ask her.

"Oh no," she laughs. "I'm all done with all that."

Fig. 17.1. Elinor Fuchs's bookshelf mirrors the author's bookshelves. Photo: Anne Davis Basting.

Contributors

Anne Davis Basting is professor emerita of English at the University of Wisconsin-Milwaukee, founder of the award-winning TimeSlips Creative Storytelling, and a MacArthur Fellow. Her books include *The Stages of Age: Performing Age in Contemporary American Culture* (1998), *Forget Memory: Creating Better Lives for People with Dementia* (2009), and *Creative Care: A Revolutionary Approach to Dementia and Elder Care* (2020).

Núria Casado-Gual is professor at the Department of Foreign Languages and Literatures of the Universitat de Lleida (Catalonia, Spain), where she teaches drama in English. She has published three co-edited volumes of essays and a co-edited special issue on age and performance for *Theatre Research in Canada*. Núria is also a theater practitioner and playwright.

Dorothy Chansky is professor emerita of theater in the School of Theatre & Dance at Texas Tech University. She is the author of *Losing It: Staging the Cultural Conundrum of Dementia and Decline in American Theatre*, *Composing Ourselves: The Little Theatre Movement and the American Audience*, and *Kitchen Sink Realisms: Domestic Labor, Dining, and Drama in American Theatre*. She is a former president of the American Theatre and Drama Society.

Elinor Fuchs (1933–2024) authored/edited five books, including *The Death of Character: Perspectives on Theater after Modernism*, winner of the George Jean Nathan Award for Dramatic Criticism, and *Making an Exit*, a family memoir about dementia and aging. She was professor emerita of dramaturgy and dramatic criticism at Yale's David Geffen School, where she taught from 1987 to 2015.

Benjamin Gillespie is assistant professor of theatre at Santa Clara University and co-editor of the *Journal of American Drama and Theatre*. His essays and reviews have been published in a wide range of journals and anthologies. He is editor of the forthcoming *Split Britches: Fifty Years On* and co-editor of *The Routledge Companion to LGBTQ+ Theatre and Performance in North America*.

R. Darren Gobert is professor of theater studies and English at Duke University, where he chairs the Department of Theater Studies and directs the Duke in New York: Creative Industries program. His publications include *The Mind-Body Stage* (Stanford University Press) and *The Theatre of Caryl Churchill* (Bloomsbury).

Margaret Morganroth Gullette, a pioneer in age studies, is the author of *American Eldercide: How It Happened, How to Prevent It* (2024), *Ending Ageism, or How Not To Shoot Old People* (2017), *Agewise* (2011), *Aged by Culture* (2004), *Declining to Decline* (1998), and *Safe at Last in the Middle Years* (1988).

Julia Henderson is assistant professor in the Department of Occupational Science and Occupational Therapy at the University of British Columbia and Chair of the North American Network in Aging Studies (2023–26). Her work is published in a range of journals and anthologies and includes arts-based research with older adults that redresses cultural ageism and promotes citizenship.

Daniel Alexander Jones is an artist and sojourner whose body of work embraces multiple disciplines. His collection of plays and performance texts, *Love Like Light*, is published by 53rd State Press. Originally from Springfield, Massachusetts, Jones holds degrees in Africana studies (Vassar College) and theater (Brown University). He maintains an active teaching practice.

Heunjung Lee is a SSHRC postdoctoral fellow at the University of Calgary. Her project, *Connecting through Culture*, investigates how a culturally tailored dance program can support the identities and creativity of Korean older adults with dementia. She serves as secretary of the North American Network in Aging Studies and editorial assistant for *Age, Culture, Humanities: An Interdisciplinary Journal.*

Valerie Barnes Lipscomb is professor of English at the University of South Florida. She is lead editor of *The Palgrave Handbook of Literature and Aging* (2024) and *Staging Age* (2010), as well as author of *Performing Age in Modern Drama* (2016). She serves as treasurer of the North American Network in Aging Studies.

Scott Magelssen is Executive Director and Floyd U. Jones Family Endowed Chair of the University of Washington School of Drama. His books include

Performing Flight: From the Barnstormers to Space Tourism, *Simming: Participatory Performance and the Making of Meaning*, and the co-edited collections *Enveloping Worlds: Toward a Discourse of Immersive Performance*, *Theater Historiography: Critical Interventions*, and *Enacting History*.

Bonnie Marranca is founding editor and publisher of PAJ Publications. Her books include *Timelines: Writings and Conversations*, *Performance Histories*, *Ecologies of Theater*, *Theatrewritings*, and *Conversations with Meredith Monk*. She has also edited the anthologies *Alchemies of Theater: Plays, Scores, Writings by Dick Higgins*, *Conversations on Art and Performance*, *New Europe: Plays from the Continent*, and *Plays for the End of the Century*.

Robbie McCauley (1942–2021) was an Obie Award–winning playwright for *Sally's Rape*, and an internationally recognized performance artist and director. Her most recent play, *Sugar*, a one-woman show about her lifelong struggle with diabetes, received wide critical acclaim. Robbie McCauley retired from the faculty of Emerson College in 2016, which conferred on her the title professor emerita.

Yana Meerzon is professor of theater studies at the University of Ottawa. She is the author of four books, including *Performing Nationalism in Russia* (Cambridge University Press, 2024). She has co-edited nine collections, including *The Palgrave Handbook of Theatre and Migration* (2023). She is co-editor of the series Palgrave Studies in Performance and Migration.

Hillary Miller is the author of *Drop Dead: Performance in Crisis, 1970s New York* (2016) and *Playwrights on Television: Conversations with Dramatists* (2020). She teaches at Queens College, City University of New York, and is an affiliate faculty member in the Theatre and Performance doctoral program at the Graduate Center (CUNY).

Jennifer Parker-Starbuck, professor of theater and performance at Royal Holloway, University of London, is author of *Cyborg Theatre* (2011), co-author of *Performance and Media* (2015), and co-editor of *Performing Animality* (2015). She is performance lead for CoSTAR National R&D Lab for Creative Industries and series editor for Theater: Theory/Text/Performance (University of Michigan Press).

Cindy Rosenthal is professor of drama at Hofstra University. She has authored/edited six books on the avant-garde, radical ensembles, playwriting, and directing, and contributed essays to the *New York Times*, *Performance Research*, *Theatre Survey*, and *TDR*. Her monograph *Ellen Stewart Presents: Fifty Years of La MaMa Experimental Theatre* won the 2017 George Freedley Prize.

Bess Rowen is assistant professor of theater at Villanova University and a theater theorist, historian, and practitioner. Her first book, *The Lines Between the Lines: How Stage Directions Affect Embodiment*, was published by University of Michigan Press in 2021. Her current book project focuses on theatrical representations of teenage girls. She is co-editor of *The Routledge Companion to LGBTQ+ Theatre and Performance in North America*.

Inesa Shevchenko-Hotsuliak is adjunct professor at the Department of Foreign Languages and Literatures of the Universitat de Lleida (Catalonia, Spain). She is a member of the European Network in Aging Studies (ENAS), a member of the research group Dedal-Lit (CELCA) at the University of Lleida, and a researcher in the project PRO-SUEDAD, funded by the Spanish Ministry of Science and Innovation.

Index

Page locators in *italics* indicate illustrations.